LINCOLN CHRISTIAN COLLEGE AND

D1162081

Psychological Treatment of

OBSESSIVE–COMPULSIVE DISORDER

Psychological Treatment of

OBSESSIVE–COMPULSIVE DISORDER

FUNDAMENTALS AND BEYOND

EDITED BY
Martin M. Antony
Christine Purdon
Laura J. Summerfeldt

AMERICAN PSYCHOLOGICAL ASSOCIATION
WASHINGTON, DC

Copyright © 2007 by the American Psychological Association. All rights reserved. Except as permitted under the United States Copyright Act of 1976, no part of this publication may be reproduced or distributed in any form or by any means, including, but not limited to, the process of scanning and digitization, or stored in a database or retrieval system, without the prior written permission of the publisher.

Published by
American Psychological Association
750 First Street, NE
Washington, DC 20002
www.apa.org

To order
APA Order Department
P.O. Box 92984
Washington, DC 20090-2984
Tel: (800) 374-2721; Direct: (202) 336-5510
Fax: (202) 336-5502; TDD/TTY: (202) 336-6123
Online: www.apa.org/books/
E-mail: order@apa.org

In the U.K., Europe, Africa, and the Middle East, copies may be ordered from
American Psychological Association
3 Henrietta Street
Covent Garden, London
WC2E 8LU England

Typeset in Goudy by Stephen McDougal, Mechanicsville, MD

Printer: Edwards Brothers, Inc., Ann Arbor, MI
Cover Designer: Berg Design, Albany, NY
Technical/Production Editor: Tiffany L. Klaff

The opinions and statements published are the responsibility of the authors, and such opinions and statements do not necessarily represent the policies of the American Psychological Association.

Library of Congress Cataloging-in-Publication Data

Psychological treatment of obsessive-compulsive disorder : fundamentals and beyond / [edited by] Martin M. Antony, Christine Purdon, Laura Summerfeldt.—1st ed.
    p. cm.
  Includes bibliographical references and index.
  ISBN-13: 978-1-59147-484-5
  ISBN-10: 1-59147-484-1
  1. Obsessive-compulsive disorder. 2. Cognitive therapy. I. Antony, Martin M. II. Purdon, Christine. III. Summerfeldt, Laura.
  [DNLM: 1. Obsessive-Compulsive Disorder—therapy. 2. Psycho-therapy—methods. 3. Obsessive-Compulsive Disorder—psychology. 4. Comorbidity. WM 176 P9737 2007]

  RC533.P78 2007
  616.85'2270651—dc22   2006023919

British Library Cataloguing-in-Publication Data
A CIP record is available from the British Library.

Printed in the United States of America
First Edition

CONTENTS

115792

CONTRIBUTORS

Jonathan S. Abramowitz, PhD, Department of Psychology, University of North Carolina at Chapel Hill

Martin M. Antony, PhD, ABPP, Department of Psychology, Ryerson University, Toronto, Ontario, Canada, and Anxiety Treatment and Research Centre, St. Joseph's Healthcare, Hamilton, Ontario, Canada

Antje Bohne, PhD, Institute of Psychology, University of Muenster, Germany

Ancy E. Cherian, PhD, Center for Anxiety and Related Disorders, Boston University, Boston, MA

Edna B. Foa, PhD, Center for the Study and Treatment of Anxiety, Department of Psychiatry, University of Pennsylvania, Philadelphia

Martin E. Franklin, PhD, Center for the Study and Treatment of Anxiety, Department of Psychiatry, University of Pennsylvania, Philadelphia

Randy O. Frost, PhD, Department of Psychology, Smith College, Northampton, MA

Abbe Garcia, PhD, Child and Adolescent Psychiatry, Brown University Medical School and Rhode Island Hospital, Providence

Deborah Roth Ledley, PhD, Adult Anxiety Clinic of Temple University and private practice, Philadelphia, PA

John S. March, MD, MPH, Department of Psychiatry, Duke University Medical Center, Durham, NC

Dean McKay, PhD, Department of Psychology, Fordham University, Bronx, NY

Christy A. Nelson, MA, Department of Psychology, University of Kansas, Lawrence

Kieron P. O'Connor, PhD, Fernand–Seguin Research Centre, Louis H. Lafontaine Hospital, and Department of Psychiatry, University of Montreal, Montreal, Quebec, Canada

Anushka Pai, BA, Department of Psychology, University of Texas at Austin

C. Alec Pollard, PhD, Anxiety Disorders Center, St. Louis Behavioral Medicine Institute, St. Louis, MO

Christine Purdon, PhD, Department of Psychology, University of Waterloo, Waterloo, Ontario, Canada

S. Rachman, PhD, Department of Psychology, University of British Columbia, Vancouver, British Columbia, Canada

Adam S. Radomsky, PhD, Department of Psychology, Concordia University, and Centre de Recherce Fernand-Seguin, Montreal, Quebec, Canada

David S. Riggs, PhD, Center for the Study and Treatment of Anxiety, Department of Psychiatry, University of Pennsylvania, Philadelphia

Karen Rowa, PhD, Anxiety Treatment and Research Centre, St. Joseph's Healthcare, and Department of Psychiatry and Behavioural Neurosciences, McMaster University, Hamilton, Ontario, Canada

Gail Steketee, PhD, Boston University School of Social Work, Boston, MA

Laura J. Summerfeldt, PhD, Department of Psychology, Trent University, Peterborough, Ontario, Canada

Richard P. Swinson, MD, FRCP(C), FRCPsych, Anxiety Treatment and Research Centre, St. Joseph's Healthcare, and Department of Psychiatry and Behavioural Neurosciences, McMaster University, Hamilton, Ontario, Canada

Steven Taylor, PhD, Department of Psychiatry, University of British Columbia, Vancouver, British Columbia, Canada

David F. Tolin, PhD, Anxiety Disorders Center, Institute of Living, Hartford Hospital, Hartford, CT

David Veale, MD, FRCPsych, South London and Maudsley Trust, Institute of Psychiatry, King's College London, and The Priory Hospital North London, England.

ACKNOWLEDGMENTS

We thank Julia Blood for her editorial assistance on several chapters of this book. Thanks also to Susan Reynolds, Judy Nemes, and the staff at the American Psychological Association for their support. Finally, we thank the authors who contributed to this book as well as several anonymous reviewers who provided comments on a draft of the manuscript.

Psychological Treatment of

OBSESSIVE– COMPULSIVE DISORDER

INTRODUCTION

MARTIN M. ANTONY, CHRISTINE PURDON,
AND LAURA J. SUMMERFELDT

Until the mid-1960s, obsessive–compulsive disorder (OCD) was considered to be a relatively untreatable condition. In the brief span of time since then, the empirical and clinical literature have converged to point to cognitive–behavioral therapy (CBT) as among the most effective psychological interventions available for any psychiatric condition. Despite the widely recognized efficacy of behavioral and cognitive treatments for OCD, however, clinicians and researchers acknowledge that there are major challenges to implementing them successfully.

In their meta-analysis of treatment outcomes for OCD, Eddy, Dutra, Bradley, and Westen (2004) observed that about half of the patients who applied for psychological treatment were excluded from the studies examined. Moreover, despite impressive group effect sizes, only about half of those who were included in treatment efficacy studies showed clinical improvement, and only one quarter recovered completely. Of equal concern, many individuals entering therapy did not complete it, although roughly two thirds of those who did complete treatment improved.

In short, at each step of the treatment process, it appears that a substantial portion of the OCD population fails to benefit from the most effective psychological treatment available. One reason for this poor outcome may be the fact that OCD is a complex and heterogeneous disorder that may not lend itself well to generic interventions. It is also associated with features that can substantially complicate the design, application, and delivery of treatment, such as treatment ambivalence, poor insight, and high comorbidity. Obsessive–compulsive disorder is also a disorder that occurs at many points across the life span, which again may compromise the success of generic, as opposed to tailored, treatment strategies.

This volume seeks to explicate both the general, underlying features of the disorder and the unique characteristics of each subtype. The chapters cover general and specific treatment approaches, along with applications of treatment to specific populations. The book is organized into three parts. The first part covers topics that are fundamental to general cognitive–behavioral treatment of OCD. In chapter 1, Steven Taylor, Jonathan S. Abramowitz, and Dean McKay introduce cognitive–behavioral models of OCD and review empirical support for the central theoretical tenets of each. In chapter 2, David F. Tolin and Gail Steketee discuss general treatment issues in OCD, such as inpatient versus outpatient therapy, group versus individual treatment, family involvement in treatment, the role of medication in treatment, and contraindications of CBT for OCD. They provide guidelines for making important treatment decisions. In chapter 3, C. Alec Pollard discusses treatment ambivalence, readiness, and resistance in OCD, reviewing empirical data and describing a program for resolving treatment resistance and improving readiness. In chapter 4, Karen Rowa, Martin M. Antony, and Richard P. Swinson review the literature on exposure and response prevention (ERP; also known as exposure and ritual prevention) and offer a detailed, pragmatic guide for conducting ERP. This part finishes with Christine Purdon's detailed discussion in chapter 5 on implementing cognitive strategies in OCD treatment.

The second part contains chapters on treating specific OCD symptom presentations. These chapters are written by leading experts in each area and feature a description of the problem, case illustrations, treatment formulations, treatment protocols, and specific troubleshooting suggestions. In chapter 6, David S. Riggs and Edna B. Foa detail treatment of contamination fears, the most common subtype in both inpatient and outpatient settings. In chapter 7, Jonathan S. Abramowitz and Christy A. Nelson describe treatment for doubting and checking concerns, which are often difficult for the average clinician to conceptualize and plan exposure for. In chapter 8, Laura J. Summerfeldt describes the treatment of incompleteness, ordering, and arranging concerns, which are less readily explained from a CBT perspective. In chapter 9, S. Rachman addresses the treatment of repugnant aggressive, sexual, and religious obsessions, which give rise to intense and diverse emotions, and yet are often concealed by patients. Finally, in chapter 10, Ancy E. Cherian and Randy O. Frost review treatment of compulsive hoarding, often considered one of the most refractory of OCD presentations.

Chapters in the final part of this volume address issues unique to the treatment of OCD in specific populations. In chapter 11, Martin E. Franklin, John S. March, and Abbe Garcia describe applications of CBT to the treatment of OCD in children and adolescents, focusing on issues and points to consider when working with a younger population. In chapter 12, David Veale discusses issues in the conceptualization and treatment of poor insight and overvalued ideation in OCD patients. In chapter 13, Deborah Roth Ledley, Anushka Pai, and Martin E. Franklin present issues in the treatment of OCD that are comorbid with mood and anxiety problems. Finally, in chapter 14, Adam S. Radomsky, Antje Bohne, and Kieron P. O'Connor review the literature on the links between OCD and such disorders of impulse control as tics and pathological skin picking.

This volume is unique in its focus on both general aspects of treatment and specific applications of CBT to diverse manifestations of OCD and to diverse populations of individuals with OCD. Each chapter is written by experts who are internationally renowned for work in their respective areas, and their treatment recommendations are based on the latest available empirical research, cognitive–behavioral theory, and extensive clinical experience. Unlike other volumes, this book acknowledges and addresses the fact that using CBT to treat OCD can be extremely challenging and full of pitfalls. This book, designed for any clinician who treats OCD, provides

- a detailed, accessible exposition of the cognitive–behavioral model of treatment of OCD;
- a pragmatic guide to understanding the use of behavioral and cognitive techniques in treatment of OCD;
- guidelines for making important treatment decisions and improving treatment readiness;
- illustrations of ways to tailor CBT techniques according to OCD subtype; and
- details on issues specific to different populations of individuals with OCD.

By making continued efforts to acknowledge and understand treatment obstacles and the heterogeneity of OCD, and by consistently making innovative and tailored applications of CBT to specific OCD presentations, clinicians have the chance to improve treatment efficacy dramatically. It is our hope that this volume will facilitate such improvements.

REFERENCE

Eddy, K. T., Dutra, L., Bradley, R., & Westen, D. (2004). A multidimensional meta-analysis of psychotherapy and pharmacotherapy for obsessive–compulsive disorder. *Clinical Psychology Review, 24,* 1011–1030.

I

FUNDAMENTALS OF PSYCHOLOGICAL TREATMENT FOR OBSESSIVE–COMPULSIVE DISORDER

1

COGNITIVE–BEHAVIORAL MODELS OF OBSESSIVE–COMPULSIVE DISORDER

STEVEN TAYLOR, JONATHAN S. ABRAMOWITZ, AND DEAN MCKAY

There are many different theories of obsessive–compulsive disorder (OCD), but comparatively few provide clear, detailed descriptions of the mechanisms thought to cause the disorder (for reviews, see D. A. Clark, 2004; Jakes, 1996; Taylor, McKay, & Abramowitz, 2005b, 2005c). Few theories have been subject to extensive empirical evaluation. Some theories account for only a subset of OCD phenomena or a subset of the empirical findings concerning the disorder. Among the most prominent theoretical approaches are the contemporary cognitive–behavioral models, which are the focus of this chapter.

We begin by introducing the clinical features of OCD and illustrating the disorder with case examples. We then discuss what a good model of OCD ought to accomplish. Contemporary cognitive–behavioral models are discussed, along with a review of how well these models have performed in empirical tests of their predictions. The question of whether the models can account for all the major findings concerning OCD is also considered. We conclude with a discussion of future directions for better understanding and treating this common and often debilitating disorder.

CLINICAL FEATURES

By all appearances, 34-year-old Kyle had it made; he had a great job, a loving wife, and two happy, healthy school-age kids. Yet, as he tearfully told his therapist, he was plagued with "terrible" thoughts and "stupid" habits. Whenever he came across a sharp object such as a knife or a screwdriver, he had a vivid, intrusive, and horrifying image of plunging it into the eyes of one of his children. Although the images were often triggered by the sight of sharp objects, they sometimes simply popped into his mind, seemingly out of the blue. Kyle feared that he might have some sort of unconscious desire to hurt the people he loved. To avoid triggering the upsetting thoughts, he tried to keep all the sharp objects in the house out of sight, and he often insisted that the family eat meals such as burgers or finger foods that didn't require utensils. Whenever he had one of his upsetting thoughts, which occurred on most days, he felt compelled to check four times on the safety of his children and insisted that they say the words "I'm OK, Dad." He felt deeply ashamed for continually making his children go through this ritual.

For as long as she could remember, Lynda had been an anxious, overly cautious person. Now in her early 20s, she had started a new job and, for the first time, had moved out of the family home into her own rented apartment. Although she had expected to relish her newly acquired freedom, Lynda found that she was frequently preoccupied with the security of her apartment. Each day she tried to quell her many lingering doubts, which she referred to as her "sticky thinking." Every morning, when she left for work, she was beset by doubts about whether she'd "properly" locked the door. Although she checked and rechecked each morning, sometimes she set off for work only to drive back for "one more check" in an attempt to assuage her concerns. When she was at home, things were no better; she frequently was troubled by doubts about whether she'd "correctly" performed all kinds of things, such as unplugging or switching off appliances and locking windows and doors. Before going to bed each night, Lynda spent up to an hour checking that things were turned off and that her apartment was "safe and secure."

Fifty-four-year-old Jim struggled with contamination problems. He was aware that other people worried about dirt and germs, but Jim knew that he was different. He felt a strong need to clean whenever he overheard foul language. Beginning in high school, he would wash until he felt that he had completely "cleaned away" thoughts of the foul word and replaced them with "good" thoughts. As he got older, the problem worsened, such that he washed even when people made disparaging remarks about people he respected (e.g., the Pope) or when people made comments about darkly powerful figures that he feared (e.g., Nostradamus). When it was inconvenient to wash immediately, Jim maintained a checklist of occurrences of unwanted thoughts, and later, when he was alone, he would wash several times to "clean away" each unwanted thought. When Jim sought treatment, his hands were red and raw from all the time spent cleaning away "bad" thoughts.

These are three examples of the many faces of OCD. The disorder is characterized by obsessions or compulsions or, most typically, both (American Psychiatric Association, 2000). *Obsessions* are upsetting thoughts, images, or urges that intrude, unbidden, into the person's stream of consciousness. Common examples include unwanted thoughts or images of harming loved ones (as in the case of Kyle); persistent, unwarranted doubts that one has locked the door (as described by Lynda); intrusive thoughts about being contaminated (e.g., those experienced by Jim); and morally or sexually repugnant sexual thoughts (e.g., intrusive thoughts of behaving in a way that violates one's morals or runs counter to one's sexual preferences).

Compulsions are repetitive, intentional behaviors or mental acts that the person feels compelled to perform, usually with a desire to resist (e.g., Jim's hand washing). Compulsions are typically intended to avert some feared event or to reduce distress. They may be performed in response to an obsession, such as repetitive hand washing evoked by obsessions about contamination. Alternatively, compulsions may be performed in accordance to certain rules, such as Kyle's checking four times that his children were unharmed. Compulsions can be overt (e.g., turning the light switch off and on 10 times) or covert (e.g., thinking a "good" thought to undo or replace a "bad" thought, as in the case of Jim). Compulsions are excessive or not realistically connected to what they are intended to prevent (American Psychiatric Association, 2000).

Epidemiological surveys and factor analytic studies show that OCD is a symptomatically heterogeneous condition (McKay et al., 2004). There are four major types or constellations of OCD symptoms: (a) obsessions (aggressive, sexual, religious, or somatic) and checking compulsions; (b) symmetry obsessions and ordering, counting, and repeating compulsions; (c) contamination obsessions and cleaning compulsions; and (d) hoarding obsessions and collecting compulsions (Taylor, 2005).

Obsessions and compulsions of insufficient frequency or duration to meet diagnostic criteria for OCD are common in the general population (e.g., Frost & Gross, 1993; Rachman & de Silva, 1978; Salkovskis & Harrison, 1984). Compared with clinical obsessions, those found in the general population—so-called normal obsessions—tend to be less frequent, shorter in duration, and associated with less distress (Rachman & de Silva, 1978; Salkovskis & Harrison, 1984). Normal and clinical obsessions and compulsions share common themes such as violence, contamination, and doubt (Rachman & de Silva, 1978; Salkovskis & Harrison, 1984). These similarities suggest that the study of normal obsessions and compulsions may shed light on the mechanisms of their clinically severe counterparts.

CHARACTERISTICS OF A GOOD MODEL OF OBSESSIVE–COMPULSIVE DISORDER

A good model of OCD should be able to do several things (Taylor et al., 2005b, 2005c). It should provide a clear description of the processes and contents of the disorder and the interactions among these conceptual elements, while being as parsimonious as reasonably possible. Thus, a good model of OCD should provide an explanation of the major clinical characteristics of the disorder (obsessions and compulsions and their interrelations) and their origins and clinical course. A good model should be able to explain the symptom heterogeneity of OCD; why do some people, for example, have checking compulsions, whereas others have contamination obsessions, and still others have hoarding rituals?

A good model should be clear in its predictions. There should be no ambiguity about what counts as evidence for or against the model. The model should also lead to predictions that are falsifiable. Finally, a good model should have treatment relevance. The model should enhance our understanding of current treatments and should suggest new ways of improving treatment outcome. For example, it should be able to help clinicians understand why some treatments are effective (e.g., exposure and response prevention) and why other treatments are largely ineffective (e.g., relaxation training; Steketee, 1993).

BRIEF HISTORICAL PERSPECTIVE

Before the development of contemporary cognitive–behavioral models of OCD, conditioning models were the dominant explanations of the disorder, at least in the research literature. Conditioning models of OCD were based on Mowrer's (1960) two-factor model of fear (e.g., Rachman, 1971; Rachman & Hodgson, 1980; Teasdale, 1974), and they proposed that obsessional fears were acquired by classical conditioning and maintained by operant conditioning. According to these models, the obsessional fear of acquiring a serious illness from doorknobs, for example, would arise from a traumatic experience in which a loved one purportedly acquired such a disease (the unconditioned stimulus) from contact with a "dirty" doorknob in a public place (the conditioned stimulus). Obsessional fears were said to be maintained by negative reinforcement—that is, avoidance of doorknobs or compulsive washing after coming into contact with a doorknob. Here, the avoidance or compulsive ritual is negatively reinforced by the reduction in discomfort and by the reduction in the perceived probability of feared consequences such as becoming contaminated.

Conditioning models led to what has been established as one of the most effective treatments for OCD: exposure and response prevention (March, Frances, Carpenter, & Kahn, 1997; also known as exposure and ritual prevention). This treatment involves being purposefully exposed to harmless but fear-evoking stimuli while delaying or refraining from performing the compulsive rituals. In terms of treatment implications, the conditioning models were highly fruitful; no other psychological treatment has consistently outperformed the efficacy of exposure and response prevention (Abramowitz, Taylor, & McKay, 2005). Tests of the mechanisms suggested by the model, however, were not so encouraging (Clark, 2004; Gray, 1982). Major problems include the following:

- Many OCD patients do not appear to have a history of relevant conditioning experiences that might lead to obsessional fears.
- The model has difficulty explaining the emergence, persistence, and content of obsessions (e.g., why would a person experience recurrent, intrusive images of strangling his or her child, even though he or she has never committed or witnessed any harm of this sort?).
- OCD symptoms may change over time (e.g., a person might be compelled to check door locks and then, some weeks later, feel compelled to repetitively check on the safety of his or her spouse).
- The model fails to explain why people with OCD display a broad range of levels of insight into the reasonableness of their obsessions and compulsions and why any given person's degree of insight can fluctuate across time and circumstance.

These and other limitations led clinical researchers to consider cognitive explanations of OCD.

CONTEMPORARY COGNITIVE–BEHAVIORAL APPROACHES

Contemporary cognitive–behavioral models of OCD fall into two broad classes: Those proposing that OCD is caused by some dysfunction in cognitive processing (general deficit models), and those postulating specific dysfunctional beliefs and appraisals as causes of obsessions and compulsions (belief and appraisal models).

General Deficit Models

Evidence suggests that people with OCD, compared with control participants, have deficits or abnormalities on a range of tasks, including tasks that are seemingly unrelated to threat or obsessional concerns. These findings have been shown for tasks of inductive reasoning, executive functioning (e.g., planning or set shifting), and some forms of learning and memory (Greisberg & McKay, 2003; Jurado, Junque, Vallejo, Salgado, & Grafman,

2002; Woods, Vevea, Chambless, & Bayen, 2002). These deficits can persist even after successful symptomatic treatment, which suggests that the cognitive impairments are not caused by heightened anxiety or other OCD symptoms (Nielen & Den Boer, 2003). People with OCD, compared with control participants, also show weakened cognitive inhibition; that is, a weakened ability to inhibit responses, even for affectively neutral responses (e.g., Enright & Beech, 1993a, 1993b; Enright, Beech, & Claridge, 1995).

Neuropsychological deficits are not found in all patients, and even when deficits are present, they tend to be mild. Nevertheless, the findings led some theorists to suggest that OCD arises from aberrations in general information-processing systems (e.g., Pitman, 1987; Reed, 1985) or dysfunctional reasoning processes (O'Connor, 2002). The deficits are general in the sense that they affect all information that is processed, including information related to the person's obsessional concerns (e.g., contamination stimuli) and affectively neutral information.

There are five major limitations of the general deficit models. First, the models do not account for the heterogeneity of OCD symptoms (e.g., Why do some people have washing compulsions whereas others have checking rituals?). Second, the models do not account for the fact that mild neuropsychological deficits have been found in many disorders, including panic disorder, social phobia, posttraumatic stress disorder, and bulimia nervosa (Taylor, 2002); the models fail to explain why such deficits give rise to OCD instead of one of these other disorders. Third, some of the models provide only sketches of the putative mechanisms (e.g., O'Connor, 2002). Fourth, most of the models have been subject to little empirical evaluation of their predictions. Fifth, the effectiveness of exposure and response prevention in treating OCD would not be predicted from the models. If dysfunctional information processing plays any causal role in OCD, it is most likely to be a nonspecific vulnerability factor that might (or might not) play a role in obsessions and compulsions.

Belief and Appraisal Models

Among the most promising contemporary models of OCD are those based on Beck's (1976) cognitive specificity hypothesis, which proposes that different types of psychopathology arise from different types of dysfunctional beliefs. Major depression, for example, is said to be associated with beliefs about loss, failure, and self-denigration (e.g., "I'm a failure"). Social phobia is thought to be associated with beliefs about rejection or ridicule by others (Beck & Emery, 1985; e.g., "It's terrible to be rejected"). Panic disorder is said to be associated with beliefs about impending death, insanity, or loss of control (Beck, 1988; D. M. Clark, 1986; e.g., "My heart will stop if it beats too fast").

Several theorists have proposed that obsessions and compulsions arise from specific sorts of dysfunctional beliefs. The strength of these beliefs influences the person's insight into his or her OCD. Among the most sophisticated of these models is Salkovskis's cognitive–behavioral approach (e.g., Salkovskis, 1985, 1989, 1996) and the models based on Salkovskis's approach (e.g., Frost & Steketee, 2002). Such models form the theoretical foundations for much of the work described in later chapters of this volume. Salkovskis's model begins with the well-established finding that most people experience intrusions (i.e., thoughts, images, and impulses that intrude into consciousness) or normal obsessions. An important task for any model is to explain why almost everyone experiences cognitive intrusions (at least at some point in their lives), yet only some people experience intrusions in the form of clinical obsessions (i.e., intrusions that are unwanted, distressing, and difficult to remove from consciousness).

Salkovskis (1985, 1989, 1996) argued that intrusions—whether wanted or unwanted—reflect the person's current concerns arising from an "idea generator" in the brain. The concerns are automatically triggered by internal or external reminders of those concerns. For example, intrusive thoughts of being contaminated may be triggered by seeing dirty objects (e.g., trash cans). Salkovskis proposed that intrusions develop into obsessions only when the individual appraises the intrusions as posing a threat for which he or she is personally responsible. An example is the intrusive image of swerving one's car into oncoming traffic. Most people experiencing such an intrusion would regard it as a meaningless cognitive event, with no harm-related implications ("mental flotsam"). Such an intrusion can develop into a clinical obsession if the person appraises it as having serious consequences for which he or she is personally responsible. The person might make an appraisal such as the following: "Having thoughts about swerving into traffic means that I'm a dangerous person who must take extra care to ensure that I don't lose control." Such appraisals evoke distress and motivate the person to try to suppress or remove the unwanted intrusion (e.g., by replacing it with a "good" thought) and to attempt to prevent any harmful events associated with the intrusion (e.g., by avoiding driving).

Compulsions are conceptualized as efforts to remove intrusions and to prevent any perceived harmful consequences. Salkovskis (1985, 1989) advanced two main reasons why compulsions become persistent and excessive. First, they are reinforced by immediate distress reduction and by temporary removal of the unwanted thought (negative reinforcement, as in the conditioning models of OCD). Second, they prevent the person from learning that their appraisals are unrealistic (e.g., the person fails to learn that unwanted harm-related thoughts do not lead to acts of harm). Compulsions influence the frequency of intrusions by serving as reminders of intrusions and thereby triggering their reoccurrence. For example, compulsive hand washing can remind the person that he or she may have become contaminated. Attempts at distracting oneself from unwanted intrusions may paradoxically increase the frequency of intrusions, possibly because the distractors become reminders (retrieval cues) of the intrusions. Compulsions can also strengthen one's perceived responsibility. That is, the absence of the feared consequence after performing the compulsion reinforces the belief that the person is responsible for removing the threat.

To summarize, when a person appraises intrusions as posing a threat for which he or she is personally responsible, the person becomes distressed and attempts to remove the intrusions and prevent their perceived consequences. This reaction increases the frequency of intrusions. Thus, intrusions become persistent and distressing. In other words, they escalate into clinical obsessions. Compulsions maintain the intrusions and prevent the person from evaluating the accuracy of his or her appraisals.

Why do some people, but not others, make harm- and responsibility-related appraisals of their intrusive thoughts? Life experiences shape the basic assumptions people hold about themselves and the world (Beck, 1976). Salkovskis (1985) proposed that assumptions about blame, responsibility, or control play an important role in OCD, as illustrated by beliefs such as "Having a bad thought about an action is the same as performing the action" and "Failing to prevent harm is the same as having caused the harm in the first place." These assumptions are thought to be acquired from a strict moral or religious upbringing or from other experiences that teach the person codes of conduct and responsibility (Salkovskis, Shafran, Rachman, & Freeston, 1999).

Beyond Responsibility

Although Salkovskis (e.g., 1985, 1989, 1996) emphasized the importance of responsibility appraisals and beliefs, a number of cognitive–behavioral theorists have proposed that other types of dysfunctional beliefs and appraisals are also important in OCD (e.g., Freeston, Rhéaume, & Ladouceur, 1996; Frost & Steketee, 2002). Thus, contemporary cognitive–behavioral theories have extended the work of Salkovskis to propose that various types of dysfunctional beliefs and appraisals, in addition to those pertaining to responsibility, play an important role in the etiology and maintenance of OCD. Although contemporary belief and appraisal models differ from one another in some ways, their similarities generally outweigh their differences.

To illustrate, Rachman (1997) proposed that "obsessions are caused by catastrophic misinterpretations of the significance of one's thoughts (images, impulses)" (p. 793). In this model, the misinterpretations are not limited to responsibility appraisals but can include any interpretation that the intrusive thought is personally significant, revealing, threatening, or even catastrophic. Such an interpretation has the effect of "transforming a commonplace nuisance into a torment" (Rachman, 1997, p. 794). The person usually interprets the intrusive thought in a personally significant way and as implying that he or she is "bad, mad, or dangerous."

TABLE 1.1
Domains of Dysfunctional Beliefs Associated
With Obsessive–Compulsive Disorder

Belief domain	Description
Excessive responsibility	Belief that one has the special power to cause or the duty to prevent negative outcomes.
Overimportance of thoughts	Belief that the mere presence of a thought indicates that the thought is significant. For example, the belief that the thought has ethical or moral ramifications or that thinking the thought increases the probability of the corresponding behavior or event.
Need to control thoughts	Belief that complete control over one's thoughts is both necessary and possible.
Overestimation of threat	Belief that negative events are especially likely and would be especially awful.
Perfectionism	Belief that mistakes and imperfection are intolerable.
Intolerance for uncertainty	Belief that it is necessary and possible to be completely certain that negative outcomes will not occur.

For example, a devoutly religious man experienced obscene images of Jesus with an erection on the cross whenever he tried to pray. He interpreted these images as meaning that he was "a vicious, lying hypocrite and that his religious beliefs and feelings were a sham." In another example, a man whose wife had just given birth to their first child had unwanted thoughts of beating the infant. He interpreted such thoughts as meaning that he was "dangerous and clearly unfit to be a parent." Such interpretations are thought to give rise to anxiety and dysphoria, with the consequence being intense resistance to the obsessions, attempts to suppress them, neutralization, and avoidance behavior. These examples illustrate "thought–action fusion" (Shafran, Thordarson, & Rachman, 1996), in which the person believes that his or her thoughts influence the external world (e.g., "I can cause an accident simply by thinking about one") or that thinking about a behavior is morally equivalent to performing the behavior itself (e.g., "Thinking about committing adultery is as bad as actually doing it").

Building on the work of Salkovskis, Rachman, and others, the most comprehensive contemporary belief and appraisal model is that developed by the Obsessive Compulsive Cognitions Working Group (OCCWG; Frost & Steketee, 2002). This is an international group of more than 40 investigators sharing a common interest in understanding the role of cognitive factors in OCD. The group began by developing a consensus regarding the most important beliefs (and associated appraisals) in OCD (Frost & Steketee, 2002; OCCWG, 1997). They identified responsibility beliefs and other belief domains, as listed in Table 1.1, which they conceptualized as giving rise to corresponding appraisals. The group developed self-report measures to assess these domains (OCCWG, 2001, 2003, 2005).

In addition to the models designed to account for OCD in general, OCCWG members and others have also developed a number of "mini-models" to account for particular types of OCD symptoms, such as compulsive hoarding (Frost & Hartl, 1996; Frost, Steketee, & Williams, 2002; see also Rachman, 1997, 1998). The development of such models is consistent with the view that OCD may be etiologically heterogeneous as well as symptomatically heterogeneous (McKay et al., 2004; Taylor, 2005). The mini-models account for symptom heterogeneity in various ways, such as by proposing that particular beliefs or patterns of beliefs are important for specific types of OCD symptoms, including highly specific beliefs in addition to the broad belief domains mentioned in Table 1.1. To illustrate, compulsive hoarding is said to arise from a constellation of etiologic factors, including dysfunctional beliefs about the value of possessions (e.g., beliefs that even worthless objects might be highly valuable or useful in the future), perfectionism, intolerance of uncertainty, and difficulty making decisions (Frost & Hartl, 1996; Frost et al., 2002).

These models have led to a promising new cognitive–behavioral therapy. As in exposure and response prevention, the therapy involves exposure and response prevention exercises. However, the exercises are framed as behavioral experiments to test appraisals and beliefs. To illustrate, a patient has recurrent images of terrorist hijackings and a compulsion to repeatedly telephone airports to warn them. This patient is found to hold a belief such as "Thinking about terrorist hijackings will make them actually occur." To challenge this belief, the patient and therapist can devise a test that pits this belief against a more realistic belief (e.g., "My thoughts have no influence on the occurrence of hijackings"). A behavioral experiment might involve deliberately bringing on thoughts of a hijacking and then evaluating the consequences. Cognitive restructuring methods derived from Beck's cognitive therapy (e.g., Beck & Emery, 1985) are also used to challenge OCD-related beliefs and appraisals.

Empirical Tests of the Belief and Appraisal Models

One of the strengths of the belief and appraisal models is that they are clearly falsifiable and have generated a large number of empirical predictions leading to a wealth of research. Twelve predictions derived from these models are listed in Table 1.2, along with a summary of their degree of empirical support. The table shows that there is encouraging support for the models, although some predictions have not been extensively evaluated and some predictions have not been supported by the research. The following sections summarize details of the findings. Space limitations preclude a detailed review of the literature; more detailed reviews can be found elsewhere (e.g., D. A. Clark, 2004; Frost & Steketee, 2002).

TABLE 1.2
Twelve Predictions Derived From the Belief and Appraisal Models of Obsessive–Compulsive Disorder

Prediction	Empirical support
1. The beliefs listed in Table 1.1 are distinct from one another.	−
2. The beliefs statistically predict or are correlated with OCD symptoms.	++
3. The beliefs should show specificity; they should be more strongly correlated with OCD symptoms than with measures of general distress (i.e., depression and general anxiety).	+
4. The beliefs interact with one another to statistically predict OCD symptoms.	−
5. OCD patients should generally score higher than control participants on measures of beliefs and appraisals.	++
6. Experimental manipulations of appraisals (e.g., increases or decreases in responsibility appraisals) lead to corresponding changes in OCD symptoms.	+
7. Naturally occurring events that increase the strength of beliefs or occurrence of appraisals (e.g., events increasing perceived responsibility) lead to increases in OCD symptoms.	+
8. OCD patients report learning histories that could give rise to the beliefs.	?
9. Efforts to suppress unwanted intrusive thoughts lead to an increased frequency of these thoughts.	+
10. Treatment-related reductions in OCD symptoms are associated with reductions in the strength of beliefs and frequency of appraisals.	+
11. Treatments that directly target beliefs and appraisals (e.g., cognitive–behavior therapy) are more effective than treatments that do not directly target these factors (e.g., exposure and response prevention).	−
12. Treatments that directly target beliefs and appraisals should be more tolerable for OCD patients (i.e., there should be fewer treatment dropouts).	+

Note. + = Preliminary support; ++ = strong support; − = not supported; ? = not yet adequately tested. Beliefs and appraisals refer to OCD-related beliefs and appraisals, such as those listed in Table 1.1.

Prediction 1: Beliefs should be distinguishable from one another. The first prediction states that the beliefs listed in Table 1.1 should be empirically distinguishable from one another. If beliefs about inflated responsibility, for example, play a specific role in OCD, then it should be possible to demonstrate that the effects of responsibility can be empirically disentangled from other beliefs. In other words, the beliefs should not be so highly correlated with one another that they form a single nonspecific or general OCD belief factor. The research does not support this prediction. Some research has examined the factor structure of two measures: the Obsessive Beliefs Questionnaire (OBQ; a measure of each belief domain listed in Table 1.1), and the Interpretation of Intrusions Inventory (III; a measure of appraisals of intrusive thoughts in which three appraisal domains are assessed—responsibility, importance of thoughts, and control of thoughts). Factor analytic research of the III indicates that the scale is unifactorial instead of consisting of the three predicted factors (OCCWG, 2005). Factor analyses of the OBQ indicate that it consists of three factors—inflated personal responsibility and the tendency to overestimate threat, perfectionism and intolerance of uncertainty, and overimportance and overcontrol of thoughts—instead of the predicted six (OCCWG, 2005). Hierarchical factor analysis of the OBQ indicates that these factors load on a single high-order factor and that the three factors account for a small proportion of the variance in OBQ scores (6%–7%) once the higher-order factor is taken into consideration (Taylor, McKay, & Abramowitz, 2005a). Thus, the findings raise the question about the merits of distinguishing among the various belief and appraisal domains such as those listed in Table 1.1.

Predictions 2 and 3: Beliefs should predict OCD symptoms and show specificity in correlations. The second and third predictions have received more support, both for the individual scales of the OBQ and III and for their factor scores. The scales and factors are each correlated with measures of OCD symptoms. The correlations with OCD symptoms tend to be larger than correlations with measures of general distress (i.e., depression and general anxiety), and the correlations with OCD symptoms remained significant even when the effects of general distress were partialled out (OCCWG, 2001, 2003). Several other studies using the OBQ or similar measures have also shown that these sorts of dysfunctional beliefs are correlated with many forms of OCD symptoms (e.g., Foa, Sacks, Tolin, Przeworski, & Amir, 2002; Tolin, Abramowitz, Brigidi, & Foa, 2003; Tolin, Woods, & Abramowitz, 2003).

Prediction 4: Beliefs should interact to predict OCD symptoms. Belief and appraisal models predict that beliefs (and possibly appraisals) should interact with one another to give rise to obsessions and compulsions; as D. A. Clark (2004) observed,

> Dysfunctional beliefs and appraisals involved in the pathogenesis of obsessions are complex. . . . Simply defining the cognitive basis of OCD in terms of single constructs will obfuscate the true, complex, interactive and multidimensional nature of cognition in OCD. (p. 109)

To illustrate the potential interactions of beliefs, one's sense of personal responsibility could influence the perceived importance of controlling one's thoughts so that harm does not occur. Alternatively, beliefs about the importance of one's thoughts (T) might inflate responsibility (R) beliefs (Thordarson & Shafran, 2002). If one conceptualizes this in terms of a path diagram, T and R could have direct effects on OCD symptoms, and T would also have an indirect (interactive) effect via its influence on R. Perfectionism (P) and T might also interact. According to Salkovskis et al. (2000), "Perfectionism is usually defined in terms which suggest more enduring personality-type characteristics, which might be expected to interact with the appraisal of intrusions, particularly when such intrusions concern the completion (or non completion) of particular actions" (p. 364). Responsibility might also inflate P (Salkovskis & Forrester, 2002). To test these predictions, we conducted a series of regression analyses in which the main effects for each belief (R, P, T) and their two- and three-way interactions were entered as predictors of measures of OCD symptoms. Main effects were significant predictors, but the interactions were not (Taylor, Abramowitz, & McKay, 2005). The findings suggest that the cognitive–behavioral models can be simplified to include only main effects.

Prediction 5: OCD patients should score higher than control participants. Research generally supports the prediction that OCD patients, compared with clinical and nonclinical control participants, score highest on the OBQ and III (OCCWG, 2003, 2005), although some of these results are trends ($p < .10$; Taylor et al., 2005a).

Prediction 6: Experimental manipulations of appraisals should influence OCD symptoms. A handful of studies have experimentally manipulated OCD-related appraisals, particularly responsibility appraisals, to assess the effects on compulsive checking (e.g., Bouchard, Rhéaume, & Ladouceur, 1999; Lopatka & Rachman, 1995; Rachman, Shafran, Mitchell, Trant, & Teachman, 1996). Research suggests that checking is more frequent when high responsibility is induced (e.g., for checking that a stove is turned off), compared with when low responsibility is induced.

Prediction 7: Events that strengthen beliefs or appraisals should increase OCD symptoms. A small number of studies have examined whether naturally occurring events that influence OCD-related beliefs or appraisals are related to the development or exacerbation of obsessions and compulsions. Childbirth, for example, increases the sense of personal responsibility for both parents. The increase in responsibility has been associated with the onset or exacerbation of OCD symptoms, at least in some individuals (Abramowitz, Khandker, Nelson, Deacon, & Rygwall, 2005; Abramowitz, Moore, Carmin, Wiegartz, & Purdon, 2001).

Prediction 8: Particular learning histories contribute to the development of OCD-related dysfunctional beliefs. Belief and appraisal models emphasize the role of learning experiences purported to give rise to the development of dysfunctional beliefs ("mal-learning") such as those listed in Table 1.1. This suggests that it should be possible to identify such learning experiences in people with OCD. This prediction has not been systematically investigated, although case studies have described such learning experiences (e.g., de Silva & Marks, 2001; Salkovskis et al., 1999; Tallis, 1994). Examples include a childhood environment that encouraged the development of rigid or extreme codes of conduct (thereby giving rise to inflated responsibility) and events in which one's thoughts were correlated with a serious misfortune (e.g., wishing that someone would die and then learning that the person had died from some mishap), which could lead to the development of beliefs about the importance of controlling one's thoughts. Controlled research is needed to determine whether most people with OCD report such experiences and whether they are more likely to have these experiences than control participants.

Prediction 9: Excessive attempts to control OCD symptoms should worsen these systems. Belief and appraisal models propose that OCD is maintained, in part, by trying too hard to control one's unwanted thoughts or by trying too hard to allay one's doubts. Consistent with this, experimental evidence suggests that repetitive checking actually increases doubt and uncertainty (van den Hout & Kindt, 2003a, 2003b). The research on attempts to control unwanted thoughts has yielded a more complex pattern of results. Experimental studies of non-OCD participants suggest that deliberate attempts to suppress unwanted thoughts often (but not invariably) lead to a paradoxical increase in the frequency of these thoughts (Wenzlaff & Wegner, 2000). Given the degree to which people with OCD strive to avoid their unwanted thoughts, this suggests that deliberate attempts to suppress obsessions should paradoxically increase the frequency of obsessions. There is inconsistent evidence that this occurs in OCD, although research indicates that people with OCD symptoms are more likely to try to suppress their unwanted, intrusive thoughts (Purdon, 2004).

Predictions 10, 11, and 12: Targeting beliefs and appraisals should improve treatment outcome. The final set of predictions concern the treatment relevance of the belief and appraisal models of OCD. Belief and appraisal models underscore the importance of cognitive factors in maintaining OCD and also predict that interventions that reduce the strength of OCD-related dysfunctional beliefs (e.g., the overestimation of threat) should improve treatment outcome. Reducing the strength of these beliefs should also lead patients to be more willing to engage in behavioral and cognitive–behavioral treatments that encourage them to confront the things that they fear, such as exposure to contaminants or to refrain from performing rituals that they believe will avert feared consequences (e.g., by refraining from compulsively repeating a prayer after having a "bad" thought about a family member).

Consistent with the belief and appraisal models, studies have shown that treatments that reduce OCD symptoms also reduce the strength of OCD-related beliefs (Bouvard, 2002; Emmelkamp, van Oppen, & van Balkom, 2002; McLean et al., 2001). Treatments that directly target OCD-related beliefs (i.e., cognitive–behavioral therapy) are associated with a lower proportion of dropouts than treatments that do not directly target these beliefs, such as exposure and response prevention (Abramowitz, Taylor, & McKay, 2005). However, cognitive–behavior therapy for OCD is no more effective than exposure and response prevention (Abramowitz, Taylor, & McKay, 2005). The latter finding might challenge the belief and appraisal models of OCD. Alternatively, these findings may simply indicate that cognitive–behavioral therapy is not as powerful a vehicle of belief changes as is exposure and response prevention. As Bandura (1977) mentioned many years ago, behavioral interventions (e.g., exposure and response prevention) may be the most potent agents of cognitive change.

Overall, the predictions summarized in Table 1.2 have mixed but generally positive support. Even so, we agree with D. A. Clark's (2004) conclusion that more research needs to be done to firmly establish that beliefs and appraisals play a causal role in OCD.

Neglected Realms of Research

As we described in the previous section, many of the predictions derived from belief and appraisal models have received encouraging empirical support. The predictions that were not supported suggest possible avenues for refining the models. As such, the models can be regarded as open concepts (Meehl, 1977), which are amenable to development and change in response to empirical findings.

A limitation of the belief and appraisal models is that they largely ignore the burgeoning research literature on the neuropsychology and neurobiology of OCD. It is unclear, for example, how the various neuropsychological deficits and reasoning abnormalities are related, if at all, to dysfunctional beliefs and appraisals in OCD. An exception is Frost's mini-model of hoarding (Frost & Hartl, 1996; Frost et al., 2002), which describes how information-processing abnormalities, such as decision-making difficulties, might be related to dysfunctional beliefs and appraisals. Yet even this model neglects the extensive research on the neurobiology of OCD.

The brain obviously forms the organic foundation from which beliefs, appraisals, and "idea generators" emerge. And brain structures and circuits are influenced by genetic factors. Thus, a more complete understanding of the etiology of OCD may arise if the belief and appraisal models can be integrated with neurobiological and genetic research. Important questions include the following: How can belief and appraisal models be reconciled with neuroimaging research, which shows that OCD is associated with structural aberrations (e.g., volumetric abnormalities) and functional brain abnormalities, including abnormalities in the orbital frontal cortex and basal ganglia (e.g., Pujol et al., 2004; Szeszko et al., 1999; Whiteside, Port, & Abramowitz, 2004)? How can the belief and appraisal models be reconciled with research suggesting that OCD sometimes abruptly emerges in previously normal people after streptococcal infection and abates when the infection is treated (e.g., Swedo, 2002)?

Belief and appraisal models emphasize the importance of various forms of mal-learning in the development of dysfunctional beliefs and appraisals in OCD. Yet what about the role of genetic factors? Research shows that various forms of beliefs are heritable, including religious and political ideologies (e.g., Rowe, 1994), and dysfunctional beliefs implicated in various forms of psychopathology have also been shown to be heritable (e.g., Jang, Stein, Taylor, & Livesley, 1999; Taylor, Thordarson, Jang, & Asmundson, 2006). Thus, the question arises as to the relative importance of genetic and environmental factors in OCD-related beliefs and appraisals.

CONCLUSION

The belief and appraisal models of OCD have many of the properties that a good model ought to have; for example, the models are falsifiable, make clear predictions, and have treatment relevance. Not surprisingly, the models have led to a rich program of research into the etiology and treatment of OCD. Although there is a good deal of empirical support for belief and appraisal conceptualizations, these models have also encountered some difficulties, such as failures to empirically support some predictions. These models are works in progress, and no doubt they will be refined in the coming years to deal with these obstacles. A more important concern, however, is that the models have been developed largely in a cognitive–behavioral vacuum; that is, they have ignored the mounting body of research on the importance of neurobiological and genetic factors in OCD. A more complete understanding of this disorder is likely to arise if theorists and researchers are willing to tackle the challenging task of integrating mind and brain—that is, beliefs and appraisals with neuroscience. Such efforts may eventually lead to a comprehensive model of OCD.

Another potentially important avenue of research is to extend the conceptual and empirical work on OCD subtypes. It is possible that the belief and appraisal models apply only to some forms of OCD. Indeed, some research suggests that some OCD patients have essentially normal scores on dysfunctional beliefs listed in Table 1.1 (Taylor, Abramowitz, McKay, Calamari, et al., 2005). Some models of OCD do not regard dysfunctional beliefs as playing an important role (Jakes, 1996; Swedo, 2002; Szechtman & Woody, 2004). Swedo's (2002) model, for example, proposes that some cases of OCD, as well as some other disorders, arise from pediatric streptococcal infection that damages the basal ganglia and associated structures. Szechtman and Woody (2004) suggested that OCD arises from a dysfunction in a noncognitive and emotion-based security motivation system located in the brain. Neither of these models includes dysfunctional beliefs as explanatory constructs. It is possible that different theoretical models apply to different subtypes of OCD. That is, models emphasizing the role of dysfunctional beliefs and appraisals might apply only to a subgroup of cases of OCD or to particular symptom presentations. Further research is needed to explore this intriguing possibility.

REFERENCES

Abramowitz, J. S., Khandker, M., Nelson, C. A., Deacon, B. J., & Rygwall, R. (2005). *The role of cognitive factors in the pathogenesis of obsessions and compulsions: A prospective study.* Manuscript submitted for publication.

Abramowitz, J. S., Moore, K., Carmin, C., Wiegartz, P., & Purdon, C. (2001). Acute onset of obsessive–compulsive disorder in males following childbirth. *Psychosomatics, 42,* 429–431.

Abramowitz, J. S., Taylor, S., & McKay, D. (2005). Potentials and limitations of cognitive therapy for obsessive–compulsive disorder. *Cognitive Behaviour Therapy, 34,* 140–147.

American Psychiatric Association. (2000). *Diagnostic and statistical manual of mental disorders* (4th ed., text rev.). Washington, DC: Author.

Bandura, A. (1977). Self-efficacy: Toward a unifying theory of behavioral change. *Psychological Review, 84,* 191–215.

Beck, A. T. (1976). *Cognitive therapy and the emotional disorders.* New York: International Universities Press.

Beck, A. T. (1988). Cognitive approaches to panic disorder: Theory and therapy. In S. Rachman & J. D. Maser (Eds.), *Panic: Psychological perspectives* (pp. 91–109). Hillsdale, NJ: Erlbaum.

Beck, A. T., & Emery, G. (1985). *Anxiety disorders and phobias: A cognitive perspective.* New York: Basic Books.

Bouchard, C., Rhéaume, J., & Ladouceur, R. (1999). Responsibility and perfectionism in OCD: An experimental study. *Behaviour Research and Therapy, 37,* 239–248.

Bouvard, M. (2002). Cognitive effects of cognitive–behavior therapy for obsessive compulsive disorder. In R. O. Frost & G. S. Steketee (Eds.), *Cognitive approaches to obsessions and compulsions: Theory, assessment, and treatment* (pp. 403–416). Oxford, England: Elsevier.

Clark, D. A. (2004). *Cognitive–behavioral therapy for OCD.* New York: Guilford Press.

Clark, D. M. (1986). A cognitive approach to panic. *Behaviour Research and Therapy, 24,* 461–470.

de Silva, P., & Marks, M. (2001). Traumatic experiences, post-traumatic stress disorder and obsessive–compulsive disorder. *International Review of Psychiatry, 13,* 172–180.

Emmelkamp, P. M. G., van Oppen, P., & van Balkom, A. J. (2002). Cognitive changes in patients with obsessive compulsive rituals treated with exposure in vivo and response prevention. In R. O. Frost & G. S. Steketee (Eds.), *Cognitive approaches to obsessions and compulsions: Theory, assessment, and treatment* (pp. 391–401). Oxford, England: Elsevier.

Enright, S. J., & Beech, A. R. (1993a). Further evidence of reduced inhibition in obsessive compulsive disorder. *Personality and Individual Differences, 14,* 387–395.

Enright, S. J., & Beech, A. R. (1993b). Reduced cognitive inhibition in obsessive compulsive disorder. *British Journal of Clinical Psychology, 32,* 67–74.

Enright, S. J., Beech, A. R., & Claridge, G. S. (1995). The locus of negative priming effects in obsessive–compulsive disorder and other anxiety disorders. *Personality and Individual Differences, 19,* 535–542.

Foa, E. B, Sacks, M. B., Tolin, D. F., Przeworski, A., & Amir, N. (2002). Inflated perception of responsibility for harm in OCD patients with and without checking compulsions: A replication and extension. *Journal of Anxiety Disorders, 16,* 443–453.

Freeston, M. H., Rhéaume, J., & Ladouceur, R. (1996). Correcting faulty appraisals of obsessional thoughts. *Behaviour Research and Therapy, 34,* 433–446.

Frost, R. O., & Gross, R. C. (1993). The hoarding of possessions. *Behaviour Research and Therapy, 31,* 367–381.

Frost, R. O., & Hartl, T. L. (1996). A cognitive–behavioral model of compulsive hoarding. *Behaviour Research and Therapy, 34,* 341–350.

Frost, R. O., & Steketee, G. (2002). *Cognitive approaches to obsessions and compulsions: Theory, assessment and treatment.* Oxford, England: Elsevier.

Frost, R. O., Steketee, G., & Williams, L. (2002). Compulsive buying, compulsive hoarding, and obsessive–compulsive disorder. *Behavior Therapy, 33,* 201–214.

Gray, J. A. (1982). *The neuropsychology of anxiety.* London: Oxford University Press.

Greisberg, S., & McKay, D. (2003). Neuropsychology of obsessive–compulsive disorder: A review and treatment implications. *Clinical Psychology Review, 23,* 95–117.

Jakes, I. (1996). *Theoretical approaches to obsessive–compulsive disorder.* Cambridge, England: Cambridge University Press.

Jang, K. L., Stein, M. B., Taylor, S., & Livesley, W. J. (1999). Gender differences in the etiology of anxiety sensitivity: A twin study. *Journal of Gender Specific Medicine, 2,* 39–44.

Jurado, M. A., Junque, C., Vallejo, J., Salgado, P., & Grafman, J. (2002). Obsessive–compulsive disorder (OCD) patients are impaired in remembering temporal order and in judging their own performance. *Journal of Clinical and Experimental Neuropsychology, 24,* 261–269.

Lopatka, C., & Rachman, S. (1995). Perceived responsibility and compulsive checking: An experimental analysis. *Behaviour Research and Therapy, 33,* 674–684.

March, J. S., Frances, A., Carpenter, L. L., & Kahn, D. (1997). Expert consensus treatment guidelines for obsessive–compulsive disorder: A guide for patients and families. *Journal of Clinical Psychiatry, 58*(Suppl. 4), 65–72.

McKay, D., Abramowitz, J. S., Calamari, J., Kyrios, M., Sookman, D., Taylor, S., & Wilhelm, S. (2004). A critical evaluation of obsessive–compulsive disorder subtypes: Symptoms versus mechanisms. *Clinical Psychology Review, 24,* 283–313.

McLean, P. D., Whittal, M. L., Thordarson, D., Taylor, S., Söchting, I., Koch, W. J., et al. (2001). Cognitive versus behavior therapy in the group treatment of obsessive compulsive disorder. *Journal of Consulting and Clinical Psychology, 69,* 205–214.

Meehl, P. E. (1977). Specific etiology and other forms of strong influence: Some quantitative meanings. *Journal of Medicine and Philosophy, 2*, 33–53.

Mowrer, O. H. (1960). *Learning theory and behavior*. New York: Wiley.

Nielen, M. M. A., & Den Boer, J. A. (2003). Neuropsychological performance of OCD patients before and after treatment with fluoxetine: Evidence for persistent cognitive deficits. *Psychological Medicine, 33*, 917–925.

Obsessive Compulsive Cognitions Working Group. (1997). Cognitive assessment of obsessive–compulsive disorder. *Behaviour Research and Therapy, 35*, 667–681.

Obsessive Compulsive Cognitions Working Group. (2001). Development and initial validation of the Obsessive Beliefs Questionnaire and the Interpretation of Intrusions Inventory. *Behaviour Research and Therapy, 39*, 987–1005.

Obsessive Compulsive Cognitions Working Group. (2003). Psychometric validation of the Obsessive Beliefs Questionnaire and the Interpretation of Intrusions Inventory: Part 1. *Behaviour Research and Therapy, 41*, 863–878.

Obsessive Compulsive Cognitions Working Group. (2005). Psychometric validation of the Obsessive Beliefs Questionnaire and the Interpretation of Intrusions Inventory: Part 2. *Behaviour Research and Therapy, 43*, 1527–1542.

O'Connor, K. (2002). Intrusions and inferences in obsessive compulsive disorder. *Clinical Psychology and Psychotherapy, 9*, 38–46.

Pitman, R. A. (1987). A cybernetic model of obsessive–compulsive pathology. *Comprehensive Psychiatry, 28*, 334–343.

Pujol, J., Soriano-Mas, C., Alonso, P., Cardoner, N., Menchon, J. M., Deus, J., & Vallejo, J. (2004). Mapping structural brain alterations in obsessive–compulsive disorder. *Archives of General Psychiatry, 61*, 720–730.

Purdon, C. (2004). Empirical investigations of thought suppression in OCD. *Journal of Behavior Therapy and Experimental Psychiatry, 35*, 121–136.

Rachman, S. (1971). Obsessional ruminations. *Behaviour Research and Therapy, 9*, 225–238.

Rachman, S. (1997). A cognitive theory of obsessions. *Behaviour Research and Therapy, 35*, 793–802.

Rachman, S., & de Silva, P. (1978). Abnormal and normal obsessions. *Behaviour Research and Therapy, 16*, 233–248.

Rachman, S., & Hodgson, R. J. (1980). *Obsessions and compulsions*. Englewood Cliffs, NJ: Prentice Hall.

Rachman, S., Shafran, R., Mitchell, D., Trant, J., & Teachman, B. (1996). How to remain neutral: An experimental analysis of neutralization. *Behaviour Research and Therapy, 34*, 889–898.

Reed, G. F. (1985). *Obsessional experience and compulsive behaviour: A cognitive structural approach*. New York: Academic Press.

Rowe, D. C. (1994). *The limits of family influence: Genes, experience, and behavior*. New York: Guilford Press.

Salkovskis, P. M. (1985). Obsessional–compulsive problems: A cognitive–behavioural analysis. *Behaviour Research and Therapy, 25*, 571–583.

Salkovskis, P. M. (1989). Cognitive–behavioural factors and the persistence of intrusive thoughts in obsessional problems. *Behaviour Research and Therapy, 27,* 677–682.

Salkovskis, P. M. (1996). Cognitive–behavioral approaches to the understanding of obsessional problems. In R. M. Rapee (Ed.), *Current controversies in the anxiety disorders* (pp. 103–134). New York: Guilford Press.

Salkovskis, P. M., & Forrester, E. (2002). Responsibility. In R. O. Frost & G. S. Steketee (Eds.), *Cognitive approaches to obsessions and compulsions: Theory, assessment and treatment* (pp. 45–61). Oxford, England: Elsevier.

Salkovskis, P. M., & Harrison, J. (1984). Abnormal and normal obsessions: A replication. *Behaviour Research and Therapy, 22,* 1–4.

Salkovskis, P. M., Shafran, R., Rachman, S., & Freeston, M. H. (1999). Multiple pathways to inflated responsibility in obsessional problems: Possible origins and implications for therapy and research. *Behaviour Research and Therapy, 37,* 1055–1072.

Salkovskis, P. M., Wroe, A. L., Gledhill, A., Morrison, N., Forrester, E., Richards, C., et al. (2000). Responsibility attitudes and interpretations are characteristic of obsessive compulsive disorder. *Behaviour Research and Therapy, 38,* 347–372.

Shafran, R., Thordarson, D. S., & Rachman, S. (1996). Thought–action fusion in obsessive–compulsive disorder. *Journal of Anxiety Disorders, 10,* 379–391.

Steketee, G. S. (1993). *Treatment of obsessive compulsive disorder.* New York: Guilford Press.

Swedo, S. E. (2002). Pediatric autoimmune neuropsychiatric disorders associated with streptococcal infections (PANDAS). *Molecular Psychiatry, 7,* S24–S25.

Szechtman, H., & Woody, E. (2004). Obsessive–compulsive disorder as a disturbance of security motivation. *Psychological Review, 111,* 111–127.

Szeszko, P. R., Robinson, D., Alvir, J. M., Bilder, R. M., Lencz, T., Ashtari, M., et al. (1999). Orbital frontal and amygdala volume reductions in obsessive–compulsive disorder. *Archives of General Psychiatry, 56,* 913–919.

Tallis, F. (1994). Obsessions, responsibility and guilt: Two case reports suggesting a common and specific aetiology. *Behaviour Research and Therapy, 32,* 143–145.

Taylor, S. (2002). Cognition in obsessive–compulsive disorder: An overview. In R. O. Frost & G. Steketee (Eds.), *Cognitive approaches to obsessions and compulsions: Theory, assessment, and treatment* (pp. 1–12). Oxford, England: Elsevier.

Taylor, S. (2005). Dimensional and categorical models of OCD: A critical analysis. In J. S. Abramowitz & A. C. Houts (Eds.), *Handbook of OCD: Concepts and controversies* (pp. 27–41). New York: Kluwer Academic.

Taylor, S., Abramowitz, J. S., & McKay, D. (2005). Are there interactions among dysfunctional beliefs in obsessive compulsive disorder? *Cognitive Behaviour Therapy, 34,* 89–98.

Taylor, S., Abramowitz, J. S., McKay, D., Calamari, J. E., Sookman, D., Kyrios, M., et al. (2005). Do dysfunctional beliefs play a role in all types of obsessive–compulsive disorder? *Journal of Anxiety Disorders, 20,* 85–97.

Taylor, S., McKay, D., & Abramowitz, J. S. (2005a). Hierarchical structure of dysfunctional beliefs in obsessive–compulsive disorder. *Cognitive Behaviour Therapy*, *34*, 216–228.

Taylor, S., McKay, D., & Abramowitz, J. S. (2005b). Is obsessive–compulsive disorder a disturbance of security motivation? Comment on Szechtman and Woody (2004). *Psychological Review*, *112*, 656–657.

Taylor, S., McKay, D., & Abramowitz, J. S. (2005c). Problems with the security motivation model remain largely unresolved: Response to Woody and Szechtman (2005). *Psychological Review*, *112*, 656–657.

Taylor, S., Thordarson, D. S., Jang, K. L., & Asmundson, G. J. G. (2006). Genetic and environmental origins of health anxiety: A twin study. *World Psychiatry*, *5*, 47–50.

Teasdale, J. D. (1974). Learning models of obsessional–compulsive disorder. In H. R. Beech (Ed.), *Obsessional states* (pp. 197–229). London: Methuen.

Thordarson, D. S., & Shafran, R. (2002). Importance of thoughts. In R. O. Frost & G. S. Steketee (Eds.), *Cognitive approaches to obsessions and compulsions: Theory, assessment and treatment* (pp. 15–28). Oxford, England: Elsevier.

Tolin, D. F., Abramowitz, J. S., Brigidi, B. D., & Foa, E. B. (2003). Intolerance of uncertainty in obsessive–compulsive disorder. *Journal of Anxiety Disorders*, *17*, 233–242.

Tolin, D. F., Woods, C. M., & Abramowitz, J. S. (2003). Relationship between obsessive beliefs and obsessive–compulsive symptoms. *Cognitive Therapy and Research*, *27*, 657–669.

van den Hout, M., & Kindt, M. (2003a). Phenomenological validity of an OCD-memory model and the remember/know distinction. *Behaviour Research and Therapy*, *41*, 369–378.

van den Hout, M., & Kindt, M. (2003b). Repeated checking causes memory distrust. *Behaviour Research and Therapy*, *41*, 301–316.

Wenzlaff, R. M., & Wegner, D. M. (2000). Thought suppression. *Annual Review of Psychology*, *51*, 59–91.

Whiteside, S. P., Port, J. D., & Abramowitz, J. S. (2004). A meta-analysis of functional neuroimaging in obsessive–compulsive disorder. *Psychiatry Research: Neuroimaging*, *132*, 69–79.

Woods, C. M., Vevea, J. L., Chambless, D. L., & Bayen, U. J. (2002). Are compulsive checkers impaired in memory? A meta-analytic review. *Clinical Psychology: Science and Practice*, *9*, 353–366.

2

GENERAL ISSUES IN PSYCHOLOGICAL TREATMENT FOR OBSESSIVE–COMPULSIVE DISORDER

DAVID F. TOLIN AND GAIL STEKETEE

The most widely tested psychological treatment for obsessive–compulsive disorder (OCD) is exposure and response prevention (ERP; also known as exposure and ritual prevention), in which patients are gradually exposed to their obsessive feared situations and asked not to engage in rituals or avoidance behaviors. This intervention typically leads to reductions in negative emotions such as anxiety, guilt, and depression; to shifts in beliefs about the probability of harm; and to increased tolerance of intrusive thoughts. It also reduces avoidance behaviors and mental and behavioral rituals that reinforce the obsessive thoughts. Formal cognitive therapy (based on Beck's model; Beck, Emery, & Greenberg, 1985) may also provide relief from OCD symptoms, as do serotonergic medications.

This chapter focuses on the clinician's decision making and implementation of interventions for OCD. We address indications and contraindications for ERP, when to consider combining ERP with cognitive therapy and medications, various formats for delivering ERP, how to do a functional analysis and select treatment targets, and the influence of comorbidity on treatment decisions. We also review motivational strategies, whether to involve family members in exposure treatment, other aspects of the patient's life that can influence treatment, and finally, how to help patients maintain their own gains. Our recommendations for ERP implementation are based on research findings that we describe briefly in each section to set the stage for clinical decision making.

JUDGING APPROPRIATENESS FOR EXPOSURE AND RESPONSE PREVENTION

In general, ERP should at least be considered for all patients with OCD, given the compelling evidence of its efficacy (e.g., Cottraux, Mollard, Bouvard, & Marks, 1993; Fals-Stewart, Marks, & Schafer, 1993; Foa et al., 2005; Lindsay, Crino, & Andrews, 1997; van Balkom et al., 1998). In addition to traditional randomized controlled trials with highly selected participants, ERP has also proved effective in clinical settings (Franklin, Abramowitz, Kozak, Levitt, & Foa, 2000; Warren & Thomas, 2001) and with medication-resistant patients (Kampman, Keijsers, Hoogduin, & Verbraak, 2002; Simpson, Gorfinkle, & Liebowitz, 1999; Tolin, Maltby, Diefenbach, Hannan, & Worhunsky, 2004). Thus, an expert consensus panel (March, Frances, Carpenter, & Kahn, 1997) wrote that cognitive–behavioral interventions such as ERP are "recommended for every patient with OCD except those who are unwilling to participate" (p. 12).

Contraindications for ERP have not been clearly delineated. Some clinicians believe that the exposure element of ERP is too stressful for some patients. Although this issue has not been assessed formally for OCD, a survey of psychologists about treatments for another anxiety disorder, posttraumatic stress disorder (PTSD), revealed that the majority were reluctant to use exposure therapy for severely suicidal or homicidal patients, or for those with a comorbid psychotic or dissociative disorder. In addition, the majority of the sample believed that exposure therapy created a risk in some patients for dissociation, substance abuse, and suicidality (Becker, Zayfert, & Anderson, 2004). In addition (and somewhat contrary to their blanket recommendation), the OCD expert consensus panel (March et al., 1997) did not recommend CBT as a first-line treatment component for patients with comorbid schizophrenia, although they did recommend CBT for patients with all other comorbid disorders, including heart disease.

Does exposure-based therapy lead to the exacerbation of anxious symptoms or create an unacceptable risk of adverse events in dissociative, suicidal, homicidal, substance-abusing, or psychotic patients? These issues have not been explored empirically in the treatment of OCD. In a study of exposure-based treatment of PTSD patients, only a minority experienced an initial increase in symptoms; it is interesting to note (and contrary to what some would predict) that patients who experienced symptom exacerbation were no more likely than others to drop out of treatment and appeared ultimately to benefit just as much as did those whose symptoms did not increase (Foa, Zoellner, Feeny, Hembree, & Alvarez-Conrad, 2002). In patients with PTSD and comorbid cocaine dependence, many treated with PTSD-directed exposure therapy dropped out of treatment, a response that may not be unique to exposure therapy. However, patients who remained in treatment experienced a decrease in not only their PTSD symptoms but also their cocaine use (Brady, Dansky, Back, Foa, & Carroll, 2001). This result is the opposite of what would be expected if exposure therapy increased the risk of substance use. Thus, there is little reason from an empirical perspective to believe that well-conducted ERP creates a high risk for treatment-emergent adverse events, even in vulnerable individuals, although many clinicians refrain from using these techniques for these reasons.

Another factor in making treatment decisions for OCD patients is to consider variables that have been shown to predict poor response to treatment. That is, even if ERP is not deemed risky, this treatment may not be particularly effective for patients with certain features. However, no reliable markers of treatment response have been identified for ERP in OCD patients. Some studies have found that higher initial severity of OCD symptoms was associated with poorer outcomes (de Haan et al., 1997; Keijsers, Hoogduin, & Schaap, 1994), whereas others have not found such an association (Cottraux, Messy, Marks, Mollard, & Bouvard, 1993; Steketee & Shapiro, 1995). Duration of OCD was unrelated to outcome in two studies of ERP (Cottraux, Messy, et al., 1993; Steketee & Shapiro, 1995). Type of OCD may also be related to outcome. Symptoms of compulsive hoarding in particular have been associated with poor response to ERP both with and without medications (Abramowitz, Franklin, Schwartz, & Furr, 2003; Black et al., 1998; Mataix-Cols, Marks, Greist, Kobak, & Baer, 2002; Saxena et al., 2002). Likewise, sexual and religious concerns have also been associated with poor response to ERP (Mataix-Cols et al., 2002), possibly because of poorer insight among patients in these subgroups (Tolin, Abramowitz, Kozak, & Foa, 2001). Research on the effects of comorbid personality disorders is similarly mixed, with some studies finding attenuated treatment response and others finding no attenuation (Fals-Stewart & Lucente, 1993; Steketee, 1990).

Some early reports suggested that pretreatment depression predicted poorer outcomes of ERP (Foa, 1979), although a later study indicated that highly and mildly depressed patients responded similarly to treatment (Foa, Kozak, Steketee, & McCarthy, 1992). In a large sample of OCD patients, only severe depression was associated with attenuated outcome of ERP, although even those patients showed significant clinical improvement (Abramowitz, Franklin, Street, Kozak, & Foa, 2000). Consistent with these findings, Steketee, Chambless, and Tran (2001) reported that comorbid major depression predicted worse outcomes for patients with OCD or agoraphobia. Lower initial motivation appeared to be associated with poorer outcome of

ERP (de Haan et al., 1997; Keijsers et al., 1994); this may be mediated by reduced follow-through with exposure exercises (de Araujo, Ito, & Marks, 1996; O'Sullivan, Noshirvani, Marks, Monteiro, & Lelliott, 1991). Insight into the irrationality of obsessive fears has been associated with poorer outcome in some studies of ERP (Foa, 1979; Neziroglu, Stevens, & Yaryura-Tobias, 1999), but not in others (Foa et al., 1983; Hoogduin & Duivenvoorden, 1988). These differences may pertain to the use of different strategies for measuring insight.

Ideally, further research on predictors of outcome will lead to the development of treatment algorithms in which patients can be matched a priori to specific treatments. However, the available body of research does not yet support such decisions, with the possible exception of compulsive hoarding, which may require specific interventions tailored to the idiosyncratic nature of hoarding-related symptoms (Hartl & Frost, 1999; Steketee & Frost, 2003).

PHARMACOLOGICAL AUGMENTATION OF EXPOSURE AND RESPONSE PREVENTION

The expert consensus panel (March et al., 1997) recommended that for more severe cases of adult OCD, ERP should be combined with serotonin reuptake inhibitor (SRI) medication. The implication, therefore, is that ERP plus SRI should be more efficacious than ERP alone. What do the available data have to say on this topic? To date, four studies have been published that permit a clear test of the efficacy of ERP alone versus ERP + SRI (for a review, see Foa, Franklin, & Moser, 2002). In a comparison ($N = 60$) of ERP + fluvoxamine (FLV), ERP + pill placebo (PBO), and FLV alone, the combined treatment appeared superior to ERP alone and FLV alone at posttreatment (as measured by ratings of daily rituals). However, at 6-month follow-up (during which many patients remained on medications), differences among the groups had largely disappeared (Cottraux et al., 1990). At 1-year follow-up, there remained no significant differences among the groups, although patients who received ERP were less likely to be on medications at that time than were patients who did not receive ERP (Cottraux, Mollard, et al., 1993).

A second study ($N = 58$) of ERP + FLV versus ERP + PBO found a greater number of treatment responders in the ERP + FLV group than in the ERP + PBO group (Hohagen et al., 1998). Outcome was measured using the Yale–Brown Obsessive–Compulsive Scale (Y–BOCS; Goodman et al., 1989). A larger ($N = 117$) study compared five conditions: cognitive therapy (CT), ERP, CT + FLV, ERP + FLV, and wait list (WL; van Balkom et al., 1998). At posttreatment, there were no significant differences among the four active treatments, and all were superior to WL, although there was a nonsignificant trend toward superiority of combined treatment over ERP or CT monotherapy. There was no follow-up assessment.

The largest study to date on the topic of ERP alone versus ERP with medications has been published (Foa et al., 2005). The size of this study and the level of detail provided allow a closer look at the comparative effects of ERP monotherapy versus combined therapy. One hundred forty-nine participants were assigned to ERP, clomipramine (CMI), ERP + CMI, or PBO. On learning of their treatment condition, 22% withdrew from the ERP condition, 23% from the CMI condition, and 19% from the PBO condition, but only 6% from the ERP + CMI condition. Although these proportions are not significantly different from one another, they hint at a higher acceptability of combined treatment over either medication or ERP alone. These withdrawals left a sample of 122 patients who entered the study. During treatment, 28% dropped out of ERP, 25% of CMI, and 23% of PBO, but 39% dropped out of ERP + CMI. Again, these proportions were not significantly different from one another, but they suggest that although the combined treatment may be more attractive initially, more patients may discontinue this treatment prematurely.

Analysis of outcome using the Y–BOCS after 12 weeks of treatment indicated that patients in all active treatment groups fared better than did those receiving placebo. Patients completing ERP alone experienced a 55% decrease on the Y–BOCS. Patients completing ERP + CMI, CMI, and PBO experienced decreases of 59%, 31%, and 11%, respectively. ERP alone led to significantly greater improvement than did CMI alone, and ERP + CMI was superior to CMI alone. However, the difference between ERP alone and ERP + CMI was not significant. The percentage of treatment-completing patients labeled "treatment responders" using the Clinical Global Impression scale (CGI; Guy, 1976) was 86% for ERP, 79% for ERP + CMI, 48% for CMI, and 10% for PBO. The percentage of patients labeled "excellent treatment responders" using the CGI was 57% for ERP, 47% for ERP + CMI, 19% for CMI, and 0% for PBO. For responder analysis, all active treatments were superior to PBO, and both treatments containing ERP were superior to CMI. However, there were no differences in the number of responders or excellent responders between ERP alone and ERP + CMI. After treatment discontinuation, treatment responders were followed for an additional 12 weeks (Simpson et al., 2004). Relapse rates were 11% for ERP and 14% for ERP + CMI, but 45% for CMI. Thus, patients receiving ERP with or without CMI were less likely to relapse after treatment discontinuation than were patients receiving CMI alone, with no significant difference between ERP and ERP + CMI.

In summary, the available data do not clearly answer the question of whether combined therapy is preferable to ERP monotherapy. Those who would argue for ERP monotherapy might note that across studies, although there is a trend for combined therapy to be more effective than ERP alone, this trend does not reach statistical significance and appears to vanish at follow-up. Furthermore, evidence from the largest and most recent trial of

ERP and CMI suggests that combined treatment may be associated with increased risk of dropout without a substantial increase in treatment efficacy.

Those who would argue for combination therapy over ERP monotherapy could note several weaknesses in the literature. First, although the available studies do not show a strong advantage for combined therapy, none of the studies speak to the expert consensus panel's recommendation that patients with more severe OCD be given combined therapy right away (March et al., 1997). Second, patients in these studies were generally selected for the absence of certain comorbid conditions such as psychosis, substance abuse, suicidality, or developmental disorders, although other conditions such as depression and personality disorders were usually allowed. Third, studies that randomly assigned patients to treatment conditions might have failed to account for the potentially large impact of patients' preferences for one treatment over the other (TenHave, Coyne, Salzer, & Katz, 2003). Patient preference may influence treatment outcome in several ways, including enrollment and attrition, homework and medication compliance, and expectancy for improvement. Finally, some comorbid conditions, such as severe depression or psychosis, might indicate the use of medications, particularly when comorbidity makes OCD treatment difficult or impossible (e.g., for a depressed patient who is unable to get out of bed and come to therapy reliably).

USING COGNITIVE THERAPY TO AUGMENT EXPOSURE AND RESPONSE PREVENTION

Currently, the best evidence suggests that ERP is an effective intervention for OCD (Cottraux, Mollard, et al., 1993; Fals-Stewart et al., 1993; Foa et al., 2005; Lindsay et al., 1997; van Balkom et al., 1998). This treatment consists of gradual, prolonged exposure to fear-eliciting stimuli or situations combined with strict abstinence from compulsive behavior. The purpose of these exercises is to allow patients to experience a reduction of their fear response and to recognize that these situations are not excessively dangerous and that their fear will not last forever. Thus, although ERP is a "behavioral" intervention, its mechanism of action may well be cognitive (Foa & Kozak, 1986), and the distinction between behavioral and cognitive therapy may be somewhat arbitrary (Maltby & Tolin, 2003). Should cognitive interventions be used in place of, or as an augmentation of, ERP? During ERP, we routinely assist patients in changing inaccurate beliefs about feared situations, such as pointing out that feared consequences did not occur or that the patient's fear did not persist indefinitely. However, a more formal cognitive intervention teaches patients to identify and correct their dysfunctional beliefs about feared situations (Whittal & O'Neill, 2003; Wilhelm, 2003). In most cases, this has involved either rational–emotive therapy (RET), in which irrational thoughts are identified and targeted via rational debate, or, more recently, cognitive therapy along the lines of Beck et al. (1985), in which Socratic questioning, behavioral experiments, and other cognitive strategies are used to challenge the validity of distorted thoughts. The overlap of behavioral experiments with ERP should be clear, and it is possible that the difference is one of emphasis. Certainly, both cognitive therapy and ERP are intended to change both OCD behavior and cognitions, and it is not clear whether the mechanisms of action differ between these two forms of treatment.

Although the specific efficacy of cognitive therapy for OCD has not been firmly established, some evidence is promising. In an early study, RET yielded results that did not differ from those of ERP (Emmelkamp, Visser, & Hoekstra, 1988). In comparative efficacy studies of adults with OCD, Beck-style cognitive therapy produced moderately strong results that also did not differ significantly from those of ERP (Cottraux et al., 2001; van Balkom et al., 1998; van Oppen et al., 1995). In a comparison study using groups to deliver the treatment, cognitive therapy yielded moderate results that were not as strong as those obtained using group ERP (McLean et al., 2001). However, when the same investigators used individual treatment, cognitive therapy was more efficacious and comparable to ERP treatment; both treatments produced high rates of recovery after treatment (67% for cognitive therapy and 59% for ERP; Whittal, Thordarson, & McLean, 2005). Little empirical attention has been paid to the question of whether the addition of cognitive therapy augments the efficacy of behavioral therapy. An early study of RET (Emmelkamp & Beens, 1991) found that adding this intervention to ERP did not appear to enhance treatment results. In a more recent study (Vogel, Stiles, & Götestam, 2004), patients were randomly assigned to ERP plus Beck-style cognitive therapy or ERP plus relaxation training (placebo). Patients receiving ERP plus cognitive therapy were less likely to drop out of treatment than were those receiving ERP plus placebo. However, there was a (nonsignificant) trend for patients receiving ERP plus placebo to show a greater reduction in OCD symptoms, depression, and anxiety.

Our preference, on the basis of these data, is to use ERP whenever possible. However, cognitive therapy is an important treatment option when ERP has not produced optimal results or when patients refuse ERP. In an open trial with five adult OCD patients who had failed to respond to pharmacotherapy and ERP, an intensive cognitive therapy program was associated with decreases in self-reported OCD symptoms (Krochmalik, Jones, & Menzies, 2001). Additional trials of cognitive therapy are currently under way (e.g., Wilhelm & Steketee, in press), and findings from these studies should provide a clearer picture of the efficacy of this treatment.

OPTIMAL FORMATS FOR EXPOSURE AND RESPONSE PREVENTION

There has been little examination of the efficacy of inpatient ERP. Part of the concern with inpatient treatment is that in most hospitals, OCD patients are treated in a milieu with non-OCD patients. Treatment is therefore unlikely to be specific to OCD (e.g., formal ERP would be unlikely). However, a small number of inpatient and residential OCD treatment centers have been developed around the United States; these include (but are not limited to) McLean Hospital in Belmont, Massachusetts; the Menninger Clinic in Houston, Texas; and Rogers Memorial Hospital in Oconomowoc, Wisconsin. We are aware of only one systematic attempt to document the effectiveness of these programs (Stewart, Stack, Farrell, Pauls, & Jenike, 2005). In that study, 486 adult and adolescent OCD patients received an average of 61 days of treatment (ERP and medications), although length of stay ranged as high as 640 days. Among patients with a planned discharge (i.e., excluding those who discontinued the program against medical advice), a 36% decrease in OCD symptoms was noted. An intent-to-treat analysis found a 26% decrease. These decreases seem encouraging, given the likely severity of these patients at admission. However, in the absence of a controlled comparison of outpatient versus inpatient treatment, the higher cost and patient burden of inpatient treatment suggest that OCD should be treated on an outpatient basis when possible. Inpatient treatment may be especially useful for patients who do not respond well to outpatient treatment.

ERP delivered by a trained therapist is the treatment of choice for OCD, but this treatment is often difficult to obtain (American Psychiatric Association, 1989; Goisman et al., 1993). ERP is also expensive (in the short term), with a 1995 survey showing an average cost of $4,370 (Turner, Beidel, Spaulding, & Brown, 1995). Although behavior therapy is less expensive over time than longer-term psychotherapy and medications (Otto, Pollack, & Maki, 2000), it still involves considerable expense. Thus, it may be useful in some cases to explore the use of self-administered treatment rather than therapist-administered treatment. There have been comparatively few controlled assessments of self-administered OCD treatment, and many such treatments have actually involved quite a bit of therapist contact (Tolin & Hannan, 2005b). Emmelkamp and Kraanen (1977) found no difference in outcome between therapist-controlled and self-controlled ERP. Their self-controlled treatment was directed by the therapist during ten 1-hour office visits, but the therapist was not physically present during the exposure exercises. Fritzler, Hecker, and Losee (1997) compared partially self-administered treatment patients (Steketee & White's [1990] self-help book plus five sessions of therapist contact to supplement the readings) with wait list patients. Treated patients showed a superior outcome to untreated patients, although only 25% met criteria for clinically significant improvement.

Another partially self-driven ERP program is the BT–STEPS program (Baer & Greist, 1997), in which instructions for conducting self-administered ERP therapy are delivered via a computerized telephone administration system. Although BT–STEPS is not purely self-directed (exposure instructions are determined by the computer on the basis of a decision-making algorithm using the patient's anxiety ratings), there are no in-person meetings between the patient and a therapist. Open trials found this treatment to be both acceptable to and clinically effective for patients with OCD (Bachofen et al., 1999; Baer & Greist, 1997). In a controlled comparison (Greist et al., 2002), patients were randomly assigned to receive self-administered treatment (BT–STEPS), therapist-administered ERP, or relaxation (placebo treatment). After treatment, 38% of patients in the BT–STEPS group, versus 60% of patients in the therapist-administered treatment group and 14% of placebo patients, were considered responders. The BT–STEPS group showed a 23% reduction on the Yale–Brown Obsessive–Compulsive Scale (Goodman et al., 1989), compared with a 32% reduction for therapist-administered treatment patients and a 7% reduction for placebo patients. It is interesting that when only the treatment-adherent patients were sampled, the therapist-administered and BT–STEPS groups showed similar outcomes, suggesting that the reason for the attenuated results in the BT–STEPS group may have been related to nonadherence to the treatment instructions in that group. Furthermore, despite its moderately positive outcomes, the BT–STEPS program has a very high dropout rate of approximately 50% (Greist et al., 1998), indicating that many patients who entered the trial did not complete it.

In an ongoing study of self- versus therapist-administered ERP in one of our clinics, patients were randomly assigned to 15 sessions of therapist-administered ERP or to a commercially available self-help manual (Foa & Wilson, 2001). Preliminary results (Tolin, Hannan, Maltby, Diefenbach, & Worhunsky, 2004) indicate that both groups showed significant improvement in OCD symptoms, with patients receiving treatment from a therapist showing greater improvement (44% Y–BOCS reduction) than did self-help patients (19% Y–BOCS reduction). CGI ratings indicated that 56% of patients receiving therapist-administered treatment were classified as treatment responders, compared with only 15% of those receiving self-administered treatment. Thus, the therapist appears to impart specific benefits over and above the technique of ERP, such as tailored psychoeducation, consultation, support, modeling of exposures, motivation, and accountability for homework compliance (Tolin & Hannan, 2005a).

Group therapy may also be a viable method for delivering ERP. Several open trials have demonstrated that ERP in a group setting results in significant decreases in OCD severity (Bouvard, 2002; Krone, Himle, & Nesse, 1991; Van Noppen, Pato, Marsland, & Rasmussen, 1998); no difference in efficacy was found between a 7- and 12-week group (Himle et al., 2001). A randomized controlled trial also found group ERP superior to the wait list condition (Volpato Cordioli et al., 2003), and two open trials suggest that group ERP may be an effective intervention for adolescents as well as adults (Himle, Fischer, Van Etten, Janeck, & Hanna, 2003; Thienemann, Martin, Cregger, Thompson, & Dyer-Friedman, 2001). Also encouraging is the fact that even patients with very different OCD symptoms (e.g., washers and checkers) seem to benefit as much from group therapy as do patients who share the same kind of symptoms (Norton & Whittal, 2004). In an early randomized controlled trial, group and individual ERP were equally effective, although individual therapy appeared to produce faster results (Fals-Stewart et al., 1993). In a direct comparison, a group-based ERP intervention appeared superior to a group based largely on cognitive restructuring (McLean et al., 2001). In light of a subsequent study of cognitive therapy and ERP delivered individually by the same investigators (Whittal et al., 2005), it appears that cognitive aspects of treatment are more difficult to translate into a group format.

DEFINING AND SELECTING TARGETS FOR TREATMENT

The first step in treatment planning is determining whether OCD symptoms or comorbid symptoms need to be addressed first or whether they can be addressed concurrently. Many clinicians adopt a functional approach, targeting the symptoms that appear to be the primary cause of the patient's overall concerns. For example, a patient may present with comorbid OCD and major depression, and during the initial interview, it becomes clear that the onset of depression followed the onset of OCD symptoms. Furthermore, it appears that the depression results primarily from distress and reduced activity subsequent to the OCD. In this case, an argument can be made that the OCD should be treated first, with the expectation that successful OCD treatment will also reduce depressive symptoms. This is, in fact, the finding in most studies; measures of depressed mood decline concurrently with reduction in OCD symptoms (e.g., Abramowitz et al., 2000; Foa et al., 1992). A concern with this approach, however, is that comorbid symptoms, even when secondary to the OCD symptoms, may become severe enough to derail the OCD treatment. So, for example, if the patient were so depressed that he or she could not reliably come to treatment, so fatigued that he or she could not complete exposure exercises, or so suicidal that treatment for OCD put the patient at risk, it would be necessary either to treat the depression first or to treat the OCD and depression concurrently. Thus, what came first is only one aspect of treatment planning; decisions must also take into account the severity of each condition and their interactive effects.

Also important in OCD treatment planning is a clear understanding of which symptoms are part of the OCD and which are not. The terms *obsession* and *compulsion* can be used quite loosely by the public and clinicians alike, and we have received many referrals for patients with "compulsive" gambling, eating, or sexual behavior or "obsessive" thoughts about wishing to be dead or about prior traumatic experiences. The obsessive thoughts in OCD must be distinguished from the repetitive distressing thoughts characteristic of intense worries in generalized anxiety disorder, ruminations about loss and worthlessness in depression, intrusive trauma memories in posttraumatic stress disorder, and many other mental phenomena. Compulsions must be distinguished from impulsive behaviors such as gambling, hair pulling, and shoplifting; stereotyped behaviors such as rocking or head-banging (as might be seen in developmental disorders); or addictive behaviors such as alcohol or drug abuse. Although some authors have characterized all of these as part of an "obsessive–compulsive spectrum" (e.g., Hollander et al., 1996), from a behavioral perspective they are quite different and require different intervention strategies.

Part of making this distinction, and also a critical part of early treatment planning, is a functional analysis of behavior. Briefly, a functional analysis consists of identifying the target behavior, external and internal antecedents to the behavior, and immediate and delayed consequences of the behavior. The *target behavior* in OCD is usually a compulsive or avoidant behavior; mental rituals are also applicable. *Antecedents* are the factors that seem to trigger the target behavior. These factors may be external to the person (e.g., environmental factors) or internal (e.g., thoughts, feelings, or physiological sensations). In identifying *consequences*, we emphasize the immediate aftereffects of the behavior that may serve as reinforcers. In most cases, the reinforcement is negative (reduction of an aversive stimulus) rather than positive (introduction of a pleasurable stimulus), as is often the case for impulsive and addictive behaviors. We also examine the delayed and often unintended consequences of the behavior, which may serve as vulnerability factors for later symptoms or may help maintain the person's fears or maladaptive beliefs.

Some examples of functional analyses are provided in Table 2.1. Although the OCD symptoms described in Table 2.1 are different, a basic functional pattern is evident in which certain environmental cues lead to intrusive thoughts and feelings of anxiety or tension. The compulsive and avoidant behaviors function not to gratify the person, but rather to reduce these unpleasant feelings. However, these behaviors also block the natural habituation that would normally occur, maintain patients' erroneous beliefs by preventing them from obtaining disconfirming evidence, teach patients that the only way to feel better is to ritualize, and often lead to marked impairment in functioning.

Most patients with OCD present with multiple symptom dimensions (Foa et al., 1995). Therefore, the clinician and patient must choose where to begin treatment. We suggest that the primary consideration should be to choose exposure exercises that are feasible and have a high probability of success (i.e., reduced fear). Early treatment successes are one of the more helpful factors that maintain a high level of patient motivation, whereas discouraging experiences early in treatment may lead to nonadherence or dropout. To the extent that moderately easy initial exposures can be identified within multiple symptom domains, we prefer to target the symptoms

TABLE 2.1

Illustrating the Components of a Functional Analysis

External antecedent	Internal antecedent	Behavior	Immediate consequence	Delayed consequence
Entering a public restroom	Thoughts of contamination; belief that contamination is dangerous; feelings of anxiety.	Avoid touching things; wash hands repeatedly.	Feeling safer; experiencing relief from anxiety.	Continued belief that all contamination is dangerous; reduced ability to travel and socialize.
Leaving the house after using oven	Thoughts of being responsible for starting a fire; doubts about memory; panic sensations.	Return home to check the oven repeatedly; avoid using the oven before departing.	Feeling reassured; experiencing relief from anxiety and panic.	Continued inability to tolerate uncertainty; problems getting to work on time.
Seeing books improperly arranged on shelf	Thought that books are not "just right"; feeling of tension.	Rearrange books until they are lined up perfectly. Avoid the room with the bookshelf.	Experiencing relief from tension.	Continued inability to tolerate imperfection; learning that the only way to feel better is to ritualize; excessive time spent arranging.
Holding infant son	Intrusive thought that "I will harm him;" panic sensations'.	Think "I love my son" over and over; put baby down.	Experiencing relief from anxiety.	Continued belief that intrusive thoughts will come true if "I don't do something"; decreased positive interactions with son (and decreased evidence of being a good parent).

that in the patient's opinion are creating the most discomfort or functional impairment.

PREPARING THE PATIENT

The first step toward effective intervention is to provide a clear and understandable description of OCD and its treatment. In most cases, this includes a description of OCD as a psychobiological disorder. Cumbersome detail and jargon are not necessary for this step; rather, the aim is merely to convey the understanding that OCD is at least partly based in brain activity and that the brains of people with OCD function differently from those of people without OCD. However, we are also quick to remind patients that the presence of biological factors does not mean that the situation is hopeless, nor does it imply that pharmacological treatment is the best option. We point out that neuroimaging studies (e.g., Baxter et al., 1992; Schwartz, Stoessel, Baxter, Martin, & Phelps, 1996) show that abnormal brain activity can be affected by either medications or by behavior therapy.

We then turn our attention to nonbiological factors that play a key role in OCD—namely, erroneous beliefs, compulsive behaviors, and experiential avoidance. *Erroneous beliefs* in OCD include exaggerated perceptions of responsibility or threat, an unrealistic need for certainty or perfection, and beliefs about the importance of and need to control one's thoughts (Frost & Steketee, 2002; Obsessive Compulsive Cognitions Working Group, 1997, 2005). Using examples from the person's own experiences, we help him or her identify likely areas of maladaptive beliefs and suggest that the exercises in treatment are designed to help weaken these beliefs. So, for example, if someone believes that thinking bad thoughts might cause a disaster to occur, we might encourage him or her to experiment with this by first thinking low-level bad thoughts that are immediately falsifiable. We might start, for example, by noticing a fly buzzing around the office and wishing for the fly to crash into the wall and die. When the fly fails to comply, the person's belief in the power of his or her thoughts is usually weakened. Using a step-by-step approach, we can demonstrate that the same principle holds for more frightening thoughts, such as wishing for an airplane to crash.

We also discuss how compulsive behaviors or mental acts might provide some temporary relief from discomfort but ultimately serve to keep the person "stuck." Using examples from the functional analysis described in the preceding section, we might point out that washing one's hands after feeling contaminated might alleviate the anxiety in the short term but tends to maintain the belief that all contamination is dangerous and that something terrible would have happened had the person not washed. An old joke sometimes helps to illustrate this process: A man is standing on a Boston street corner, clapping his hands and stomping his feet. Another man walks by and asks him what he is doing. He replies, "I'm making all this noise to keep the alligators away." The other man looks around, perplexed, and says, "What are you talking about? There are no alligators here." The man smiles and says, "You see, it's working!" The absurdity of the joke, of course, is that even if the man was not clapping his hands and stomping his feet, no alligators would attack him. He is safe not because of his actions, but because alligators do not roam the streets of Boston. However, his actions prevent him from learning this basic fact, so he continues. In the same fashion, the person with contamination fears is safe not because of the repeated washing, but because of the fundamental fact that most germs are not deadly. However, the act of repeated washing prevents the person from fully appreciating this truth. The person attributes his or her survival to the compulsions, rather than to the objective safety of the situation.

A pretreatment discussion of the harmful effects of experiential avoidance is also useful. OCD patients' symptoms are often characterized by the excessive use of thought suppression or other maladaptive thought control strategies (Abramowitz, Whiteside, Kalsy, & Tolin, 2003; Amir, Cashman, & Foa, 1997). Although attempts to suppress thoughts may be effective for limited periods of time, evidence suggests that with time, these thoughts will paradoxically increase (Abramowitz, Tolin, & Street, 2001; Wegner, Schneider, Carter, & White, 1987). This paradoxical effect appears to be particularly acute among OCD patients (Tolin, Abramowitz, Przeworski, & Foa, 2002). Furthermore, when thought suppression attempts eventually fail, OCD patients appear to attribute such failure not to the inherent unworkability of thought suppression, but rather to internal factors such as mental weakness or the "badness" of the thought itself (Tolin, Abramowitz, Hamlin, Foa, & Synodi, 2002). Such attributions in turn may further enhance the perceived need to try harder to suppress such thoughts.

Similar arguments can be made for attempts to avoid unwanted emotions, situations, or activities that elicit unwanted thoughts and feelings. We often use strategies from acceptance-based therapies (e.g., Hayes, Strosahl, & Wilson, 1999) to help the patient recognize that the immediate aim of treatment is not necessarily to control or eliminate bad thoughts or feelings, but rather to teach him or her to tolerate them and to live a life that is not controlled by OCD—in other words, not to think and feel better, but to live better (Hannan & Tolin, 2005). Thus, paradoxically, one of the messages to convey to the patient during ERP is that unwanted thoughts and feelings will get better only when the patient stops trying so hard to make them better. We occasionally evoke the character George Costanza from the television sitcom Seinfeld. In one episode, George found that his quality of life improved dramatically when he did the exact opposite of what his instincts told him to do (Cowan, David, Seinfeld, & Cherones, 1994). In many respects, ERP is an example of "Costanza therapy"—by doing the opposite of what OCD wants them to do, patients gradually recognize that they are becoming stronger and OCD is becoming weaker. Thus, to implement ERP, we routinely tell patients that if their OCD wants them to be extra clean, they should strive to be dirty. If OCD wants them to be perfect, they should strive to be imperfect. If OCD wants them to be certain, they should strive to be uncertain.

One of the more difficult aspects of ERP is that patients must eventually be willing to face their highest fears, and these exposures often seem very risky to them. For instance, one patient's most feared exposure might be touching a toilet in a public restroom. To help patients make judgments about the appropriateness of an exposure, we often use the principle of acceptable risk in defining the range of possible exposures. No exposure is risk free. However, if the risk of the exposure is similar to risks commonly taken every day, it is an acceptable risk. For instance, the patient who balks at touching a toilet seat without washing may be asked to compare the risk of this exposure with that of a camping trip, wherein cleanliness is often delayed for days or weeks, or to the risk of driving to the therapy session on a busy street or highway. We also find it helpful to encourage patients to assume that a situation is safe unless there is clear evidence to the contrary; typically, OCD patients tend to assume that a situation is dangerous unless they can find clear evidence of safety (which is often difficult to obtain). Therapists can influence the patient's willingness to engage in more difficult exposures by preparing the patient for these at an early stage, by maintaining the expectation that exposures will be done, and by collaboratively engaging in exposures along with the patient. With this in mind, it is also important to pace the level of anxiety elicited during exposures. Exposures should elicit anxiety, but not so much that the patient feels overwhelmed. Obtaining regular subjective units of distress scale (SUDS) ratings (0–100, where 100 = the most discomfort the patient has ever felt can help clinicians gauge levels of anxiety to pace exposures according to the patient's abilities.

Approximately 25% of OCD patients refuse ERP (Franklin & Foa, 1998), perhaps because of apprehension about the difficulty and intensity of the treatment. To address this, Tolin et al. (Maltby & Tolin, 2005; Tolin & Maltby, in press) developed a brief four-session readiness intervention consisting of psychoeducation, a videotaped example of an ERP session, motivational interviewing techniques (Miller & Rollnick, 1991), and a phone conversation with a former ERP patient. This program was tested in a small sample of OCD patients who refused to enter ERP. When explaining their reasons for treatment refusal, most patients expressed a desire to change, suggesting that their treatment refusals were not the result of apathy or poor insight. They also expressed a high level of expectancy for change with ERP, indicating that their refusals were not because of disbelief in the efficacy of ERP. However, they reported that despite their interest and high expectation, they were too afraid of exposures to start ERP. Results from this pilot study were encouraging: 87% of patients receiving the readiness intervention chose to begin ERP, whereas only 20% of patients in a wait-list condition entered ERP. The key factor in helping these patients transition to ERP appeared to be reducing their fear of exposures via small, graded exposures to the treatment process itself. Another potential strategy for facilitating treatment enrollment in reluctant patients is to begin with cognitive therapy and gradually introduce first behavioral experiments and then prolonged exposures and response prevention. Alternatively, some patients may benefit from medications to reduce their OCD symptoms enough that ERP is no longer overwhelming.

INVOLVING THE FAMILY

Because of OCD's substantial impact on family functioning, as well as the risk of family members accommodating (and inadvertently reinforcing) patients' compulsions (Amir, Freshman, & Foa, 2000; Calvocoressi et al., 1995), family intervention may also be indicated as a supplement to traditional ERP and pharmacological interventions. Although early studies yielded mixed findings on the advantage of including spouses or other family members in treatment (Emmelkamp, de Haan, & Hoogduin, 1990; Emmelkamp & de Lange, 1983; Mehta, 1990), more recent studies have shown that in individual and group settings, inclusion of family members resulted in superior outcomes to those of individual ERP (Grunes, Neziroglu, & McKay, 2001; Van Noppen, Steketee, McCorkle, & Pato, 1997). Van Noppen (1999; Van Noppen & Steketee, 2003) developed an 18-session multifamily behavioral treatment (MFBT) delivered in a group setting of five to seven families. The major goals of MFBT (Van Noppen & Steketee, 2003) are

- to establish a therapeutic alliance with the patient and family and to provide a supportive context for change;
- to provide education about OCD and ERP;
- to develop and implement a behavioral treatment plan;
- to reduce maladaptive family behaviors such as hostile criticism, overinvolvement, and excessive accommodation;
- to promote feelings of empathy and support while decreasing feelings of stigma and shame;
- to teach patients to use self-instruction during ERP; and
- to provide behavioral strategies to manage the recurrence of OCD symptoms.

Family intervention may be particularly helpful in the treatment of children with OCD. Parents may be trained to use ERP methods at home (Knox, Albano, & Barlow, 1996), thus serving as "surrogate therapists" during homework exercises. This type of involvement seems to be more helpful for younger children, whereas adolescents and teenagers may prefer to do the work on their own and may resent parental overinvolvement. In such cases, the therapist may choose to work with the parents on setting appropriate boundaries and allowing the child to take more responsibility for his or her own treatment. In many cases, it is also helpful for the therapist to examine carefully the degree to which parents or other family members accommodate the child's OCD by participating in rituals (e.g., showering and changing clothes immediately upon coming home from work), facilitating avoidance (e.g., not touching things that appear contaminated or not bringing contaminated objects into the home), or providing excessive reassurance (Calvocoressi et al., 1995). Such family behaviors may help reduce the child's level of distress (and subsequently the amount of tension in the home) in the short term but are unhelpful (and perhaps even harmful) in the long term. Thus, the therapist should work with the family to reduce these forms of excess accommodation and to learn to tolerate the child's potentially intense (but temporary) distress.

Another area in which family intervention may be helpful for children with OCD is when high levels of expressed emotion are present in the family. *Expressed emotion* is defined as critical, hostile, or emotionally overinvolved patterns of interaction between family members and the patient. Such family patterns appear to predict poor initial response to OCD treatment or relapse following successful treatment (Leonard et al., 1993). In a study of OCD and agoraphobic outpatients treated with ERP, emotional overinvolvement and hostility in family members were associated with more dropout, and hostility and patients' perceptions of criticism in their relative predicted worse outcome (Chambless & Steketee, 1999). The therapist might work with the family by providing education about the harmful effects of expressed emotion, using cognitive strategies to reframe the patient's behavior as manifestations of an illness rather than as a personality flaw or malicious behavior, and providing strategies to improve coping strategies among family members (Van Noppen & Steketee, 2003).

DEALING WITH QUALITY-OF-LIFE ISSUES

People with OCD often face considerable financial and social costs that reduce their quality of life. A poll of members of the Obsessive Compulsive Foundation indicated that 41% could not work because of OCD symptoms and that they had lost an average of 2 years of wages (Hollander, Rowland, Stein, Broatch, & Himelein, 1995). Adults with OCD tend to drop out of college and to earn low salaries, and up to one quarter of a sample reported receiving some form of financial assistance (Henderson & Pollard, 1988). In addition, OCD carries tremendous social costs for patients and their families when obsessions and compulsions pervade daily behavior and interfere with social functioning. Hollander et al. (1995) found that 64% of the OCD sufferers surveyed lowered their career aspirations, and 62% reported difficulty maintaining relationships because of their symptoms. For clinical OCD patients, rates of nonmarriage are much higher than the U.S. population norm (Steketee, 1997). Most family members of those with OCD experience personal disruptions, with more than 60% of relatives reporting family problems, loss of interpersonal relationships, lack of leisure time, and financial problems (Cooper, 1996).

These figures suggest that ERP will necessarily be conducted in the context of a variety of family, social, economic, and employment problems that have adversely affected patients' quality of life. Although few studies indicate that demographic characteristics (e.g., age, gender, marital status) influence the outcome of behavioral treatment (see Steketee & Shapiro, 1995), there is little guiding information about whether the type or extent of these quality-of-life problems has adverse effects on the outcome of ERP. It is safe to assume that socioeconomic and family stresses will put extra strain on patients who are engaging in a demanding therapy such as ERP. Our own strategy is to identify these stressors at the outset of therapy and to determine whether patients have sufficient supports available to address these stressors so that their primary focus during the treatment phase can be learning and practicing the ERP interventions. As ERP begins to have positive effects, some of these stressors may reduce. For example, family members may become less frustrated as the patient's rituals and dependence on others are reduced. Bosses may find that the person is less often absent or late to work. Patients may begin to socialize more, especially when this becomes part of their exposure procedures. Studies of ERP outcomes suggest that improvements in social, family, and work functioning do occur (Marks, Stern, Mawson, Cobb, & McDonald, 1980; Tolin, Maltby, Diefenbach, Hannan, & Worhunsky, 2004; Van Noppen et al., 1997), although they lag behind the improvements in symptoms, as might be expected.

In general, the primary emphasis in ERP is the reduction of obsessive thoughts and compulsive behaviors. However, as described previously in this chapter, we often use quality-of-life issues as a means toward encouraging patients to decrease the amount of time and energy spent in direct attempts to control thoughts and feelings and to increase the amount of time spent engaged in activities that are consistent with the person's values (Hannan & Tolin, 2005). A clear example of this process is a patient who values being a competent wife and mother but is unable to touch her family members until they have engaged in extensive cleaning rituals and refuses to accompany them on outings for fear of becoming contaminated. Through Socratic discussion, the therapist might help this patient to understand that her OCD behaviors are in direct conflict with her stated values and that overcoming OCD may well involve doing those things that would be frightening to her in the short term but ultimately rewarding in the long term.

END-OF-TREATMENT ISSUES

As patients near the end of their treatment, the therapist must make sure that they are able to manage their OCD on their own, without the oversight of the therapist. During active treatment, the therapist not only provides expert education and consultation, but also is a source of support and someone to whom the patient feels accountable for completing exposure homework (Tolin & Hannan, 2005a). Without an appropriate transition, patients may revert to old patterns and may relapse. One of the best ways to maximize the patient's self-reliance is to gradually fade the therapist's involvement during the latter portions of treatment. Around the midpoint in treatment, we begin to increase the patient's role in deciding what exposures to do and when. Often, a late-treatment exposure session begins with the therapist asking, "What kind of exposure do you think would be helpful for you to do today?" Similarly, in cognitive therapy, patients are encouraged to take more responsibility for designing their own homework assignments (Wilhelm & Steketee, 2006). Thus, the patient is recruited as a cotherapist with increasing responsibilities as the treatment progresses. It may also be helpful, particularly for patients who have been receiving intensive (daily) treatment, to space some of the later sessions progressively farther apart (Rowe & Craske, 1998). By increasing the length of time between sessions, the patient has greater intersession opportunity for self-directed practice, thus strengthening his or her level of self-efficacy and reducing reliance on the therapist.

Another important late-treatment component is relapse prevention and management. The aims of relapse prevention, originally developed for substance abuse treatment, are to prevent the return of symptoms and to help patients get "back on track" if lapses occur (Parks, Anderson, & Marlatt, 2001). In the area of substance abuse, relapse prevention interventions have been shown to improve the durability of treatment effects and to reduce the severity of relapses when they do occur (Carroll, 1997). The model of relapse prevention has been applied to a wide range of clinical disorders. McKay and colleagues (McKay, 1997; McKay, Todaro, Neziroglu, & Yaryura-Tobias, 1996) tested a relapse prevention program on six patients with OCD. The program consisted of one psychoeducational session about relapse and brief phone contacts twice monthly for 6 months. All patients maintained gains on OCD symptoms and anxiety, but depressed mood remained elevated up to a 2-year follow-up. Another study by Hiss, Foa, and Kozak (1994) showed that patients who received relapse prevention training following ERP were less likely to relapse at 6-month follow-up than were patients whose ERP was followed by an associative therapy (placebo) treatment. Thus, effective relapse prevention requires specific, focused efforts to help patients reduce and manage the occurrence of symptom increases.

One relapse prevention strategy involves educating the patient about the likely precursors to relapse. Fear may return when the person is placed under unusual stress (e.g., major life events or an accumulation of daily hassles) or faces a new situational or environmental context that had not been addressed during exposure exercises (e.g., Bouton, 2002). Helping patients identify their likely high-risk situations may help reduce the probability that they will respond to these situations with compulsions or avoidance. Also, taking a cue from substance abuse treatment, relapse prevention for OCD may include a discussion of the *abstinence violation effect*, in which an isolated occurrence of the problem behavior cues the patient to give up trying and to return to old habits. We discuss the distinction between a lapse (a single, isolated occurrence of compulsive behavior) and a relapse (full-blown return of OCD symptoms). We inform patients that lapses do not need to turn into relapses and that even if they find themselves engaging in compulsive or avoidant behavior, it is never too late for them to combat OCD by reintroducing exposure exercises. Although the emergence of new obsessive fears following successful treatment is not common, we help prepare patients for this possibility by asking them questions about what they would do if new fears developed. Questions such as, "What would you do if you suddenly developed, say, a fear of trees?" or "What if you developed a fear that you would hurt children?" can be used to ascertain whether the patient understands that the appropriate way to manage fears, even unpracticed ones, is to identify and expose himself or herself to the triggers of fear rather than engage in avoidance or compulsions.

Finally, we emphasize that long-term recovery from OCD involves permanent lifestyle changes. An analogy from weight loss strategies such as the Atkins diet (Atkins, 1981) helps illustrate this point. Such diets are commonly divided into two phases. During the first phase, the patient works at losing weight with high intensity, often following procedures that are highly unusual. Once people reach their target weight, they move to Phase 2, in which their weight loss efforts are less intense and they resume more normal eating patterns. Two characteristics of Phase 2 are particularly noteworthy: This phase lasts for the rest of the person's life, and it involves ways of eating different from their prediet patterns. Even though the individual is no longer dieting vigorously (as in Phase 1), he or she can never go back to eating large quantities of junk food. Taking this analogy to OCD, Phase 1 of the treatment is ERP proper. During this phase, the person does a number of highly unusual and intense activities aimed at bringing OCD under control. When the symptoms are well controlled, the person enters Phase 2, in which he or she sees the therapist not at all or only sporadically. However, for the rest of his or her life, he or she will remain "in recovery" and will make an effort to never go back to avoidant or compulsive behavior, to be mindful of fears as they emerge, and to combat these fears with periodic self-directed exposure exercises.

REFERENCES

Abramowitz, J. S., Franklin, M. E., Schwartz, S. A., & Furr, J. M. (2003). Symptom presentation and outcome of cognitive–behavioral therapy for obsessive–compulsive disorder. *Journal of Consulting and Clinical Psychology, 71*, 1049–1057.

Abramowitz, J. S., Franklin, M. E., Street, G. P., Kozak, M. J., & Foa, E. B. (2000). Effects of comorbid depression on response to treatment for obsessive–compulsive disorder. *Behavior Therapy, 31*, 517–528.

Abramowitz, J. S., Tolin, D. F., & Street, G. P. (2001). Paradoxical effects of thought suppression: A meta-analysis of controlled studies. *Clinical Psychology Review, 21*, 683–703.

Abramowitz, J. S., Whiteside, S., Kalsy, S. A., & Tolin, D. F. (2003). Thought control strategies in obsessive–compulsive disorder: A replication and extension. *Behaviour Research and Therapy, 41*, 529–540.

American Psychiatric Association. (1989). *Psychiatrist activity survey (1988–1989).* Unpublished manuscript.

Amir, N., Cashman, L. A., & Foa, E. (1997). Strategies of thought control in obsessive–compulsive disorder. *Behaviour Research and Therapy, 35*, 775–777.

Amir, N., Freshman, M., & Foa, E. B. (2000). Family distress and involvement in relatives of obsessive–compulsive disorder patients. *Journal of Anxiety Disorders, 14*, 209–217.

Atkins, R. C. (1981). *Dr. Atkins' diet revolution.* New York: Bantam Doubleday Dell.

Bachofen, M., Nakagawa, A., Marks, I. M., Park, J. M., Greist, J. H., Baer, L., et al. (1999). Home self-assessment and self-treatment of obsessive–compulsive disorder using a manual and a computer-conducted telephone interview: Replication of a UK–US study. *Journal of Clinical Psychiatry, 60*, 545–549.

Baer, L., & Greist, J. H. (1997). An interactive computer-administered self-assessment and self-help program for behavior therapy. *Journal of Clinical Psychiatry, 58*(Suppl. 12), 23–28.

Baxter, L. R., Jr., Schwartz, J. M., Bergman, K. S., Szuba, M. P., Guze, B. H., Mazziotta, J. C., et al. (1992). Caudate glucose metabolic rate changes with both drug and behavior therapy for obsessive–compulsive disorder. *Archives of General Psychiatry, 49*, 681–689.

Beck, A. T., Emery, G., & Greenberg, R. L. (1985). *Anxiety disorders and phobias: A cognitive perspective.* New York: Basic Books.

Becker, C. B., Zayfert, C., & Anderson, E. (2004). A survey of psychologists' attitudes towards and utilization of exposure therapy for PTSD. *Behaviour Research and Therapy, 42*, 277–292.

Black, D. W., Monahan, P., Gable, J., Blum, N., Clancy, G., & Baker, P. (1998). Hoarding and treatment response in 38 nondepressed subjects with obsessive–compulsive disorder. *Journal of Clinical Psychiatry, 59*, 420–425.

Bouton, M. E. (2002). Context, ambiguity, and unlearning: Sources of relapse after behavioral extinction. *Biological Psychiatry, 52*, 976–986.

Bouvard, M. (2002). Un programme de thérapie cognitive et comportementale en groupe danse le trouble obsessionnel compulsif: Résultats préliminaires. [A standardized cognitive–behavioral group treatment program for obsessive compulsive disorder: Preliminary outcomes]. *Encephale, 28,* 439–446.

Brady, K. T., Dansky, B. S., Back, S. E., Foa, E. B., & Carroll, K. M. (2001). Exposure therapy in the treatment of PTSD among cocaine-dependent individuals: Preliminary findings. *Journal of Substance Abuse Treatment, 21,* 47–54.

Calvocoressi, L., Lewis, B., Harris, M., Trufan, S. J., Goodman, W. K., McDougle, C. J., & Price, L. H. (1995). Family accommodation in obsessive–compulsive disorder. *American Journal of Psychiatry, 152,* 441–443.

Carroll, K. M. (1997). Relapse prevention as a psychosocial treatment: A review of controlled clinical trials. In G. A. Marlatt & G. R. VandenBos (Eds.), *Addictive behaviors: Readings on etiology, prevention, and treatment* (pp. 697–717). Washington, DC: American Psychological Association.

Chambless, D. L., & Steketee, G. (1999). Expressed emotion and behavior therapy outcome: A prospective study with obsessive compulsive and agoraphobic outpatients. *Journal of Consulting and Clinical Psychology, 67,* 658–665.

Cooper, M. (1996). Obsessive–compulsive disorder: Effects on family members. *American Journal of Orthopsychiatry, 66,* 296–304.

Cottraux, J., Messy, P., Marks, I. M., Mollard, E., & Bouvard, M. (1993). Predictive factors in the treatment of obsessive–compulsive disorders with fluvoxamine and/or behavior therapy. *Behavioural Psychotherapy, 21,* 45–50.

Cottraux, J., Mollard, E., Bouvard, M., & Marks, I. (1993). Exposure therapy, fluvoxamine, or combination treatment in obsessive–compulsive disorder: One-year followup. *Psychiatry Research, 49,* 63–75.

Cottraux, J., Mollard, E., Bouvard, M., Marks, I., Sluys, M., Nury, A. M., et al. (1990). A controlled study of fluvoxamine and exposure in obsessive–compulsive disorder. *International Clinical Psychopharmacology, 5,* 17–30.

Cottraux, J., Note, I., Yao, S. N., Lafont, S., Note, B., Mollard, E., et al. (2001). A randomized controlled trial of cognitive therapy versus intensive behavior therapy in obsessive compulsive disorder. *Psychotherapy and Psychosomatics, 70,* 288–297.

Cowan, A., David, L., Seinfeld, J. (Writers), & T. Cherones (Director). (1994). The opposite [Television series episode]. In J. Seinfeld, P. Mehlman, M. Gross, & S. Greenberg (Producers), *Seinfeld.* Beverly Hills, CA: Castle Rock Entertainment.

de Araujo, L. A., Ito, L. M., & Marks, I. (1996). Early compliance and other factors predicting outcome of exposure for obsessive–compulsive disorder. *British Journal of Psychiatry, 169,* 747–752.

de Haan, E., van Oppen, P., van Balkom, A. J., Spinhoven, P., Hoogduin, K. A., & Van Dyck, R. (1997). Prediction of outcome and early vs. late improvement in OCD patients treated with cognitive behaviour therapy and pharmacotherapy. *Acta Psychiatrica Scandinavica, 96,* 354–361.

Emmelkamp, P. M., & Beens, H. (1991). Cognitive therapy with obsessive–compulsive disorder: A comparative evaluation. *Behaviour Research and Therapy, 29,* 293–300.

Emmelkamp, P. M., de Haan, E., & Hoogduin, C. A. (1990). Marital adjustment and obsessive–compulsive disorder. *British Journal of Psychiatry, 156,* 55–60.

Emmelkamp, P. M., & de Lange, I. (1983). Spouse involvement in the treatment of obsessive–compulsive patients. *Behaviour Research and Therapy, 21,* 341–346.

Emmelkamp, P. M., & Kraanen, J. (1977). Therapist-controlled exposure in vivo versus self-controlled exposure in vivo: A comparison with obsessive–compulsive patients. *Behaviour Research and Therapy, 15,* 491–495.

Emmelkamp, P. M., Visser, S., & Hoekstra, R. J. (1988). Cognitive therapy vs exposure in vivo in the treatment of obsessive–compulsives. *Cognitive Therapy and Research, 12,* 103–144.

Fals-Stewart, W., & Lucente, S. (1993). An MCMI cluster typology of obsessive–compulsives: A measure of personality characteristics and its relationship to treatment participation, compliance and outcome in behavior therapy. *Journal of Psychiatric Research, 27,* 139–154.

Fals-Stewart, W., Marks, A. P., & Schafer, J. (1993). A comparison of behavioral group therapy and individual behavior therapy in treating obsessive–compulsive disorder. *Journal of Nervous and Mental Disease, 181,* 189–193.

Foa, E. B. (1979). Failure in treating obsessive–compulsives. *Behaviour Research and Therapy, 17,* 169–176.

Foa, E. B., Franklin, M. E., & Moser, J. (2002). Context in the clinic: How well do cognitive–behavioral therapies and medications work in combination? *Biological Psychiatry, 52,* 987–997.

Foa, E. B., Grayson, J. B., Steketee, G. S., Doppelt, H. G., Turner, R. M., & Latimer, P. R. (1983). Success and failure in the behavioral treatment of obsessive–compulsives. *Journal of Consulting and Clinical Psychology, 51,* 287–297.

Foa, E. B., & Kozak, M. J. (1986). Emotional processing of fear: Exposure to corrective information. *Psychological Bulletin, 99,* 20–35.

Foa, E. B., Kozak, M. J., Goodman, W. K., Hollander, E., Jenike, M. A., & Rasmussen, S. A. (1995). DSM–IV field trial: Obsessive–compulsive disorder. *American Journal of Psychiatry, 152,* 90–96.

Foa, E. B., Kozak, M. J., Steketee, G., & McCarthy, P. R. (1992). Treatment of depressive and obsessive–compulsive symptoms in OCD by imipramine and behaviour therapy. *British Journal of Clinical Psychology, 31*(Part 3), 279–292.

Foa, E. B., Liebowitz, M. R., Kozak, M. J., Davies, S., Campeas, R., Franklin, M. E., et al. (2005). Randomized, placebo-controlled trial of exposure and ritual prevention, clomipramine, and their combination in the treatment of obsessive–compulsive disorder. *American Journal of Psychiatry, 162,* 151–161.

Foa, E. B., & Wilson, R. (2001). *Stop obsessing! How to overcome your obsessions and compulsions* (rev. ed.). New York: Bantam Books.

Foa, E. B., Zoellner, L. A., Feeny, N. C., Hembree, E. A., & Alvarez-Conrad, J. (2002). Does imaginal exposure exacerbate PTSD symptoms? *Journal of Consulting and Clinical Psychology, 70,* 1022–1028.

Franklin, M. E., Abramowitz, J. S., Kozak, M. J., Levitt, J. T., & Foa, E. B. (2000). Effectiveness of exposure and ritual prevention for obsessive–compulsive disorder: Randomized compared with nonrandomized samples. *Journal of Consulting and Clinical Psychology, 68,* 594–602.

Franklin, M. E., & Foa, E. B. (1998). Cognitive–behavioral treatments for obsessive–compulsive disorder. In J. M. Gorman (Ed.), *A guide to treatments that work* (pp. 339–357). New York: Oxford University Press.

Fritzler, B. K., Hecker, J. E., & Losee, M. C. (1997). Self-directed treatment with minimal therapist contact: Preliminary findings for obsessive–compulsive disorder. *Behaviour Research and Therapy, 35,* 627–631.

Frost, R. O., & Steketee, G. (Eds.). (2002). *Cognitive approaches to obsessions and compulsions: Theory, assessment, and treatment.* New York: Pergamon Press.

Goisman, R. M., Rogers, M. P., Steketee, G. S., Warshaw, M. G., Cuneo, P., & Keller, M. B. (1993). Utilization of behavioral methods in a multicenter anxiety disorders study. *Journal of Clinical Psychiatry, 54,* 213–218.

Goodman, W. K., Price, L. H., Rasmussen, S. A., Mazure, C., Fleischmann, R. L., Hill, C. L., et al. (1989). The Yale–Brown Obsessive Compulsive Scale: I. Development, use, and reliability. *Archives of General Psychiatry, 46,* 1006–1011.

Greist, J. H., Marks, I. M., Baer, L., Kobak, K. A., Wenzel, K. W., Hirsch, M. J., et al. (2002). Behavior therapy for obsessive–compulsive disorder guided by a computer or by a clinician compared with relaxation as a control. *Journal of Clinical Psychiatry, 63,* 138–145.

Greist, J. H., Marks, I. M., Baer, L., Parkin, J. R., Manzo, P. A., Mantle, J. M., et al. (1998). Self-treatment for obsessive compulsive disorder using a manual and a computerized telephone interview: A U.S.–U.K. study. *MD Computing, 15,* 149–157.

Grunes, M. S., Neziroglu, F., & McKay, D. (2001). Family involvement in the behavioral treatment of obsessive–compulsive disorder: A preliminary investigation. *Behavior Therapy, 32,* 803–820.

Guy, W. (1976). *Assessment manual for psychopharmacology.* Washington, DC: U.S. Government Printing Office.

Hannan, S. E., & Tolin, D. F. (2005). Mindfulness and acceptance-based behavior therapy for obsessive–compulsive disorder. In S. M. Orsillo & L. Roemer (Eds.), *Acceptance and mindfulness-based approaches to anxiety: Conceptualization and treatment* (pp. 271–299). New York: Springer Publishing Company.

Hartl, T. L., & Frost, R. O. (1999). Cognitive–behavioral treatment of compulsive hoarding: A multiple baseline experimental case study. *Behaviour Research and Therapy, 37,* 451–461.

Hayes, S. C., Strosahl, K. D., & Wilson, K. G. (1999). *Acceptance and commitment therapy: An experiential approach to behavior change.* New York: Guilford Press.

Henderson, J. G., Jr., & Pollard, C. A. (1988). Three types of obsessive compulsive disorder in a community sample. *Journal of Clinical Psychology, 44,* 747–752.

Himle, J. A., Fischer, D. J., Van Etten, M. L., Janeck, A. S., & Hanna, G. L. (2003). Group behavioral therapy for adolescents with tic-related and non-tic-related obsessive–compulsive disorder. *Depression and Anxiety, 17,* 73–77.

Himle, J. A., Rassi, S., Haghighatgou, H., Krone, K. P., Nesse, R. M., & Abelson, J. (2001). Group behavioral therapy of obsessive–compulsive disorder: Seven vs. twelve-week outcomes. *Depression and Anxiety, 13,* 161–165.

Hiss, H., Foa, E. B., & Kozak, M. J. (1994). Relapse prevention program for treatment of obsessive–compulsive disorder. *Journal of Consulting and Clinical Psychology, 62,* 801–808.

Hohagen, F., Winkelmann, G., Rasche-Ruchle, H., Hand, I., Konig, A., Munchau, N., et al. (1998). Combination of behaviour therapy with fluvoxamine in comparison with behaviour therapy and placebo: Results of a multicentre study. *British Journal of Psychiatry, 35,* 71–78.

Hollander, E., Kwon, J. H., Stein, D. J., Broatch, J., Rowland, C. T., & Himelein, C. A. (1996). Obsessive–compulsive and spectrum disorders: Overview and quality of life issues. *Journal of Clinical Psychiatry, 57*(Suppl. 8), 3–6.

Hollander, E., Rowland, C., Stein, D. J., Broatch, J., & Himelein, C. (1995). A pharmacoeconomic and quality of life study of obsessive compulsive disorder [Abstract]. *Psychopharmacology Bulletin, 31,* 526.

Hoogduin, C. A., & Duivenvoorden, H. J. (1988). A decision model in the treatment of obsessive–compulsive neuroses. *British Journal of Psychiatry, 152,* 516–521.

Kampman, M., Keijsers, G. P., Hoogduin, C. A., & Verbraak, M. J. (2002). Addition of cognitive–behaviour therapy for obsessive–compulsive disorder patients non-responding to fluoxetine. *Acta Psychiatrica Scandinavica, 106,* 314–319.

Keijsers, G. P., Hoogduin, C. A., & Schaap, C. P. (1994). Predictors of treatment outcome in the behavioural treatment of obsessive–compulsive disorder. *British Journal of Psychiatry, 165,* 781–786.

Knox, L. S., Albano, A. M., & Barlow, D. H. (1996). Parental involvement in the treatment of childhood obsessive–compulsive disorder: A multiple-baseline examination incorporating parents. *Behavior Therapy, 27,* 93–115.

Krochmalik, A., Jones, M. K., & Menzies, R. G. (2001). Danger Ideation Reduction Therapy (DIRT) for treatment-resistant compulsive washing. *Behaviour Research and Therapy, 39,* 897–912.

Krone, K. P., Himle, J. A., & Nesse, R. M. (1991). A standardized behavioral group treatment program for obsessive–compulsive disorder: Preliminary outcomes. *Behaviour Research and Therapy, 29,* 627–631.

Leonard, H. L., Swedo, S. E., Lenane, M. C., Rettew, D. C., Hamburger, S. D., Bartko, J. J., & Rapoport, J. L. (1993). A 2- to 7-year follow-up study of 54 obsessive–compulsive children and adolescents. *Archives of General Psychiatry, 50,* 429–439.

Lindsay, M., Crino, R., & Andrews, G. (1997). Controlled trial of exposure and response prevention in obsessive–compulsive disorder. *British Journal of Psychiatry, 171,* 135–139.

Maltby, N., & Tolin, D. F. (2003). Overview of treatments for OCD and spectrum conditions: Conceptualization, theory and practice. *Brief Treatment and Crisis Intervention, 3,* 127–144.

Maltby, N., & Tolin, D. F. (2005). A brief motivational intervention for treatment-refusing OCD patients. *Cognitive Behaviour Therapy, 34,* 176–184.

March, J. S., Frances, A., Carpenter, D., & Kahn, D. A. (1997). The expert consensus guideline series: Treatment of obsessive–compulsive disorder [Entire issue]. *Journal of Clinical Psychiatry, 58*(Suppl. 4).

Marks, I. M., Stern, R. S., Mawson, D., Cobb, J., & McDonald, R. (1980). Clomipramine and exposure for obsessive–compulsive rituals: I. *British Journal of Psychiatry, 136,* 1–25.

Mataix-Cols, D., Marks, I. M., Greist, J. H., Kobak, K. A., & Baer, L. (2002). Obsessive–compulsive symptom dimensions as predictors of compliance with and response to behaviour therapy: Results from a controlled trial. *Psychotherapy and Psychosomatics, 71,* 255–262.

McKay, D. (1997). A maintenance program for obsessive–compulsive disorder using exposure with response prevention: 2-year follow-up. *Behaviour Research and Therapy, 35,* 367–369.

McKay, D., Todaro, J. F., Neziroglu, F., & Yaryura-Tobias, J. A. (1996). Evaluation of a naturalistic maintenance program in the treatment of obsessive–compulsive disorder: A preliminary investigation. *Journal of Anxiety Disorders, 10,* 211–217.

McLean, P. D., Whittal, M. L., Thordarson, D. S., Taylor, S., Sochting, I., Koch, W. J., et al. (2001). Cognitive versus behavior therapy in the group treatment of obsessive–compulsive disorder. *Journal of Consulting and Clinical Psychology, 69,* 205–214.

Mehta, M. (1990). A comparative study of family-based and patient-based behavioural management in obsessive–compulsive disorder. *British Journal of Psychiatry, 157,* 133–135.

Miller, W. R., & Rollnick, S. (1991). *Motivational interviewing: Preparing people to change addictive behaviors.* New York: Guilford Press.

Neziroglu, F., Stevens, K., & Yaryura-Tobias, J. A. (1999). Overvalued ideas and their impact on treatment outcome. *Revista Brasileira de Psiquiatria, 21,* 209–214.

Norton, P. J., & Whittal, M. L. (2004). Thematic similarity and clinical outcome in obsessive–compulsive disorder group treatment. *Depression and Anxiety, 20,* 195–197.

Obsessive Compulsive Cognitions Working Group. (1997). Cognitive assessment of obsessive–compulsive disorder. *Behaviour Research and Therapy, 35,* 667–681.

Obsessive Compulsive Cognitions Working Group. (2005). Psychometric validation of the Obsessive Beliefs Questionnaire and the Interpretation of Intrusions Inventory: Part 2. Factor analyses and testing of a brief version. *Behaviour Research and Therapy, 43,* 1527–1542.

O'Sullivan, G., Noshirvani, H., Marks, I., Monteiro, W., & Lelliott, P. (1991). Six-year follow-up after exposure and clomipramine therapy for obsessive compulsive disorder. *Journal of Clinical Psychiatry, 52,* 150–155.

Otto, M. W., Pollack, M. H., & Maki, K. M. (2000). Empirically supported treatments for panic disorder: Costs, benefits, and stepped care. *Journal of Consulting and Clinical Psychology, 68,* 556–563.

Parks, G. A., Anderson, B. K., & Marlatt, G. A. (2001). Relapse prevention therapy. In N. Heather, T. J. Peters, & T. Stockwell (Eds.), *International handbook of alcohol dependence and problems* (pp. 575–592). New York: Wiley.

Rowe, M. K., & Craske, M. G. (1998). Effects of an expanding-spaced vs. massed exposure schedule on fear reduction and return of fear. *Behaviour Research and Therapy, 36,* 701–717.

Saxena, S., Maidment, K. M., Vapnik, T., Golden, G., Rishwain, T., Rosen, R. M., et al. (2002). Obsessive–compulsive hoarding: Symptom severity and response to multimodal treatment. *Journal of Clinical Psychiatry, 63,* 21–27.

Schwartz, J. M., Stoessel, P. W., Baxter, L. R., Jr., Martin, K. M., & Phelps, M. E. (1996). Systematic changes in cerebral glucose metabolic rate after successful behavior modification treatment of obsessive–compulsive disorder. *Archives of General Psychiatry, 53,* 109–113.

Simpson, H. B., Gorfinkle, K. S., & Liebowitz, M. R. (1999). Cognitive–behavioral therapy as an adjunct to serotonin reuptake inhibitors in obsessive–compulsive disorder: An open trial. *Journal of Clinical Psychiatry, 60,* 584–590.

Simpson, H. B., Liebowitz, M. R., Foa, E. B., Kozak, M. J., Schmidt, A. B., Rowan, V., et al. (2004). Post-treatment effects of exposure therapy and clomipramine in obsessive–compulsive disorder. *Depression and Anxiety, 19,* 225–233.

Steketee, G. (1990). Personality traits and disorders in obsessive–compulsive disorder. *Journal of Anxiety Disorders, 4,* 351–364.

Steketee, G. (1997). Disability and family burden in obsessive–compulsive disorder. *Canadian Journal of Psychiatry, 42,* 919–928.

Steketee, G., Chambless, D. L., & Tran, G. Q. (2001). Effects of axis I and II comorbidity on behavior therapy outcome for obsessive–compulsive disorder and agoraphobia. *Comprehensive Psychiatry, 42,* 76–86.

Steketee, G., & Frost, R. O. (2003). Compulsive hoarding: Current status of the research. *Clinical Psychology Review, 23,* 905–927.

Steketee, G., & Shapiro, L. J. (1995). Predicting behavioral treatment outcome for agoraphobia and obsessive–compulsive disorder. *Clinical Psychology Review, 15,* 315–346.

Steketee, G., & White, K. (1990). *When once is not enough: Help for obsessive–compulsives.* Oakland, CA: New Harbinger.

Stewart, S. E., Stack, D. E., Farrell, C., Pauls, D. L., & Jenike, M. A. (2005). Effectiveness of intensive residential treatment (IRT) for severe, refractory obsessive–compulsive disorder. *Journal of Psychiatric Research, 39,* 603–609.

TenHave, T. R., Coyne, J., Salzer, M., & Katz, I. (2003). Research to improve the quality of care for depression: Alternatives to the simple randomized clinical trial. *General Hospital Psychiatry, 25,* 115–123.

Thienemann, M., Martin, J., Cregger, B., Thompson, H. B., & Dyer-Friedman, J. (2001). Manual-driven group cognitive–behavioral therapy for adolescents with obsessive–compulsive disorder: A pilot study. *Journal of the American Academy of Child and Adolescent Psychiatry, 40,* 1254–1260.

Tolin, D. F., Abramowitz, J. S., Hamlin, C., Foa, E. B., & Synodi, D. S. (2002). Attributions for thought suppression failure in obsessive–compulsive disorder. *Cognitive Therapy and Research, 26,* 505–517.

Tolin, D. F., Abramowitz, J. S., Kozak, M. J., & Foa, E. B. (2001). Fixity of belief, perceptual aberration, and magical ideation in obsessive–compulsive disorder patients. *Journal of Anxiety Disorders, 15,* 501–510.

Tolin, D. F., Abramowitz, J. S., Przeworski, A., & Foa, E. B. (2002). Thought suppression in obsessive–compulsive disorder. *Behaviour Research and Therapy, 40,* 1255–1274.

Tolin, D. F., & Hannan, S. E. (2005a). The role of the therapist in behavior therapy. In J. S. Abramowitz & A. C. Houts (Eds.), *Handbook of obsessive–compulsive spectrum disorders* (pp. 317–332). New York: Springer Publishing Company.

Tolin, D. F., & Hannan, S. E. (2005b). What's in a name? The distinction between self-directed and self-conducted treatment. In J. S. Abramowitz & A. C. Houts (Eds.), *Handbook of obsessive–compulsive spectrum disorders* (pp. 347–352). New York: Springer Publishing Company.

Tolin, D. F., Hannan, S., Maltby, N., Diefenbach, G. J., & Worhunsky, P. (2004, November). Self-administered vs. therapist-administered cognitive–behavioral therapy for medication nonresponders with obsessive–compulsive disorder. In M. Whittal (Chair), *Variables impacting treatment outcome in OCD.* Symposium presented at the annual meeting of the Association for Advancement of Behavior Therapy, New Orleans, LA.

Tolin, D. F., & Maltby, N. (in press). Motivating treatment-refusing patients with obsessive–compulsive disorder. In H. Arkowitz, H. A. Westra, W. R. Miller, & S. Rollnick (Eds.), *Clinical applications of motivational interviewing.* New York: Guilford Press.

Tolin, D. F., Maltby, N., Diefenbach, G. J., Hannan, S. E., & Worhunsky, P. (2004). Cognitive–behavioral therapy for medication nonresponders with obsessive–compulsive disorder: A wait-list-controlled open trial. *Journal of Clinical Psychiatry, 65,* 922–931.

Tolin, D. F., Maltby, N., Diefenbach, G. J., & Worhunsky, P. (2004, November). Motivating treatment-refusing obsessive–compulsive disorder patients. In D. J. Dozois (Chair), *Motivational interviewing and related strategies for the treatment of anxiety and depression.* Symposium presented at the annual meeting of the Association for Advancement of Behavior Therapy, New Orleans, LA.

Turner, S. M., Beidel, D. C., Spaulding, S. A., & Brown, J. M. (1995). The practice of behavior therapy: A national survey of costs and methods. *Behavior Therapist, 18,* 1–4.

van Balkom, A. J., de Haan, E., van Oppen, P., Spinhoven, P., Hoogduin, K. A., & van Dyck, R. (1998). Cognitive and behavioral therapies alone versus in combination with fluvoxamine in the treatment of obsessive compulsive disorder. *Journal of Nervous and Mental Disease, 186,* 492–499.

Van Noppen, B. L. (1999). Multi-family behavioral treatment (MFBT) for OCD. *Crisis Intervention, 5,* 3–24.

Van Noppen, B. L., Pato, M. T., Marsland, R., & Rasmussen, S. A. (1998). A time-limited behavioral group for treatment of obsessive–compulsive disorder. *Journal of Psychotherapy Practice and Research, 7,* 272–280.

Van Noppen, B. L., & Steketee, G. (2003). Family responses and multifamily behavioral treatment for obsessive–compulsive disorder. *Brief Treatment and Crisis Intervention, 3,* 231–247.

Van Noppen, B. L., Steketee, G., McCorkle, B. H., & Pato, M. (1997). Group and multifamily behavioral treatment for obsessive compulsive disorder: A pilot study. *Journal of Anxiety Disorders, 11,* 431–446.

van Oppen, P., de Haan, E., van Balkom, A. J., Spinhoven, P., Hoogduin, K., & van Dyck, R. (1995). Cognitive therapy and exposure in vivo in the treatment of obsessive compulsive disorder. *Behaviour Research and Therapy, 33,* 379–390.

Vogel, P. A., Stiles, T. C., & Götestam, K. G. (2004). Adding cognitive therapy elements to exposure therapy for obsessive compulsive disorder: A controlled study. *Behavioural and Cognitive Psychotherapy, 32,* 275–290.

Volpato Cordioli, A., Heldt, E., Braga Bochi, D., Margis, R., Basso de Sousa, M., Fonseca Tonello, J., et al. (2003). Cognitive–behavioral group therapy in obsessive–compulsive disorder: A randomized clinical trial. *Psychotherapy and Psychosomatics, 72,* 211–216.

Warren, R., & Thomas, J. C. (2001). Cognitive–behavior therapy of obsessive–compulsive disorder in private practice: An effectiveness study. *Journal of Anxiety Disorders, 15,* 277–285.

Wegner, D. M., Schneider, D. J., Carter, S. R., & White, T. L. (1987). Paradoxical effects of thought suppression. *Journal of Personality and Social Psychology, 53,* 5–13.

Whittal, M. L., & O'Neill, M. L. (2003). Cognitive and behavioral methods for obsessive–compulsive disorder. *Brief Treatment and Crisis Intervention, 3,* 201–215.

Whittal, M. L., Thordarson, D. S., & McLean, P. D. (2005). Treatment of obsessive–compulsive disorder: Cognitive behavior therapy vs. exposure and response prevention. *Behaviour Research and Therapy, 43,* 1559–1576.

Wilhelm, S. (2003). Cognitive treatment of obsessions. *Brief Treatment and Crisis Intervention, 3,* 187–199.

Wilhelm, S., & Steketee, G. (2006). *Cognitive therapy for obsessive–compulsive disorder: A guide for professionals.* Oakland, CA: New Harbinger.

3

TREATMENT READINESS, AMBIVALENCE, AND RESISTANCE

C. ALEC POLLARD

After learning about his problem on the *Oprah Winfrey Show*, Jim immediately called the Obsessive Compulsive Foundation to find a provider in his area who worked with obsessive–compulsive disorder (OCD). Dr. Smith, an OCD specialist, had an office nearby and was able to see Jim the next day. Dr. Smith confirmed Jim's diagnosis and outlined the evidence-based treatments currently available for OCD. Jim enthusiastically agreed to a trial of outpatient cognitive–behavioral therapy (CBT). He arrived on time for every appointment and completed all therapy homework assignments exactly as Dr. Smith prescribed. Jim asked thoughtful, sometimes challenging questions, but he never argued with Dr. Smith and was careful not to waste time in sessions defending the irrational nature of his OCD. Dr. Smith also met with Jim's family. They learned how to modify their behavior to facilitate Jim's recovery and, like Jim, followed Dr. Smith's guidelines conscientiously. After 15 sessions, Jim was significantly better. He sustained all treatment gains, relying only on periodic maintenance sessions with Dr. Smith and the relapse prevention strategies Jim learned in therapy.

There is good news and bad news about Jim's story. The good news is some people with OCD recover much like Jim did. The bad news is that most of them do not. Only a minority of individuals with OCD receive CBT (Goodwin, Koenen, Hellman, Guardino, & Struening, 2002; Hantouche,

Bouhassira, & Lancrenon, 2000; Pollard, Henderson, Frank, & Margolis, 1989). Approximately 25% to 30% of those with access to CBT are likely to refuse it (Foa, Steketee, Grayson, & Doppelt, 1983; Kozak, Liebowitz, & Foa, 2000), and a similar proportion drop out of therapy prematurely (Kozak et al., 2000). Among those who complete exposure and response prevention (ERP; also known as exposure and ritual prevention), about 25% do not respond to treatment, at least in part because of nonadherence (de Araujo, Ito, & Marks, 1996; O'Sullivan, Noshirvani, Marks, Monteiro, & Lelliott, 1991).

Greater recognition of the number of people with OCD who avoid, refuse, discontinue, or fail to participate adequately in CBT has stimulated growing interest in concepts related to *treatment readiness,* or an individual's willingness or ability to pursue help and engage in treatment. Prochaska and DiClemente's (1982) transtheoretical model outlines different stages and processes of human behavior change and emphasizes the clinical importance of matching interventions with the appropriate stage of change. The model was meant to be applicable to problem behavior in general, but it can be readily applied to OCD. For example, an active, change-oriented intervention like ERP would be considered an appropriate intervention for an OCD patient in the action stage of change. However, attempting to administer ERP to a patient in a preaction stage (e.g., the contemplative or precontemplative stages) will almost certainly fail.

Experience with treatment-resistant substance abusers led Miller and Rollnick (1991) to develop the motivational interviewing approach. In motivational interviewing, active treatment of the presenting problem is delayed until the therapist believes that the patient is ready for therapy. Fostering treatment readiness involves helping patients clarify their motivation for recovery. According to Miller and Rollnick, attempting to treat someone who is insufficiently motivated is likely to be ineffective and to waste valuable resources. Motivational interviewing strategies were originally developed for use with substance abusers, but they have also been applied to patients with OCD (Maltby & Tolin, 2003; Steketee & Frost, in press).

Several authors have discussed cognitive and behavioral strategies for dealing with treatment resistance in general (e.g., Ellis, 1985; Goldfried, 1982; Lazarus & Fay, 1982; Leahy, 2001; Meichenbaum & Gilmore, 1982; Turkat & Meyer, 1982), but little discussion has been devoted specifically to the application of strategies for OCD patients. In this chapter, I discuss issues involved in promoting treatment readiness and managing ambivalence and resistance in OCD patients.

DEFINING TREATMENT READINESS, AMBIVALENCE, AND RESISTANCE

When discussed in reference to treatment, the terms *ambivalence* and *resistance* have not been used consistently. *Resistance,* for example, is often used in medicine to indicate the failure of an illness to respond to a particular treatment (e.g., Rasmussen & Eisen, 1997; Stein, Seedat, Shapira, & Goodman, 2001). In the psychotherapy literature, *resistance* is typically used to describe a patient's reluctance or refusal to participate in some aspect of therapy. The latter use of the word is the one I address in this chapter.

For psychodynamic therapists, resistance and ambivalence are inextricably tied to underlying motivations and conflicts and often focus on the patient's response to the therapist (Wachtel, 1982). Guidano and Liotti (1983) used the term *ambivalence* to describe an individual's conflicted self-concept. Turkat and Meyer (1982) defined *resistance* as "client behavior that the therapist labels as antitherapeutic" (p. 158). One advantage of Turkat and Meyer's definition is that acceptance of a particular theoretical model is not required. In addition, a distinction is made between resistant behavior and the factors believed to influence resistant behavior. Turkat and Meyer also pointed out that no single behavior can be universally classified as a sign of resistance. Context must be considered before a behavior can be judged inconsistent with the goals of treatment.

Although context is an important consideration, certain behaviors are more likely than others to interfere with treatment. Behavior commonly perceived by the therapist as antitherapeutic I refer to in this chapter as *treatment-interfering behavior* (TIB). A TIB is any behavior the therapist believes is incompatible with effective participation in therapy or the pursuit of recovery. Failure to complete therapy homework assignments is a common TIB. Other common examples include missing therapy appointments, dishonest or inaccurate reporting, and reflexive arguing with the therapist. A behavior must occur repeatedly to qualify as a TIB. A single missed appointment, for example, would not be considered a TIB. Furthermore, a TIB is defined by the functional outcome of the behavior, not by the hypothesized intention of the behavior. Exhibit 3.1 contains a list of TIBs commonly found in OCD patients. This checklist was developed at our center to assist therapists and patients in identifying behaviors that may need to be addressed in treatment (VanDyke & Pollard, 2005).

Resistance, ambivalence, and readiness can be thought of as different points along a continuum of treatment engagement. Levels of treatment engagement can be distinguished by the severity of TIB present. Resistance is indicated by TIB so persistent or otherwise significant that benefit from treatment is improbable. At the opposite end of the continuum is a patient who engages almost exclusively in treatment-facilitating behavior. This patient would be considered ready for treatment, as indicated by the relative absence of TIB. Ambivalence represents an intermediate condition, in which TIB is moderate and comparatively easy to modify. The clinical management implications of these three levels of treatment engagement I discuss later in the chapter.

EXHIBIT 3.1
Treatment-Interfering Behavior Checklist

Patient name: _____ Date: _____

Treatment-interfering behavior (TIB) is any behavior that is incompatible with successful treatment and recovery. Please check each TIB this patient exhibits:

_____ 1. Does not acknowledge having a problem.
_____ 2. Does not adequately or consistently acknowledge the problem's severity or its impact on others.
_____ 3. Does not identify clear goals for treatment.
_____ 4. Argues with, repeatedly questions, or otherwise dismisses the therapist's presentation of the nature of the problem or the treatment plan.
_____ 5. Attempts to change the focus of sessions to issues not on the treatment plan.
_____ 6. Has difficulty explaining the treatment plan or the rationale behind it.
_____ 7. Has difficulty answering questions in a timely fashion (e.g., provides information not relevant to the question, provides too much detail).
_____ 8. Is frequently late or does not show up for treatment sessions.
_____ 9. Has difficulty following the treatment plan (e.g., does not complete therapy assignments, doesn't take medication as prescribed) when
_____ accompanied by staff.
_____ not accompanied by staff.
_____ 10. Provides information to the treatment team that is inaccurate, misleading, or inconsistent (e.g., does not adequately report difficulties, reports different things to different clinicians, leaves out critical details).
_____ 11. Engages in, threatens to engage in, or hints at engaging in self-destructive acts.
_____ 12. Speaks or acts in a way that makes others feel physically threatened.
_____ 13. Other: _____

FACTORS ASSOCIATED WITH TREATMENT AMBIVALENCE AND RESISTANCE

Although ambivalence and resistance have not been formally studied in OCD patient samples, some studies have examined relevant behavior such as failure to seek treatment, treatment refusal, dropout, and nonadherence. A survey of National Anxiety Disorders Screening Day participants who reported disabling obsessive–compulsive symptoms indicated that those who had not received treatment were less likely than treated individuals to have panic attacks and more likely to be a minority group member (Goodwin et al., 2002). Among those who had not been treated, willingness to be treated was associated with the presence of panic, posttraumatic stress disorder, and suicidal symptoms. Reluctance to seek treatment was more likely to be reported by respondents who were employed and who felt that they could handle their problem without assistance from others. Notably, level of functioning was not a predictor of willingness to receive treatment. One factor that might predict treatment seeking, however, is the type of OCD an individual develops. Simonds and Thorpe (2003) found that a sample of college students perceived harm obsessions as more shameful and socially unacceptable than those involving washing or checking. The authors suggested that negative attitudes inhibit help seeking and that individuals with harm obsessions may be less likely to pursue treatment than those with other types of OCD.

Type of OCD may also be related to a patient's ability to complete therapy. Mataix-Cols, Marks, Greist, Kobak, and Baer (2002) found patients with hoarding compulsions more likely than patients with other types of OCD to withdraw prematurely from treatment. In recognition of the prevalence of TIB in this patient population, Steketee and Frost (in press) added motivational interviewing strategies to the initial phase of their hoarding treatment manual. Variables other than type of OCD may also be associated with dropping out of treatment. Hansen, Hoogduin, Schaap, and de Haan (1992) found that compared with OCD patients who completed CBT, those who dropped out of therapy early were more likely to have incongruent expectations of therapy, to be more critical of their therapist, and to have less pressure to stay in treatment from people close to them. It is interesting that patients who dropped out were also more likely to have less severe OCD and less anxiety while carrying out therapy homework, which suggests that at least some treatment dropout is related to a lower level of impairment and, perhaps, a lower level of motivation.

Level of motivation may also influence those who complete therapy but are nonadherent. It is reasonable to speculate that highly motivated patients will be more treatment adherent than less motivated patients. Compliance with therapy homework (de Araujo et al., 1996; O'Sullivan et al., 1991) and higher levels of motivation for treatment (de Haan et al., 1997; Keijsers, Hoogduin, & Schaap, 1994) have both been associated with successful treatment outcome in OCD patients. Nonadherence and motivation may be especially important to address in OCD patients. Hand (1998) reported that therapists in his anxiety disorders clinic were less likely to rate OCD patients as compliant compared with patients with agoraphobia or social phobia. Perhaps the challenges of implementing response prevention provide more opportunities for nonadherence to emerge.

FACILITATING TREATMENT READINESS

Most OCD patients come to therapy with at least some ambivalence. After all, it is no secret that CBT involves discomfort, not to mention the expenditure of time, effort, and money. OCD patients can be keenly aware of the costs of CBT without being comparably convinced of the benefits. In addition, new patients often possess one or more inaccurate notions about the hazards of therapy (e.g., "The therapist will force me to do things against my will," "Treatment will make me go crazy"). How therapists manage these issues can influence a patient's level of engagement in treatment.

Common ambivalence can usually be addressed adequately in the first few sessions. However, patients who continue to exhibit TIB will need more than standard treatment preparation. Before describing the management of TIB, I will discuss the assessment of treatment readiness and standard strategies therapists can use to help patients overcome ambivalence.

Assessing Treatment Readiness

In addition to evaluating the nature and severity of a patient's OCD, therapists should also assess a patient's readiness for treatment when conducting the initial evaluation. Four assessment questions in particular should be explored: (a) How well does the patient understand OCD and the CBT model? (b) How realistic are the patient's treatment expectations? (c) What is the patient's level of motivation to change? (d) Are there any other treatment obstacles that need to be addressed?

A few instruments have been developed to assist clinicians in assessing treatment readiness. The Treatment Ambivalence Questionnaire (Purdon, Rowa, & Antony, 2004) surveys patients' concerns about treatment. Another instrument, the Treatment Perceptions Questionnaire (Deacon et al., 2004), assesses patients' attitudes and preconceptions about therapy. The Psychotherapy Decisional Balance Scale (Medeiros, 1987; O'Connell, 1986) was developed to ascertain an individual's opinions of the pros and cons of entering psychotherapy. The transtheoretical model led to the development of instruments that measure the extent to which an individual endorses items related to

- each of four stages of behavior change (Stages of Change Scale; McConnaughy, DiClemente, Prochaska, & Velicer, 1989);
- each of 12 types of strategies or activities for changing problem behaviors (Processes of Change Questionnaire; Prochaska, Velicer, DiClemente, & Fava, 1988); and
- each of several causal categories (e.g., cognitive, biological, situational) involved in problem behavior (Levels of Attribution and Change Scale; Norcross, Prochaska, & Hambrecht, 1985).

Therapists can use these instruments to identify concerns, attitudes, or motivational issues that should be targeted for intervention to enhance readiness.

The practical utility of these instruments with ambivalent or resistant OCD patients has not been demonstrated clearly. In addition, none of these instruments has been studied adequately with large samples of OCD patients. Most important, the heuristic value of these instruments for predicting therapy behavior or for designing treatment readiness interventions has yet to be determined. A study at our center found that compared with scores on the Stages of Change Scale, therapists' predictions that were based on clinical interviews more accurately predicted which anxiety disorder patients would drop out of therapy prematurely (Carter-Sand, 2004). Nonetheless, self-report measures might complement the clinical interview and provide therapists with another method for detecting patients who need additional preparation before proceeding with ERP. Responses to individual items may also assist therapists in identifying specific targets for pre-ERP intervention.

Whether or not self-report instruments are used, much of the information on treatment readiness status will come from the clinical interview. The patient's ability to articulate treatment goals is a particularly important source of information about his or her level of motivation to change. Patients should be asked to identify both long-term or life goals (e.g., go to college, find and keep a job, get married) and short-term or treatment goals (e.g., read and write normally, complete tasks within a normal amount of time, touch objects that have been touched by others). Difficulty articulating goals is an indication that the patient may need motivational enhancement. Another source of information in assessing treatment readiness is, of course, the patient's observable behavior. TIB can be evident early in treatment, sometimes even before the first visit; examples include having someone else make the appointment, missing or rescheduling appointments, failing to complete assessment questionnaires, and engaging in uninformed criticism of CBT or the therapist.

Once the initial assessment has been completed, the therapist must decide what level of intervention will be necessary to prepare a patient adequately for ERP. There are three basic options: (a) standard treatment preparation followed by ERP, (b) standard treatment preparation with special attention to an identified readiness issue, or (c) delay of ERP and a temporary refocus of the treatment on TIB.

Managing Ambivalence: Preparing Patients to Engage in Treatment

Very few studies have examined strategies for preparing OCD patients to engage effectively in ERP. However, several authors have discussed the things they do to promote treatment engagement in OCD patients (Abramowitz, Franklin, & Cahill, 2003; Clark, 2004; Maltby & Tolin, 2003; Rachman, 2003). In this section, I will integrate some of their suggestions. The strategies they describe can be conceptualized as attempts to instill proper insight about OCD or CBT, to promote realistic expectations about therapy and the recovery process, or to enhance motivation for change. Accordingly, it is usually helpful for the therapist to do the following:

- *Provide accurate information about the symptoms and nature of OCD.* Information should be provided in a way that discourages guilt and shame and encourages patients to assume responsibility for their efforts to recover.
- *Present the CBT model in a way the OCD patient can easily understand.* Complex models are of little clinical value if the patient cannot grasp and remember the concepts. The clinician should keep it simple by drawing a diagram on a marker board or piece of paper and giving the patient something to take home and review. The model should give patients a more useful way to understand their OCD symptoms and provide a rationale for the CBT procedures they will be following (see chap. 1 in this volume).
- *Allow for biology.* Many OCD patients believe that OCD is biological, and some of them are taking antiobsessional medication when they begin CBT. Polemic refutation of the biological model creates confusion and engenders unnecessary resistance in certain patients. Resistance to psychological models of OCD can usually be circumvented by emphasizing the reciprocal relationship between brain and behavior. It is sometimes helpful to refer to brain imagery studies of OCD patients that document changes in brain activity following CBT (e.g., Baxter et al., 1992). Therapists can also provide examples of medical disorders (e.g., diabetes) that are treated in part with behavioral interventions (e.g., exercise, stress management, skills training to enhance adherence to diet and medication).
- *Include supportive concepts, metaphors, and information that might help patients understand and accept the CBT model.* Abramowitz et al. (2003) discussed four main points they emphasized in getting patients to grasp the CBT model: (a) the normal occurrence of intrusive thoughts, (b) the paradoxical effects of thought suppression, (c) the nature of thought–action fusion, and (d) the futility of pursuing certainty. Whatever the strategy, the objective is to help patients grasp an alternative way of understanding the meaning of their symptoms and the factors that maintain their condition.
- *Clarify the role and duties of patient and therapist.* The therapist should emphasize the collaborative and complementary nature of the relationship. Each person has a job. Patients are the experts on what they would like to change. Therapists are the experts on how to make that change happen. Therapists should also clarify that their job is to advise, guide, encourage, and support the patient and that it is not the therapist's job to order the patient around. Patients need to know up front what will

be required of them (e.g., regular homework assignments, rearranging their schedule and priorities), especially if they have never been given homework assignments between psychotherapy sessions. Before starting ERP, it is helpful to ask patients to determine the amount of time they are willing to devote to therapy each week, the current responsibilities or activities they will temporarily suspend to make time for homework assignments, and the specific times and days of the week they will be reserving to complete those assignments.

Therapists can supplement the psychoeducation they provide with other sources of information to help prepare patients for CBT. Patients can be asked to read one of several consumer books that contain informative descriptions of the cognitive–behavioral treatment of OCD (e.g., Baer, 1991, 2001; Foa & Wilson, 1991; Grayson, 2003; Hyman & Pedrick, 1999; Neziroglu & Yaryura-Tobias, 1991; Penzel; 2000; Steketee & White, 1990). Helpful information can also be obtained on the Internet at the Web sites of reputable organizations like the Obsessive Compulsive Foundation (http://www.ocfoundation.org), Anxiety Disorders Association of America (http://www.adaa.org), and Obsessive Compulsive Information Center (http://www.miminc.org/aboutocic.html).

Pretreatment access to other OCD patients can sometimes be valuable. In their treatment package designed to promote treatment readiness, Maltby and Tolin (2003) included two interventions that involved other OCD patients, watching videotaped demonstrations of ERP and speaking with patients who have already been through treatment. We have a similar program at our center, called the "patient liaison program," in which ambivalent OCD patients discuss their questions and concerns with someone who has successfully completed CBT. Some patients need special attention to motivational issues. Maltby and Tolin's treatment readiness package also involves motivational interviewing. In this approach, it is important that therapists help patients objectively assess the reasons for and against participating in CBT. This requires therapists to maintain a nonconfrontational, nonjudgmental composure and to encourage patients to make their own decisions. A related method used at our clinic is called the impact analysis, which helps patients assess the impact OCD has had on their lives. Patients list all of the positive and negative ways in which OCD has affected them. We also ask them to conduct a survey to determine the impact their OCD has had on the lives of key family members, coworkers, and friends. The therapist reviews the results of the impact analysis with the patient in an effort to clarify his or her motivation for treatment.

Once the therapist believes that a patient has adequate knowledge, realistic expectations, and sufficient motivation, the active phase of treatment (e.g., ERP) can be implemented. A state of treatment readiness should be

signaled by the relative absence of TIB. If the patient still exhibits significant TIB, more attention should be devoted to readiness issues before proceeding with ERP. In some cases, TIB will not be apparent in the initial
phase of therapy but will emerge once ERP is initiated. Whenever a pattern
of significant TIB is identified, the therapist should consider discontinuing
the ERP. It is not necessary to terminate treatment altogether, but the focus
of therapy should be redirected to helping the patient overcome TIB.

MANAGING RESISTANCE: TREATING THE PATIENT'S TREATMENT-INTERFERING BEHAVIOR

The efficacy of strategies to manage treatment resistance has not been
studied extensively in OCD patients. Two attempts to circumvent treatment
resistance I have referred to previously in this chapter (Maltby & Tolin,
2003; Steketee & Frost, in press), both of which include motivational interviewing (Miller & Rollnick, 2002). As of yet, Steketee and Frost (in press)
have not reported outcome data on the specific contributions of motivational interviewing to the treatment of hoarding. However, Maltby and Tolin
(2003) reported that 60% of the group of OCD patients who received their
treatment readiness package chose to begin ERP, compared with only 20%
of patients in the wait-list control group. These promising results suggest
that a pretreatment intervention can increase an OCD patient's willingness
to begin ERP. It is still undetermined, however, if this kind of intervention
facilitates treatment participation or, ultimately, the outcome of ERP.

Another promising approach to working with treatment resistance is
cognitive therapy (see chap. 5 in this volume). The independent effects of
cognitive therapy in the absence of some form of ERP cannot yet be isolated
given the status of existing research. However, interventions derived from
cognitive models may help promote treatment readiness in some OCD patients who are resistant to ERP. Sookman and Pinard (1999) developed an
approach they called *integrative cognitive therapy* specifically to address the
needs of OCD patients who were not able to participate adequately in ERP.
In their approach, treatment targets different levels of cognition (e.g., appraisals, core beliefs) and attempts to address general cognitive domains and
issues that may contribute to OCD or to the resistant patient's inability to
participate in CBT. No controlled outcome data are available, but Sookman
and Pinard reported significant symptom reductions in seven OCD patients
who were previously unresponsive to ERP.

Another approach to the management of treatment resistance in OCD
was developed at our center in St. Louis, Missouri (VanDyke & Pollard, 2005).
This approach uses an integrative cognitive–behavioral model to formulate

and develop interventions to modify TIB. We call this approach *readiness treatment*. I describe the components of readiness treatment in some detail as an example of one way to approach treatment resistance.

For cognitive–behavioral therapists, the concepts and interventions that together form readiness treatment should be familiar. The approach draws from a variety of sources within the cognitive–behavioral field (e.g., Beck, Emery, & Greenberg, 1985; Goldfried & Davidson, 1994; Hayes, Strosahl, & Wilson, 1999; Linehan, 1993; Nezu, Nezu, & Lombardo, 2004; Resick, 1993). Principles and strategies consistent with motivational interviewing are also incorporated (Miller & Rollnick, 2002). The more distinctive aspects of readiness treatment are the breadth of cognitive–behavioral components included in the approach and the requirement that therapists formally terminate OCD treatment and redirect the target of analysis and treatment to the TIB. Formal redirection of the focus of therapy has significant implications for what the therapist does in treatment. For example, cognitive interventions in readiness treatment are directed at beliefs associated with the TIB, not necessarily at beliefs directly related to OCD. Readiness treatment includes six major steps, described in the sections that follow.

Identifying Treatment-Interfering Behavior

In the first component of readiness treatment, the therapist and patient collaboratively determine any TIB that might be responsible for the patient's inadequate response to treatment. The success of readiness treatment begins with and relies on the accurate identification of relevant TIB. It is important to introduce patients to the concept of TIB in a way that helps them fully appreciate the negative impact of the behavior without generating excessive defensiveness. To accomplish this, the therapist needs to present and describe the patient's TIB objectively. Pejorative, judgmental language or unnecessary interpretations of behavior or underlying motivations should be avoided. It is also important to emphasize the functional significance of the behavior, rather than the intention of the behavior. The therapist should be careful not to imply that the patient is trying to sabotage treatment. Instead, the effect of the behavior on treatment should be pointed out. When TIB is discussed in this manner, most patients display little or no defensiveness.

Selecting the Behavior to Target for Treatment

The next step is to determine which TIB to address first. If a patient has only one TIB, this is an uncomplicated decision. When the patient has more than one TIB, the therapist must select which TIB will become the initial focus of readiness treatment. Usually, the target TIB is selected on the basis of its primacy. In other words, the therapist tries to determine which TIB has the most fundamental or significant impact on treatment. For example, failure to acknowledge having a problem is more fundamental than not completing homework assignments consistently. A person who denies having a problem is unlikely to follow through with therapy exercises. Typically, only one TIB is addressed at a time. Once the target TIB has been modified sufficiently, the therapist and patient can elect to target another TIB, if needed. In some cases, resolution of one TIB eliminates the others.

Setting Readiness Goals and Objectives

After the target TIB has been selected, the therapist and patient discuss the criteria for completion of readiness work. In other words, what changes in behavior should be evident before ERP is initiated or resumed? This step involves setting a goal and related objectives. A goal is a general statement about changes in the TIB that should occur as a result of readiness treatment (e.g., "Jack will stop arguing with his therapist when discussing exposure homework"). Objectives are statements that describe more specific behavioral changes indicating when the goal has been reached (e.g., "For five consecutive therapy sessions, Jack will discuss ERP without questioning the therapist's judgment or stating that therapy is 'stupid' or 'won't work'"). The therapist and the patient must agree that the criteria outlined in the goals and objectives indicate meaningful change in the TIB. OCD treatment is not resumed until these criteria are met.

Identifying Factors Contributing to the Target Behavior

The next step of readiness treatment is to conduct a cognitive–behavioral analysis and develop hypotheses about factors that might be contributing to the TIB. Identifying contributing factors is an essential step in readiness treatment, because these factors are the targets for intervention. There are four categories of factors that potentially contribute to the maintenance of a TIB: (a) beliefs that are incompatible with active participation in therapy (e.g., "OCD makes me special," "Treatment doesn't work"); (b) skill deficits (e.g., poor time management, problems with assertion); (c) emotional dysregulation (e.g., excessive guilt or anger); and (d) incentive or motivation deficits. These categories are not presumed to be orthogonal; a single intervention might affect more than one factor. Identification of factors contributing to a TIB relies on the clinician's ability to thoroughly examine available assessment data and systematically consider each category of factors. Methods included to assess each category vary somewhat depending on the patient. For more discussion of the cognitive behavioral analysis of TIB, the reader is referred to VanDyke and Pollard (2005).

Designing and Implementing Interventions to Address Contributing Factors

Once a factor is hypothesized as contributing to a TIB, interventions are selected to address that factor. For example, nonadherence because of a patient's poor time management skills would be treated with time management training, a patient with insufficient motivation would receive motivational interviewing, and cognitive interventions would be used to address TIB associated with treatment-incompatible beliefs.

Resuming Treatment of the Obsessive–Compulsive Disorder

When the patient meets the readiness objectives and achieves the readiness goal, readiness treatment for the target TIB can be terminated. Unless another significant TIB remains, therapy for the OCD is resumed.

EFFECTIVENESS OF READINESS TREATMENT

In a preliminary report, readiness treatment was successful in reducing TIB in 7 of 11 treatment-resistant OCD patients (VanDyke & Pollard, 2005). However, controlled studies evaluating the effectiveness of readiness treatment have not yet been conducted. Furthermore, the ultimate effect of this approach on a patient's ability to participate in and respond favorably to ERP has not been examined. Until the appropriate research has been conducted, readiness treatment and other approaches (Maltby & Tolin, 2003; Pollard, 2000; Salkovskis, Richards, & Forrester, 2000; Sookman & Pinard, 1999; Steketee & Frost, in press) to treatment-resistant OCD should be considered experimental.

CONCLUSION

Now that ERP has been shown to be an effective treatment for many OCD patients, it is time to develop ways to help those who do not currently benefit from therapy. A primary research objective should be to increase the number of people with OCD who seek, find, actively participate in, and adequately respond to treatment. One way to achieve this objective is to develop strategies that help resistant people with OCD participate more effectively in ERP. Current strategies are in the experimental stage of development, and more research is needed. Nonetheless, the approaches I describe in this chapter suggest that practitioners of CBT have more to offer treatment-resistant OCD patients than the invitation to "come back when you're ready."

REFERENCES

Abramowitz, J. S., Franklin, M. E., & Cahill, S. P. (2003). Approaches to common obstacles in the exposure-based treatment of obsessive–compulsive disorder. *Cognitive and Behavioral Practice, 10*, 14–21.

Baer, L. (1991). *Getting control.* Boston: Little, Brown.

Baer, L. (2001). *Imp of the mind.* New York: Penguin Putnam.

Baxter, L. R., Schwartz, J. M., Bergman, K. S., Szuba, M. P., Guze, B. H., Mazziotta, J. C., et al. (1992). Caudate glucose metabolic rate changes with both drug and behavior therapy for obsessive–compulsive disorder. *Archives of General Psychiatry, 49*, 681–689.

Beck, A. T., Emery, G., & Greenberg, R. L. (1985). *Anxiety disorders and phobias: A cognitive perspective.* New York: Penguin.

Carter-Sand, S. A. (2004). Examining the utility of the transtheoretical model with psychotherapy for anxiety disorders. *Dissertation Abstracts International, 65,* 2008. (UMI No. 3130017)

Clark, D. A. (2004). *Cognitive–behavioral therapy for OCD.* New York: Guilford Press.

de Araujo, L. A., Ito, L. M., & Marks, I. (1996). Early compliance and other factors predicting outcome of exposure for obsessive–compulsive disorder. *British Journal of Psychiatry, 169*, 747–752.

de Haan, E., van Oppen, P., van Balkom, A. J., Spinhoven, P., Hoogduin, K. A., & van Dyck, R. (1997). Prediction of outcome and early vs. late improvement in OCD patients treated with cognitive behavior therapy and pharmacotherapy. *Acta Psychiatrica Scandinavica, 96*, 354–361.

Deacon, B., Schwartz, S., Whiteside, S., Kalsy, S., Moore, K., & Abramowitz, J. (2004, November). *Patients' perceptions of pharmacological and cognitive–behavioral treatment of OCD.* Paper presented at the annual meeting of the Association for Advancement of Behavior Therapy, New Orleans, LA.

Ellis, A. (1985). *Overcoming resistance: Rational-emotive therapy with difficult clients.* New York: Springer Publishing Company.

Foa, E. B., Steketee, G., Grayson, J. B., & Doppelt, H. G. (1983). Treatment of obsessive–compulsives: When do we fail? In E. B. Foa & P. M. G. Emmelkamp (Eds.), *Failures in behavior therapy* (pp. 10–34). New York: Wiley.

Foa, E. B., & Wilson, R. (1991). *Stop obsessing! How to overcome your obsessions and compulsions.* New York: Bantam Books.

Goldfried, M. R. (1982). Resistance and clinical behavior therapy. In P. L. Wachtel (Ed.), *Resistance: Psychodynamic and behavioral perspectives* (pp. 95–114). New York: Plenum Press.

Goldfried, M. R., & Davidson, G. C. (1994). *Clinical behavior therapy* (expanded ed.). New York: Wiley.

Goodwin, R., Koenen, K. C., Hellman, F., Guardino, M., & Struening, E. (2002). Helpseeking and access to mental health treatment for obsessive–compulsive disorder. *Acta Psychiatrica Scandinavica, 106*, 143–149.

Grayson, J. (2003). *Freedom from obsessive–compulsive disorder*. New York: Tarcher/Penguin.

Guidano, V. F., & Liotti, G. (1983). *Cognitive processes and emotional disorders*. New York: Guilford Press.

Hand, I. (1998). Out-patient, multi-modal behaviour therapy for obsessive–compulsive disorder. *British Journal of Psychiatry, 173*(Suppl. 35), 45–52.

Hansen, A. M., Hoogduin, C. A., Schaap, C., & de Haan, E. (1992). Do drop-outs differ from successfully treated obsessive–compulsives? *Behaviour Research and Therapy, 30*, 547–550.

Hantouche, E. G., Bouhassira, M., & Lancrenon, S. (2000). Prospective follow-up over a 12 month period of a cohort of 155 patients with obsessive–compulsive disorder: Phase III National DRT–TOC study. *Encephale, 26*, 73–83.

Hayes, S. C., Strosahl, K. D., & Wilson, K. D. (1999). *Acceptance and commitment therapy: An experiential approach to behavior change*. New York: Guilford Press.

Hyman, B. M., & Pedrick, C. (1999). *The OCD workbook*. Oakland, CA: New Harbinger.

Keijsers, G. P., Hoogduin, C. A., & Schaap, C. P. (1994). Predictors of treatment outcome in the behavioural treatment of obsessive–compulsive disorder. *British Journal of Psychiatry, 165*, 781–786.

Kozak, M. J., Liebowitz, M. R., & Foa, E. B. (2000). Cognitive behavior therapy and pharmacotherapy for obsessive–compulsive disorder: The NIMH-sponsored collaborative study. In W. K. Goodman, M. V. Rudorfer, & J. Maser (Eds.), *Obsessive–compulsive disorder: Contemporary issues in treatment* (pp. 501–530). Mahwah, NJ: Erlbaum.

Lazarus, A. A., & Fay, A. (1982). Resistance or rationalization? A cognitive–behavioral perspective. In P. L. Wachtel (Ed.), *Resistance: Psychodynamic and behavioral perspectives* (pp. 115–132). New York: Plenum Press.

Leahy, R. (2001). *Overcoming resistance in cognitive therapy*. New York: Guilford Press.

Linehan, M. M. (1993). *Cognitive–behavioral treatment of borderline personality disorder*. New York: Guilford Press.

Maltby, N., & Tolin, D. F. (2003). Overview of treatments for obsessive–compulsive disorder and spectrum conditions: Conceptualization, theory, and practice. *Brief Treatment and Crisis Intervention, 3*, 127–144.

Mataix-Cols, D., Marks, I. M., Greist, J. H., Kobak, K. A., & Baer, L. (2002). Obsessive–compulsive symptom dimensions as predictors of compliance with and response to behaviour therapy: Results from a controlled trial. *Psychotherapy and Psychosomatics, 71*, 255–262.

McConnaughy, E., DiClemente, C., Prochaska, J., & Velicer, W. (1989). Stages of change in psychotherapy: A follow-up report. *Psychotherapy: Theory, Research, and Practice, 20*, 368–375.

Medeiros, M. (1987). [Inter-rater agreement on the Psychotherapy Decisional Balance Scale]. Unpublished raw data.

Meichenbaum, D., & Gilmore, J. B. (1982). Resistance from a cognitive–behavioral perspective. In P. L. Wachtel (Ed.), *Resistance: Psychodynamic and behavioral perspectives* (pp. 133–156). New York: Plenum Press.

Miller, W. R., & Rollnick, S. (1991). *Motivational interviewing: Preparing people to change addictive behavior*. New York: Guilford Press.

Miller, W. R., & Rollnick, S. (2002). *Motivational interviewing: Preparing people to change* (2nd ed.). New York: Guilford Press.

Neziroglu, F., & Yaryura-Tobias, J. (1991). *Over and over again*. Lexington, MA: Lexington Books.

Nezu, A. M., Nezu, C. M., & Lombardo, E. (2004). *Cognitive–behavioral case formulation and treatment design: A problem-solving approach*. New York: Springer Publishing Company.

Norcross, J., Prochaska, J., & Hambrecht, M. (1985). Levels of Attribution and Change (LAC) scale: Development and measurement. *Cognitive Therapy and Research, 9,* 631–649.

O'Connell, D. (1986). *The decisional balance sheet and its relation to the stages of change model in weight loss and control*. Unpublished master's thesis, University of Rhode Island, Kingston.

O'Sullivan, G., Noshirvani, H., Marks, I., Monteiro, W., & Lelliott, P. (1991). Six-year follow-up after exposure and clomipramine therapy for obsessive compulsive disorder. *Journal of Clinical Psychiatry, 52,* 150–155.

Penzel, F. (2000). *Obsessive–compulsive disorders*. New York: Oxford University Press.

Pollard, C. A. (2000). Inpatient treatment of refractory obsessive–compulsive disorder. In W. K. Goodman, M. V. Rudorfer, & J. D. Maser (Eds.), *Obsessive–compulsive disorder: Contemporary issues in treatment* (pp. 223–231). Mahwah, NJ: Erlbaum.

Pollard, C. A., Henderson, J. G., Jr., Frank, M., & Margolis, R. B. (1989). Help-seeking patterns of anxiety disordered individuals in the general population. *Journal of Anxiety Disorders, 3,* 131–138.

Prochaska, J., & DiClemente, C. (1982). Transtheoretical therapy: Toward a more integrative model of change. *Psychotherapy: Theory, Research, and Practice, 19,* 276–288.

Prochaska, J., Velicer, W., DiClemente, C., & Fava, J. (1988). Measuring processes of change: Applications to the cessation of smoking. *Journal of Consulting and Clinical Psychology, 4,* 520–528.

Purdon, C., Rowa, K., & Antony, M. (2004, November). *Treatment fears in individuals awaiting treatment for OCD*. Paper presented at the annual meeting of the Association for Advancement of Behavior Therapy, New Orleans, LA.

Rachman, S. (2003). *The treatment of obsessions*. New York: Oxford University Press.

Rasmussen, S. A., & Eisen, J. L. (1997). Treatment strategies for chronic and refractory obsessive–compulsive disorder. *Journal of Clinical Psychiatry, 58*(Suppl. 13), 9–13.

Resick, P. (1993). *Cognitive processing therapy for rape victims: A treatment manual*. Newbury Park, CA: Sage.

Salkovskis, P. M., Richards, C., & Forrester, E. (2000). Psychological treatment of refractory obsessive–compulsive disorder and related problems. In W. K. Goodman, M. V. Rudorfer, & J. D. Maser (Eds.), *Obsessive–compulsive disorder: Contemporary issues in treatment* (pp. 201–219). Mahwah, NJ: Erlbaum.

Simonds, L. M., & Thorpe, S. J. (2003). Attitudes toward obsessive–compulsive disorder: An experimental investigation. *Social Psychiatry and Psychiatric Epidemiology, 38,* 331–336.

Sookman, D., & Pinard, G. (1999). Integrative cognitive therapy for obsessive–compulsive disorder: A focus on multiple schemas. *Cognitive and Behavioral Practice, 6,* 351–362.

Stein, D. J., Seedat, S., Shapira, N. A., & Goodman, W. K. (2001). Management of treatment resistant obsessive–compulsive disorder. In M. T. Pato & J. Zohar (Eds.), *Current treatments of obsessive–compulsive disorder* (2nd ed., pp. 221–237). Washington, DC: American Psychiatric Publishing.

Steketee, G., & Frost, R. (in press). *Treatment manual for compulsive hoarding.* New York: Oxford University Press.

Steketee, G., & White, K. (1990). *When once is not enough.* Oakland, CA: New Harbinger.

Turkat, D., & Meyer, V. (1982). The behavior-analytic approach. In P. Wachtel (Ed.), *Resistance* (pp. 157–158). New York: Plenum Press.

VanDyke, M., & Pollard, C. A. (2005). Treatment of refractory obsessive–compulsive disorder: The St. Louis model. *Cognitive and Behavioral Practice, 12,* 30–39.

Wachtel, P. L. (1982). *Resistance: Psychodynamic and behavioral approaches.* New York: Plenum Press.

4

EXPOSURE AND RESPONSE PREVENTION

KAREN ROWA, MARTIN M. ANTONY, AND RICHARD P. SWINSON

Historically, obsessive–compulsive disorder (OCD) has been a perplexing disorder to treat. It was not until the 1960s that researchers identified techniques that proved to be effective for managing obsessive thoughts and compulsive behaviors. These techniques were first reported in case studies by Meyer (1966), who exposed clients to anxiety-evoking stimuli and prevented them from engaging in compulsive rituals. As discussed in previous chapters, this method of treatment has become known as exposure and response prevention (ERP; also known as exposure and ritual prevention). In the 1970s and 1980s, ERP underwent empirical scrutiny and emerged as the gold standard psychological treatment for OCD. Currently, ERP continues to be the standard against which other treatments are compared and is the only psychological intervention for OCD to be recognized as an empirically supported psychological treatment (DeRubeis & Crits-Christoph, 1998). A review of treatment outcome research indicates that between 63% and 83% of participants across multiple studies obtained some benefit following ERP, and many of these gains were maintained across long-term follow-up (Abramowitz, 1997; Foa & Kozak, 1996; Stanley & Turner, 1995). In this chapter, we review the empirical status of ERP, including how this treatment has fared against other psychological and medication treatments, and then provide a description of how to implement ERP in clinical practice. We conclude the chapter with a case example to illustrate the use of ERP with a client with OCD.

Current versions of ERP retain similarity to the techniques Meyer (1966) described. In this treatment, clients are asked to purposely expose themselves to triggers, cues, or situations that evoke anxiety and obsessional thoughts. This type of exposure is termed *in vivo exposure* because exposure is completed in the actual feared situation. For example, a client with contamination fears may be asked to touch "dirty" or "contaminated" objects such as doorknobs or public faucets, and a client with the need to arrange objects symmetrically may be asked to leave objects purposely askew. After exposing themselves to these cues, clients are then instructed to refrain from using compulsive rituals until their anxiety, fear, or discomfort substantially subsides. Another significant part of ERP includes identifying cues or situations the client may be avoiding for fear of triggering obsessional concerns. In treatment, clients are asked to conduct exposure and response prevention exercises in avoided situations. For example, an individual with obsessions about sexually molesting children may avoid being around children, changing children's diapers, or being alone with young children. ERP for this client would involve exposure to these very situations and discouragement of the use of rituals.

In contrast to the in vivo approach, exposure can also be done in imagination, called *imaginal exposure*. Clients expose themselves to feared thoughts (e.g., thoughts of hurting a loved one), images (e.g., blasphemous images), or imagined consequences of not using rituals. For example, a person might be asked to repeatedly imagine not checking the lock on the door, walking away, and having the door be unlocked or someone burgling the person's house as a result of not checking.

EMPIRICAL STATUS OF EXPOSURE AND RESPONSE PREVENTION

In this section, we review the empirical status of ERP including its effectiveness compared to other treatments and the variables that affect outcome.

Findings Regarding Outcome

Extensive research has examined the efficacy of ERP for OCD, beginning in the 1970s with a series of studies by Marks, Rachman, and Hodgson (e.g., Hodgson, Rachman, & Marks, 1972; Marks, Rachman, & Hodgson, 1975; Rachman, Marks, & Hodgson, 1971, 1973). These early studies found that exposure was significantly more effective than relaxation training. Subsequent to these influential early studies, further trials have confirmed the effectiveness of ERP (e.g., Foa & Goldstein, 1978). In reviews of the outcome literature, ERP has been found to be more effective than relaxation and similarly effective to cognitive therapy (Abramowitz, 1997), although other controlled trials have indicated a slight advantage for ERP over cognitive therapy (see Eddy, Dutra, Bradley, & Westen, 2004, for a review). It should be noted that the cognitive therapy used in these studies often contains a behavioral component similar to ERP, and we await the results of ongoing studies that compare "pure" cognitive therapy with ERP.

A meta-analysis by Kobak et al. (Kobak, Greist, Jefferson, Katzelnick, & Henk, 1998) found that ERP was more effective than the SSRIs, although when methodological differences between studies were controlled (e.g., method of calculating effect size, presence of a control group), ERP was found to be similarly effective to the SSRIs and clomipramine. ERP also appears to be similarly effective to the combination of ERP and medication (Foa et al., 2005; van Balkom et al., 1998), although one meta-analysis suggested that the combination of pharmacotherapy and psychotherapy may be the most effective intervention compared with monotherapies (Eddy et al., 2004). Although studies generally support the effectiveness of ERP, many early studies were not randomized controlled trials. However, ERP has proved its effectiveness in the handful of randomized controlled trials that have been conducted. For example, a study comparing ERP with anxiety management techniques found a significant advantage of ERP in the reduction of OCD symptoms (Lindsay, Crino, & Andrews, 1997). In fact, participants in the anxiety management group demonstrated no change on obsessive–compulsive symptoms across the 15 hours of therapy, whereas participants receiving ERP showed significant improvement on OCD symptoms, confirming that ERP is specifically effective for these symptoms.

Trials have also confirmed the short- and long-term effectiveness of ERP. In a meta-analysis, Abramowitz (1998) found that clinically meaningful change after ERP was maintained across a 5-month follow-up period. Reviews by Marks (1981) and O'Sullivan and Marks (1990) found that treatment gains following ERP were maintained for periods lasting from 1 to 6 years, with 79% of participants classified as improved or much improved. Although some individuals reported exacerbation of symptoms during the years following treatment, one study found that almost half of participants reported maintaining their gains or making further improvements in the 6 years after treatment ended (O'Sullivan, Noshirvani, Marks, Monteiro, & Lelliott, 1991). ERP may also reduce the need for antidepressant medication in the months after treatment (Cottraux, Mollard, Bouvard, & Marks, 1993).

Moderating Factors

With the general effectiveness of ERP established, researchers have also focused on variables that may affect the outcome of ERP. For example, studies suggest that therapist modeling of exposure exercises does not significantly add to the effects of in vivo exposure (Marks, 1981). There is mixed evidence regarding the benefit of adding imaginal exposure exercises to in vivo exposures. A meta-analysis found that this combination was superior to in vivo exposure alone (Abramowitz, 1996), although some individual studies have found no such benefit (de Araujo, Ito, Marks, & Deale, 1995; Ito, Marks, de Araujo, & Hemsley, 1995). Individual therapy appears to yield better results than group therapy (Eddy et al., 2004), despite early indications that the two were similarly effective (Fals-Stewart, Marks, & Schafer, 1993).

A great deal of research has focused on the superiority of exposure guided by a therapist versus self-directed exposure (i.e., exposure conducted by the client outside of the therapist's office). This remains an important question for several reasons. First, therapist involvement in exposures can be time consuming and therefore costly to provide. Furthermore, it may be difficult for individuals to find a therapist who is trained to administer ERP, and individuals living in remote areas may have difficulty gaining access to treatment. Indeed, studies suggest that individuals with OCD often receive treatments other than behavioral treatments like ERP for their symptoms, despite the clear evidence supporting ERP (e.g., Goisman et al., 1993; Rowa, Antony, Brar, Summerfeldt, & Swinson, 2000). Is it necessary for ERP to be therapist guided? Studies generally support the superiority of exposures conducted within sessions, with a therapist present, as compared with self-directed exposures (Abramowitz, 1996), although self-directed exposure still does result in a significant reduction of OCD symptoms (Fritzler, Hecker, & Losee, 1997; see chap. 2 for a more detailed discussion). Therefore, if possible, ERP provided under the guidance of a therapist appears to be the most desirable option. However, self-administered ERP is a reasonable choice for clients without access to the services of a therapist.

A number of variables hypothesized to improve the outcome of ERP have been shown to make little difference compared with standard therapist-administered ERP. For example, inpatient ERP has been shown to be equivalent to outpatient ERP (van den Hout, Emmelkamp, Kraaykamp, & Griez, 1988), 7-week group ERP was as effective as 12-week group ERP (Himle et al., 2001), and twice-weekly ERP demonstrated similar outcomes to intensive outpatient ERP (i.e., daily sessions; Abramowitz, Foa, & Franklin, 2003). A study by our group compared ERP offered in the therapist's office with ERP administered at a client's home or other environment where symptoms may occur. Results suggested that both treatments were similarly effective at posttreatment and 3-month follow-up, both on clinician and self-ratings of OCD symptoms and on measures of functional impairment (Rowa, Antony, Summerfeldt, Purdon, & Swinson, 2004). Franklin and colleagues compared the outcomes of ERP for clients from randomized controlled trials with those of clients offered ERP outside of a trial. They found that both groups significantly benefited from ERP, suggesting that this is a useful treatment both within the context of a study with carefully selected participants and in a general clinical practice (Franklin, Abramowitz, Kozak, Levitt, & Foa, 2000).

To summarize, ERP has been shown to be an effective treatment for OCD, resulting in significant reductions in OCD symptoms for those who complete treatment. When compared with alternative treatments, ERP is more effective than relaxation or general anxiety management strategies and is as effective as or perhaps more effective than cognitive therapy and medication treatments. ERP can be offered in a number of formats, and it appears that most of these format variations or modifications in delivery have a negligible impact on its effectiveness. One exception is the involvement of a therapist in exposure exercises; the literature suggests that therapist involvement can lead to superior results compared with self-directed exposure. Thus, ERP is a potent, flexible treatment for OCD. We now turn to a discussion of how to implement this treatment in clinical practice.

PRACTICE AND APPLICATION

Presenting the Treatment Rationale

An integral part of any cognitive or behavioral treatment is the presentation of a sound, well-explained rationale for why the client should engage in these particular treatment strategies. Not only does the provision of a rationale help foster clients' understanding of what they will be doing and enhance their trust in the therapy, but research also suggests that the client's acceptance of the rationale can enhance treatment outcome. For example, Addis and Jacobson (2000) found that early acceptance of the rationale in cognitive–behavioral therapy for depression made a unique and independent contribution to change in treatment and ultimate outcome, even when homework compliance ratings were controlled in the analyses.

Chapter 2 of this volume presents many points that should be covered during the presentation of the rationale for ERP. We briefly highlight two of these. The first involves a behavioral explanation. In an OCD cycle, obsessional thoughts, images, or impulses are associated with a sharp increase in anxiety or distress, and compulsive rituals are used to provide relief from this distress (Rachman & Hodgson, 1980). Although the relief from distress is a normal and understandable goal, using compulsions to "cut off" this distress disrupts the process of extinction, during which levels of anxiety and distress decline. Unfortunately, if using a compulsive ritual works for an individual, the likelihood of using the ritual becomes strengthened through negative reinforcement (i.e., the ritual is more likely to be used again because it removed the aversive state of anxiety or distress). In ERP, clients are asked to purposely allow obsessions and anxiety to occur, but then are asked to stop using rituals to allow the natural process of fear reduction to occur. With repeated exposure to the same cue or trigger without using compulsions, anxiety and distress reactions also decrease until the cue becomes significantly less bothersome.

Research illustrates the process by which compulsive rituals disrupt the process of fear reduction. Rachman, Shafran, Mitchell, Trant, and Teachman (1996) conducted an experiment with undergraduate students in which students were asked to write an anxiety-evoking statement in the lab (e.g., "I hope Joe has a car accident"). After writing this statement, half of the participants were told that they could do whatever they wanted to neutralize the statement. Students engaged in behaviors such as crumpling up the paper, crossing the offending statement out, or writing another statement with good intentions—all behaviors akin to a compulsive ritual. The other half of participants were asked to simply sit in a room and wait for the experimenter without doing anything to the original statement. Results indicated that students who were allowed to neutralize their statement showed a rapid decrease in anxiety levels, whereas students asked to refrain from neutralizing found that their anxiety eventually decreased, but over a much longer period of time, presumably through the normal learning processes, such as extinction.

The second part of the rationale for ERP involves a cognitive explanation of why it is important to eliminate compulsive rituals. Through the process of exposing oneself to fearful thoughts, cues, and situations without using rituals, individuals are able to test their predictions and to learn that their feared outcomes will not take place. Some authors argue that the acquisition of new information also helps the process of fear reduction through the modification of fear structures thought to maintain obsessional concerns (Foa & Kozak, 1986). This view suggests that cognitive processes may be involved in ERP.

The following dialogue between a therapist and a client with OCD illustrates the description of a rationale that incorporates these learning processes:

> Therapist: Let's spend a few minutes to understand how an OCD cycle works for you. You mentioned that a big problem for you involves the thought that things need to be lined up perfectly on your desk and a tendency to spend lots of time arranging these items.
>
> Client: Yes, I get really uncomfortable if things are out of order on my desk.
>
> Therapist: How strong is that discomfort?
>
> Client: Very strong! If anything is even a tiny bit out of place, my anxiety skyrockets. I'm afraid that something bad will happen to

someone in my family if things aren't arranged in their exact spot.

Therapist: It's pretty understandable that you would want to do something to relieve that anxiety once it's skyrocketed. What do you do?

Client: That's when I rearrange things on my desk and spend lots of time making sure things are exactly where they should be.

Therapist: Once you've arranged everything, what happens to your anxiety?

Client: It drops off a lot.

Therapist: OK, so if you spend enough time, and you get the objects just right, your anxiety will almost go away?

Client: Yes . . . usually.

Therapist: Lots of people with OCD say the same thing. Using a compulsion often helps reduce anxiety. But why isn't it a good long-term strategy for you?

Client: Well, lots of reasons. For one, it takes so much of my time. I probably spend an extra 2 hours at work every day because of this. It's also embarrassing if someone comes by and sees me doing it. And sometimes, it doesn't even work—I still feel anxious, even after spending an hour arranging my desk.

Therapist: The reasons you're giving for why compulsions are a problem are very similar to reasons we've heard from lots of clients with OCD [see Exhibit 4.1 for problems with compulsions]. We know that compulsions are also a problem because they prevent you from learning two important things about your OCD cycle. One is that your anxiety would reduce on its own, even without using a compulsion, if you sat with it long enough. The other is that your fears about someone getting hurt if things are out of order aren't true. You probably know this, logically, but your OCD is convincing you that you can't take the chance to find out, so you'd better arrange your desk.

Client: Yes, that's exactly what it feels like.

Therapist: Well, the treatment we are going to do together is designed to help you learn these two pieces of information. The treatment is called *exposure and response prevention*. The exposure part initially involves figuring out the triggers for your obsessions and anxiety, followed by directly confronting these triggers. For you, this might involve moving something a little bit out of place on your desk. The point of exposure is to actually get your anxiety and obsessions going. The response prevention part involves sitting with your anxiety and fears instead of using a compul-

EXHIBIT 4.1
Problems With Using Compulsions to Reduce Anxiety

- Compulsions provide only temporary relief.
- Compulsions sometimes do not work and may make my anxiety worse.
- Compulsions are time consuming.
- Compulsions prevent me from learning that my fears do not actually come true.
- Compulsions prevent me from learning that I can handle this anxiety.
- I feel foolish doing my compulsions.
- Compulsions often involve other people and may bother my family or friends.
- Compulsions may make me feel bad about myself (i.e., by leading to other distressing emotions).
- Compulsions often grow in complexity and in the length of time they take to complete.
- I feel like I've lost control when I'm doing my compulsions.

sion to get rid of the anxiety right away. Over time, the anxiety will decrease on its own.

Client: This sounds scary.

Therapist: The treatment does require some courage, but we will design it so that you start with exposure exercises that you find manageable. In other words, you don't have to mess up your entire desk right away—we'll start with moving a small item on your desk that you feel you can manage. If you work on that small item over and over again, what do you think will happen?

Client: I guess I may start to believe that nothing bad will happen if something is out of order on my desk. And maybe I'd be able to stand it more.

Therapist: That's the exact idea.

In this example, the therapist had the client articulate why the current cycle of behavior was not helpful in the long run in an effort to engage the client in wanting to change. When presenting the rationale, it is most useful for the therapist to use examples from the client's own personal experience.

Developing an Exposure Hierarchy

Most contemporary ERP therapists advocate a gradual plan of exposure for several reasons, the main reason being that gradual exposure is more tolerable for clients than is mass flooding, although flooding may still be an appropriate and useful treatment for particular clients (e.g., Fontenelle et al., 2000). Studies suggest that the two methods have comparable outcomes (e.g., Abramowitz, 1996; Boersma, den Hengst, Dekker, & Emmelkamp, 1976). As a result of the preference for gradual exposure in clinical practice, an important step in therapy is the construction of an *exposure hierarchy*, which outlines a series of exposures ranging from moderately difficult to the most

TABLE 4.1
Example of an Exposure Hierarchy for Symmetry Concerns

Item	SUDS rating
Allow my wife to put away my clothes in any order.	100
Let the kids play in the living room.	90
Put my shirts away with no color coordination.	80
Put fingerprints on mirrors in bathrooms.	75
Use a hand towel in the bathroom without straightening it afterward.	65
Make my bed within five minutes.	60
Purposely shave one sideburn slightly longer than the other.	55
Put away towels in the linen closet in any order.	45
Leave a dishtowel in the kitchen askew.	35

Note. SUDS = Subjective Units of Distress Scale.

anxiety-provoking situations and cues. Item difficulty is rated using Subjective Units of Distress Scale (SUDS) ratings. This rating scale of 0 to 100 allows clients to label each item with the corresponding level of anxiety or distress it would cause them. An example of an exposure hierarchy for OCD can be found in Table 4.1.

Hierarchies can be constructed from two main sources of information. First, details ascertained from the initial assessment of OCD symptoms can provide information about the cues and triggers of an individual's anxiety. During the assessment phase, many specialty clinics use the Yale–Brown Obsessive–Compulsive Scale (Y–BOCS), a clinician-administered interview detailing obsessions, compulsions, and avoidance behaviors (Goodman, Price, Rasmussen, Mazure, Delgado, et al., 1989; Goodman, Price, Rasmussen, Mazure, Fleischmann, et al., 1989). Information from an instrument such as this (or from a detailed clinical interview) can be used to generate possible items for a hierarchy. For example, if a person reports feared thoughts of hurting his or her children and avoids being alone with the children for this reason, a possible exposure may be to purposely spend time alone with the children and to use knives or sharp objects around children if the client has avoided them because of these fears.

Another excellent source of information for constructing a hierarchy is asking a client to complete monitoring sheets (Steketee, 1993). Typically, clients are asked to monitor external triggers of their obsessions and compulsions (e.g., using a knife, touching the taps in a public washroom, turning on an appliance); internal triggers (e.g., having horrific thoughts, experiencing uncomfortable feelings that things are not right); and avoided situations, people, or activities (e.g., avoiding walking into a room for fear of making footprints in the carpet). Specific examples reported on monitoring forms are included as items in the exposure hierarchy.

There are a number of issues to consider when constructing an exposure hierarchy. One involves the number of items to include. It is not uncommon for clients with OCD to provide numerous pages of triggers, cues, and avoided situations. If all these examples were included on a hierarchy, the hierarchy could be many pages long as well. Given the time-limited course of ERP in most settings and the overwhelming effort needed to address as many as 40 or 50 exposure goals, it may be useful to restrict the length of an exposure hierarchy. Typically, hierarchies should include 10 to 15 items, on average, with some clients including fewer than this and others including up to 20 or more items. To reduce long lists of information to just 10 to 15 items, the therapist can ask clients to pick their most important goals to work on, to select items that are good representations of key symptoms, or to construct multiple hierarchies, each with the desired number of items. This last suggestion is especially relevant for clients who present with OCD symptoms in multiple domains (e.g., concerns about contamination, sexual thoughts, hoarding, and excessive checking). Instead of trying to incorporate all symptom domains into one hierarchy, it may be more manageable to construct a hierarchy for each domain and then to sequentially work through each hierarchy.

An important point to continually remind clients of is that hierarchies are exposure and response prevention hierarchies. In other words, the assumption underlying the inclusion of each item on the hierarchy is that the client will complete the exposure without using an accompanying ritual or compulsion. Early work by Marks (1987) suggested that avoidance or compulsions during an exposure are not necessarily problematic, as long as steps are taken to ensure that avoidance does not become complete and that it does not provide feelings of safety for the client; for example, Marks described repeatedly "contaminating" a client while he or she engaged in ritualized washing. Although this style may be an option for some therapists, the therapist cannot always be present to play this role, and therefore the combination of exposure and response prevention appears to be the strategy most conducive to symptom reduction. Furthermore, research supports the superior effectiveness of the combined techniques versus either technique used alone (Steketee, Foa, & Grayson, 1982).

Creating an exposure hierarchy can sometimes require creativity on the part of the therapist. For example, some clients may present with a series of cues and triggers that are all in the 90 to 100 SUDS range. It is the therapist's responsibility to figure out how to develop initially more manageable goals that address these cues and triggers. The following is an example of an exchange between therapist and client to establish a workable hierarchy:

Therapist: From your monitoring sheets, it looks like your biggest concern comes from taking tests and writing papers.

Client: Yes, when I have to take a test or hand in a major paper, I have all these thoughts about whether I've cheated, whether this is really my work, and whether I copied my neighbor's answers.

Therapist:	You've rated taking tests and writing papers as 90 and 100 on the SUDS scale. Do these activities ever cause you less anxiety?
Client:	No, they are always really stressful.
Therapist:	Well, let's brainstorm a bit to figure out some items for your hierarchy that may be a little easier for starting your exposures. Does the topic of the paper make a difference?
Client:	Well, I guess a research paper for my sociology class would be the worst, because there are so many citations in it.
Therapist:	If the sociology paper is worst, which is the easiest to write, in comparison?
Client:	Hmm . . . I guess papers for art history are a bit easier.
Therapist:	OK, that's useful. Writing an art history paper might be a little lower on your hierarchy. What about writing a paper for me or one of my colleagues, instead of for school? Do you think that would make it any easier?
Client:	Yeah, I would be much less worried if I was just giving the paper to you. But it would still bug me.
Therapist:	How high would your SUDS rating be if you wrote a paper, sort of like a sociology paper, but handed it in to me instead of your professor?
Client:	If I still had to cite papers without checking the source, my SUDS would be about 60.
Therapist:	Good, there are a couple of ideas for hierarchy items we can include.

This exchange illustrates how creativity and flexibility are useful tactics for a therapist to use when planning a client's exposure hierarchy.

Guidelines for Conducting Exposure Practices

Once an exposure hierarchy is constructed, the therapist and client can begin planning a schedule of exposure and response prevention exercises. In this section, we review some of the guidelines that therapists should keep in mind for conducting exposure practices.

Predictability and Control

Many clients report having been forced to touch something they did not want to touch or a well-meaning loved one physically blocking them from completing rituals. They report such events as negative, and it appears that allowing clients greater control and predictability over exposure exercises is a more optimal strategy. Although the literature is equivocal on this topic, some studies of other phobic disorders support the utility of predictable exposures for client outcome. For example, a study of snake-fearful individuals found that predictable exposure to a snake led to less avoidance of the phobic object than did unpredictable exposure (Lopatka, 1989). Furthermore, some studies suggest that having control over exposure intensity can yield better outcomes (e.g., McGlynn, Rose, & Lazarte, 1994), though other studies have found this form of control to have no impact (e.g., McGlynn, Rose, & Jacobson, 1995). Indeed, as mentioned earlier in this chapter, therapist-assisted exposure has been shown to be more effective than self-administered exposure (Abramowitz, 1996), even though self-administered exposure provides the ultimate in client control. Thus, a combination of allowing the client as much control and predictability as possible while continuing to push and challenge the client during exposure appears to be the best strategy.

Distraction During Exposure

Theoretically, distraction during exposure and response prevention should hamper the effect of this treatment; during exposure, it would seem important to maintain some degree of focus on the feared stimulus for fear reduction to occur. However, studies on the effect of distraction during exposure for phobic disorders have yielded mixed results. Some studies have found that distraction interferes with exposure (Weir & Marshall, 1980), especially during high-intensity exposure (Rodriguez & Craske, 1995). However, other studies have found no effects of distraction on exposure outcome (Antony, McCabe, Leeuw, Sano, & Swinson, 2001), and others have found that distraction may enhance the effects of exposure (Craske, Street, Jayaraman, & Barlow, 1991; Johnstone & Page, 2004; Oliver & Page, 2003). In studies examining distraction specifically in ERP for OCD, results suggest that focusing on anxiety-provoking stimuli leads to greater reduction of anxiety between exposure sessions (Grayson, Foa, & Steketee, 1982) and within an exposure session as compared with using distraction during exposure practices (Grayson, Foa, & Steketee, 1986). Within-session anxiety reduction in this study by Grayson and colleagues (1986) was observed only for physiological measures of anxiety, whereas participants reported greater subjective reduction of anxiety in the distraction condition.

A related issue is the use of thought suppression during exposure practices. Individuals with OCD commonly suppress or push away feared thoughts, which can be considered a form of distraction. Although the literature is inconsistent about whether the act of suppressing one's thoughts paradoxically leads to an increased frequency of thoughts (see Purdon, 1999, for a review), some research suggests that concerns about not being able to successfully suppress unwanted thoughts contributed to increased distress over obsessive thoughts and a decline in mood state for participants with OCD (Purdon, Rowa, & Antony, 2005). In other words, failures in effective suppression (or perhaps distraction) during exposure practices may cause heightened distress for clients.

Given the inconsistencies in the literature and current knowledge of the impact of failures in thought suppression for clients with OCD, it seems prudent to encourage as much focus on the feared stimulus during exposure practices as possible, while keeping in mind that some distraction during ERP is not likely to be adverse. To encourage clients to focus, we routinely ask them to focus on the task at hand, to review out loud what they are doing (e.g., "I just touched the door of a public washroom, and now I'm eating a snack without washing my hands"), and to keep casual conversation with the therapist to a minimum. In fact, it may be helpful to let the client know in advance that the therapist will be unusually quiet during an exposure practice to allow the client to focus on the task at hand.

Length and Spacing of Exposure Practices

In a review of treatment outcome studies, exposure sessions for OCD ranged from 30 to 120 minutes, with an average of almost three sessions per week (range = 1–5 per week; Abramowitz, 1996). With such widely discrepant frequencies and lengths of sessions, it is important to examine the most optimal spacing and length of exposures for OCD. In his meta-analysis of treatment outcome studies for OCD, Abramowitz (1996) found that longer sessions were correlated with larger effect sizes on measures of OCD symptoms. Theoretically, longer sessions would allow for greater within-session fear reduction, one possible reason for this finding. Thus, 90- to 120-minute sessions may be the most useful length of session.

Though there is little research that speaks to the ideal spacing of exposure sessions in OCD, studies in agoraphobia and other phobic disorders suggest that more frequent or massed exposure (e.g., daily practice) is more effective than spaced exposure (e.g., weekly practice; Foa, Jameson, Turner, & Payne, 1980). Therefore, frequent treatment sessions or frequent homework assignments (ideally daily) are important for maximizing outcomes in ERP.

Safety Behaviors During Exposure Practices

The use of safety behaviors during exposure seems to hamper outcomes for phobic populations. Powers et al. (2002) found that allowing people with claustrophobia to use safety behaviors (e.g., medications, distraction) during exposure interfered with fear reduction during exposure. In fact, even the availability of safety behaviors interfered with fear outcome, suggesting that clinicians should encourage clients to eliminate both the use of and access to safety cues during exposure.

Abramowitz, Franklin, and Cahill (2003) discussed the potentially deleterious impact of seeking reassurance (a form of a safety behavior or compulsion) during ERP. They argued that any provision of information during exposure practices interferes with the goal of exposure, which is to achieve full exposure to the possibility of the feared outcome and to learn to live with uncertainty about what will happen. Thus, these authors encouraged discussing the role of reassurance directly with clients if it comes up, accompanied by a gentle refusal to answer questions that appear to have the purpose of increasing safety.

An issue related to providing reassurance is the question of whether therapist modeling of or participation in exposure practices is a useful addition to ERP or simply constitutes a form of reassurance itself. Therapist modeling of exposure exercises does not appear to significantly add to the effects of in vivo exposure alone (Marks, 1981), but treatment programs often continue to use this technique (e.g., Van Noppen, Pato, Marsland, & Rasmussen, 1998), and experienced clinicians often recommend modeling exposures, at least at the outset of ERP (e.g., Steketee, 1993). We encourage caution when considering the use of therapist modeling. For some clients, especially those who seek excessive reassurance, modeling may simply be another form of reassurance (i.e., "If my therapist is OK with doing this, then it can't be that dangerous"). Clients are often aware of the possibility that modeling could make the exposure easier for them (i.e., provide reassurance), providing a clear contraindication to using this technique. Conversely, it is sometimes apparent that modeling serves a useful purpose for other clients, and in these cases therapists should use it as needed. When unsure, it is best not to use modeling or to use it judiciously while monitoring the impact on a client's anxiety level.

Guidelines for Response Prevention

Although the notion of response prevention appears clear, we highlight several considerations for therapists when implementing this technique.

Complete Versus Gradual Response Prevention

An important consideration is whether to use complete versus partial response prevention. Many leading treatment manuals advocate complete response prevention (e.g., no checking in any situation once ERP has begun; Kozak & Foa, 1997). Research supports the idea that complete response prevention is superior to partial response prevention (Abramowitz, 1996). Indeed, it makes clinical sense that engaging in rituals outside of particular exposure practices would continue to feed the OCD cycle, reminding the individual that rituals or compulsions provide immense relief from high levels of anxiety.

Complete response prevention is not always practical or feasible, however. In outpatient programs, especially with weekly or twice weekly sessions, a great deal of the impetus for response prevention falls on the shoulders of the client, who may find this overwhelming. Moreover, clients may refuse to continue treatment if forced to engage in complete response prevention. If a client has numerous rituals or has been engaging in rituals for years, the task of abruptly stopping these rituals will be daunting. Abramowitz, Franklin, et al. (2003) pointed out that expectations for complete response prevention may be too rigid for perfectionistic clients, who may catastrophize over an occasional slip into a ritual. For these reasons, a gradual approach to response prevention may be indicated for some clients.

In a gradual response prevention program, the therapist should articulate several points to the client. First, it is important that the client understand the risks of continuing to engage in some rituals. In other words, the client should be informed that engaging in rituals will maintain the OCD cycle for longer than complete abstinence from rituals. Furthermore, the client and therapist together should develop a clear plan to achieve a decrease in rituals. An example of a gradual response prevention plan can be found in Abramowitz, Franklin, et al. (2003), and suggestions for gradual response prevention can be found in Kyrios (2003). When rituals are decreased in one domain of a client's symptoms, the client should be vigilant that rituals do not grow or develop in other symptom domains.

Other Response Prevention Strategies

Clients can use other strategies than complete response prevention during ERP. For example, clients who use a ritual during exposure could re-expose themselves to the original trigger or "ruin" the ritual if they noticed themselves using it (Abramowitz, Franklin, et al., 2003). A common example of needing re-exposure occurs with contamination exposures. Because it is necessary for clients to wash their hands at various points during the day (e.g., after using the bathroom), clients working on contamination exposures should continuously touch contaminated objects or stimuli after these naturally occurring interruptions in exposure take place. In our center, we commonly provide the client with a cloth or towel that has been contaminated with the feared stimulus, allowing the client to continuously recontaminate himself or herself throughout the day.

Another strategy used if complete response prevention is impossible or contraindicated is to delay or change the ritual (see Kyrios, 2003, for examples of alternative response prevention strategies). Although this strategy is less useful than eliminating the ritual, it provides a more tolerable step toward response prevention for some clients.

Involvement of Family Members or Supportive Others

Given that therapist-guided exposure appears to be superior to self or computer-administered exposure (Abramowitz, 1996), perhaps because therapists provide the support and accountability necessary to keep clients on task during ERP, does the involvement of family members or friends in ERP enhance outcome and commitment to the exercises? As reviewed in chapter 2, research suggests that family factors are related to various indexes of OCD

EXHIBIT 4.2
Guidelines for Family Members and Friends

- Learn more about OCD. For example, what are *obsessions, compulsions, reassurance,* and *avoidance*? Read the materials your family member or friend brings home from treatment.
- Provide support to the person, but don't help the OCD. Often friends and family members feel that they are being supportive by helping an individual with his or her compulsions or rituals, by complying with his or her requests (even unreasonable ones), or by providing reassurance when he or she is upset or anxious. Of course, no one likes seeing a loved one in distress. However, the best way you can help your family member or friend is to help him or her resist doing anything that quickly relieves the anxiety (e.g., a compulsion). In other words, it is more helpful if you and the individual can agree that you will not provide reassurance and will not help with rituals while he or she is working on the OCD.
- Keep in mind that your family member or friend is supposed to feel anxious while completing exposure exercises. Although the anxiety is unpleasant, it is not dangerous. Encourage him or her to do homework exercises, even on difficult days. Help with exposures if the person desires.
- Be encouraging if setbacks occur. It is not uncommon to have setbacks during and after treatment.
- Try to reduce other sources of stress and conflict as much as possible during treatment.
- Allow your family member or friend to maintain control and predictability over his or her exposure exercises.
- Encourage the person to try increasingly difficult exercises, but also respect his or her pace.
- Do not force the individual into doing an unplanned exposure exercise if he or she does not want to.

severity and that involving family members in treatment has a positive effect on OCD symptom severity.

Some indicators of improvement show similar change both with and without family involvement, however (Van Noppen, Steketee, McCorkle, & Pato, 1997). A safe conclusion is that family involvement is preferable but may not be necessary for positive outcome in ERP. At the very least, it would be useful to involve family members in some sessions of therapy or to provide them with information about what is and is not useful during their loved one's involvement in ERP. An example of a handout for family members and friends can be found in Exhibit 4.2.

Imaginal Exposure

There are some symptoms for which in vivo exposure and response prevention are impossible or difficult. Examples include horrific thoughts (e.g., thoughts of stabbing loved ones), fears of disastrous consequences (e.g., fears that one's house will flood because one has not checked that faucets are turned off), or scenarios that cannot be re-created in reality (e.g., fears of going to hell for having blasphemous thoughts). In such scenarios, it may be useful to consider using imaginal exposure, in which individuals are exposed to their

EXHIBIT 4.3
Imaginal Exposure Script

My doorbell rings, and I answer the door. It's my daughter dropping off my two grand-daughters for the day. My daughter leaves, and I am alone with my young grand-daughters. The eldest is wearing a white blouse, and the youngest is wearing a pink T-shirt. They ask me for a snack, so we go into the kitchen. I start to cut fruit with a very sharp knife and then begin to feel unsteady. My anxiety is quickly rising, and my hand starts to shake. I have a horrible urge to use the knife on my granddaughters. Before I know it, I turn around and plunge the knife into the older one's stomach. Blood starts to spurt out everywhere. I pull my hand away with the knife still in it. I have blood on my hands, face, and body. She is staring at me with blood pouring out of her stomach. Her white blouse is stained red. Her face is pale, there are tears streaming down her face, and she is clutching her bloody stomach. My younger granddaughter is screaming. There is blood all over her as well. I feel sick. The room feels over-whelmingly hot. It starts to spin. My horror is unbelievable. The knife falls from my hands, and I collapse on the floor in a pool of blood as my granddaughter collapses beside me in a heap.

fearful thoughts or images in a repetitive, prolonged fashion. Just as live situational exposure can lead to reduced discomfort in the presence of feared objects or situations, exposure in imagination can lead to a reduction in discomfort associated with feared thoughts or images.

Imaginal exposure involves constructing a script of the individual's feared scenario, written in the first person and containing sufficient detail to evoke an anxiety response. Some authors recommend that the scenario be 3 to 5 minutes in length (e.g., Hyman & Pedrick, 1999), but clinically we have had success with much shorter narratives. Clients are encouraged to write a scenario as if they were writing it for an actor in a movie scene. Once an anxiety-evoking scenario is created, clients can either repeatedly read the scenario out loud until their anxiety decreases or record the scenario on an audiotape and repeatedly listen to the tape. The rationale for imaginal exposure is similar to that for in vivo exposure, with the focus being on getting used to one's thoughts, just as individuals get used to external fear triggers (e.g., touching a contaminated object). An example of an imaginal exposure script is found in Exhibit 4.3.

Imaginal exposure, just like in vivo exposure, can be done at a gradual pace. Some clients find it overwhelming to confront the very thoughts they have been suppressing for months or years and may not be willing to do so at first for their most feared scenarios. Thus, an exposure hierarchy for imaginal exposure may be a useful tool. At the same time, it is useful for the therapist to know when to push or challenge the client during an imaginal exposure exercise. If a client becomes overwhelmed and stops the exposure session, a novice therapist may feel uncomfortable pushing the client to resume reading the script. However, stopping an imaginal exposure exercise is akin to avoidance of the feared thoughts, the exact opposite of the goal of exposure. Thus, the therapist needs to balance respect for the client's readiness with his or her own discomfort in encouraging a client to do something that is obviously painful and difficult.

The evidence is mixed with respect to whether the addition of imaginal exposure provides benefit to in vivo ERP. Generally, it may not be necessary to add imaginal exposure for all clients. Instead, this technique is likely most useful for clients who are frightened of their thoughts (usually clients with religious, sexual, or aggressive obsessions).

TROUBLESHOOTING: ISSUES THAT MAY ARISE DURING ERP

ERP, though effective, is a difficult treatment for many clients to complete. Furthermore, issues can arise throughout a course of treatment, creating difficulties for the therapist and client. About 20% to 30% of people with OCD refuse to begin ERP or terminate treatment prematurely (Stanley & Turner, 1995). This section outlines some potential problems that may arise during ERP and suggestions for how to deal with them.

Motivational Issues

Involvement in ERP assumes that the individual is ready and willing to change. Indeed, to most therapists it is almost unfathomable why individuals with OCD would not be ready to reduce and eliminate their uncomfortable and distressing symptoms. However, it is clear that many individuals with OCD and other anxiety disorders experience ambivalence about change. Furthermore, level of readiness for change significantly predicts treatment attrition and outcome following treatment in a number of anxiety disorders, including pharmacotherapy for generalized anxiety disorder (Wilson, Bell-Dolan, & Beitman, 1997), pharmacotherapy for panic disorder (Beitman et al., 1994), and cognitive–behavioral therapy for panic disorder (Dozois, Westra, Collins, Fung, & Garry, 2004).

A study by Purdon, Rowa, and Antony (2004) found that treatment ambivalence concerns were widely reported by individuals with OCD about to embark on ERP, and their concerns fell into four categories: (a) fears that treatment would fail, (b) fears that treatment would succeed (e.g., "Others will demand more of me if I'm well"), (c) fears that treatment would cause an increase in anxiety, and (d) general treatment concerns (e.g., "I will have to miss work" or "It will be embarrassing to disclose these things to others"). Clinically, therapists are likely all too familiar with signs of ambivalence about change, including missed appointments, hesitancy to complete exposure exercises in session, refusal to complete homework exposures, answers of "yes, but . . . ," and early withdrawal from treatment. When these signs appear, it may be useful to briefly change the focus of the treatment session from the exposure exercises themselves to the source of the ambivalence or

TABLE 4.2
Costs and Benefits of Engaging in Exposure and Response Prevention

Benefits	Costs
I may be able to stop some of my checking. (80%)	The anxiety may be overwhelming. (100%)
I will save time in my day. (90%)	The house may burn down, and it would be my fault. (100%)
My spouse will be happy. (75%)	
I will feel a sense of accomplishment. (40%)	I may not be able to concentrate at work if I am worried about the house. (80%)
I will be able to get to work on time. (80%)	My family may expect more of me than I am ready to handle. (60%)

Note. The percentages in parentheses indicate the importance of the benefit or cost.

fear. In some cases, hesitancy may arise from a misunderstanding of the treatment rationale, confusion about how to complete an exposure exercise, or an attempt to try an exercise that is too challenging. Providing information or breaking an exposure down into more manageable steps may eradicate the hesitation. In other cases, hesitancy or refusal may be more complex, and the client may not even realize where it comes from. At this point, it may be more useful to explore the costs and benefits of engaging in treatment versus the costs and benefits of not changing. Table 4.2 provides an example of a cost and benefit list generated by a client with OCD who began ERP but began having difficulty completing exposures partway into treatment. This client wrote down the pros and cons of working on his symptoms and also rated the importance of each point in parentheses. From his list, it became more evident why change was difficult, and the exercise helped him understand why he was stuck.

Other motivational enhancement strategies have been developed to help clients with anxiety disorders recognize reasons for being stuck and investigate options for moving forward with treatment. Many of these strategies are borrowed from the stages of change model and motivational interviewing techniques for substance use problems (Prochaska & DiClemente, 1984; Prochaska, Norcross, & DiClemente, 1994) and have been adapted for use with anxiety and depression (Westra & Phoenix, 2003). Strategies include encouraging the client to voice reasons for change (e.g., switching roles with the therapist and providing a rationale for completing an exposure), exploring future costs and benefits of change, and having the client provide suggestions for hypothetical clients with similar problems. Chapter 2 of this volume evaluates these strategies for an OCD population.

Subtle Avoidance and Reassurance Seeking

In many cases, both client and therapist clearly recognize the OCD symptoms. However, in some cases, symptoms are more subtle. For example, some clients may be so good at asking for or otherwise seeking reassurance that they don't even realize they are doing it. One client from our center completed ERP with her husband present and watched his face and body language for signs that he disapproved of her exposure tasks. If he did not look worried or hesitant, this provided her with reassurance that what she was doing could not be that bad.

Avoidance behaviors can also be subtle. We worked with a client who avoided seeing imperfections in the state of her house by keeping lights dim or off. If the lights were on, she would notice dust, smudges, or other problems, but with the lights off she was able to pretend that these imperfections did not exist. In cases of subtle avoidance or reassurance, the most important task for both client and therapist is to monitor and recognize these subtle or tricky forms of OCD symptoms. We have found it useful to warn clients that subtle symptoms may be present, to have them and their support persons actively look for these symptoms, and to use a rule of thumb that if it feels like it might be OCD (even if the client is unsure), then it probably is OCD and should be treated as such. Therapists should make clients aware of these issues when presenting the rationale for ERP at the outset of therapy, and further reminders should be consistent with clients' understanding of how this therapy works. Therapists and clients should also be vigilant for questions that may be attempts to seek reassurance, and the therapist should seek the client's agreement that the therapist will refrain from answering questions during sessions if the answer may provide some form of reassurance.

Working With Mental Compulsions

A common challenge in ERP is the identification and prevention of mental compulsions. During the assessment process, it is important to be clear about which mental phenomena reported by a client are obsessions and which might be mental compulsions. Usually, mental compulsions are carried out in a particular way, are voluntarily performed by a client, and are designed to reduce discomfort; obsessions, in contrast, are unwanted mental phenomena that occur outside of voluntary control. In other words, mental compulsions are the functional equivalent of physical compulsions. Examples of mental compulsions include engaging in ritualized praying, reviewing events or conversations in a repetitive or ritualized way, or replacing "bad" thoughts with "good" thoughts or images. In our center we saw a man who had a mental compulsion of having to "blow up" a negative image each time it occurred by picturing the obscene image exploding into a million pieces.

When working with mental compulsions in ERP, the challenge is helping the client resist these automatic and often difficult-to-control mental actions. If it is challenging for a client to resist repetitive hand washing or checking, it may be even more difficult for him or her to resist something outside of his or her physical control. In the case of mental rituals, one useful step is for clients to increase awareness of their use of these rituals through journaling, monitoring forms, or similar tools. With increased awareness, the client is in a better position to catch and then stop mental rituals. However, awareness is often not enough. When the client is aware of the use of mental compulsions but still finds it difficult to interrupt them, it may be useful for him or her to "spoil" the compulsion if it is initiated or to use distraction instead of allowing the compulsion to be carried out. An example of spoiling a mental compulsion for the client who imagined blowing up obscene images would be for him to purposely invite a negative image back into his mind after blowing it up. Although the use of distraction during exposure is controversial, as discussed earlier in this chapter, distraction is preferable to engaging in mental compulsions. Thus, if a client had to mentally review conversations to ensure he said something "perfectly," we would encourage the client to put his mind to some other use (e.g., focusing on the task at hand) whenever the urge to review a conversation emerged.

Knowing When to Stop Treatment

When should ERP for OCD end? Some possibilities include stopping when the hierarchy is complete, when the client generally feels more comfortable with symptoms, or when the client has successfully pushed himself or herself past the point of comfort. Each option carries its own advantages and disadvantages. For example, trying to push a client past his or her level of comfort may disrupt rapport and may, in some cases, put the client in danger. But not pushing a client far enough leaves open the possibility of relapse. The more symptoms that remain at the end of treatment, the greater the likelihood that the symptoms will fester and return.

We recommend encouraging clients to go as far as they can without crossing ethical boundaries and without engaging in exposures that the average person without OCD would see as dangerous or inappropriate. It is appropriate to ask clients to do things that are disgusting or anxiety provoking (e.g., touching a toilet seat in a public bathroom), but we recommend against having them do exposures that are associated with significant realistic risks (e.g., handling raw chicken without washing afterward). When discussing with the client how far to take exposures, it is useful to discuss the advantages of pushing oneself as far as possible (i.e., to provide the greatest protection against relapse), while still respecting the client's right to stop exposures if he or she deems it necessary. Practical considerations may also need to be considered: Many programs offer a set number of sessions, or clients may have a certain amount of coverage for sessions. In these cases, it is best to encourage clients to complete as much of the hierarchy as possible and to provide guidance and a plan for them to continue exposures once treatment has ended.

"Bad Luck" Events

There are times when an individual's worst fear has actually occurred or occurs during the course of therapy. Rhéaume et al. highlighted several case examples of "bad luck" contributing to the development of OCD symptoms (Rhéaume, Freeston, Léger, & Ladouceur, 1998). What should a therapist do if the client has experienced his or her worst fear or experiences an untoward outcome during an exposure? For clients who have experienced real-life adverse outcomes, one possible avenue is to compare the realistic probability that the feared outcome will occur again with the energy and time spent preventing this. For an individual who was robbed after leaving a door unlocked, the comparison would be between the hours spent checking the door, driving back home to ensure the door is locked, and so forth versus the realistic chances that he or she would leave the door unlocked again and someone would happen to try to break into the house again. If even more serious consequences have occurred (e.g., making a family member seriously ill by bringing home a contaminant or by not cooking food properly), it may be useful to help the individual engage in gradual response prevention instead of encouraging him or her to abandon all rituals right away. For example, if an individual overcooks food and checks expiry dates excessively because he or she cooked something improperly in the past, it may be useful to help the client set limits on checking and time spent cooking and to gradually make the limits more challenging as treatment progresses. Individuals could consult cookbooks and trusted friends or family members to gather a range of examples of what is "normal" when it comes to cooking particular foods and then try to follow these guidelines.

To help prepare a client for a possible untoward experience during the course of therapy (if the outcome is realistically possible), it is useful to have a frank discussion about this possibility before exposures start. For example, it is entirely possible that someone could contract a minor illness like a cold from completing exposures involving touching things that many others have touched. Clients should be made aware of this, and therapists can help decatastrophize this possibility. Furthermore, therapists can explore with clients the other possible explanations of why people may contract a cold (e.g., from being around coworkers or family members carrying cold germs), rather than attributing the complete responsibility to their exposures.

If a client experiences something very upsetting or traumatic during an exposure, the therapist's reaction is important in determining how the client views this outcome. A therapist should be empathic and understanding about how difficult the experience was for the client but should avoid catastrophizing the outcome. In other words, if the therapist models a reasonable, tempered, and sympathetic response to an upsetting event, this may help a client put the outcome into perspective without feeling that exposures have to be abandoned.

CASE VIGNETTE: REBECCA'S CONTAMINATION FEARS

Rebecca was a 32-year-old married woman who presented for assessment and treatment of severe contamination and harm-related concerns. At the time of treatment, Rebecca had a 2-year-old daughter and was pregnant with her second child. She lived with her husband and daughter and worked part-time as a teacher. Rebecca's concerns revolved around fears of harming others by serving undercooked meats or improperly prepared foods, by inadvertently feeding someone a food he or she was allergic to, by accidentally tripping someone she passed without realizing it, or by causing someone to slip and fall by splashing water on the ground. Rebecca's OCD symptoms dated back to her teenage years and were successfully treated pharmacologically through her 20s. However, she experienced a surge in symptoms after the birth of her first child, and she was experiencing another surge in symptoms as the pregnancy of her second child progressed. After a thorough diagnostic assessment that highlighted OCD as the primary problem, the therapist explained the rationale for ERP to Rebecca, and she indicated strong interest in participating.

The therapist spent the initial sessions providing psychoeducation about OCD. Rebecca readily identified personal examples of the various definitions and indicated comfort with the rationale for completing ERP. From daily monitoring forms, Rebecca and her therapist developed an exposure hierarchy, highlighting some of the most important goals Rebecca wished to work on. Her hierarchy can be found in Table 4.3. Monitoring forms also revealed the compulsions Rebecca used to try to relieve her anxiety, including excessive checking to ensure that things were cooked properly (i.e., using a meat thermometer numerous times during cooking), seeking opinions and reassurance from her husband or mother that meat looked cooked, prefacing her offering of food to others with warnings about the ingredients (i.e., that a product might contain nuts or some other allergen), mentally reviewing the process of preparing a meal to ensure that she had not done something careless, and checking excessively that she did not trip or hurt someone (e.g., looking behind her as she walked, calling coworkers she thought she may have tripped to ensure that they were OK, excessively wiping bathroom counters and floors in case she had dripped water). Rebecca also acknowledged sometimes avoiding cooking for others and avoiding using certain "high-risk" foods as a result of her fears. For example, she did not use dented cans for fear that there was something wrong with the food inside, and she often avoided cooking with foods that had expiry dates like milk, sour cream, and eggs. One of the main reasons Rebecca presented for treatment was her husband's concern that she was not able to cook for her 2-year-old daughter; she often threw meals out and resorted to "safe" foods like pasta with tomato sauce.

Once Rebecca's hierarchy was established, she began completing exposures with the therapist, meeting the therapist twice a week with daily home-

TABLE 4.3
Rebecca's Exposure Hierarchy

Item	SUDS rating
Cooking roast chicken for family.	100
Baking cookies or brownies with nuts for daughter and friends.	95
Cooking spaghetti sauce with ground beef for family.	90
Purposely dripping water on bathroom floor at work.	90
Baking cookies without nuts to send to daycare.	85
Using a dented can of food in meal for family.	80
Cooking fish for family.	75
Leaving hands damp after using washroom at work.	70
Making eggs for daughter.	70
Thinking of tripping a colleague.	60
Walking down hallway at work during lunch hour.	60
Purposely dripping water on the bathroom floor at mom's house.	55
Preparing frozen precooked chicken for family.	45

Note. SUDS = Subjective Units of Distress Scale.

work between sessions. The first difficulty occurred almost immediately, when Rebecca found it difficult to begin cooking for her family without the support of the therapist. To circumvent this difficulty, the therapist suggested having Rebecca's husband attend a session, at which he could learn how to be her coach during exposure sessions that had to be conducted at Rebecca's home. Rebecca agreed with this idea and brought her husband, Scott, to the following session. This turned out to be particularly useful, because Scott revealed that he often inadvertently provided reassurance to his wife by assuring her that she had cooked something long enough and taking the first bite of anything to "prove" to her that it was cooked enough. The therapist spent time explaining the function of this type of reassurance to Rebecca and Scott, as illustrated in the following exchange:

Therapist: It's pretty understandable why you try to help Rebecca out when she's cooking by answering her questions and checking the food for her. What is it like for you to see her so upset?

Scott: It's really difficult. It upsets me to see her so upset.

Therapist: Your reaction is the natural reaction of loved ones—they want to do whatever it takes to relieve their loved one's distress. But can either of you think of any downfalls of providing this kind of reassurance and help?

Rebecca: From what we've talked about, reassurance seeking may be a type of compulsion.

Therapist: That's right. And remind me why you don't want to use compulsions as your main strategy to handle the anxiety anymore?

Rebecca: Mainly because it doesn't help my anxiety in the long run. I know that when Scott checks the food for me, I feel much better for a little while, but then I start to doubt myself again quite quickly. I guess the point is that I need to cook the food and serve it, without him saying anything.

Therapist: Scott, does that make sense to you?

Scott: It does. I hadn't realized that I shouldn't be answering her questions. But what if she's really upset or asks me over and over?

Therapist: Good question. Maybe we need to spend some time as a group deciding what Scott should do in these kinds of circumstances. Rebecca, what do you think is reasonable for Scott to do in that situation?

At this point, the therapist helped Rebecca and Scott agree on guidelines for how Scott could continue to be supportive of Rebecca without providing reassurance that only fed the OCD cycle. For example, Rebecca agreed to try not to ask Scott for any reassurance and also gave Scott permission to refuse to answer her questions if she did ask for reassurance. Additionally, Rebecca and Scott agreed that Scott could best support her through this exposure by encouraging her to hang in there and reminding her of why she was doing this treatment (e.g., to be able to more comfortably cook for her daughter and future child). With Scott's support, Rebecca was able to try her first cooking exposure at home, where she baked precooked frozen chicken for her family's dinner without overcooking it or throwing it out.

As therapy progressed, Rebecca began to experience success with numerous items on her hierarchy. Rebecca encountered another difficulty when she began baking items for her family and her daughter's daycare. Her first exposure was to bake chocolate chip cookies for a family gathering. Rebecca's compulsions when baking included excessively checking the expiry date of ingredients like milk and eggs, overbaking the cookies, and then mentally reviewing the process between the time of baking and serving the cookies. Although Rebecca was able to resist compulsions of checking and overbaking, she ran into difficulty restraining herself from engaging in the mental reviews. She brought this difficulty into a therapy session:

Rebecca: I'm having trouble stopping myself from playing my mental mind games. It just seems to happen automatically!

Therapist: That's understandable. Mental compulsions are notoriously difficult to stop. How aware are you that you're engaging in mental compulsions?

Rebecca: Very aware. At first, I didn't realize it. But since I started the monitoring forms, I am fully aware that I review my steps of baking in my head to make sure I didn't do something wrong.

Therapist: There are a couple of options for preventing the mental reviewing. One is to try and "ruin" the reviewing process by purposely

> picturing yourself doing something "wrong" during baking, even if you didn't.

Rebecca: You mean like picturing myself using expired eggs in the cookies?

Therapist: Exactly. What do you think the purpose of doing this might be?

Rebecca: I guess to make sure I don't get any relief from the mental mind games that might reinforce the OCD.

Therapist: That's right. What do you think of this strategy?

Rebecca: It sounds awfully hard. I'll probably have a panic attack if I imagine something that awful.

Therapist: Well, another strategy people sometimes use is distraction. So, even though I don't want you to distract yourself during most exposures, you could use distraction to stop the mental rituals. What's something you could do to get your mind off the mental ritual, but still allow yourself to remember your exposure?

Rebecca: That's a tough one. Maybe talk to Scott about the exposure but not review the steps of baking?

Therapist: Great suggestion. Could you start with that strategy and see how it goes?

Rebecca was able to successfully use distraction to stop her mental rituals, and after five further sessions she was able to start ruining her mental compulsions if she noticed herself doing them. Over the course of 25 sessions, Rebecca tackled most items on her hierarchy and was enjoying a significant reduction in OCD symptoms. Because of limits on the number of sessions the clinic was able to offer, after 25 sessions, twice per week, Rebecca and her therapist contracted for four further booster sessions to focus on relapse prevention.

CONCLUSION

ERP is an effective and flexible psychological treatment for OCD. To the naive observer, it may appear that treatment of obsessions and compulsions by ERP is straightforward (e.g., "Just stop washing your hands so much"). Although this is one of the goals of ERP, treatment is most helpful when provided with therapist support and a sound rationale for treatment goals and when treatment moves at a gradual pace over which the client has some control. Furthermore, longer sessions provided more frequently (i.e., twice per week) appear to be the most useful. Beyond these basic tenets, this chapter outlined some of the challenges that often arise during a course of ERP and provided practical suggestions for managing these challenges. OCD is a tenacious and difficult disorder, and successful treatment requires creativity, optimism, and persistence on the part of both client and therapist.

REFERENCES

Abramowitz, J. S. (1996). Variants of exposure and response prevention in the treatment of obsessive compulsive disorder: A meta-analysis. *Behavior Therapy, 27,* 583–600.

Abramowitz, J. S. (1997). Effectiveness of psychological and pharmacological treatments for obsessive–compulsive disorder: A quantitative review. *Journal of Consulting and Clinical Psychology, 65,* 44–52.

Abramowitz, J. S. (1998). Does cognitive–behavioral therapy cure obsessive–compulsive disorder? A meta-analytic evaluation of clinical significance. *Behavior Therapy, 29,* 339–355.

Abramowitz, J. S., Foa, E. B., & Franklin, M. E. (2003). Exposure and ritual prevention for obsessive–compulsive disorder: Effects of intensive versus twice-weekly sessions. *Journal of Consulting and Clinical Psychology, 71,* 394–398.

Abramowitz, J. S., Franklin, M. E., & Cahill, S. P. (2003). Approaches to common obstacles in the exposure-based treatment of obsessive–compulsive disorder. *Cognitive and Behavioral Practice, 10,* 14–22.

Addis, M. E., & Jacobson, N. S. (2000). A closer look at the treatment rationale and homework compliance in the cognitive–behavioral treatment of depression. *Cognitive Therapy and Research, 24,* 313–326.

Antony, M. M., McCabe, R. E., Leeuw, I., Sano, N., & Swinson, R. P. (2001). Effect of exposure and coping style on in vivo exposure for specific phobia of spiders. *Behaviour Research and Therapy, 39,* 1137–1150.

Beitman, B. D., Beck, N. C., Deuser, W., Carter, C., Davidson, J., & Maddock, R. (1994). Patient stages of change predict outcome in a panic disorder medication trial. *Anxiety, 1,* 64–69.

Boersma, K., den Hengst, S., Dekker, J., & Emmelkamp, P. M. G. (1976). Exposure and response prevention in the natural environment: A comparison with obsessive–compulsive patients. *Behaviour Research and Therapy, 14,* 19–24.

Cottraux, J., Mollard, E., Bouvard, M., & Marks, I. (1993). Exposure therapy, fluvoxamine, or combination treatment in obsessive–compulsive disorder: One-year follow-up. *Psychiatry Research, 49,* 63–75.

Craske, M. G., Street, L. L., Jayaraman, J., & Barlow, D. H. (1991). Attention versus distraction during in vivo exposure: Snake and spider phobias. *Journal of Anxiety Disorders, 5,* 199–211.

de Araujo, L. A., Ito, L. M., Marks, I. M., & Deale, A. (1995). Does imagined exposure to the consequences of not ritualizing enhance live exposure for OCD? A controlled study: I. Main outcome. *British Journal of Psychiatry, 167,* 65–70.

DeRubeis, R. J., & Crits-Christoph, P. (1998). Empirically supported individual and group psychological treatments for adult mental disorders. *Journal of Consulting and Clinical Psychology, 66,* 37–52.

Dozois, D. J. A., Westra, H. A., Collins, K. A., Fung, T. S., & Garry, J. K. F. (2004). Stages of change in anxiety: Psychometric properties of the University of Rhode Island Change Assessment (URICA) scales. *Behaviour Research and Therapy, 42,* 711–729.

Eddy, K. T., Dutra, L., Bradley, R., & Westen, D. (2004). A multidimensional meta-analysis of psychotherapy and pharmacotherapy for obsessive–compulsive disorder. *Clinical Psychology Review, 24,* 1011–1030.

Fals-Stewart, W., Marks, A. P., & Schafer, J. (1993). A comparison of behavioral group therapy and individual behavior therapy in treatment obsessive–compulsive disorder. *Journal of Nervous and Mental Disease, 181,* 189–193.

Foa, E. B., & Goldstein, A. (1978). Continuous exposure and complete response prevention in the treatment of obsessive–compulsive neurosis. *Behavior Therapy, 9,* 821–829.

Foa, E. B., Jameson, J. S., Turner, R. M., & Payne, L. L. (1980). Massed versus spaced exposure sessions in the treatment of agoraphobia. *Behaviour Research and Therapy, 18,* 333–338.

Foa, E. B., & Kozak, M. J. (1986). Emotional processing of fear: Exposure to corrective information. *Psychological Bulletin, 99,* 20–35.

Foa, E. B., & Kozak, M. J. (1996). Psychological treatment for obsessive–compulsive disorder. In M. R. Mavissakalian & R. F. Prien (Eds.), *Long-term treatments of anxiety disorders* (pp. 285–309). Washington, DC: American Psychiatric Press.

Foa, E. B., Liebowitz, M. R., Kozak, M. J., Davies, S., Campeas, R., Franklin, M. E., et al. (2005). Randomized, placebo-controlled trial of exposure and ritual prevention, clomipramine, and their combination in the treatment of obsessive–compulsive disorder. *American Journal of Psychiatry, 162,* 151–161.

Fontenelle, L., Soares, I. D., Marques, C., Rangé, B., Mendlowicz, M. V., & Versiani, M. (2000). Sudden remission of obsessive–compulsive disorder by involuntary, massive exposure. *Canadian Journal of Psychiatry, 45,* 666–667.

Franklin, M. E., Abramowitz, J. S., Kozak, M. J., Levitt, J. T., & Foa, E. B. (2000). Effectiveness of exposure and ritual prevention for obsessive–compulsive disorder: Randomized compared with nonrandomized samples. *Journal of Consulting and Clinical Psychology, 68,* 594–602.

Fritzler, B. K., Hecker, J. E., & Losee, M. C. (1997). Self-directed treatment with minimal therapist contact: Preliminary finding for obsessive–compulsive disorder. *Behaviour Research and Therapy, 35,* 627–631.

Goisman, R. M., Rogers, M. P., Steketee, G. S., Warshaw, M. G., Cuneo, P., & Keller, M. B. (1993). Utilization of behavioral methods in a multicenter anxiety disorders study. *Journal of Clinical Psychiatry, 54,* 213–218.

Goodman, W. K., Price, L. H., Rasmussen, S. A., Mazure, D., Delgado, P., Heninger, G. R., & Charney, D. S. (1989). The Yale–Brown Obsessive–Compulsive Scale: Part II. Validity. *Archives of General Psychiatry, 46,* 1012–1016.

Goodman, W. K., Price, L. H., Rasmussen, S. A., Mazure, D., Fleischmann, R. L., Hill, C. L., et al. (1989). The Yale–Brown Obsessive–Compulsive Scale: Part I. Development, use and reliability. *Archives of General Psychiatry, 46,* 1006–1011.

Grayson, J. B., Foa, E. B., & Steketee, G. S. (1982). Habituation during exposure treatment: Distraction vs attention-focusing. *Behaviour Research and Therapy, 20*, 323–328.

Grayson, J. B., Foa, E. B., & Steketee, G. S. (1986). Exposure in vivo of obsessive–compulsives under distracting and attention-focusing conditions: Replication and extension. *Behaviour Research and Therapy, 24*, 475–479.

Himle, J. A., Rassi, S., Haghighatgou, H., Krone, K. P., Nesse, R. M., & Abelson, J. (2001). Group behavioral therapy of obsessive–compulsive disorder: Seven vs. twelve-week outcomes. *Depression and Anxiety, 13*, 161–165.

Hodgson, R., Rachman, S., & Marks, I. M. (1972). The treatment of chronic obsessive–compulsive neurosis: Follow-up and further findings. *Behaviour Research and Therapy, 10*, 181–189.

Hyman, B. M., & Pedrick, C. (1999). *The OCD workbook: Your guide to breaking free from obsessive–compulsive disorder*. Oakland, CA: New Harbinger Publications.

Ito, L. M., Marks, I. M., de Araujo, L. A., & Hemsley, D. (1995). Does imagined exposure to the consequences of not ritualizing enhance live exposure for OCD? A controlled study: II. Effect of behavioural v. subjective concordance of improvements. *British Journal of Psychiatry, 167*, 71–75.

Johnstone, K. A., & Page, A. C. (2004). Attention to phobic stimuli during exposure: The effect of distraction on anxiety reduction, self-efficacy and perceived control. *Behaviour Research and Therapy, 42*, 249–275.

Kobak, K. A., Greist, J. H., Jefferson, J. W., Katzelnick, D. J., & Henk, H. J. (1998). Behavioral versus pharmacological treatments of obsessive compulsive disorder: A meta-analysis. *Psychopharmacology, 136*, 205–216.

Kozak, M. J., & Foa, E. B. (1997). *Mastery of your obsessive compulsive disorder: Therapist guide*. New York: Oxford University Press.

Kyrios, M. (2003). Exposure and response prevention for OCD. In R. G. Menzies & P. de Silva (Eds.), *Obsessive–compulsive disorder: Theory, research and treatment* (pp. 259–274). Chichester, England: Wiley.

Lindsay, M., Crino, R., & Andrews, G. (1997). Controlled trial of exposure and response prevention in OCD. *Psychiatry, 171*, 135–139.

Lopatka, C. L. (1989). *The role of unexpected events in avoidance*. Unpublished master's thesis, University at Albany, State University of New York.

Marks, I. M. (1981). Review of behavioural psychotherapy: I. Obsessive–compulsive disorders. *American Journal of Psychiatry, 138*, 584–592.

Marks, I. M. (1987). *Fears, phobias, and rituals*. New York: Oxford University Press.

Marks, I. M., Rachman, S., & Hodgson, R. (1975). Treatment of chronic obsessive–compulsive neurosis by in vivo exposure. *British Journal of Psychiatry, 127*, 263–267.

McGlynn, F. D., Rose, M. P., & Jacobson, N. (1995). Effects of control and of attentional instructions on arousal and fear during exposure to phobia-cue stimuli. *Journal of Anxiety Disorders, 9*, 451–461.

McGlynn, F. D., Rose, M. P., & Lazarte, A. (1994). Control and attention during exposure influence arousal and fear among insect phobias. *Behavior Modification, 18*, 371–388.

Meyer, V. (1966). Modification of expectations in cases with obsessional rituals. *Behaviour Research and Therapy, 4*, 273–280.

Oliver, N. S., & Page, A. C. (2003). Fear reduction during in-vivo exposure to blood injection stiumuli: Distraction vs. attentional focusing. *British Journal of Clinical Psychology, 42*, 13–25.

O'Sullivan, G., & Marks, I. M. (1990). Long-term outcome of phobic and obsessive–compulsive disorders after exposure: A review. In R. Noyes, M. Roth, & G. Burrows (Eds.), *Handbook of anxiety* (Vol. 4, pp. 87–108). Amsterdam: Elsevier.

O'Sullivan, G., Noshirvani, H., Marks, I., Monteiro, W., & Lelliott, P. (1991). Six-year follow-up after exposure and clomipramine therapy for obsessive compulsive disorder. *Journal of Clinical Psychiatry, 52*, 150–155.

Powers, M. B., Smits, J. A. J., Ngoc Bui, T., Harness, A., Caudwell, J., Barera, P., & Telch, M. J. (2002, November). *The effect of safety-behavior availability or utilization on claustrophobic fear reduction: A treatment study.* Poster presented at the meeting of the Association for Advancement of Behavior Therapy, Reno, NV.

Prochaska, J. O., & DiClemente, C. C. (1984). *The transtheoretical approach: Crossing traditional boundaries of therapy.* Homewood, IL: Dow Jones/Irwin.

Prochaska, J. O., Norcross, J. C., & DiClemente, C. C. (1994). *Changing for good: A revolutionary six-stage program for overcoming bad habits and moving your life positively forward.* New York: Avon.

Purdon, C. (1999). Thought suppression and psychopathology. *Behaviour Research and Therapy, 37*, 1029–1054.

Purdon, C., Rowa, K., & Antony, M. M. (2004, November). Treatment fears in individuals awaiting treatment for obsessive–compulsive disorder. In C. L. Purdon (Chair), *Treatment ambivalence, readiness, and resistance in obsessive–compulsive disorder.* Symposium presented at the meeting of the Association for Advancement of Behavior Therapy, New Orleans, LA.

Purdon, C., Rowa, K., & Antony, M. M. (2005). Thought suppression and its effects on thought frequency, appraisal and mood state in individuals with obsessive–compulsive disorder. *Behaviour Research and Therapy, 43*, 93–108.

Rachman, S. J., & Hodgson, R. J. (1980). *Obsessions and compulsions.* Englewood Cliffs, NJ: Prentice Hall.

Rachman, S., Marks, I. M., & Hodgson, R. (1971). The treatment of chronic obsessive–compulsive neurosis. *Behaviour Research and Therapy, 9*, 237–247.

Rachman, S., Marks, I. M., & Hodgson, R. (1973). The treatment of chronic obsessive–compulsive neurotics by modeling and flooding in vivo. *Behaviour Research and Therapy, 11*, 463–471.

Rachman, S., Shafran, R., Mitchell, D., Trant, J., & Teachman, B. (1996). How to remain neutral: An experimental analysis of neutralization. *Behaviour Research and Therapy, 34*, 889–898.

Rhéaume, J., Freeston, M. H., Léger, E., & Ladouceur, R. (1998). Bad luck: An underestimated factor in the development of obsessive–compulsive disorder. *Clinical Psychology and Psychotherapy, 5,* 1–12.

Rodriguez, B. I., & Craske, M. G. (1995). Does distraction interfere with fear reduction during exposure? A test among animal-fearful subjects. *Behavior Therapy, 26,* 337–349.

Rowa, K., Antony, M. M., Brar, S., Summerfeldt, L. J., & Swinson, R. P. (2000). Treatment histories of patients with three anxiety disorders. *Depression and Anxiety, 12,* 92–98.

Rowa, K., Antony, M. M., Summerfeldt, L. J., Purdon, C., & Swinson, R. P. (2004, November). *The effectiveness of office-based versus home-based exposure with response prevention for obsessive compulsive disorder.* Poster presented at the meeting of the Association for Advancement of Behavior Therapy, New Orleans, LA.

Stanley, M. A., & Turner, S. M. (1995). Current status of pharmacological and behavioral treatment of obsessive–compulsive disorder. *Behavior Therapy, 26,* 163–186.

Steketee, G. S. (1993). *Treatment of obsessive–compulsive disorder.* New York: Guilford Press.

Steketee, G. S., Foa, E. B., & Grayson, J. B. (1982). Recent advances in the behavioral treatment of obsessive–compulsives. *Archives of General Psychiatry, 39,* 1365–1371.

van Balkom, A. J., de Haan, E., van Oppen, P., Spinhoven, P., Hoogduin, K.A., & van Dyck, R. (1998). Cognitive and behavioural therapies alone versus in combination with fluvoxamine in the treatment of obsessive compulsive disorder. *Journal of Nervous and Mental Disease, 186,* 492–499.

van den Hout, M., Emmelkamp, P., Kraaykamp, H., & Griez, E. (1988). Behavioral treatment of obsessive–compulsives: Inpatient vs outpatient. *Behaviour Research and Therapy, 26,* 331–332.

Van Noppen, B. L., Pato, M. T., Marsland, R., & Rasmussen, S. A. (1998). A time-limited behavioral group for treatment of obsessive–compulsive disorder. *Journal of Psychotherapy Practice and Research, 7,* 272–280.

Van Noppen, B., Steketee, G., McCorkle, B. H., & Pato, M. (1997). Group and multifamily behavioral treatment for obsessive compulsive disorder: A pilot study. *Journal of Anxiety Disorders, 11,* 431–446.

Weir, R. O., & Marshall, W. L. (1980). Relaxation and distraction in experimental desensitization. *Journal of Clinical Psychology, 36,* 246–252.

Westra, H. A., & Phoenix, E. (2003). *Motivational enhancement therapy in two cases of anxiety disorder: New responses to treatment refractoriness.* Unpublished manuscript, London Health Sciences.

Wilson, M., Bell-Dolan, D., & Beitman, B. (1997). Application of the stages of change scale in a clinical drug trial. *Journal of Anxiety Disorders, 11,* 395–408.

5

COGNITIVE THERAPY FOR OBSESSIVE–COMPULSIVE DISORDER

CHRISTINE PURDON

Successful treatment of obsessive–compulsive disorder (OCD) was elusive until the benefits of exposure to the obsession with simultaneous ritual prevention were recognized (Foa, Franklin, & Kozak, 1998; Foa & Tillmans, 1980; Rachman & Hodgson, 1980). Exposure and response prevention (ERP; also known as exposure and ritual prevention) has proved to be an effective treatment for OCD. For example, in a meta-analysis of existing treatment studies, Abramowitz (1996) reported a large effect size for ERP. Similarly, in a comprehensive review of treatment outcome studies, Foa and Kozak (1996) reported an average immediate response rate of 83% and a long-term follow-up success rate of about 76%. ERP is behavioral, with no emphasis on identification and modification of thoughts

With such a high success rate for ERP, what is the utility of examining the role of cognitive factors in the development of OCD and of adding cognitive techniques to its treatment? There are two central reasons why the addition of a cognitive component to the treatment of OCD is valuable. First, the behavioral view from which ERP is derived does not adequately account for salient aspects of the disorder. Salkovskis (1988) and Rachman and Hodgson (1980) observed that rituals are not always performed in response to the obsession. For example, when the therapist is present, the individual is less likely to perform checking rituals. Salkovskis (1998) also argued that the behavioral account is unable to differentiate among the theoretical conceptualization of different anxiety disorders, noting that the two-process theory on which exposure is based (i.e., obsessions as anxiety-inducing stimuli and compulsions as anxiety-reducing acts) could be applied equally to specific phobia and agoraphobia and to OCD.

Foa and McNally (1996) noted that the mechanism of change in exposure-based interventions has been perceived to be an actual change in existing *fear structures*, or the structures that consist of information about the feared stimulus situation, information about responses to the situation, and information about the meaning of the stimulus and response elements of the structure (Foa & Kozak, 1986, p. 20). Yet more recent empirical evidence has suggested that fear reduction occurs not from the weakening of existing stimulus–response associations, but rather from the formulation of new associations. The implication is that after successful therapy, old fear structures remain intact but are overridden by the ones learned in treatment. Thus, factors that promote accessibility of the new structure and help inhibit activation of the old structure need to be identified and incorporated into treatment. Furthermore, Foa and McNally (1996) observed that although ERP is extremely effective in reducing anxiety and fear responses, individuals with OCD report various other negative emotional responses to the obsessive stimulus, including guilt, fear, and disgust. Such emotions involve complex representations of the self that are not readily changed by exposure alone. They suggested that treatment involving a cognitive component may be more helpful when the emotional response is complex.

Others have argued that despite the strong treatment efficacy statistics for ERP, actual treatment success rates of ERP may be much lower when treatment refusal and dropout rates are taken into consideration (Freeston et al., 1997; Salkovskis, 1988, 1996, 1998) For example, about 20% to 30% of individuals with OCD refuse to begin ERP or terminate treatment prematurely, and another 20% to 30% who complete treatment are nonresponders (Stanley & Turner, 1995), meaning that the actual treatment success rate could be as low as 50%. A central reason for refusal and dropout is fear of the treatment itself (Foa, Steketee, Grayson, & Doppelt, 1983). Salkovskis (e.g., Salkovskis & Warwick, 1985) suggested that if fear of obsessions can be reduced by identifying and modifying erroneous or exaggerated appraisals of their meaning before commencing exposure, treatment success may improve considerably. Taken together, these observations indicate that a more comprehensive conceptualization of the etiological and maintaining factors in obsessional problems is warranted.

EFFICACY OF COGNITIVE THERAPY

Until the past decade or so, there were no large-scale treatment outcome studies on cognitive therapy for OCD. Early studies examined the efficacy of ERP combined with rational-emotive therapy (RET) in addressing general irrational beliefs about obsessions as compared with ERP alone. The interventions were found to have an equal impact on reducing symptoms, and adding exposure to the cognitive component did not enhance treatment effects (Emmelkamp & Beens, 1991; Emmelkamp, Visser, & Hoekstra, 1988).

Several studies have examined the efficacy of treatment protocols derived from the current cognitive model. For simplicity, I refer to protocols that include a formal ERP component in addition to cognitive restructuring as *cognitive–behavioral therapy* (CBT) and to those that include a formal cognitive component with no ERP as *cognitive therapy* (CT). Ladouceur, Freeston, Gagnon, Thibodeau, and Dumont (1995) examined the efficacy of CBT in a multiple baseline case study of three people with OCD. They found that CBT resulted in a significant reduction in discomfort and an increase in professional or interpersonal functioning or both for all three and that treatment gains were maintained at 8- to 11-month follow up. Freeston et al. (1997) found that CBT resulted in a significant reduction in OCD symptoms posttreatment and at 6-month follow-up compared with no intervention (wait-list control group). van Oppen et al. (1995) offered the first comparison of ERP to CT and found CT to be modestly superior, with equal dropout rates. In a small sample of OCD patients, Vogel, Stiles, and Götestam (2004) found that CBT was equivalent to ERP (with a relaxation control group for the formal cognitive component) in reducing symptoms. The treatment dropout rate was lower in the CBT condition.

In a larger scale study comparing group treatment with "pure" CT, ERP, and wait-list control groups, McLean et al. (2001) found that ERP was marginally more effective than CT both posttreatment and at 3-month follow-up and that both were superior to no intervention. However, there were more dropouts in the ERP condition. They suggested that CT in group format may not be the most effective means of offering treatment and that there may be advantages to offering CT individually. Warren and Thomas (2001) had an 84% treatment response using CBT (ERP + cognitive restructuring) in a routine clinical practice setting, suggesting that the treatment is fairly generalizable to settings in which most people receive their care.

O'Connor, Todorov, Robillard, Borgeat, and Brault (1999) compared CBT alone, selective serotonin reuptake inhibitors (SSRIs) alone, and the combination of SSRIs with CBT with a wait-list control condition. The combined treatment was superior to the individual active treatments, which in turn were more efficacious than no treatment. van Balkom et al. (1998) examined the efficacy of adding cognitive therapy or ERP to medication (fluvoxamine) at Week 9 to that of each psychotherapy alone and to a wait-list control group. All treatment groups were found to be equally effective compared with the wait-list control condition. In a large-scale (N = 122) double-blind, multisite treatment efficacy study comparing ERP with discussion of appraisal during exposure to this treatment plus an SSRI, Foa et al.

(2005) found that the groups were equal in effectiveness but superior to a placebo. In a meta-analysis of studies comparing psychotherapy and ERP, CBT, or CT, Eddy, Dutra, Bradley, and Westen (2004) concluded that CBT and ERP were marginally more effective than CT, although all were strong. Furthermore, there was a stronger effect size when these treatments were administered on an individual basis rather than in group format.

Rhéaume and Ladouceur (2000) examined change in appraisal of the obsession in relation to changes in the frequency of checking rituals in participants receiving ERP versus CBT in a small ($N = 15$) time series analysis. They found that for all those in the ERP group and for one third of those in the CBT group, change on at least one type of appraisal preceded a decrease in checking rituals, although for each participant, decreased checking rituals also preceded change in appraisal at least once. These findings support the link between appraisal and compulsions, asserted by cognitive models, and also suggest that changes in appraisal may actually cause change in the use of compulsive strategies. Thus, appraisal appears to play an important role in treatment success, whether it is addressed directly, as in CT, or not.

In sum, at this point few studies have compared "pure" CT or CBT with ERP. CBT, CT, and ERP appear to be effective treatments of OCD to about the same degree. However, there is some indication that there may be a therapeutic advantage to retaining an ERP component to treatment and for administering CT in an individual, rather than group, format. There is limited evidence that treatment dropout rates may be lower for CT interventions compared with ERP. Given the limited empirical evidence, all conclusions must be made with caution.

THE COGNITIVE–BEHAVIORAL MODEL OF OBSESSIVE–COMPULSIVE DISORDER

The cognitive–behavioral model of OCD is grounded in the general cognitive–behavioral model of psychological distress, which assumes that negative automatic thoughts drive problematic emotional and behavioral responses, which in turn solidify the negative thoughts, the assumptions from which they derive, and the core beliefs that generate the assumptions. According to the cognitive–behavioral model of OCD, obsessions lie on a continuum with the normal thoughts everyone experiences. When obsessional thoughts give rise to negative automatic thoughts that the obsession is dangerous, unnatural, or harmful and that action must be taken to prevent the feared outcome, problems occur. First, this "catastrophic misinterpretation" of the obsession leads to anxiety, guilt, shame, disgust, fear, discomfort, and other negative states (Rachman, 1997, 1998; Salkovskis, 1985, 1989, 1999). Compulsive rituals are then enacted to ameliorate this distress. The reduction in distress (or the perceived relative reduction in distress relative to the distress expected if nothing were done) serves as negative reinforcement for the compulsive act, so the person will repeat the act when the obsession occurs again (Foa & Tillmans, 1980; Rachman, 1976, 1997, 1998; Rachman & Hodgson, 1980; Salkovskis, 1999). The person takes the nonoccurrence of the event the obsession is appraised as portending as evidence that the compulsion was successful (Salkovskis, 1999). Thus, no new learning about the thought's actual meaning is possible.

Avoidance strategies such as overt avoidance and covert avoidance (thought suppression) are also used to prevent the thought from occurring or to dismiss the thought when it does occur. These strategies terminate exposure to the obsession so that no new learning takes place, and termination disallows the exposure to the obsession necessary for the aversive emotional response to extinguish (Rachman & Hodgson, 1980). Thought suppression may result in a paradoxical increase in thought frequency (Rachman, 1997, 1998; Salkovskis, 1999), or at the very least, failures in thought control may intensify appraisals about the thought's meaning (Purdon, Rowa, & Antony, 2005). Finally, thought suppression requires hypervigilance to thought occurrences, increasing the salience of thought-relevant cues and therefore thought occurrences (e.g., Salkovskis, 1999).

TYPES OF APPRAISAL

Six types of appraisal are considered relevant to the development and persistence of OCD (Taylor, Kyrios, Thordarson, Steketee, & Frost, 2002): overestimation of threat, intolerance of uncertainty, responsibility, overimportance of thoughts, mental control, and perfectionism.

Overestimation of Threat

Overestimation of threat refers to a tendency to overestimate the severity and the likelihood of the imagined negative consequences of an obsession (Steketee, Frost, & Cohen, 1998). Examples of such beliefs include "I believe that the world is a dangerous place," "Bad things are more likely to happen to me than to other people," and "When anything goes wrong in my life, it is likely to have terrible effects" (as summarized by Sookman & Pinard, 2002, p. 64). For example, C, a lawyer, was plagued with sudden impulses to say something extremely inappropriate in court. Even though she had no history of impulsive behavior and was known for being very calm and controlled in the courtroom, she estimated the probability of acting on these impulses at 65%.

Intolerance of Uncertainty

Some persons with OCD believe that perfect certainty can and should be achieved before they can safely proceed. Examples of such beliefs are "If I am uncertain, there is something wrong with me," "If I'm not absolutely sure of something, I'm bound to make a mistake," and "It is essential for me to consider all the possible outcomes of a situation." Y was plagued by doubts that he might be a child molester. In addition to believing that he would not be having these thoughts unless there was some truth to them, he also believed that until he could achieve 100% certainty that he was not a child molester, he considered himself a danger to children; 99.99% certainty was not good enough because as long as the chance that he was a child molester was bigger than 0, he needed to protect children from himself as if he was absolutely sure that he was a child molester.

L had intrusive thoughts that maybe he was sexually aroused by violence and therefore might be capable of rape. He spent hours reading about rapists and matching known qualities of rapists with his own qualities. He was so intolerant of uncertainty about this that even learning that he was in fact a potential rapist would be a relief; at least then he could withdraw from society and forgo having friends and a family of his own with full confidence that he was doing the right thing.

P was very afraid of becoming contaminated. Before preparing food, she scoured her counters with a strong solution of antibacterial soap, but she never felt absolutely certain that all contaminants had been eradicated. In the absence of full certainty that the counter was uncontaminated, she was unable to proceed with food preparation. Another client, C, feared becoming contaminated from using skin care products. She knew that each product had been tested for safety before being released on the market, but she reasoned that a combination of skin care products (e.g., facial scrub, moisturizer, and sunscreen) might interact with each other to produce a carcinogen. She rated the probability of this as being about 70%. Each day, then, she chose one product and one product only to use, but she feared contact with other people in the event that the skin care products they had used would rub off on her and create the carcinogen.

Responsibility

Salkovskis's model (1985, 1989, 1996, 1998, 1999; Salkovskis, Richards, & Forrester, 1995) proposes that obsessions develop when normal thoughts activate overvalued beliefs about one's responsibility to protect oneself and others from harm. Salkovskis defined *responsibility* as

> the belief that one has the power which is pivotal to bring about or prevent subjectively crucial negative outcomes. These outcomes may be actual, that is, having consequences in the real world, and/or at a moral level. (Salkovskis, Rachman, Ladouceur, & Freeston, cited in Salkovskis et al., 1995, p. 285)

Examples of responsibility beliefs include the following: "Having a thought about an action is like performing an action," "Failing to prevent (or failing to try to prevent) harm to self or others is the same as having caused the harm in the first place," "Responsibility is not attenuated by other factors (e.g., low probability of occurrence)," "Not neutralizing when an intrusion has occurred is similar or equivalent to seeking or wanting the harm involved in that intrusion to happen," and "One can and should control one's thoughts" (Salkovskis, 1985, p. 579).

In essence, then, *responsibility* refers to the belief that if one has any influence over a negative outcome whatsoever, then one is responsible for doing whatever one can to prevent that outcome and indeed is honor bound to do so, no matter how minute the probability of that negative outcome. For example, K noticed that when the wind blew in a certain direction, the branches of a tree on the street corner near his house interfered with a clear view of a stop sign. He called the city and reported the problem, but no action was taken. Shortly thereafter, an accident happened at the intersection. K felt 100% responsible for the accident, because he thought he should have done more to convince the city to trim the tree or should have done it itself. For K, not having ensured that the branches were trimmed made him as criminally negligent as if he had actually taken the stop sign.

Another client, J, was studying at the library and decided to eat her peanut butter cookie. After she left the library, she suddenly thought, "What if there are crumbs from my cookie on the desk, and the next person who sits there has a peanut allergy, touches my crumbs, has a full-blown anaphylactic reaction, and doesn't have an epinephrine injection and dies? It would be entirely my fault!" J felt as guilty and distressed over her carelessness in leaving cookie crumbs behind as she might if she had directly attempted to harm someone.

Q's home was packed so full of objects that he could no longer use his living space in normal ways. He continued to acquire new objects out of fear that he might run out in the future and that he would be responsible for having squandered them without replacing them. He was extremely reluctant to discard newspapers and magazines out of concern that he might need that information in the future and would be responsible for any harm that would come from not having that information should he have discarded it. Q found it hard to put any items out of sight for fear that he would forget about them and would not be able to benefit from them in future when he needed them (i.e., they would be technically "lost"). Q also shopped when items he might have future use for were on sale; if he did not buy them on sale immediately and had to pay full price later, he would be responsible for having wasted money. Q would never lend out any of his possessions because he felt wholly responsible for their welfare; if something happened to the item, it would be as if he had betrayed it.

Overimportance of Thoughts

Rachman (1998) introduced the idea of *thought–action fusion* to describe the belief that having an unacceptable thought increases the likelihood of the negative event represented in the thought coming true and that having a morally repugnant thought is the moral equivalent of committing a morally repugnant deed. This overemphasis on the meaning of a thought's occurrence can also manifest itself in beliefs that "obsessional thoughts indicate something significant about oneself" (e.g., that one is terrible, weird, abnormal), and "negative intrusive thoughts must be important merely because they have occurred" (Thordarson & Shafran, 2002, p. 15). Rachman (1997) provided a number of examples of these kinds of thoughts: "This thought reflects my true evil nature," "Having this thought means I am a bad person," "If I think this, I must really want it to happen," "Thinking this can make the event more likely to happen," "If others knew I thought this, they would think I am an evil person," and "Having this thought means I am likely to lose control over my mind or my behavior" (p. 793).

For example, G had images of engaging in a sexual act with someone who was not his wife and to whom he was not at all attracted. G believed that having this thought meant the same thing as actually cheating on his wife, that he had been unfaithful, and that he was therefore an immoral person. Other examples also illustrate the ways in which one type of belief is linked to another. In the week before the fatal space shuttle *Challenger* launch in 1986, B, who was an avid follower of the space program, had a sudden image of the shuttle exploding. She was horrified and did her best to keep it out of her head, believing that thinking about it would cause it to happen. She avoided all news stories on the shuttle and stopped watching TV and reading the newspaper altogether during that week. When the disaster happened, B believed that her thoughts had caused it to happen and that because she bore some influence over that outcome, she was wholly responsible for the disaster. She was guilt ridden 2 decades later that she had not contacted NASA and informed them about her images of the shuttle blowing up.

L was riddled by doubts as to whether she had turned appliances off. In addition to perceiving herself as responsible for any harm that could occur from leaving an appliance on, she also believed that she would not be having a doubt about whether she had turned something off unless there was good reason. Similarly, V was terrified of becoming contaminated, and when he had a thought that something might be contaminated, he assumed that he would not have this thought unless there was some truth to it.

Mental Control

Mental control refers to "overevaluation of the importance of exerting complete control over intrusive thoughts, images or impulses, and the belief that this is both possible and desirable" (Purdon & Clark, 2002, p. 37). Examples of such beliefs include "I would be a better person if I gained more control over my thoughts," "If I exercise enough willpower, I should be able to gain complete control over my mind," and "Being unable to control unwanted thoughts will make me physically ill." For example, D was a traveling sales representative who had frequent intrusive images of driving his car into oncoming traffic. He believed that it was very dangerous to allow himself to have these thoughts for fear that his loss of control over the thought might lead to a loss of control over his behavior. X believed that her inability to control her obsessional thoughts meant that she had lost her sanity.

Perfectionism

Steketee (1999) defined *perfectionism* as the "tendency to believe that there is a perfect solution to problems, that doing something without mistakes is possible and desirable and that even minor errors will have serious consequences" (p. 146). Examples of such beliefs include "In order to be a worthwhile person, I must be perfect at everything I do," "If I fail at something, then I am a failure as a person," "I must keep working at something until it is done exactly right," "There is only one right way to do things," and "Even minor mistakes mean a job is not complete." Y was preoccupied with ordering and arranging her household, to the point that every item had a specific place. If an item was out of place, Y felt that she had failed as a wife. R checked and rechecked his work, fearful of having made a mistake and blown the assignment entirely. This checking process took so long that he was unable to complete much of his work in a timely fashion. Z had many collections of different types of objects, but she viewed them all as entirely incomplete because she did not possess every single object of each type. She was overwhelmed with distress when one bag of items was inadvertently discarded, making one collection even less complete. Z had considerable difficulty organizing her collections, because no organizational strategy was perfect.

DOES THE COGNITIVE MODEL APPLY TO ALL TYPES OF OCD?

OCD is a heterogeneous disorder. For example, the Yale–Brown Obsessive–Compulsive Scale (Goodman et al., 1989) features eight categories of obsessions (39 separate specific obsessions) and seven types of compulsions (26 specific compulsions), plus room for "other" examples within each type of obsession and compulsion. Does the cognitive model explain the extreme myriad of clinical presentations of the disorder? Certainly, many individuals have no obvious negative interpretations of their obsessional thoughts. Salkovskis (1999) suggested that for such individuals, "the neutralizing and avoidance behaviors have become automatic responses which pre-empt the perception of threat" (pp. S37–S38). He drew an analogy between completing the compulsion and braking for a red light. It is difficult to reconstruct the sense of threat that actually drives the braking behavior, because that behavior is so automatic. According to Salkovskis, then, it is possible that in cases in which there is no salient sense of threat over the obsession, it is simply because the compulsion has been used to preempt threat for so long that the association between the obsession and threat is lost.

However, there are people whose obsessional fears are very much like phobias. For example, some people with OCD fear becoming contaminated, but they do not fear thoughts about becoming contaminated; that is, they no more fear thoughts about contamination than dog phobics fear thoughts about dogs. For example, D was afraid of becoming contaminated by objects that originated, or passed through, the city in which his estranged father lived. His compulsions were triggered by external stimuli, such as vehicles that drove between his and his father's cities, maps of his father's city, and so forth. He was unable to describe what harm the contamination might cause, other than leading him to feel "dirty," and he reported no avoidance of thoughts of becoming contaminated or fear of such thoughts. As in a phobia, the thoughts occurred only when triggered by an external stimulus or in anticipation of encountering a relevant external stimulus.

Some individuals with symmetry or exactness concerns also report no negative appraisal of their thoughts that objects are not aligned properly or are out of place. Instead, they describe simply having an unpleasant feeling, comparable to an intense itch that will not recede until symmetry or exactness is achieved. The two-factor theory of fear may best account for the symptoms of such individuals, and they may best be served by a behavioral approach that emphasizes ERP as opposed to CT.

OVERVIEW OF COGNITIVE THERAPY

Cognitive therapy is a structured, short-term, present-oriented intervention that is widely applied to Axis I and Axis II disorders (J. S. Beck, 1995). CT works to help clients identify and modify excessive, rigid, and incorrect beliefs, assumptions, and thoughts (the cognitive component) and at the same time to modify behavior that serves to maintain symptoms (the behavioral component). Successful modification of thoughts and behavior relies on an excellent formulation of the client's problem in cognitive terms. The therapist must have a solid understanding of the thoughts that are associated with the problematic emotional and behavioral responses for that particular person.

The formulation allows individuals to make sense of their problems. Often individuals with OCD believe that they are, or are going, "crazy" because their symptoms make so little sense. Also, when the client is presented with a solid case formulation as to what is responsible for the persistence of the problem, it can engender hope and motivation. What before were puzzling and alarming symptoms acquire some rational context. Thus, the assessment and formulation of the individual's idiosyncratic system of thoughts, feelings, and actions is critical in CT for OCD (e.g., Freeston, Rhéaume, & Ladouceur, 1996; Ladouceur et al., 1995; Salkovskis, 1999).

Development of a solid formulation also communicates the therapist's empathy for the problem, which in turn fosters the therapeutic alliance. In OCD, behavior change often requires acceptance of calculated risks, risks that the person has organized her or his life around avoiding. The client must trust that the therapist has her or his best interests in mind and has a genuine empathy for the client to accept interventions for change, especially exposure and behavioral experiments (Salkovskis, 1999). Furthermore, the key element of cognitive restructuring is the evaluation of negative automatic thoughts. The therapeutic alliance must be strong for the client to accept the idea that alternative ways of viewing obsessions are available and potentially more accurate; that is, the client must trust that the therapist understands the problem and has his or her best interests in mind to feel confident enough to accept the possibility of relinquishing his or her beliefs about the thought's meaning. In sum, then, the development and communication of a solid case formulation helps build the therapeutic alliance and may serve to reduce treatment resistance and noncompliance.

Cognitive therapy also emphasizes collaboration and active participation. The "collaborative empiricism" described by A. T. Beck (A. T. Beck, Rush, Shaw, & Emery, 1979) and Greenberger and Padesky (1995) is tied in with the sound therapeutic alliance but goes one step further in that the therapist seeks to learn with the client about the problem and the thoughts and behaviors that maintain it. The client thus becomes an active participant in, rather than a passive recipient of, therapy and thereby shares responsibility for treatment. In treatment of OCD, this shared responsibility may be especially helpful for clients inclined to transfer responsibility for negative outcomes to the therapist.

Another therapeutic advantage of the collaborative nature of the work is that it has more potential for being effective. Clients typically believe that the evidence supporting their negative thoughts is highly valid and credible. If the therapist takes a noncollaborative approach and passes judgment on the validity of the evidence prematurely, he or she will lose credibility, because such a "balanced" view is not based on a comprehensive understanding of the issues important to the client. In treatment of OCD, the therapist's credibility is crucial, because clients perceive the stakes of giving up their concerns as being very high. Furthermore, the therapist who does not fully collaborate with the client to explore and examine evidence for negative thoughts is likely to rupture the therapeutic alliance, because he or she is not exhibiting empathy for the client's view. Indeed, when cognitive restructuring is done in a noncollaborative manner, clients may perceive that their thoughts are on trial, as if they were on the witness stand before the prosecution, which is highly unpleasant. Finally, a noncollaborative approach may evoke considerable defense of the evidence supporting the negative thought and may therefore backfire, with the client being unwilling to back down from the position that the negative thought is valid.

A final unique feature of CBT is that when its mechanisms of change are made explicit, the client is empowered to actively participate in treatment by making informed decisions about how to manage thoughts and behavior. In CBT for OCD, the client has the knowledge and understanding necessary both to make good decisions about the use of avoidance and compulsive acts and to set up behavioral experiments that test appraisal of the obsession. This knowledge base maximizes the effectiveness of between-session work and may serve to reduce posttreatment relapse.

In sum, then, development of a solid case formulation and client education about that model are key elements of CBT for OCD. These activities build the therapeutic alliance, qualm fears, instill hope, foster active participation in treatment, lay the groundwork for effective cognitive and behavioral interventions, empower the client, and potentially reduce treatment resistance and relapse.

Educating the Client About the Model

Once the assessment has been completed and client and therapist have agreed that the target of treatment will be OCD symptoms, the therapist then develops comprehensive knowledge of the thoughts, feelings, and behaviors relevant to the client's obsession. It is helpful to interview the client first about the content of the obsessions, the strategies used to manage the obsessions (e.g., compulsions, thought suppression, avoidance), the feelings the obsession evokes, and the client's appraisal of the obsession (e.g., "What are you afraid might happen if you did not do [the compulsive ritual]?" "What does having the thought mean about you?") using a recent example from the client's life. Appraisal can be assessed using self-report measures such as the Interpretation of Intrusions Inventory (III; Obsessive Compulsive Cognitions Working Group [OCCWG], 1997) and the Obsessive Beliefs Questionnaire (OCCWG, 2001). The client can then monitor obsessions, the emotions evoked by the obsessions, compulsions, and avoidance over 1 week using diary records (e.g., a five-column table listing date, obsession, emotion, compulsions, and avoidance). Clients need to be made aware that some of their compulsions and avoidance strategies may be so habitual that they no longer notice they are doing them and should be asked to try to identify these. Because obsessions can occur frequently, the therapist and client should work out a reasonable plan for completing the diaries, such as having the client report on one obsession each morning, afternoon, and evening.

Once the therapist has a basic working model of the client's idiosyncratic presentation, he or she can introduce the model to the client. The therapist's formulation will continually evolve as more information (e.g., about appraisals, assumptions) is obtained. The client can be educated about the model using the following text as a template:

In our understanding of OCD, *obsessions* are thoughts that make you feel upset in some way—in your case, your obsessions make you feel _____. Your feelings about _____ make sense, given your view that having the obsession means _____, _____, and _____ [this information is gleaned from the interview and self-report tool]. The things you do to deal with the obsession, such as _____ [compulsions], _____ [avoidance], and _____ [thought suppression] also make sense, given that you believe the obsession to mean _____, _____, and _____. I know that these strategies help you in the short term, but they also cost you in terms of time and effort —that is one of the reasons you are here today. And not only do these strategies for managing the obsession cost you, but they also serve to make your problem worse. Here is how: First, when you use your compulsions, they reduce your distress, or at the very least you may perceive that your distress would be substantially worse if you did not do them. The reason you do them, again, is that they worked to reduce your distress. However, the compulsions are so closely linked to your obsessions that the compulsion itself and any cues for the compulsion, such as _____ [e.g., water, soap, cleaning products], are apt to trigger the obsession, making it happen more often.

Second, when you do your compulsion and avoid things that trigger the obsession, you do not experience the obsession itself in its distressing form. This means that you don't have the opportunity to learn anything new about how dangerous it actually is to have the obsession without acting on it. For example, the obsession may not be dangerous to have at all, but by completing the compulsion, you don't have the chance to learn this; instead, if the event you fear does not happen, you are likely to assume that it is because you did the compulsion and that the probability of the feared event happening would be much higher if you had not done it. If you avoid places, people, objects, and so forth, that trigger the obsession, you are likely to assume that no harm came because you did not have the dangerous obsession.

Finally, when you suppress or control your obsession, you may ironically be making it happen more often over the long term than if you did not attempt to control it. There are several reasons for this. First, suppressing an obsession requires you to be on the lookout for signs that the obsession is about to occur, so that you can quickly distract yourself by thinking about something else. The "something else" you use to distract yourself with will become associated with the obsession, and when you encounter it again, it may trigger the obsession. Second, no matter how hard you try to suppress your obsession, it will return. We know from research that no one can perfectly suppress an unwanted thought. When the thought occurs despite your best efforts to keep it away, however, it is likely that you interpret it as being especially meaningful—why would it persist otherwise?

One very important point here is that the key element in this cycle is how you interpret or appraise your obsessional thoughts. If you did not appraise them as highly significant and meaningful, you would not feel distressed, nor would you feel the need to use compulsions, avoidance, and suppression.

Consider Susan and John. Susan has a thought of swerving into the next lane while driving. She thinks, "What an odd thought for someone like me to have, because I'm not the kind of person who would harm anyone. Must be my creative mind at work! I wonder what I should make for dinner." John, having the same thought, thinks, "Oh my gosh, why did I have that thought? Maybe I am a murderer at heart! What if I act on it? I can't have this thought again, because what if having it makes me do it? I am a terrible person for having this thought! I don't really want to drive if I'm in danger of harming people!" How does Susan feel about the thought? [Neutral.] What will she do next? [Keep driving, plan dinner.] How does John feel about the thought? [Anxious, scared, ashamed.] What will he do next? [Slow down his driving, monitor his thoughts, begin looking into himself for any other evidence that he is a murderer.]

You can see how two different interpretations lead to very different emotions and actions. As a prominent OCD researcher, Dr. Paul Salkovskis (1999), said, "Maybe you are not dangerous, but rather are very worried about being dangerous" (p. S35). The difference between people with OCD and those without OCD is in their interpretation of the thought; we know from considerable research that most people have obsessional thoughts, even very violent, aggressive ones. We also know from research that people without OCD interpret their obsessional thoughts as being harmless rather than harmful. [Show client a list of normal obsessions, e.g., from Rachman & de Silva, 1978, or Purdon & Clark, 1993, 1994.]

So how do we go about treating OCD? Well, appraisal is a key element in the cycle, and we also know that in OCD, appraisals of obsessions are incorrect or too extreme and are often based on assumptions that have never really been brought to mind and questioned. *Appraisals* are interpretations that happen automatically, leaving you with impressions about the obsessions before you are even aware that these impressions are based on a series of assumptions. Our minds are geared to work very efficiently, and we often take mental shortcuts. For example, when you see a table, you see a table; however, somewhere in the back of your mind, your brain has processed the visual data it has received about this series of inclined planes and generated the conclusion that it is a table, without you even knowing that that level of processing has taken place.

Here's another example: Sarah gets out of her limousine and begins walking briskly down the street. She is wearing her fur coat and her designer sunglasses and sports a large diamond ring on her finger. She is in a hurry because she is late for her appointment with a manicurist. A panhandler is sitting on the street near the entrance to the beauty spa where she is headed. Answer the following question with a yes or no answer immediately: Will she give him any money—yes or no? What was your immediate, honest answer? Now, let's discuss what led you to generate an answer. [Discuss reasoning.]

Your answer, then, was based on an automatic processing of the information you were given and reflected views you have about _____, _____, and _____ [Wealthy people, women, people who wear fur coats.] Now let's take the time to think fully about the situation. Let's consider the fact that she was rushing—could this mean that she has demonstrated some consideration for others' time, and so may be empathic and considerate enough to donate money to someone? Do we actually have enough information about Sarah to give an answer with confidence? This is the beauty of revisiting automatic impressions of events, including your own thoughts; it gives you the opportunity to think about your automatic appraisals in a conscious, fully aware way. You can take the time to consider all the angles, seek new information about a situation, and draw a conclusion based on all the available data, rather than taking your immediate opinion for granted.

To overcome OCD, you must be able to identify the automatic appraisals of your obsessions that lead you to believe that something is threatening or dangerous. In treatment, we will be working together to weigh and balance these appraisals to determine whether they are accurate. You can then modify appraisals that are not accurate to reflect a balanced view of the meaning of your obsessions, a view that is based on many sources of information and that takes alternate explanations into account." [If ERP is to be included in treatment, this is a good time to provide the rationale for exposure. It is not covered here because ERP is covered in detail in chap. 4 of this volume.]

This psychoeducational component is best done in an interactive way, stopping periodically to gauge the client's level of comprehension by asking the client to repeat key concepts in her or his own words (e.g., "So let's review here—what do you see as the key link between the obsession and the emotions and behaviors it evokes?") and asking questions (e.g., "So given what we have discussed here, what do you think would happen if you were to interpret the obsession as meaning that you have a creative mind?" "Suppose your friend came to you saying she had an obsession about _____ and compulsions of _____. What would you tell her about why her obsessions and compulsions keep occurring?").

The therapist must keep in mind that the goal is to make this psychoeducational component therapeutic as opposed to strictly didactic. The didactic nature of this and other interventions in CT (e.g., evidence weighing) can result in the emergence of a countertherapeutic dynamic in which the client experiences the therapist as a potentially punitive figure of authority and feels like a potentially recalcitrant student.

Identification of Appraisals

As in any course of cognitive therapy, clients must become adept at accurately identifying their negative automatic thoughts or appraisals that lead to problematic emotional and behavioral responses. Therapists treating OCD can refer to numerous sources on how to increase clients' awareness, including A. T. Beck et al. (1979), J. S. Beck (1995), Greenberger and Padesky (1995), Purdon and Clark (2005), and Steketee (1999). The goal of this stage of treatment is for clients to become aware of underlying appraisals and assumptions. The therapist can then use the downward arrow technique to get past the accurate, descriptive appraisal of the situation (e.g., "I hate this; this is awful!") to the underlying appraisals that make the situation awful. The downward arrow technique involves initially asking the client, "What makes it awful?" and then responding to his or her answer with, "What is the worst part about that for you?" and repeating that question after every response until the thoughts listed fully account for the emotional intensity of the reaction to the thought. To help clients identify the appraisal, they may find it helpful to ask themselves the following questions, on the basis of Purdon and Clark (2005):

- "What does this obsession mean about my personality or character?"
- "What does this obsession mean for the near future? What does it mean for the distant future?"
- "What does it mean that the obsession keeps coming back?"
- "What will happen if I do not do my compulsion, avoidance, or suppression?"

At first, many clients report that what bothers them the most about having the obsession is that someone is in danger. The clients' desire to protect others from harm is wholly appropriate and rational; the goal of treatment is never to make people develop a callous attitude toward others or to trivialize the consequences of harm. Instead, the goal is to help clients question the view that having the obsession itself is the route by which harm might occur. The downward arrow technique, then, should focus not on thoughts about how bad it would be if another was harmed (unless the degree of perceived harm is highly exaggerated) but, rather. on the appraisals that lead the individual to believe that the obsession itself is a harbinger of harm.

The client can next begin learning to identify his or her appraisals through the use of thought records between sessions. In this phase, it may be most useful to have a four-column thought record with columns labeled *date*, *obsession*, *emotions*, and *thoughts*. The client can complete this for a week, ideally daily (e.g., once every morning, afternoon, and evening, or whenever obsessional thoughts occur). Learning to accurately identify negative automatic thoughts is a skill, and therapists should expect that clients will need 2

EXHIBIT 5.1
Sample Thought Record for a Nursing Student
With Obsessive–Compulsive Disorder

Date	Obsession	Feelings and SUDS ratings	Appraisal
Jan. 28, morning	Impulse to kick out the crutch of an injured person.	Fear: 90 Shame: 80	Am I a psychopath? I wouldn't be having thoughts like this unless part of me truly wanted to do it. Should I be changing careers? The more I have these thoughts, the more likely I am to act on them. I am a menace to society. I am a bad person for having these thoughts.
Jan. 28, afternoon	What if some water spilled on the floor from the drinking fountain and someone slipped and hurt himself or herself?	Fear: 80 Guilt: 90	I don't think any water spilled, but maybe it did, and if anything happened, it would be all my fault. Not going back to clean up any water is just like actually tripping someone.
Jan. 28, evening	Urge to trip elderly person.	Fear: 90 Guilt: 90 Shame: 90	I am a bad person. These thoughts keep happening even though I don't want them to! They must be a sign of something. Maybe I want to do it; maybe I am a cold, callous person at heart, and this is a sign that I shouldn't go into nursing. I'm going to lose control and do it. Not controlling this thought is the same as actually tripping someone.

Note: SUDS = Subjective Units of Distress Scale. From *Overcoming Obsessive Thoughts* (p. 52), by C. Purdon and D. A. Clark, 2005, Oakland, CA: New Harbinger. Copyright 2005 by New Harbinger. Adapted with permission.

or 3 weeks to do it well. Each thought record should be reviewed in session and fleshed out. One good rule of thumb is to identify thoughts that, in and of themselves, account for the range and intensity of the emotions reported. When the client is able to accurately identify his or her most upsetting appraisals, he or she can begin the phase of questioning and restructuring the appraisal. See Exhibit 5.1 for a sample completed thought record used to monitor appraisals.

Between-Session Work

A few comments about between-session assignments are warranted at this point, as between-session work is a key ingredient of the psychoeducational and active treatment components of therapy. First, it may be helpful to present between-session work as the "application of the principles learned in session to your real life" rather than as "homework." The term *homework* can have negative associations (e.g., something that is abstract with little practical utility or that is burdensome and whose purpose is not obvious) and can evoke the punitive teacher–recalcitrant student dynamic when it is experienced as something imposed by the therapist, as opposed to a mutually agreed on strategy for tackling the OCD. The former description communicates both the goal of the between-session assignment and the expectation that the client is an active participant in overcoming his or her OCD. One analogy that can be helpful is the following:

> Suppose you decided to see a fitness trainer to get into better physical shape. If you met with the trainer once a week but did not do any of the exercises the trainer recommended, by the end of the program your knowledge of fitness might be greater, but your overall physical shape will not have changed. The same is true for this kind of work; to overcome your problem with OCD, we need to help you apply what we discuss in our 1 hour together to your real life.

Clients will be less likely to complete between-session work if they do not understand its purpose or do not anticipate that its obvious costs (e.g., time, effort) outweigh its benefits, which are less obvious in the initial stages of therapy and which the client must accept on trust from the therapist. Padesky and Greenberger (1995) offered nine strategies for increasing client compliance with between-session work:

1. Make assignments small.
2. Assign tasks within the client's skill level.
3. Make assignments relevant and interesting.
4. Collaborate with the client in developing learning assignments.
5. Provide a clear rationale for the assignment and a written summary.
6. Begin the assignment during the session.
7. Identify and solve impediments to the assignment.
8. Emphasize learning, not a desired outcome.
9. Show interest, and follow up in the next appointment.

If the client does not complete between-session tasks, this needs to be handled constructively and nonpunitively (Padesky & Greenberger, 1995). The therapist must seek to understand why the client did not do the work and must work collaboratively with the client to identify solutions. Many clients have difficulty telling the therapist that the point of the exercise was not clear or that it did not seem worth it. Instead, they may just say that they did not have time or that they find making time for themselves too hard.

Before heading into a discussion of how to make the time or of how worthy the client truly is of taking that time, it may be worthwhile first to explore other possible reasons for the noncompliance (e.g., "Even though the between-session exercises make sense in session, sometimes people find it hard to see their relevance once they try applying it to real life. What was it like for you; did the assignment seem relevant and worthwhile once you got home, or not really?").

Noncompliance with between-session work can create considerable strain on the therapeutic relationship, and therapists need to avoid using coercive tactics to try to gain compliance (e.g., threatening to withdraw services unless the client complies). Such strategies may yield grudging compliance, but they are not therapeutic because the client is doing the exercises with the mindset of avoiding punishment rather than learning skills for overcoming the problem. Again, the therapist and the client have to be in agreement regarding compliance, with both viewing failure to complete between-session work as a problem, before treatment can proceed productively.

Salkovskis (1999) observed that in some cases, the client's therapy goals are to be reassured or to find more effective ways of conducting rituals. The goals of CBT are quite different. Treatment cannot proceed productively if the client and therapist do not have common goals. Salkovskis offered several strategies for helping clients shift their perspective on treatment goals. For clients who are very concerned about the consequences of treating their obsessions differently than they do currently, Salkovskis suggested pointing out that although therapists cannot guarantee that harm will not occur, they can guarantee that clients will continue to experience obsessional problems if they are unwilling to change their view of the meaning of the obsession (p. S39). It can be helpful to add that the price of excessive caution is currently very high. I find it also helpful to point out that everyone in the world accepts the same kind of risks that will be asked of the client in therapy; that is, the difference between people with OCD and those without OCD is that those without OCD are willing to live their lives in accordance with the balance of probabilities, whereas those with OCD organize their lives around preventing outcomes that have miniscule probabilities. The risks in treatment are calculated ones, and not ones that the therapist himself or herself would be unwilling to make.

One assumption therapists often make is that the client is ready and willing to change, and they interpret resistance behaviors (e.g., failing to complete between-session work) negatively ("This client does not accept my authority," "This client is lazy," "This client does not want to get better," "I'm failing as a therapist") as a result. However, clients may have considerable ambivalence about treatment. Purdon, Rowa, and Antony (2004) examined treatment ambivalence in a sample of individuals diagnosed with OCD and waiting for group CBT. The vast majority reported treatment fears, which included fear of treatment failure ("I will be a hopeless case!"), fear of treatment success ("If my OCD improves, people's expectations of me will be too high, and I won't meet them"), fear that treatment will increase anxiety or other symptoms, and general treatment fears (e.g., fear of disclosing to strangers). It is important to be sensitive to these issues and to address them openly. If noncompliance with between-session work is not readily overcome by open discussion, it may be that the client's overall ambivalence is too high or that he or she simply is not ready to make changes. Chapter 3 provides a detailed discussion of treatment readiness and resistance, and Purdon and Clark (2005) provided suggestions for helping clients overcome treatment fears.

COGNITIVE TECHNIQUES IN TREATMENT OF OCD

Cognitive–behavioral therapy for OCD draws on the same repertoire of general strategies for cognitive restructuring as used in treatment of other problems. These strategies include evidence weighing using thought records, Socratic dialogue, behavioral experiments, and formulation of new assumptions and beliefs, as described in detail in numerous sources (J. S. Beck, 1995; Greenberger & Padesky, 1995; Steketee, 1999). As Salkovskis (1999) asserted, the goal of cognitive restructuring is for the "patient and therapist to work together to construct and test a new, less threatening explanation of the patient's experience, and then to explicitly examine the validity of the contrasting accounts" (p. S36). That is, the client and therapist work together to determine which explanation is better: that the client is truly harmful or that the client is simply worried about being harmful. Salkovskis suggested specific techniques organized according to appraisal type.

As in cognitive interventions for any other type of problem, the crux of change is the client's ability to generate alternative ways of viewing a problem or thinking about a situation. The therapist's role is to facilitate insight through guided discovery (Padesky & Greenberger, 1995). This tenet is crucial, because when clients themselves go through the process of weighing and balancing a thought, they generate a balanced alternative that is credible. When the therapist provides the alternative, it is likely to have little credibility, because the client is likely to think, "She's my therapist, she has to say that" or "But he doesn't know all the bad stuff about me!" Thus, there is far less therapeutic effectiveness when the therapist feeds clients the alternatives. Although it may take considerably longer for the client to produce alternative explanations and balanced thoughts, therapy will ultimately be more efficient, because the client will believe his or her own alternative or balanced view more quickly.

Overestimation of Threat

To address overestimation of threat, a therapist will find it useful to identify whether the person overestimates the chance of danger or the extent or consequences of the danger (van Oppen & Arntz, 1994). One technique for addressing overestimations of probability is to identify the sequence of events leading to the catastrophe, calculating the probability of each event, and then multiplying these probabilities together to get the event's overall probability.

In the example of J, who was afraid that she would cause someone to die by leaving cookie crumbs on her desk in the library, she identified a number of steps toward this catastrophe. She identified the probability of this catastrophe as being about 15%; not terribly high, but certainly not negligible, given how awful the consequence was. To address this probability overestimation, we first identified the probability that she had left enough crumbs to cause an anaphylactic reaction. J had brushed the crumbs into a napkin and deposited them in a nearby wastebasket before leaving, and she did not remember seeing any crumbs on the desk. She rated the probability of there being enough peanut residue to cause a reaction as being about 10%. We then examined the probability that the next person who sat at the desk had a peanut allergy so extreme that contact with peanut residue would cause a full anaphylactic reaction. This required a bit of research, but according to recent statistics posted on an authoritative Web site, about 1.3% of adults in the United States report peanut allergies of all severities. Thus, the estimated probability that the next person at the desk would have a severe peanut allergy was less than 1.3%. We then examined the probability that someone with such a severe allergy would not have an epinephrine injection on hand, and J reasoned that it was probably about 1%. The probability of someone dying because of exposure to her peanut cookie crumbs would be calculated as follows: $0.10 \times 0.013 \times 0.01 = 0.000013$, at the very most. Thus, the probability of this consequence *not* happening was at least 99.999987%.

To address overestimations of the consequences of an event, one may find it helpful to seek normative information. van Oppen and Arntz (1994) gave the example of a man who feared that if he made an error on a bank transfer, it would lead to his bankruptcy, because the money would not be transferred and he would not get the money back. They advised that he write a letter to the bank asking about what really happens when such an error occurs. van Oppen and Arntz also suggested setting up behavioral experiments to test negative predictions about the consequences of negative events, for example, by having the individual in their example actually make an error on a bank transfer.

As van Oppen and Arntz (1994) and others (e.g., Clark, 2004; Freeston et al., 1997; Rachman & Hodgson, 1980; Salkovskis, 1999) have observed, however, addressing probability overestimations is unlikely to succeed on its own, because as long as the probability of the feared event is not absolutely 0, the person with OCD is likely to continue to work to avoid the outcome because of overvalued responsibility (i.e., any influence over an outcome is equivalent to full responsibility for that outcome) and intolerance of uncertainty (i.e., unless there is perfect certainty that an event has not happened or will not happen, the person must behave as if it has happened or will happen). Working with probabilities is useful as a means of reducing anxiety over the event coming true, but when working with individuals who fear that their thoughts themselves are the vehicle through which the event might happen, treatment must then address the erroneous appraisal of the obsession, rather than the content of the obsession.

For example, in treatment of the obsession "Maybe I am a pedophile," initially it would be critical to determine what evidence the individual has for believing this thought could be true (see chap. 9 in this volume) and to establish a realistic probability that he or she is not a pedophile. However, from that point on, treatment should not focus on whether the person is a pedophile; instead, treatment needs to focus on appraisals of responsibility (e.g., "As long as the probability of my not being a pedophile is not 0, for certain, then I must organize my life around protecting children from me"), importance of thoughts (e.g., "This thought wouldn't keep occurring unless it was meaningful; it must mean that I am a pedophile at heart"), and control ("I can and should be able to control this thought"). Focusing on evidence for and against one's status as a pedophile is likely to serve as reassurance (i.e., tallying all the evidence that one is not a pedophile and finding that it outweighs the evidence that one might be a pedophile), but it does not address the appraisal of the thought itself that is causing the individual to entertain the idea that there is truth value to the thought itself.

As another example, C had doubts about whether clothes he purchased at an army surplus store had been contaminated with depleted uranium. He had the clothes tested at a lab, and the result was negative. He felt reassured enough by this to wear the clothes in public. However, within 24 hours the doubt returned. Assuming that the doubt would not have returned unless it was meaningful, he began to think of reasons why the lab results could be faulty. He wondered if the lab staff had made a mistake and had given him the wrong results. Within 48 hours, he was wracked with guilt over having worn the clothes and with fear that he had contaminated people. He began scouring the news for stories about epidemics of radiation sickness, and he checked his own body frequently for signs of illness.

C sealed the clothes in a bag and locked them in a shed, but he soon became concerned that the bag was not sufficient to contain the radiation. Unsure of how to safely dispose of the clothes, he ordered a second lab test, and it, too, came back negative. His relief over the lab test was fleeting, dissipating completely when he began to doubt whether the lab's equipment was sensitive enough to detect the depleted uranium. C's fears over having contaminated people when he wore the clothes were now constant and strengthened his appraisal that the fears would not occur unless there was good reason. He had the clothes tested again. This time, the negative result gave no relief from his anxiety, because he now had a powerful feeling that the clothes were indeed contaminated but that the labs had either erred or had faulty equipment. His fear did not begin to dissipate until he addressed his appraisal of the thought's meaning, rather than its content.

Intolerance of Uncertainty

Intolerance of uncertainty is often driven by the need to know. Freeston et al. (1996) suggested a behavioral experiment in which the client tolerates the doubt about whether something has or has not happened without engaging in any strategy to seek certainty. The client tracks the intensity of the need to know over time and is likely to find that it dissipates over time. The point is that the "need" to know is not an actual need at all. Some clients have a need to remember information for certain. Steketee (1999) recommended having a client do a cost–benefit analysis of seeking certainty of information: How often has the client been able to recall a piece of information with perfect certainty in the past? Is the effort worth it? She also recommended having the client place on a continuum information that is vital to know accurately and information that is unimportant and to use this as a guide when the need to recall something accurately arises—is there a genuine need to know this information for certain, or is there simply a feeling that one can ignore?

Responsibility

The pie chart technique can be used to address the idea that if one has any responsibility for a harmful outcome, then one is fully responsible for its prevention. The procedure has been described in numerous sources (e.g., Salkovskis, 1999; van Oppen & Arntz, 1994). The therapist first draws a circle representing responsibility for the negative event. The client then makes a list of all the influences on that outcome, starting with her or his own. Proportion of responsibility is assigned to each item, beginning at the bottom of the list, so that the client's influence comes last. The therapist structures this discussion but lets the client generate the items and the proportions. The therapist then charts each reason on the pie chart according to its proportion and asks the client to revisit the idea that any responsibility is the equivalent of full responsibility in light of the chart.

Discussion can address why the client feels more responsible for protecting a person from harm than the person himself or herself does. Salkovskis (1999) noted that the therapist can also introduce a discussion of how "potent" the client's act of commission or omission was in causing the event—by asking, for example, "Isn't washing one's hands a good way to commit murder?" The pie chart can also be used to launch a discussion of how the client might advise his or her best friend if the best friend felt guilty and

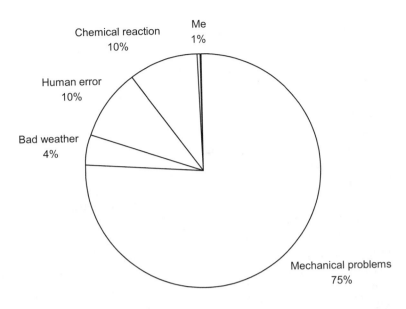

Chemical reaction
10%

Me
1%

Human error
10%

Bad weather
4%

Mechanical problems
75%

Figure 5.1. B's pie chart allocating responsibility for the space shuttle *Challenger* disaster.

responsible for the same harm for the same reasons. The pie chart strategy is especially useful when the client's influence over the outcome is vague and remote, as in the example of B, who felt 100% responsible for the space shuttle *Challenger* disaster in 1986 because she had had images of it exploding and had failed to inform NASA. B's pie chart is presented in Figure 5.1. Salkovskis (1999) also recommended using this strategy when the client believes that some act of omission on his or her part in the past led to a negative outcome. This strategy may not be useful when the perceived "victim" of harm is truly powerless (i.e., could not possibly anticipate or defend against the danger, such as a pedestrian walking on a sidewalk) or is expected to be protected by society (e.g., children, people with disabilities).

Freeston et al. (1996) suggested that the therapist have the client act as a prosecuting attorney to argue the case against himself or herself and then have the client switch roles and argue for the defense. Purdon and Clark (2005) offered another strategy for challenging the idea that failing to prevent harm is as bad, morally, as causing harm: The therapist draws a line and at one end writes the words "committing premeditated murder against a helpless person" and at the other "taking my life to save another." The client then plots all the actions that he or she has committed and feels guilty about and responsible for (e.g., not fixing a mat that was turned up at the corner, not stopping to mop up water that spilled from a drinking fountain, leaving the bathroom without having achieved perfect certainty as to whether one's hands are uncontaminated). This can help the individual gain perspective on the role of intention in harm, on direct versus highly indirect routes to harm, and on the morality of acts of omission versus deliberate acts of commission that result in harm. Discussion can then address the pros and cons of organizing one's life around protecting others from vague and low-probability events at substantial personal expense.

It can be worthwhile to help clients examine the morality of organizing their lives around low-probability events at the expense of family, work, friends, and so forth. For example, K had contamination fears. She would not dine out because she was afraid that her contamination fears would make her anxious and therefore nauseous and that she might throw up, causing great offense and discomfort to the other diners (she had never thrown up in public before, even when highly anxious). Although her family enjoyed dining out, and although dining out once a week would alleviate some of the stress of their very busy schedules, her feeling of responsibility for the dining experience of the other patrons was too high for her to be able to eat in a restaurant; she did not feel that it was morally correct to put the other diners at risk for an unpleasant experience. We discussed the morality of protecting these unknown diners from a very low probability event versus the morality of repeatedly letting her family down. We then discussed how people without OCD determine their responsibility to others, identifying event probability, the potency of an action or inaction in causing the event, and the relationship one had to the potential victim of harm as central guiding factors. Eventually, K was able to develop adaptive guidelines for accepting responsibility for outcomes.

Finally, it can be productive to discuss whether other people should be as cautious as the client is. What would the world look like if everyone organized their lives around preventing events of very low probability?

Clark (2004) described a behavioral experiment that can be used to help clients modify responsibility appraisals. In this experiment, the client transfers responsibility for harm to the therapist for 1 week and then monitors his or her obsessions, compulsions, and feelings over that week. It is likely that the client will have many fewer obsessions and much less anxiety during the week than previously. In session, the therapist and client compare the experience of feeling responsible with not feeling responsible as a means of conveying the importance of appraisal in the persistence of the disorder. This transference of responsibility can be accomplished by having the therapist put in writing that he or she will take full responsibility for all harm that occurs (Lopatka & Rachman, 1995). Another behavioral experiment is to have the client scout out a "dangerous" public situation, such as an upturned mat or spilled water, and then discreetly observe what happens. Most people will spot the problem and avoid tripping, and the consequences for those who trip are not catastrophic. Furthermore, it is likely that someone will correct the placement of the mat or mop up the water. This observation helps the client develop a realistic sense of the probability and severity of harm, as well as the extent to which others are willing to share responsibility for preventing harm.

Overimportance of Thoughts

A primary strategy in correcting faulty appraisal of the importance of thoughts is to normalize them (Freeston et al., 1996; Rachman, 2003; Salkovskis, 1999). When the client understands that his or her thoughts are identical to thoughts that others experience, it helps dispute the idea that the thought must "come from" his or her personality. If a morally repugnant thought occurred only to highly immoral people, than the vast majority of individuals would be immoral. The lists of obsessional thoughts referred to in the section on educating the client about the model can be used for this purpose (e.g., Rachman & deSilva, 1978). Clients can also ask their close friends and family about whether they have ever had thoughts about immoral actions.

To overcome "moral fusion," or the belief that having a thought about an immoral deed is just as bad, morally, as committing that deed, Purdon and Clark (2005) recommended examining thoughts within the context of deeds. The therapist asks the client to identify the most moral person he or she has heard of (e.g., Mother Teresa) and the most immoral person he or she has heard of (e.g., Hitler). The therapist draws a line, putting one name at one end and the other name at the other. The client then maps his or her best friend, spouse, and himself or herself on the line. Typically, clients fall close to their best friend and spouse. There are many discussion points from here on. First, clients can identify at what point on the line they would put their best friend if their best friend had the same kinds of immoral thoughts the client is reporting. This can lead to a discussion of how one's morality is established; is it by the deeds one commits, or is it by the transient thoughts one has? Is the immoral thought the only relevant piece of information about the client's morality? Do intent and action matter more than simply having the thought?

To address the concern that having the thought means that the individual is in danger of losing control and acting on it, Purdon and Clark (2005) recommended discussing the steps that occur between thought and action. The client can consider a time when he or she was tempted to do something and decided not to do it (e.g., eat a donut that was offered at work) and then analyze what happened when the temptation occurred. It is likely that as soon as the temptation to eat the donut arose, so did all the pros and cons of eating it. Some people are concerned that because they have behaved impulsively in the past, they may behave impulsively again and act on an unwanted violent or sexual urge. Freeston et al. (1996) recommended having the client examine acceptable thoughts that he or she has not acted on. If behavioral control can be inhibited even when the action is a desirable one, then the client is likely to have sufficient control to inhibit a repugnant, undesirable behavior. Purdon and Clark suggested a behavioral experiment in which the client attempts to make himself or herself lose control. The client can be instructed to go to a public place and try to scream or do something else inappropriate. While doing so, the client is to observe all of the strategies he or she uses to inhibit the behavior.

It can be helpful to point out that many times when people behave impulsively, it is because there is some form of instant gratification (e.g., pleasure, retribution). The therapist can ask the client whether acting on the obsession would provide any pleasure. If not, then to act on the obsession, the client would have to not only go against his or her morals and values, but also engage in an activity that he or she finds repugnant. Some clients express doubt as to whether they would enjoy the activity, especially if the obsession evokes physical sensations that are mistaken for sexual arousal. This line of discussion may not be productive for such individuals.

One variant of the likelihood fusion is that having a thought increases the probability of the event it represents coming true. To address this concern, Freeston et al. (1996) suggested asking clients to make themselves win a lottery by thinking about winning each day for at least half an hour or to cause an appliance to break down by thinking about it breaking down 100 times per day.

Purdon and Clark (2005) described a number of behavioral experiments that can be done to address faulty appraisals of the meaning of thought recurrences. One exercise is to have the client construct an especially vivid image (e.g., a white poodle wearing a red and black polka dot bikini) and focus on it for several minutes. They are then instructed *not* to have that image for the next week but to keep track of when the image occurs should it happen anyway. In the next session, discussion can focus on how easy or difficult it was not to have the thought and the circumstances under which the thought appeared. Chances are that its appearance was fairly predictable, as opposed to mysterious. For example, it may have been triggered by stimuli evocative of the image (dogs, polka dots, items that are black and red) or by recalling the therapist or therapy. Discussion can then focus on the "meaning" of the thought's recurrence: What is the most likely explanation for the thought's recurrence—that images people try to control become more salient and difficult to control, or that the client is developing a fetish for dogs, bikinis, or polka dots?

Many clients believe that the thought "comes from" their personality and so may not find this exercise compelling, because the thought was imposed by the therapist. An exercise that can address this concern is to have the client monitor all distinctive thoughts over the course of the week. How many silly, foolish, or strange thoughts did the client experience? Did having a strange thought make the client strange? Did having a silly thought make the client silly? Clark (2004) suggested another exercise in which the client identifies all the obsessional thoughts he or she has had that were readily dismissed and all the ones that were not. What made it easier to dismiss one thought but not another? Rowa, Purdon, Summerfeldt, and Antony (2005) compared people's most versus least upsetting obsession and found that what distinguished the two was the extent to which the obsession reflected current concerns and violated important and valued aspects of the self. This information can be used to explore the extent to which any particular thought is objectively meaningful.

Freeston et al. (1996) noted that some clients have superstitious or magical thinking (e.g., "If I don't walk around the table three times, something dreadful might happen to my family"). This kind of appraisal can be tougher to crack, because the perceived harm is vague, uncertain, and in the future. The client can attain no certainty as to whether harm has in fact been averted, and because harm can occur at any time in the future (even after the client is dead), the consequences of not acting on the thought seem high. Freeston et al. (1996) noted that this kind of OCD is more often associated with poor insight.

One strategy for addressing this kind of concern is to take an approach more like that used in treatment of health anxiety. This approach involves helping the client come to terms with uncertainty and lack of control over important outcomes such as the illness or death of a loved one. The therapist can point out that the loved one can be harmed in a multitude of ways other than through the client's failure to complete a ritual and that these other avenues of harm are actually much higher in probability (e.g., car crash, cancer). Everyone must live every day with the knowledge that a loved one or oneself can be seriously harmed, and because death is inevitable and people have very little control over when it will happen, they need to accept the idea of death and enjoy the present. A cost–benefit analysis of the compulsions, taking into account that there is no certainty that the compulsion will truly protect the family member and that the family member may be harmed in many other ways anyway, may help reduce investment in the rituals. Another facet of this manifestation of OCD is the vague sense that there is a being that is privy to one's thoughts and has the potential to act malevolently. For example, clients may feel that their thoughts are being monitored and that if they are arrogant (i.e., if they do not engage in the compulsion), they are tempting that being to punish them for their arrogance. It may be helpful to have the client articulate this idea and examine it openly. Who is the being? What makes the being malevolent? Numerous other strategies for challenging thought–action fusion and the overimportance of thoughts appraisals appear in chapter 9, which details treatment of repugnant obsessions.

Mental Control

Several behavioral experiments are very useful in addressing exaggerated beliefs about the necessity of being able to control one's thoughts. Often these appraisals are based on a misunderstanding of how thoughts and attentional processes work. Purdon and Clark (2005) recommended an exercise that is based on one described by Freeston and Ladouceur (1999). In this exercise, clients are instructed to focus on "white bears" for 2 minutes and to record any instances when they notice their thoughts wandering. Then they are to *not* have any thoughts about white bears for 2 minutes but to keep track of such thought occurrences should they happen anyway. Typically, people are surprised by the extent to which their mind has "a mind of its own," wandering when it is supposed to be focused and allowing in thoughts that it has been told not to; perfect suppression of a thought is almost never achieved. Furthermore, the client is likely to find himself or herself somewhat sensitized to stimuli evoking thoughts of white bears. The point of this exercise is to illustrate that people simply do not have perfect control over their attention and thoughts, even when they try very hard. The costs versus benefits of thought control can then be examined; is it worth the effort to work so hard to obtain so little control? (The poodle exercise described in the section on the overimportance of thoughts can also assist in making this point.)

Clark (2004) recommended an exercise in which clients alternate days they try to control their obsession as usual with days they do not try to control the obsession. The client keeps track of the frequency of obsessions and the distress they cause. Clients are likely to find that they are bothered less by the obsession on the days when they do not try to control it. This kind of strategy is best implemented once the client has begun to modify his or her appraisal of the dangerousness of the obsession; otherwise, it will be too difficult for the client to do.

Perfectionism

Perfectionism is characterized by black-and-white, all-or-nothing thinking. Treatment of perfectionism needs to address this rigidity. It is helpful to identify the elusiveness of perfection and this elusiveness as a key factor in the client's distress. The therapist can also discuss differences between the client and other people whose work the client admires. Does the admired person make mistakes? If so, what are the consequences? How is that person's work judged—by the presence of a few errors or by the overall quality? The therapist can also explore reasons why the client feels that he or she must be held to different standards of performance than others. Some clients are concerned that if they relax their standards at all, they will decline to the point at which they are sloppy and careless. This concern can be addressed by framing treatment goals in terms of reducing standards that interfere with performance but leaving intact standards that enhance performance. The therapist can use a graph to demonstrate that perfectionistic standards are functional only to a certain point and then begin to have diminishing returns (e.g., by drawing the inverted U that describes the relationship between standards [Y axis] and performance [X axis]).

Steketee (1999) described behavioral experiments in which the client deliberately makes errors to see if the predicted catastrophic consequences do occur. Another strategy she recommended is having the client complete a cost–benefit analysis of striving for perfection (e.g., for perfect recall, for perfect comprehension). Clark (2004) described a variant of this in which the client is instructed to increase his or her standards of perfectionism (e.g., from 85% perfect to 95% perfect) and then weigh the increase in effort required to do this against the benefit of achieving better performance.

APPLICATION OF COGNITIVE RESTRUCTURING

Therapists can use the exercises and behavioral experiments suggested in this chapter to help decrease clients' belief in the validity of their original appraisal of the obsession's meaning and to increase their belief in a benign appraisal of the obsession. For this shift to occur, clients need to work at identifying and weighing appraisal in their real lives. These exercises are meant to help clients develop a repertoire of disconfirming evidence for use in this endeavor. It will be very useful, then, for clients to complete thought records in which they identify their most upsetting appraisal (the "hot" thought) and modify it, just as in treatment of other disorders. A variation of the six-column thought record developed by Greenberger and Padesky (1995) is useful, with columns labeled *obsession, emotions, appraisal, evidence for the hot thought, evidence against the hot thought,* and *balanced appraisal.* The client can rate the intensity of the emotional response before and after the evidence weighing in the emotions column.

INTEGRATION OF COGNITIVE TECHNIQUES WITH EXPOSURE AND RESPONSE PREVENTION

Therapists should use their best clinical judgment about the pacing and timing of cognitive interventions with ERP. If the client has very little appraisal (e.g., in symmetry or exactness concerns with no perfectionism or magical thinking), then the therapist may want to move into exposure. If the client has highly repugnant obsessions that he or she is very afraid of (e.g., if the perceived awfulness of the event coming true is high), then it may be useful to reduce the sense of personal meaning and degree of threat the obsession carries before commencing ERP. If cognitive restructuring exercises stall and yield no real shift in appraisal, it may be useful to introduce exposure, as there is evidence that ERP leads to shifts in appraisal.

CONCLUSION

Cognitive therapy for OCD is relatively new but shows promise in that it appears to be about as effective as ERP alone and may be associated with lower treatment dropout. At this point, it appears that there may be a slight advantage to retaining an ERP component in treatment, so therapists may want to plan to use CBT, as opposed to CT, in treatment. This chapter identified five domains of appraisal of obsessions that are targets for treatment, and cognitive restructuring exercises and behavioral experiments were suggested that address each type of appraisal. The therapist can use his or her clinical judgment in the integration of cognitive techniques with ERP.

REFERENCES

Abramowitz, J. S. (1996). Variants of exposure and response prevention in the treatment of obsessive–compulsive disorder: A meta-analysis. *Behavior Therapy, 27,* 583–600.

Beck, A. T., Rush, A. J., Shaw, B. F., & Emery, G. (1979). *Cognitive therapy of depression.* New York: Guilford Press.

Beck, J. S. (1995). *Cognitive therapy: Basics and beyond.* New York: Guilford Press.

Clark, D. A. (2004). *Cognitive–behavioral therapy for OCD.* New York: Guilford Press.

Eddy, K. T., Dutra, L., Bradley, R., & Westen, D. (2004). A multidimensional meta-analysis of psychotherapy and pharmacotherapy for obsessive–compulsive disorder. *Clinical Psychology Review, 24,* 1011–1030.

Emmelkamp, P. M., & Beens, H. (1991). Cognitive therapy with obsessive–compulsive disorder: A comparative evaluation. *Behaviour Research and Therapy, 29,* 293–300.

Emmelkamp, P. M., Visser, S., & Hoekstra, R. J. (1988). Cognitive therapy vs exposure in vivo in the treatment of obsessive–compulsives. *Cognitive Therapy and Research, 12,* 103–114.

Foa, E. B., Franklin, M. E., & Kozak, M. J. (1998). Psychosocial treatments for obsessive–compulsive disorder. In R. P. Swinson, M. M. Antony, S. Rachman, & M. A. Richter (Eds.), *Obsessive–compulsive disorder: Theory, research and treatment* (pp. 258–276). New York: Guilford Press.

Foa, E. B., & Kozak, M. J. (1986). Emotional processing of fear: Exposure to corrective information. *Psychological Bulletin, 99,* 20–35.

Foa, E. B., & Kozak, M. J. (1996). Psychological treatment for obsessive–compulsive disorder. In M. R. Mavissakalian & R. F. Prien (Eds.), *Long-term treatments of anxiety disorders* (pp. 285–309). Washington, DC: American Psychiatric Publishing.

Foa, E. B., Liebowitz, M. R., Kozak, M. J., Davies, S., Campeas, R., Franklin, M. E., et al. (2005). Randomized, placebo-controlled trial of exposure with response prevention, clomipramine, and their combination in the treatment of obsessive–compulsive disorder. *American Journal of Psychiatry, 162,* 151–161.

Foa, E. B., & McNally, R. J. (1996). Mechanisms of change in exposure therapy. In R. M. Rapee (Ed.), *Current controversies in the anxiety disorders* (pp. 329–343). New York: Guilford Press.

Foa, E. B., Steketee, G., Grayson, J. B., & Doppelt, H. G. (1983). Treatment of obsessive–compulsives: When do we fail? In E. B. Foa & P. M. G. Emmelkamp (Eds.), *Failures in behavior therapy* (pp. 10–34). New York: Wiley.

Foa, E. B., & Tillmanns, A. (1980). The treatment of obsessive–compulsive neurosis. In A. Goldstein & E. B. Foa (Eds.), *Handbook of behavioral interventions: A clinical guide* (pp. 416–499). New York: Wiley.

Freeston, M. H., & Ladouceur, R. (1999). Exposure and response prevention for obsessional thoughts. *Cognitive and Behavioral Practice, 6,* 362–383.

Freeston, M. H., Ladouceur, R., Gagnon, F., Thibodeau, N., Rhéaume, J., Letarte, H., & Bujold, A. (1997). Cognitive–behavioral treatment of obsessive thoughts: A controlled study. *Journal of Consulting and Clinical Psychology, 65,* 405–413.

Freeston, M. H., Rhéaume, J., & Ladouceur, R. (1996). Correcting faulty appraisals of obsessional thoughts. *Behaviour Research and Therapy, 34,* 433–446.

Goodman, W. K., Price, L. H., Rasmussen, S. A., Mazure, C., Fleischmann, R. L., Hill, C. L., et al. (1989). The Yale–Brown Obsessive–Compulsive Scale: I. Development, use, and reliability. *Archives of General Psychiatry, 46,* 1006–1011.

Greenberger, D., & Padesky, C. (1995). *Mind over mood: Change how you feel by changing the way you think.* New York: Guilford Press.

Ladouceur, R., Freeston, M. H., Gagnon, F., Thibodeau, N., & Dumont, J. (1995). Cognitive behavioral treatment of obsessions. *Behavior Modification, 19,* 247–257.

Lopatka, C., & Rachman, S. (1995). Perceived responsibility and compulsive checking: An experimental analysis. *Behaviour Research and Therapy, 33,* 673–684.

McLean, P. D., Whittal, M. L., Sochting, I., Koch, W. J., Paterson, R., Thordarson, D. S., et al. (2001). Cognitive versus behavior therapy in the group treatment of obsessive–compulsive disorder. *Journal of Consulting and Clinical Psychology, 69,* 205–214.

Obsessive Compulsive Cognitions Working Group. (1997). Cognitive assessment of obsessive–compulsive disorder. *Behaviour Research and Therapy, 35,* 667–681.

Obsessive Compulsive Cognitions Working Group. (2001). Development and initial validation of the Obsessive Beliefs Questionnaire and the Interpretation of Intrusions Inventory. *Behaviour Research and Therapy, 39,* 987–1006.

O'Connor, K., Todorov, C., Robillard, S., Borgeat, F., & Brault, M. (1999). Cognitive behaviour therapy and medication in the treatment of obsessive–compulsive disorder: A controlled study. *Canadian Journal of Psychiatry, 44,* 64–71.

Padesky, C., & Greenberger, D. (1995). *Clinician's guide to mind over mood.* New York: Guilford Press.

Purdon, C., & Clark, D. A. (1993). Obsessional intrusive thoughts in nonclinical subjects: Part I. Content and relation with depressive, anxious and obsessional symptoms. *Behaviour Research and Therapy, 31*, 713–720.

Purdon, C., & Clark, D. A. (1994). Obsessional intrusive thoughts in nonclinical subjects: Part II. Cognitive appraisal, emotional response and thought control strategies. *Behaviour Research and Therapy, 32*, 403–410.

Purdon, C., & Clark, D. A. (2002). The need to control thoughts. In R. Frost & G. Steketee (Eds.), *Cognitive approaches to obsessions and compulsions: Theory, assessment and treatment* (pp. 29–43). Amsterdam: Elsevier/Pergamon.

Purdon, C., & Clark, D. A. (2005). *Overcoming obsessive thoughts.* Oakland, CA: New Harbinger.

Purdon, C., Rowa, K., & Antony, M. M. (2004, November). Treatment fears in individuals awaiting treatment of OCD. In C. Purdon & A. Pollard (Chairs), *Treatment ambivalence, readiness and resistance.* Symposium presented at the meeting of the Association for Advancement of Behavior Therapy, New Orleans, LA.

Purdon, C., Rowa, K., & Antony, M. M. (2005). Thought suppression and its effects on thought frequency, appraisal and mood state in individuals with obsessive–compulsive disorder. *Behaviour Research and Therapy, 43*, 93–108.

Rachman, S. (1976). The modification of obsessions: A new formulation. *Behaviour Research and Therapy, 14*, 437–443.

Rachman, S. (1997). A cognitive theory of obsessions. *Behaviour Research and Therapy, 35*, 793–802.

Rachman, S. (1998). A cognitive theory of obsessions: Elaborations. *Behaviour Research and Therapy, 36*, 385–401.

Rachman, S. J. (2003). *The treatment of obsessions.* Oxford, England: Oxford University Press.

Rachman, S. J., & de Silva, P. (1978). Abnormal and normal obsessions. *Behaviour Research and Therapy, 16*, 233–248.

Rachman, S. J., & Hodgson, R. J. (1980). *Obsessions and compulsions.* Englewood Cliffs, NJ: Prentice Hall.

Rhéaume, J., & Ladouceur, R. (2000). Cognitive and behavioural treatment of checking behaviour: An examination of individual and cognitive change. *Clinical Psychology and Psychotherapy, 7*, 118–127.

Rowa, K., Purdon, C., Summerfeldt, L. J., & Antony, M. M. (2005). Why are some obsessions more upsetting than others? *Behaviour Research and Therapy, 43*, 1453–1465.

Salkovskis, P. M. (1985). Obsessional–compulsive problems: A cognitive–behavioural analysis. *Behaviour Research and Therapy, 23*, 571–584.

Salkovskis, P. M. (1988). Intrusive thoughts and obsessional disorders. In D. Glasgow & N. Eisenberg (Eds.), *Current issues in clinical psychology: Vol. 4.* London: Gower.

Salkovskis, P. M. (1989). Cognitive–behavioural factors and the persistence of intrusive thoughts in obsessional problems. *Behaviour Research and Therapy, 27*, 677–682.

Salkovskis, P. M. (1996). Cognitive–behavioural approaches to the understanding of obsessive–compulsive problems. In R. M. Rapee (Ed.), *Current controversies in the anxiety disorders* (pp. 103–133). New York: Guilford Press.

Salkovskis, P. M. (1998). Psychological approaches to the understanding of obsessional problems. In R. P. Swinson, M. M. Antony, S. Rachman, & M. A. Richter (Eds.), *Obsessive–compulsive disorder: Theory, research and treatment* (pp. 33–50). New York: Guilford Press.

Salkovskis, P. M. (1999). Understanding and treating obsessive–compulsive disorder. *Behaviour Research and Therapy, 37*, S29–S52.

Salkovskis, P. M., Richards, H. C., & Forrester, E. (1995). The relationship between obsessional problems and intrusive thoughts. *Behavioural and Cognitive Psychotherapy, 23*, 281–299.

Salkovskis, P. M., & Warwick, H. M. C. (1985). Cognitive therapy of obsessive compulsive disorder: Treating treatment failures. *Behavioural Psychotherapy, 13*, 243–255.

Sookman, D., & Pinard, G. (2002). Overestimation of threat and intolerance of uncertainty in obsessive–compulsive disorder. In R. Frost & G. Steketee (Eds.), *Cognitive approaches to obsessions and compulsions: Theory, assessment and treatment* (pp. 63–89). Amsterdam: Elsevier/Pergamon.

Stanley, M. A., & Turner, S. M. (1995). Current status of pharmacological and behavioral treatment of obsessive–compulsive disorder. *Behavior Therapy, 26*, 163–186.

Steketee, G. (1999). *Overcoming obsessive–compulsive disorder: A behavioral and cognitive protocol for the treatment of OCD*. Oakland, CA: New Harbinger.

Steketee, G., Frost, R. O., & Cohen, I. (1998). Beliefs in obsessive–compulsive disorder. *Journal of Anxiety Disorders, 12*, 525–537.

Taylor, S., Kyrios, M., Thordarson, D. S., Steketee, G., & Frost, R. O. (2002). Development and validation of an instrument for measuring intrusions and beliefs in obsessive compulsive disorder. In R. Frost & G. Steketee (Eds.), *Cognitive approaches to obsessions and compulsions: Theory, assessment and treatment* (pp. 118–138). Amsterdam: Elsevier/Pergamon.

Thordarson, D. S., & Shafran, R. (2002). Importance of thoughts. In R. Frost & G. Steketee (Eds.), *Cognitive approaches to obsessions and compulsions: Theory, assessment and treatment* (pp. 15–28). Amsterdam: Elsevier/Pergamon.

van Balkom, A. J. L., de Haan, E., van Oppen, P., Spinhoven, P., Hoogduin, K., & Dyke, R. (1998). Cognitive and behavioral therapies alone versus in combination with fluvoxamine in the treatment of obsessive compulsive disorder. *Journal of Nervous and Mental Disease, 186*, 492–499.

van Oppen, P., & Arntz, A. (1994). Cognitive therapy for obsessive–compulsive disorder. *Behaviour Research and Therapy, 32*, 79–87.

van Oppen, P., de Haan, E., van Balkom, A. J. L. M., Spinhoven, P., Hoogduin, K., & van Dyck, R. (1995). Cognitive therapy and exposure in vivo in the treatment of obsessive compulsive disorder. *Behaviour Research and Therapy, 4*, 379–390.

Vogel, P., Stiles, T. C., & Götestam, K. G. (2004). Adding cognitive therapy elements to exposure therapy for obsessive compulsive disorder: A controlled study. *Behavioural and Cognitive Psychotherapy, 32*, 275–290.

Warren, R., & Thomas, J. C. (2001). Cognitive–behavior therapy of obsessive compulsive disorder in private practice: An effectiveness study. *Journal of Anxiety Disorders, 15*, 277–285.

II

STRATEGIES FOR SPECIFIC OBSESSIVE–COMPULSIVE DISORDER PRESENTATIONS

6

TREATING CONTAMINATION CONCERNS AND COMPULSIVE WASHING

DAVID S. RIGGS AND EDNA B. FOA

The *Diagnostic and Statistical Manual of Mental Disorders, Fourth Edition* (American Psychiatric Association, 1994) does not formally distinguish among subtypes of obsessive–compulsive disorder (OCD), with the exception of identifying clients with poor insight. However, several classification schemes categorize people with OCD according to the topography of the ritualistic activity (i.e., compulsions). Because many individuals with OCD manifest multiple obsessions and compulsions (e.g., washing, checking, and repeating), it is common to classify individuals by their most prominent type of symptoms. In this chapter, we focus on clients who manifest significant symptoms of washing or cleaning rituals.

Ritualistic washing, the most common compulsion, is typically performed to decrease discomfort associated with obsessional fears about germs or diseases. For example, individuals who fear contact with "AIDS germs" clean themselves excessively to prevent either contracting AIDS or spreading it to others. In addition to washing themselves excessively, some washers clean their environment to excess. Ritualistic washing may involve multiple repetitions, radical cleansers (e.g., bleach, alcohol), or ritualized patterns of washing.

We illustrate the application of exposure and response prevention (ERP; also known as exposure and ritual prevention) to issues that arise when treating compulsive washing. Using a composite case example, we discuss the importance of careful assessment in identifying obsessional fears, compulsive rituals, and the functional relationship between them to develop an effective treatment plan. We also discuss potential difficulties that might arise at various stages of the treatment.

CASE COMPOSITE

Carol, a 31-year-old, married woman with a 4-year-old son, presented with severe washing rituals. Carol represents a composite of different cases, allowing us to protect the confidentiality of specific clients and to illustrate a greater variety of clinical issues than would ordinarily arise in a single case.

History

Carol reported that she first developed obsessions and compulsions in high school. At that time, her obsessions focused on potential dangers to herself and her immediate family. Most of her rituals involved repeating "good" thoughts or brief prayers to protect her family. In college, Carol became preoccupied with the potential of contracting a serious illness and began washing and cleaning compulsively. Despite the academic and social difficulties that her OCD caused, Carol was able to complete college and meet her future husband. To a great extent, she concealed her rituals from her husband-to-be by washing only when she was alone and avoiding contact with potential contaminants whenever possible. She also found that portable washing tools (e.g., wiping a contaminated hand on a premoistened paper towel) could substitute for a full wash as long as she knew that she could complete a full wash before the end of the day. This meant that she was often up late to completely and repeatedly scour her body when she returned home after a date.

Carol's symptoms declined somewhat after she was married and were manageable until her son was born about 4 years later. While Carol was pregnant, her symptoms increased substantially, and she was no longer able to hide them from her husband. In fact, he was co-opted into some rituals by joining his wife in washing and rewashing surfaces in their home and agreeing to disrobe in the laundry room before entering the main house from outside. After her son was born, Carol became obsessed that he would contract an illness, and her fears also generalized to concerns about her husband. Her washing became more extensive, particularly when caring for her son. Because of this, Carol's mother took on a substantial role in the care of her grandson. About 2 years before she presented at our clinic, Carol was placed on serotonin reuptake inhibitor (SRI) medication. She had tried several alternative medications with little or no relief from her OCD. Her doctor recommended that she try an antipsychotic medication to augment the SRI, but she was concerned about doing so because she wanted to have another child, and she would need to stop whatever medication she was taking at the time. Therefore, she wished to try a psychological approach to therapy so that she might avoid taking the medication.

Presentation

When she presented for treatment, Carol continued to fear that she or a member of her family would contract a fatal illness. Much of her fear focused on AIDS, but at times she would obsess about other illnesses, including pneumonia, cancer, and influenza. She spent about 120 minutes each day showering. Typically, she would shower once in the morning, again when she returned home from any activity outside (e.g., shopping, visiting family, taking her son to the doctor), and a third time before going to bed. Also, she washed her hands 30 to 40 times throughout the day. Carol also washed surfaces in her home that might have come into contact with people or objects that had been outside. Thus, after returning from the supermarket, Carol would wash all of the surfaces in the kitchen. Carol's husband continued to change clothes in the laundry room, and her mother put on a housecoat any time she came to watch her grandson (as she did most days). Carol also required her mother to wash her hands before touching the child.

In addition to her washing and cleaning rituals, Carol had an extensive list of places, objects, and situations that she avoided so as to reduce her potential exposure to germs. She planned her days so that she had to leave the house only once each day. She would try to avoid any contact between her skin and anything that had not been cleaned. To this end, she wore gloves whenever possible without drawing attention to herself. To prevent contact with contaminants, she pulled her sleeve over her hand, used plastic bags or tissues to pick things up, and waited for someone else to open a door. She limited physical contact with people, refusing to shake hands or sit next to anyone other than family members. To limit the spread of contamination, she rarely held, hugged, or kissed her son unless she had first washed ritualistically.

In addition to OCD, Carol was moderately depressed and anxious in social situations. The social anxiety likely arose from her OCD and was largely related to becoming contaminated or appearing strange as she engaged in rituals. She and her husband reported that her symptoms were contributing to marital difficulties. Carol was motivated to be rid of her symptoms, although somewhat reluctant to engage in treatment given the nature of the therapy.

TREATMENT USING EXPOSURE AND RESPONSE PREVENTION

On the basis of information collected in the initial evaluation, the therapist begins to develop an idea of how treatment will proceed and what potential stumbling blocks may turn up along the way. These impressions can be used to ease the client into treatment and to provide an initial framework for the treatment plan that will be developed in collaboration with the client.

Exposure and response prevention has proved to be a highly effective treatment for OCD (for a review, see Franklin & Foa, 2002) and is considered the psychosocial treatment of choice (March, Frances, Kahn, & Carpenter, 1997). It is thought that repeated exposure to feared stimuli and voluntary abstinence from rituals promotes habituation to feared thoughts and situations and disconfirms mistaken beliefs about risk and responsibility (Foa & Kozak, 1986). One study found that the combination of exposure and response prevention is superior to either component alone (Foa, Steketee, Grayson, Turner, & Latimer, 1984). Clinically, we make use of these findings when discussing the rationale for treatment with clients before they commit to a course of ERP, and sometimes we use dramatic and colorful graphs of the data Foa et al. (1984) provided to drive home this critical point for clients and families alike.

Most contemporary ERP programs include in vivo exposure, in which clients confront the feared object or situation directly, and some programs also include imaginal exposure, in which clients imagine feared consequences. Typically, exposure exercises are conducted in a graduated fashion, with moderately distressing situations confronted before more upsetting ones. In the case of a washer afraid of contamination, exposure to the floor of the therapist's office would typically precede exposure to a public restroom. The therapist and client plan the order of exposures before treatment is initiated on the basis of the client's predicted distress level, as we will illustrate later in this chapter. It is important to note that the specified order of exposures is not set in stone and may change as treatment progresses.

Despite the name of this treatment, therapists do not actually prevent clients from engaging in rituals. Instead, therapists provide a clear rationale and instructions for response prevention, encourage clients to refrain from rituals on their own, and reinforce successful abstinence. During treatment of washing rituals, the therapist does not intercede to stop a clients from turning on the water or washing their hands, but encourages them to refrain from ritualistic washing and reminds them of why it is crucial to do so. Clients are asked to record violations of abstinence between sessions so that the therapist can develop strategies to help them refrain from future rituals.

There are variations in the manner in which ERP treatments are administered. For example, many ERP programs include daily sessions (e.g., Foa et al., 2005; Franklin, Abramowitz, Kozak, Levitt, & Foa, 2000), but studies have found that programs that hold sessions twice or once weekly are also effective (e.g., Abramowitz, Foa, & Franklin, 2003; Warren & Thomas, 2001). Without a large randomized study to base their decisions on, therapists must rely on clinical impressions when deciding how frequently to hold sessions for a given client. Generally, we find that less frequent sessions may suffice for clients with mild to moderate OCD symptoms. Clients with severe symptoms or those who have difficulty complying with treatment instructions are likely to benefit from more frequent sessions. In Carol's case, her reluctance to restrict her washing, as well as the severity of her OCD symptoms, suggested that an intensive treatment regimen should be tried.

Clients who began treatment by confronting the most distressing situations have achieved gains similar to those made by clients who worked up from less distressing situations (Hodgson, Rachman, & Marks, 1972). However, clients seem to prefer a gradual approach. Because it is important to maximize compliance and motivation, we usually begin treatment with exposure to moderately difficult situations and complete several intermediate steps leading up to the most distressing exposures. We structure this using a hierarchy developed collaboratively with the client.

One issue that arises in ERP treatment planning is whether to include imaginal exposure or only in vivo exposure. Studies of the question are inconclusive, with some showing a positive effect of including imaginal exposure (Foa, Steketee, Turner, & Fischer, 1980; Steketee, Foa, & Grayson, 1982) and others not (de Araujo, Ito, Marks, & Deale, 1995). Clinically, we find imaginal exposure to be very useful for clients whose obsessional fears include disastrous consequences (e.g., killing one's child) or whose fears are not readily translated into in vivo exposure exercises (e.g., physical contact with a dead relative). In Carol's case, her fear focused on the possibility of contracting a disease. Because this outcome may occur as much as several years after exposure to the infecting agent, it was impossible to disconfirm her fear with time-limited in vivo exposure exercises. Therefore, it was important to include exercises involving imaginal exposure to being ill.

The client must refrain from ritualizing while engaging in programmatic exposure exercises (Foa et al., 1984). Therapists can assist clients by providing support, encouragement, and suggestions about how to refrain from rituals in particular situations. Self-monitoring may also serve to promote abstinence by increasing client awareness and providing an alternative activity when urges to ritualize are high. In our experience, ERP treatment without an effort to eliminate all rituals results in poor outcome. Retaining some rituals appears to negate many of the positive effects of exposure. In essence, holding on to the rituals enables clients to maintain the belief that the feared situations are dangerous. When agreeing to provide treatment in which total response prevention is not initiated at the outset, the therapist must be clear that the ultimate goal is to eliminate all rituals.

APPLICATION OF EXPOSURE AND RESPONSE PREVENTION TO CAROL'S CONTAMINATION FEARS AND WASHING RITUALS

At its core, ERP aims to encourage the client to confront his or her greatest fear and refrain from behaviors (rituals) that provide a sense of safety. Given the intensity of the fear, this may be the emotional equivalent of asking the client to face an armed attacker without fighting back and with only the therapist's assurance that the client will not be harmed. For example, Carol was asked to risk the possibility that she or someone she loved would contract a deadly disease. Although the therapist realized that the risk of using a public restroom is small, to Carol it was difficult to distinguish this level of risk from that involved in sharing a needle with a person with AIDS. To facilitate ERP, the therapist must work to help clients develop a sense of trust in the therapist, the therapy, and themselves so that they will be able to take the risks involved in the treatment. One way to promote this trust is to communicate clearly to the client the expectations, goals, and rationale for the treatment. The therapist can also use a variety of techniques to encourage, reinforce, and support clients as they engage in treatment.

Initial Meetings

In our center's standard ERP protocol, the first 4 hours of treatment are used to gather information about the client's symptoms and, with the client, to develop a treatment plan. These sessions also provide the foundation for the therapeutic relationship. One important mechanism for facilitating this relationship is for the therapist and client to develop a sense that they are a team working together to treat the symptoms—in essence, this is a shared battle against the OCD. In Carol's case, it was important to identify areas in which the OCD symptoms were creating problems. Her OCD symptoms made child rearing difficult, and she also feared that her symptoms might become worse when her second child was born, as they had when her first was born. Building on this information, the therapist pointed out how Carol's symptoms had already affected her husband and son. By sharing the goal of getting rid of her symptoms so that she could improve her family's lives, the therapist and Carol were able to sidestep potential conflicts over the completion of difficult exercises.

During these initial sessions, we also introduce our model of OCD and the rationale for ERP treatment. This process begins even before the first treatment session. We typically describe the basic treatment protocol to clients when they are evaluated at our clinic. Also, when the initial treatment session is scheduled, we tell clients what to expect. Specifically, we tell them that the first session will be used to get to know one another and to develop a treatment plan. This provides clients with clear expectations and may reduce anticipatory anxiety.

We also educate clients about the OCD symptoms and the relationship between the symptoms and the treatment plan. We usually spend a portion of the first hour describing the model and carefully defining the terms we use during treatment. For example, ERP treatment is based on the idea that there is a functional relationship between obsessions (which increase anxiety) and compulsive rituals (which decrease anxiety). However, many of our clients are unaware of these relationships. A therapist might begin as follows:

> We've talked about your compulsive washing and cleaning and some of the fears that drive your need to clean. It seems pretty clear that you find the need to wash so often and the fears themselves unpleasant and that they interfere with other things you want to do. The treatment program we are going to begin is designed to help you get rid of the need to wash and the fears that the compulsions help reduce. Before we start, I need to understand as much as I can about your symptoms, and you and I need to agree about how we are going to treat them. So in this and the next session, I am going to ask you to help me understand your struggle. First, though, I want to talk a little bit about how we understand OCD and make sure that you and I are on the same page as we talk about your symptoms.
>
> We think about obsessions and compulsions as two sides of a coin. *Obsessions* are thoughts or images that come to your mind, even though you don't want them. Most of your obsessions involve your fear of contracting or spreading an awful disease. When these thoughts come to your mind, you get very upset, and just like anyone else who feels bad, you want to do something to make the bad feeling go away. The things that you have found to reduce the fear and distress, at least for a short time, are what we call *compulsions* or *rituals*. For example, you wash yourself or something that you feel has become contaminated. Unfortunately, as you know, the relief you get from the rituals doesn't last, and soon you are just as upset as if you hadn't washed at all. You get caught going around and around this circle, with obsessions driving up your anxiety and compulsions giving you a brief sense of relief that is soon replaced by more fear. The treatment we are about to begin is designed to break this cycle and get you some longer-lasting relief.

The collaborative approach influences all interactions with the client. From the perspective of the therapist, potential obstacles to forming the alliance typically result from neglecting the skills of good therapy, such as active listening, reflection, and empathy. It is vitally important to use these skills when talking with clients about their symptoms and distress and about the treatment plan. Unfortunately, the structure of ERP and the fact that it is manualized can lead clinicians to neglect these basic skills in favor of the treatment techniques. In training and supervision, we often remind clinicians to be good therapists first and good users of manualized treatments second. This is not to say that we drift far from the ERP techniques; rather, we find that the techniques work much better in the context of a strong therapeutic alliance.

We worked to ensure that Carol understood the rationale for ERP. The program would require Carol to abandon her washing and temporarily experience substantial discomfort. If she did not understand how this would help her in the long run, she would be unlikely to comply with treatment. Making a strong link between the model of OCD and the therapeutic techniques in the introduction to the therapy also would allow the therapist to return to this rationale in later sessions should Carol resist certain exercises. We presented the treatment rationale to Carol as follows:

> The treatment we use is called *exposure and response prevention. Exposure* refers to having you confront situations that increase your obsessions, such as touching something contaminated. *Response prevention* means that we will ask you not to use rituals, such as washing, to manage your anxiety. The treatment aims to break two associations that people with OCD often have. The first is the association between certain objects, situations, or thoughts and your feelings of anxiety, like when you bring something into the house from outside and begin to fear that you might also be bringing in germs. These are the connections that set off your obsessions. The second association we want to break is the one between your rituals, like washing your hands, and relief from anxiety. The problem with these connections is that you feel better only for a short time, and then you feel contaminated and anxious again. The exposure and response prevention will help break these automatic connections. It is important to note that when you confront situations that trigger your obsessions and you don't ritualize, you will find that your feared catastrophes do not happen.

Information Gathering

Information gathering is one of the critical aspects of ERP. Without a detailed knowledge of a client's symptoms and the functional relations between his or her obsessions and compulsions, the therapist and client cannot develop an effective treatment plan. Information gathering does not stop when treatment begins; the therapist should continue to collect information about obsessions, rituals, and the links between them throughout treatment and update or revise the treatment plan as appropriate. Carol's therapist began this process with the following statement:

> Carol, I need to understand, as completely as I can, what your experience of OCD is like. The more you can teach me about what you struggle with, the better we'll be able to develop a plan to help you. Ultimately, what I need to get is a list of situations that distress you or cause you to obsess and a list of the rituals you use to reduce or manage the distress that comes from your obsessions. Why don't you begin by telling me about some situations that can lead to obsessions or anxiety?

In addition to obsessions and rituals, we ask clients to identify situations that would raise obsessive concerns were they not avoided (e.g., using a public restroom). Sometimes clients discount these situations because they do not presently cause problems. It is important for the therapist to ask whether obsessions would arise should the client be in this situation in the future. Unless we are absolutely sure that the situation will not lead to obsessions, we include it the treatment plan.

The primary problems that arise during information gathering involve the therapist's failure to obtain all the information necessary to develop a complete treatment plan. The therapist might fail to ask detailed questions, but some clients are also reticent about describing symptoms because they find them embarrassing or too frightening. We have developed several approaches to help therapists ask all necessary questions. First, in training and supervision, we emphasize the need to obtain detailed information about symptoms. Second, we provide therapists with a session outline that instructs them to elicit lists of stimuli that cue obsessions and compulsions as well as avoided situations. Third, we provide specific prompt questions designed to obtain detailed information. For example, the therapist can ask the client to describe his or her experience of obsessions and compulsions on a typical day. As the client describes this day, the therapist can intersperse questions to get additional detail. The information obtained through the description of a day helps identify situations that lead to obsessions and ways rituals are used to counter the obsessions.

Again, the therapist needs to ask detailed questions to ensure a full understanding of the obsessions and rituals. The therapist must become comfortable with asking clients about all their activities, including many that clients would not typically discuss even with a therapist, at least in the first or second session of therapy. In treating Carol, for example, the therapist needed to discuss issues such as grooming, toileting, eating, dressing, sex, and sleeping. Even aspects of the client's life that seem relatively benign, such as opening doors, using the telephone, and shopping, must be explored in detail to identify aspects that lead to obsessions, rituals, or situations that the client simply avoids altogether.

Sometimes clients fail to fully describe their OCD symptoms even when the therapist asks the right questions. We find three main reasons for this. First, some clients overlook symptoms because they have become almost automatic or because the symptoms have been a part of their lives for so long that they seem normal. Also, some symptoms reflect extensions of culturally accepted practices and may not be identified as symptoms. Thus, Carol may recognize that her hand washing is excessive, but she may insist that it is normal to wash after using the toilet and that this should not count as a compulsion, regardless of the fact that it reduces her anxiety. Similarly, instructions to medical professionals to wash sufficiently to reduce the risk of infection and cleansing rituals that are part of religious practices can be seen as normal, although they also reduce obsessions.

Second, some clients find the content of their obsessions or the specifics of their rituals embarrassing. Again, therapists using ERP must remember to use good therapeutic skills to encourage clients to share necessary information. It also may be helpful to normalize these feelings. As the therapist becomes more familiar with the presentation of OCD, he or she may find it useful to offer educated hypotheses about the client's fears. Sharing hypotheses allows the client to confirm or deny the content of the fears, rather than having to express them completely. If the therapist is accurate, it offers a normalizing experience for the client (i.e., "I am not the only person who feels this way"), and the therapist can gain credibility.

Given Carol's fears, it seemed likely that she had concerns about sexual activity with her husband. However, when initially asked about situations that elicited obsessions, she did not mention sexual activity. When the therapist returned to the topic and mentioned that many people with contamination concerns had some anxiety about sexual contact, she acknowledged that sexual activity with her husband was quite limited in frequency and also rigid in terms of the activities in which they engaged. On further questioning, she revealed that the couple engaged in sexual activity about once a month and that it involved only intercourse, with little touching before or after. When asked if she had to prepare before or after intercourse, she acknowledged that both she and her husband had to have washed immediately before intercourse and that she would wash again afterward. She also told the therapist that she would not touch her own or her husband's genitals with her bare hands, which limited their activities a great deal.

A third reason that clients may resist discussing symptoms is because talking about them increases their anxiety either because attention is focused on the obsession or because they believe that verbalizing the fear makes it more likely that the consequence will occur (e.g., "If I say that I fear my son will get sick and die, then it will happen"). Again, clinical skills and offering hypothesized fears can help. Another strategy is to give the client permission to complete a ritual to "undo" the obsession once the discussion is completed. Also, discussing less severe fears may make it easier for clients to describe their worst fears (much as gradual exposure serves to encourage confronting the hardest items). Therefore, we often skip areas that the client is having a difficult time talking about and return later in the discussion.

Treatment Planning

In the treatment planning stage of ERP, the therapist and client collaborate to develop a hierarchy of situations and stimuli that cue obsessions and a list of rituals to be eliminated. To develop the hierarchy, the client rates the degree of fear or distress caused by the situations identified during information gathering. We have the client rate each situation on a subjective units of distress scale (SUDS) ranging from 0 (no distress) to 100 (the worst fear I could imagine). On the basis of these ratings, we develop the hierarchy and a plan for confronting each situation as part of treatment. Carol's hierarchy of feared situations is presented in Exhibit 6.1.

The most common problems during the development of an exposure hierarchy reflect the interaction between the task demands (i.e., generating a complete and accurate hierarchy) and the client's obsessive nature. Clients may find it difficult to rate each situation because they feel the need to provide precise and accurate answers. The goal is to develop a working hierarchy with five to six steps from the first item to be used in treatment to the top of the hierarchy, not to get the "right" answer. We typically target the first exposure exercise to an item rated about 50% of the most difficult item and move up in steps of about 10 SUDS rating points. Thus, a distinction of a few SUDS points is rarely important for clinical purposes. The therapist can also remind the client that the ratings need not be perfectly accurate and that they may be adjusted later if necessary. Also, it can be helpful to encourage clients to "round off" the rating to the nearest 5 or 10 SUDS points.

Clients may present with multiple obsessive themes (e.g., contamination by germs and eternal punishment for blasphemy). Practically, the structure of ERP encourages a single hierarchy. However, therapists may find it useful for organizational purposes to have the client rate items on multiple lists first and then combine the lists into a single hierarchy.

The biggest problem that might arise during treatment planning is the client's rejection of some aspect of the plan. Typically, this occurs when the client does not agree to confront one or more situations on the hierarchy, usually the hardest ones. Thus, Carol might agree to expose herself to most items on her hierarchy (Exhibit 6.1), but she might absolutely rule out shaking hands with a homeless person or touching blood. Our clinical experience, as well as the limited data available, suggests that addressing all the symptoms results in more persistent gains. Therefore, we hesitate to eliminate objects from the treatment plan. Instead, we educate the client as to why it is important to include the contentious exposures in treatment, using three lines of reasoning:

1. We reiterate the rationale for ERP.
2. We inform the client that data and our experience indicate that it is important to address all the obsessive concerns as completely as possible and that ruling out some exposure exercises is likely to lead to the problems returning later.

EXHIBIT 6.1
Hierarchy of Exposure Items for Carol

Situation	SUDS rating[a]	Planned for session number
Touch blood.[b]	100	6
Shake hands with a homeless person.	100	6
Touch trash in a dumpster.	100	6
Use a public restroom.	98	6
Go to the AIDS library (i.e., to be around people likely to be HIV positive).	95	6 hw[c]
Touch surfaces (not toilet) in a public restroom.	90	5
Bring a piece of trash from the street into the house.	90	5 hw
Use food from a dented can (or other "contaminated" packaging).	90	5 hw
Eat food from a street vendor.	88	5
Eat food from a takeout restaurant.	85	4 hw
Use the toilet at home or in the clinic.	85	4
Eat at a restaurant.	80	4
Touch the street or sidewalk.	80	3
Touch the bottom of her shoes.	80	3
Let her husband enter the house without changing clothes.	70	3 hw
Bring groceries into the house.	70	3 hw
Pick up son without washing her hands.	68	3 hw
Touch surfaces outside.	65	2
Go into a hospital.	60	2
Eat a picnic.	60	3 hw
Touch surfaces in the bathroom at home.	55	2 hw
Touch the floor of the office waiting room.	55	1
Sitting on the floor in the therapist's office.	50	1
Touch the floor at home.	40	1 hw
Touch something her husband has used at the office.	40	1 hw
Sit on the grass.	30	1 hw
Touch the front door at home.	25	1 hw

Note. SUDS = Subjective Units of Distress Scale. [a]All SUDS ratings are made assuming that no cleaning or washing will be done after exposure. [b]We keep on hand a supply of animal blood from a scientific supply house for use in blood exposures. At the time of the initial exposure, we inform the client of the nature of this blood, but additional requests for information are typically interpreted as reassurance seeking and are dealt with appropriately. [c]Items designated hw are planned as homework assignments.

3. We discuss the concept of overcorrection. That is, because the client's tendency is to be overly cautious, we need to push far in the other direction during treatment to overcome this tendency (this may be particularly useful when the client relies on the argument that "normal people wouldn't do that" in objecting to a particular exposure).

This discussion is not designed to take control away from the client, but rather to explain why every exposure exercise is important. The therapist's aim is to have clients agree to participate fully in the treatment, not to force them into it. If these efforts fail, the therapist is faced with a difficult decision: to proceed with treatment while eliminating some proposed exercises or to suggest that the client try an alternative treatment for OCD (or delay ERP until he or she is ready to engage in all of the exercises). At this point, we tend toward initiating treatment even when the client resists some exposures. However, we strongly encourage therapists to form an agreement with the client to revisit the issue later in treatment. The therapist should also explore alternative exposure exercises that approximate the ones that the client resists. Finally, the therapist must ensure that the client understands that by limiting the exposures to be done, he or she may be limiting the effectiveness of the treatment.

In Vivo Exposure

The basic intervention in ERP is the in vivo exposure exercise, during which clients confront situations that raise obsessive fears. Theoretically, the exercises serve to activate the client's cognitive fear structure and allow new information (e.g., "Nothing bad happened when I used the public toilet") to be integrated into the system. Ideally, the exercises last a sufficient length of time (30–45 minutes) to allow the client's anxiety to decrease and are done repeatedly.

Obviously, the first challenge for the client is to actually engage in the exposure. The therapist should remember how difficult these exercises are for clients and empathize with their struggle. Several approaches can help clients engage in the exercises and are appropriate for most clients. First, therapists can remind the client of the rationale for exposure, with emphasis on the expected long-term gains. Second, therapists should provide clients with concrete instructions so that the expectations for the exercise are clear. Third, the therapist should be willing to model the exposure. If the client is still unable to complete the exposure, the therapist and client may develop a series of small exercises (essentially a brief hierarchy to be completed in the session) that end with the exposure originally planned for that day. It is also important that the therapist reinforce the client's attempts to complete exposure exercises.

Carol and her therapist elected to begin the exposure exercises by sitting on the floor of the therapist's office, an item Carol gave a SUDS rating of 50. Initially she refused to participate in the exercise, stating that she felt that it would be too dangerous to do without washing afterwards, particularly because she would have to get into her car, which would then become contaminated. The therapist empathized with Carol's fears and calmly reminded her of the treatment plan and how confronting these situations would help her in the long run. Carol acknowledged that she knew that she "had to do this" but wondered if the exposure could begin with something a little easier. The therapist asked Carol what she would be willing to try and suggested touching the floor of the office with her fingers as an initial step. At the same time, the therapist demonstrated this by bending down and touching the floor. Carol hesitantly agreed and reached down to touch the floor briefly before quickly raising her hand. Once she had touched the floor, it was apparent that she was keeping the hand from touching anything else, indicating that she was anxious that she might spread the contamination.

The therapist verbally reinforced and encouraged her for taking the first step, suggested that she could touch the floor and leave her hand there for a while rather than immediately lifting it, and again demonstrated the task. Carol complied, and again the therapist reinforced her effort. The therapist continued to model additional exposures (e.g., touching clothes, arms, and face with "contaminated" hands) and reinforced Carol when she was able to complete each task. Throughout the exercise, the therapist asked Carol to provide current SUDS ratings to assess her arousal level. The initial goal had a rating of 50, and the therapist worked to maintain Carol's arousal at this level by increasing the level of exposure. Finally, the therapist suggested that they try to complete the original exercise, and he invited Carol to sit on the floor with him. Both Carol and the therapist sat on the floor, where they continued the exposure until she had successfully habituated to the situation. Given Carol's concern about contaminating her car, the therapist extended the exercise to include accompanying Carol to the parking lot, where she touched as many surfaces in the car as possible.

Another problem that might interfere with effective in vivo exercises is the failure of the exercise to elicit anxiety. Three possible reasons may lead to this failure. First, the situation that is the focus of the exposure may not actually activate the client's obsessive fears. It is possible that the client inaccurately rated the item or that previous exposures successfully addressed the same concerns as this exercise. Second, the exercise may be designed poorly such that it does not elicit the desired response. For example, some clients with contamination fears isolate parts of their environment to keep them "safe." If Carol's fear of contamination focused only on whether she would spread the contamination to a previously safe area like her car, then exposure to the floor might not elicit any anxiety until she had to enter the car. If the therapist conducted only the initial exposure to the floor, it might not elicit anxiety. Finally, it is possible that the fear is not elicited because the client is engaging in rituals that function to control the anxiety. In Carol's case, holding her hand away from her body after touching the floor effectively reduced her anxiety by preventing the perceived spread of contamination. It is possible for clients to develop substitute rituals; for example, a client with washing rituals might rub her hands on her clothes to remove contaminants. In one case, a client first substituted hand rubbing for his washing, and when the therapist advised him to stop rubbing his hands together, he substituted a subtle rubbing of his fingers. The therapist must be alert to such substitutions, because even if they are more subtle than the original, they function in the same manner and will interfere with treatment.

When an exercise does not elicit distress, the therapist must determine why. Typically, we first explore whether we missed an important variable or whether the exposure was poorly designed. We usually do this through a dialogue with the client in which we discuss ways to make the exercise more anxiety evoking. Once we have a plan, we adjust the exercise.

If the exposure exercise includes the vital elements, the therapist must determine if the client is engaging in rituals (or other behaviors) to limit arousal. The therapist must remember to make this inquiry as nonthreatening and noncritical as possible. The therapist should provide concrete instructions for refraining from the identified behavior as well as any other behaviors that reduce anxiety during exposure. It can also be useful to remind the client of the rationale for treatment and of the goal of the exercise—to experience anxiety and learn from it.

If the exercise incorporates the client's anxiety cues and the client uses no rituals, then the therapist can conclude that the situation no longer elicits anxiety (or perhaps never did). Generally, we ask the client to complete similar exposures in other settings (e.g., at home, in the office, with children) to ensure that the absence of anxiety is not specific to one setting. If the client does not experience anxiety in other settings, then the item may be removed from the hierarchy (although the therapist may try a similar exposure in a later session to be sure that the anxiety has been addressed).

Imaginal Exposure

We typically include imaginal exposure exercises in our OCD treatment, but it is most important to incorporate them when aspects of the client's fear cannot be activated through in vivo exercises. In Carol's case, for example, her fear of contracting a deadly illness or passing it to her son could not be incorporated into in vivo exercises. Another reason to incorporate imaginal exposures into treatment is to use them as initial steps toward eventual in vivo exposure. For example, the therapist might have Carol imagine touching surfaces in a public restroom during the session before the one in which they complete the in vivo exposure to a restroom to allow Carol to habituate to the idea of touching a toilet before actually doing it.

Potential problems during imaginal exposure exercises are similar to those during in vivo exercises. Clients may refuse to engage in the exercise, or the exercise may fail to elicit anxiety. Also, some clients find it difficult to generate an image of their feared consequence. This may reflect a difficulty using their imagination, but often it means that the therapist has misidentified some aspect of the fear. As with in vivo exposures, the therapist must work with the client to identify what needs to be changed, omitted, or added so that the imagery elicits anxiety.

If the client reports that the imagery is accurate, then a failure to elicit the anxiety suggests that the client is ritualizing to reduce arousal. Again, the therapist must carefully ask the client if he or she is doing, saying, or thinking anything that might function as a ritual. Some likely candidates include self-reassurance, in which clients repeatedly assure themselves that the consequences will not actually happen; silent prayers; distraction; and discounting the practice as "simply an exercise." If the client is using rituals, the therapist must remind the client that the rituals defeat the purpose of the exercise, and the two should work to develop a strategy that will allow the client to experience anxiety during the exposure.

Response Prevention

Compliance with response prevention is often more difficult than compliance with exposure exercises. Exposures are typically planned, time-limited exercises that are completed first with the therapist as an observer and coach and then as part of specific homework assignments. In contrast, response prevention requires the client to change his or her behavior in many aspects of life with only limited supervision. At the most basic level, the response prevention intervention requires the client to resist all urges to engage in compulsions or rituals, regardless of the situation. Ideally, the client stops all rituals beginning with the initial day of treatment. However, there will undoubtedly be occasions when clients resort to rituals to manage their anxiety. We have developed several approaches to maximize response prevention and address problems that arise when rituals do occur.

Carol's rituals focused on washing herself and her environment to prevent contamination with germs introduced from outside. She had designated specific areas (e.g., her home, her car) that were kept "clean." Even within these areas, there were gradients of contamination, so that when she moved from one area to another (e.g., from her bathroom to her bedroom), she had to be sure that germs did not accompany her by performing brief rituals to clean herself. Before initiating response prevention, the therapist identified as many of her rituals as possible. For example, although she washed compulsively after using the toilet, Carol also performed a short ritual of wiping her hands and feet as she left the bathroom. The therapist must convey the importance of stopping all rituals, not only the ones that create the largest disruptions in the client's life.

Several aspects of ERP are designed, wholly or in part, to provide the foundation for response prevention. For example, when first describing treatment, we voice the expectation that clients will be able to inhibit most rituals once treatment begins. Second, we have clients monitor their rituals during treatment planning. This heightens attention to the rituals, and in some cases clients report that the monitoring alone seems to decrease their frequency and duration. Self-monitoring continues throughout treatment, although we tell clients that we expect few rituals to be reported after response prevention is initiated. Third, during information gathering, the therapist identifies links between specific obsessional cues and compulsive rituals. This information can be used to ease the task of preventing rituals by eliminating exposure to some obsessional cues early in treatment. For example, were Carol to enter a public restroom, her urges to wash would become so strong that it would be extremely difficult for her resist them. Therefore, it is better to limit her contact with public restrooms early in treatment rather than to allow the ritual washing to occur. Typically, when faced with the choice between avoiding an obsessional cue and confronting that cue followed by using a ritual, we prefer that the client avoid the cue temporarily. However, the treatment plan must incorporate planned exposures to the obsessional cues when appropriate given the SUDS ratings. Thus, we might encourage Carol to avoid public restrooms at the beginning of treatment, but once we have completed an exposure exercise in a public restroom (at about Session 5 or 6), we would ask her to stop avoiding them while continuing to resist her rituals.

The most common problem during response prevention is that clients "slip" and give in to the urge to ritualize. In fact, slips are so common that we predict that they will occur when we give the initial response prevention instructions. We often point out that we do not expect clients to be perfect at their attempts to resist rituals. When clients report that they have ritualized, the therapist can work with them to develop strategies to better resist the urges in the future. The therapist can reiterate the basic instructions and rationale but must be careful not to be punitive. It is important for the therapist to remember how difficult this task is for the client and to reinforce clients' attempts to resist their urges to ritualize.

A second problem arises when a client refuses to refrain from rituals. If the refusal is general (i.e., the client refuses to give up any rituals or agrees to give up only a few), then ERP is probably not an appropriate treatment approach. Such clients should be referred for an alternative form of treatment. It is more likely that clients will agree to eliminate most compulsions but will want to retain one or two "really important" ones. This problem parallels that of clients who do not agree to complete all of the planned exposure exercises, and the therapist is faced with a similar decision. Should the therapist insist that the client resist all rituals or agree that some rituals may be retained during the early part of treatment and addressed later?

In our experience, we have found that initiating ERP treatment without eliminating all rituals is difficult. Retaining some rituals negates many benefits of exposure exercises and prevents clients from experiencing complete fear reduction. By continuing to ritualize, clients never challenge the belief that the feared situations and thoughts are dangerous and that only the rituals protect them. We treat clients who continue their rituals, but the treatment is more difficult and potentially less effective. When we agree to begin treatment without full response prevention, we emphasize that the ultimate goal of treatment is to eliminate all rituals. As in the case of slips, it is helpful to minimize the need for rituals, so the therapist may instruct the client to avoid some situations to reduce the frequency of rituals.

A third potential problem arises when the response prevention instructions conflict with the demands of everyday life. In this case, clients do not refuse to prevent their rituals out of hand, but compliance conflicts with other demands. For example, we would instruct Carol to refrain from washing (i.e., hand washing, showering, perhaps even brushing her teeth) for 3-day periods early in treatment. However, this may create problems with child care and food preparation (e.g., it is appropriate to wash one's hands when preparing meals). The therapist could instruct Carol to avoid situations in which she cannot refrain from washing (this is made easier by the degree to which her family already performs some tasks for her). The therapist must also remember that the goal of response prevention is to break the association between rituals and the sense of safety. Thus, washing itself may not be a problem, but washing to decontaminate is. Therefore, one way to modify response prevention when it is unrealistic for clients to refrain from rituals entirely is to find a way to "undo" them (this strategy can also be used to counter slips when they occur). To undo Carol's washing ritual, we would find a behavior that reverses the decontamination process. For example, she might "recontaminate" her hands after she washes them by touching something that was previously contaminated. The result is that the client is clean but contaminated, and the washing will have failed to eliminate her anxiety about germs.

Homework

Homework is a vital component of ERP and usually consists of 1 to 3 hours of additional exposure exercises to be done each day. The primary problem with homework is lack of compliance. Therapists can improve compliance by planning homework assignments carefully and reinforcing the expectation that the client will complete the assignments. Homework should include exercises that have been successfully completed in session so that the client has already had a chance to experience some reduction in fear. For example, Carol's therapist would not assign a homework assignment of touching the toilet in her home before having her complete an exposure exercise in which she touched the toilet in the clinic. Therapists should also consider ways to incorporate exposure homework into naturally occurring activities. For example, Carol experienced a great deal of anxiety when returning home from outside. Her therapist might plan a homework exercise of contaminating her home immediately on returning from her treatment session, rather than asking her to set aside additional time to plan a separate trip. It is also likely that some exposures assigned for homework will be difficult to maintain for the 30 to 45 minutes necessary for the client's anxiety to decrease. For example, although Carol could continue touching the toilet in the clinic or at her home for an extended period, it would be unrealistic for her to maintain a similar exposure to a public toilet in a local restaurant. Therefore, the therapist would need to work with Carol to develop a plan that would allow prolonged exposure. In this case, we suggested that she contaminate a handkerchief on the toilet seat of the public restroom and carry this "contamination rag" in a pocket to maintain the exposure. This is also a convenient way for clients to recontaminate should they find it necessary to wash.

CONCLUSION

The combination of exposure and response prevention has proved to be one of the most effective programs for treating OCD, including compulsive washing. The application of these techniques requires the therapist to balance the demands of an intervention designed to elicit increased anxiety or distress and to encourage clients to persist for an extended period of time, on the one hand, with the needs of a client who is deathly afraid of contact with seemingly harmless objects, on the other. Although the therapist, and even the client, may recognize the irrationality of the client's fears, the fear itself is real and powerful. An empathic clinician who can develop and maintain an effective and caring therapeutic relationship with the client is likely to be more successful than one who does not project such empathy. In the absence of a good working relationship, both clinician and client are likely to find the experience frustrating and disappointing.

REFERENCES

Abramowitz, J. S, Foa, E. B., & Franklin, M. E. (2003). Exposure and ritual prevention for obsessive–compulsive disorder: Effects of intensive versus twice-weekly sessions. *Journal of Consulting and Clinical Psychology, 71,* 394–398.

American Psychiatric Association. (1994). *Diagnostic and statistical manual of mental disorders* (4th ed.). Washington, DC: Author.

de Araujo, L. A., Ito, L. M., Marks, I. M., & Deale, A. (1995). Does imagined exposure to the consequences of not ritualising enhance live exposure for OCD? A controlled study: I. Main outcome. *British Journal of Psychiatry, 167,* 65–70.

Foa, E. B., & Kozak, M. J. (1986). Emotional processing of fear: Exposure to corrective information. *Psychological Bulletin, 99,* 20–35.

Foa, E. B., Liebowitz, M. R., Kozak, M. J., Davies, S., Campeas, R., Franklin, M. E., et al. (2005). Randomized, placebo-controlled trial of exposure and ritual prevention, clomipramine, and their combination in the treatment of obsessive–compulsive disorder. *American Journal of Psychiatry, 162,* 151–161.

Foa, E. B., Steketee, G., Grayson, J. B., Turner, R. M., & Latimer, P. (1984). Deliberate exposure and blocking of obsessive–compulsive rituals: Immediate and long-term effects. *Behavior Therapy, 15,* 450–472.

Foa, E. B., Steketee, G., Turner, R. M., & Fischer, S. C. (1980). Effects of imaginal exposure to feared disasters in obsessive–compulsive checkers. *Behaviour Research and Therapy, 18,* 449–455.

Franklin, M. E., Abramowitz, J. S., Kozak, M. J., Levitt, J., & Foa, E. B. (2000). Effectiveness of exposure and ritual prevention for obsessive compulsive disorder: Randomized compared with non-randomized samples. *Journal of Consulting and Clinical Psychology, 68,* 594–602.

Franklin, M. E., & Foa, E. B. (2002). Cognitive–behavioral treatment of obsessive compulsive disorder. In P. Nathan & J. Gorman (Eds.), *A guide to treatments that work* (2nd ed., pp. 367–386). New York: Oxford University Press.

Hodgson, R., Rachman, S., & Marks, I. M. (1972). The treatment of chronic obsessive–compulsive neurosis: Follow-up and further findings. *Behaviour Research and Therapy, 10,* 181–189.

March, J., Frances, A., Kahn, D., & Carpenter, D. (1997). Expert consensus guidelines: Treatment of obsessive–compulsive disorder. *Journal of Clinical Psychiatry, 58*(Suppl. 4), 1–72.

Steketee, G. S., Foa, E. B., & Grayson, J. B. (1982). Recent advances in the treatment of obsessive–compulsives. *Archives of General Psychiatry, 39,* 1365–1371.

Warren, R., & Thomas, J. C. (2001). Cognitive–behavior therapy of obsessive–compulsive disorder in private practice: An effectiveness study. *Journal of Anxiety Disorders, 15,* 277–285.

7

TREATING DOUBTING AND CHECKING CONCERNS

JONATHAN S. ABRAMOWITZ AND CHRISTY A. NELSON

Obsessional doubting and compulsive checking are among the most common presentations of obsessive–compulsive disorder (OCD; Antony, Downie, & Swinson, 1998). These phenomena consistently cluster together in factor and cluster analytic studies of OCD symptoms (Abramowitz, Franklin, Schwartz, & Furr, 2003), suggesting that they form a reliable dimension or subtype of OCD. In this chapter, we review the descriptive psychopathology of obsessional doubting and compulsive checking, provide a cognitive–behavioral conceptual model of these symptoms, and address the cognitive–behavioral treatment (CBT) of doubting and checking concerns using a case illustration.

THE NATURE OF DOUBTING AND CHECKING SYMPTOMS

Obsessional Doubting

Individuals with OCD often report recurrent, anxiety-evoking (obsessional) doubts related to specific situations, items, or actions. Although the

169

content of such doubts is highly patient specific and therefore virtually boundless, most of these obsessions fall into five descriptive categories: (a) responsibility for damage or injury in the home, (b) responsibility for harm that could befall others, (c) "hit-and-run" obsessions, (d) doubts about one's own health or identity, and (e) scrupulosity obsessions. These categories are described in the sections that follow.

Responsibility for Damage or Injury in the Home

Many patients have obsessional doubts that they will come to be responsible for something terrible happening in their home, perhaps because of carelessness or negligence. They may worry that fires will start because they have left the stove on or the curling iron plugged in or that the house will be robbed because they failed to lock the windows and doors. Although these doubts sometimes occur spontaneously, they are typically evoked by external triggers such as driving away from the house or seeing a fire engine or police car. The level of distress associated with the doubts is often reduced if responsibility can be transferred to another person. For example, a patient with obsessional doubts over whether she had locked the front door to her apartment building experienced discomfort only when she knew that she was the last person to leave the premises.

Responsibility for Harm That Could Befall Others

Doubts that one's actions may inadvertently harm others are common in OCD. In some cases, the content represents a gross overestimate of a realistic hazard. For example, one man feared that he would accidentally drop his medications and that an unsupervised child would find the pills, swallow them, and die. Another felt responsible for warning passersby about patches of ice on the sidewalk. In other cases, the fears seem to have a magical quality. For example, some patients feel that coming across unlucky numbers or saying negative words will lead to harm (e.g., "If I say the word *death* while thinking about Mother, Mother will die").

Hit-and-Run Obsessions

Whereas the categories in the preceding sections relate to consequences that could occur in the future, individuals with hit-and-run obsessions are plagued with doubts that they might have already caused harm. Often the imagined victim is an innocent person. Examples include "Did I hit a pedestrian with my car and then leave the scene of the accident?" "Could I have pushed an elderly person into traffic?" and "Am I sure that I didn't curse at the boss?"

Doubts About One's Own Health or Identity

Somatic obsessions concern doubts about one's own physical health (e.g., "Do I have cancer?") and overlap substantially with those observed in people with severe health anxiety (i.e., hypochondriasis; Abramowitz & Braddock, 2006; Abramowitz, Schwartz, & Whiteside, 2002). Other obsessive doubts are triggered by intrusive thoughts that strongly conflict with personal values. For example, a young mother had images of drowning her baby and doubts about whether she was really the gentle-hearted woman she thought she was. Also common are doubts about sexual preference. For example, a heterosexual man experienced unwanted thoughts with homosexual themes and had doubts about whether he was becoming gay.

Scrupulosity Obsessions

Scrupulosity obsessions involve doubts regarding whether one has committed a sin. Patients with such symptoms worry that they have violated religious rules for which even religious authorities would not assign culpability. Examples include doubts about whether swallowing too much saliva during Yom Kippur (a Jewish day of fasting) violates the fast and the fear that intrusive thoughts about sexual encounters are morally equivalent to committing adultery.

Compulsive Checking and Related Behaviors

Despite their superficial differences in content, the various types of doubts described in the preceding sections all evoke obsessional distress. A cardinal feature of OCD is that compulsive behavior is performed to neutralize obsessional distress or prevent the occurrence of some feared consequence, or both.

Overt Checking

Among individuals with OCD, checking is the most common response to obsessional doubts. Checking serves to reduce doubt, prevent misfortune, and protect oneself or others from harm. Rachman (2002) described the function of compulsive checking in OCD as follows:

> Compulsive checking occurs when people who believe that they have a special, elevated responsibility for preventing harm, mainly to others, are unsure that a perceived threat has been reduced or removed. They repeatedly check that all is safe. The intensity and duration of the checking is determined by the sense of responsibility, probability of harm, and anticipated seriousness of the harm. (p. 626)

Classic examples of checking include a woman who repeatedly checked that the appliances were unplugged to allay her obsessive doubts about causing fires, a man with obsessive fears that he had hit a pedestrian who repeatedly circled around the block to check that no one was harmed, and a woman who checked the TV news and called relatives to be sure that no one she knew had been killed. Often, the person recognizes the senselessness and excessiveness of the urge to check yet engages in the ritual because it reduces unacceptable levels of doubt and uncertainty. Checking can be carried out by proxy—for example, by asking others to check the door locks before coming to bed. It may also be covert, such as excessive monitoring of one's own body for signs of inappropriate sexual arousal. Sometimes the checking involves exhaustive investigation to achieve perfect resolution of the obsessional doubt. For example, one patient continually researched what murderers "are like" to ensure that he wasn't one of them.

Because it is rarely possible to achieve certainty about the kinds of obscure or vague doubts often featured in obsessions (e.g., "Is God angry with me?" "Will I develop a serious illness?"), most compulsive checking has no natural conclusion. It is common, therefore, for patients to become frustrated by and increasingly distressed as a result of their checking (Rachman, 1976). Rachman (1976) further pointed out the following features of checking rituals:

- They occur primarily in the person's own home.
- They are usually performed when the person is alone.
- They intensify when the person is feeling depressed.
- Their intensity is related to the degree of perceived responsibility for the feared outcome.

Covert (Mental) Checking and Reviewing

In addition to overt (observable) checking rituals, individuals may engage in covert (mental) checking strategies—for example, mentally reviewing one's behavior to gain reassurance that one made no egregious mistakes. One patient engaged in a 2-hour mental ritual each day after coming home from work at a pizza restaurant. The ritual entailed trying to remember each pizza she made to reassure herself that she did not mix in any poisonous substances such as cleaning solutions or rat poison. The ritual was aided by a list that she kept of each customer she served that day and what they ordered on their pizza.

Reassurance Seeking

Reassurance seeking is a subtle way of involving others in checking rituals and usually entails persistently asking relatives, friends, or authorities questions to allay obsessional doubts (e.g., "Do you think I will really kill the baby?" "Did you see me turn off the stove?"). Patients with scrupulous doubts often pursue spiritual leaders with persistent questions (or confessions) regarding religious rules and obligations (e.g., "Will I go to hell if I think of having sex while I am in church?"), and those with health-related doubts might pursue doctors with similar inquiries. We have had individuals contact us repeatedly to gain assurance that they have OCD and not a more severe problem such as schizophrenia. The reassurance rarely provides the absolute guarantee that the patient is seeking, because complete certainty often cannot be achieved. In some cases, the reassurance seeking is subtle, such as watching others' reactions or asking the same question in different ways.

A COGNITIVE–BEHAVIORAL MODEL OF DOUBTING AND CHECKING

What are the factors that contribute to the development and maintenance of obsessional doubts and compulsive checking? Clinical observations and research findings suggest that obsessional doubts originate from normal intrusive thoughts that become anxiety provoking when they are misappraised as significant or threatening (Rachman, 1997). Indeed, most people have unwanted thoughts about possible negative (or even disastrous) consequences (Rachman & de Silva, 1978), and these may be especially prevalent when a person is experiencing increased stress or responsibility (e.g., Abramowitz, Schwartz, & Moore, 2003). Individuals who hold dysfunctional beliefs such as those described in chapter 1 of this volume are at risk of misinterpreting thoughts and images of disasters as highly significant. For example, as a result of their intolerance for uncertainty, individuals with OCD experience the mere possibility of feared consequences as highly anxiety evoking ("If I can picture it, it could happen, and I can't take that chance"). Appraisal of intrusive thoughts as highly significant evokes urges to take action (e.g., checking or seeking assurance) to ensure against the dreaded outcome.

But why, following repeated checking and assurance seeking, do the senseless obsessive doubts persist and evoke such severe distress? Research on the factors that maintain obsessive doubts and checking rituals suggests that checking produces an immediate (albeit temporary) anxiolytic effect (Rachman & Hodgson, 1980), providing a temporary sense of certainty regarding the obsession (even if the senselessness of the ritual itself increases subjective frustration). However, rituals have deleterious long-term effects. Because they immediately reduce obsessional fear, checking prevents the natural extinction of anxiety. That is, by obtaining reassurance that the lights have been turned off or that everyone is safe, the person never learns to become comfortable living with acceptable levels of uncertainty (indeed, no one can predict the future with certainty). Moreover, checking rituals rob the person of the opportunity to disconfirm their dysfunctional beliefs about risk, intrusive thoughts, and uncertainty. As a result, dysfunctional beliefs and misinterpretations of intrusive thoughts persist over time, thereby maintaining the obsessional fear. Moreover, the maladaptive checking behavior is negatively reinforced by the reduction in obsessional distress it engenders, thus increasing its frequency. Research also suggests that compulsive checking produces memory distrust (van den Hout & Kindt, 2003) and therefore

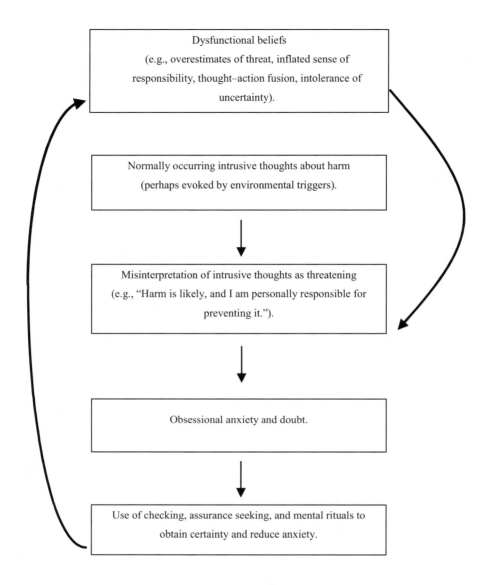

Figure 7.1. Cognitive–behavioral model of doubting and checking symptoms.

additional uncertainty. A simplified version of this model is displayed in Figure 7.1.

TREATMENT FORMULATION

In this section we describe CBT procedures for OCD doubting and checking concerns. To illustrate our methods of case formulation and therapy, we present the case of Sam, whose OCD complaints were characterized by obsessional doubts about harm and compulsive checking routines. Subsequently, we present a brief treatment protocol that draws on the core CBT interventions outlined in Part 1 of this volume.

Sam's Case Description

Sam was a 33-year-old married man with two young children. He worked as the manager of a bookstore and had experienced OCD for about 20 years, having failed numerous trials of medications and "talk therapy." Sam's primary symptoms included persistent obsessive doubts about being responsible for harming other people and excessive checking and reassurance seeking to ensure against such harm. For instance, at work he frequently worried that customers would drop food and drink (purchased from a food counter within the bookstore) or books and other objects on the floor, which would become hazards for those browsing through the shelves. He persistently checked the floors for anything that might cause injury, such as spills, coins, sharp objects, and fallen books. Although Sam was able to manage with his OCD symptoms from day to day, the quality of his work, social, and family life was substantially impaired. When not at work, he frequently called the store to double check that "everything was OK."

Sam's most severe obsession involved the fear that he might drop his OCD medication, Celexa (citalopram hydrobromide), on the floor and that a child could find the loose pills, ingest them, and die. He was afraid to leave his medicine at home because his own young children could be in danger. Thus, he carried his pills with him in his pants pocket. He kept the pills in their bottle, which he encased within five self-sealing plastic bags. Yet Sam still feared that somehow a pill would escape and end up killing a child. As a result, he avoided public places as much as possible and would retrace his steps while checking the floor if he saw children nearby. At work, Sam had a "safe path" that he would use when walking through the store, although he frequently had to retrace his steps and check the floors anyway. Furthermore, he avoided the store's children's books section as much as possible. Although he spent hours checking for pills he might have lost and counting those in his possession (to be sure he had not dropped any), Sam constantly worried that children might consume his medication. On a daily basis, he either telephoned his doctor or the local poison control center for information regarding what effects accidental ingestion of Celexa might have on a small child.

Case Conceptualization

The conceptualization of doubting and checking symptoms in OCD involves both nomothetic and idiographic components. The cognitive–behavioral model of OCD (see chap. 1 of this volume) and the model presented earlier in this chapter serve as functional templates or guides for un-

TABLE 7.1
Assessment Instruments Used to Formulate
a Conceptualization and Treatment Plan

Instrument	Purpose
Symptom checklist of the Yale–Brown Obsessive–Compulsive Scale (Y–BOCS; Goodman et al., 1989)	Assesses the presence of a wide range of obsessional doubts and their environmental triggers and allows the therapist to understand the patient's full repertoire of avoidance, checking, and other safety-seeking strategies.
Y–BOCS Severity scale (Goodman et al., 1989)	Measures the clinical severity of doubting and checking symptoms.
Brown Assessment of Beliefs Scale (Eisen et al., 1998)	Assesses *insight,* or the degree to which the patient understands that his or her doubts and checking rituals are senseless.
Hamilton Rating Scale for Depression (Hamilton, 1960)	Assesses the severity of depressive symptoms.
Obsessive Beliefs Questionnaire (Obsessive–Compulsive Cognitions Working Group, 2003)	Assesses cognitive distortions relevant to OCD regarding overestimates of threat and responsibility, the importance of and need to control intrusive thoughts, and perfectionism and intolerance of uncertainty.
Interpretation of Intrusions Inventory (Obsessive–Compulsive Cognitions Working Group, 2003)	Assesses patients' appraisals of their specific intrusive thoughts.

derstanding the symptoms and ways to decrease them. However, the patient's idiosyncratic triggers, obsessional thoughts, cognitions, and avoidance strategies must also be considered. This formulation serves as a working hypothesis that is continually tested by collecting information from the patient and by measuring the effects of treatment procedures that are used. In our clinic, the collection of such data is guided by the use of several psychometrically validated instruments listed in Table 7.1. The remainder of this section illustrates how such data were used to generate a treatment formulation in Sam's case.

Sam's obsessive doubts were conceptualized as having originated from normal intrusive thoughts such as "A child could swallow my pills and become sick." These intrusions had become associated (via classical conditioning) with various stimuli (e.g., children, the workplace) that now triggered the intrusions. Assessment revealed that Sam overestimated both the probability of dropping his pills and his degree of responsibility for unsupervised children swallowing them. He was also interpreting his intrusive thoughts as highly significant (e.g., "If I am thinking about it, then it must be important") and as having implications for his responsibility to prevent harm (e.g., "Now that I've thought about something that could go wrong, I have a responsibility to make sure it doesn't happen"). Moreover, he evidenced an intolerance of uncertainty. These cognitions were considered to be the basis of Sam's obsessional fears.

Sam's desire to keep his medication with him at all times, his need to have the pill bottle tightly wrapped in numerous bags, and his avoidance of situations that evoked obsessional doubts were conceptualized as strategies to prevent his feared disasters from occurring. Checking rituals were viewed as anxiety-reduction responses to obsessions that could not be altogether avoided. All of these safety-seeking behaviors were evoked by the mere possibility that harm could occur (intolerance of uncertainty), and Sam performed them to reduce the chances of being responsible for harm. Clinical observations suggest that individuals with doubting and checking concerns base their beliefs about danger on the absence of evidence that guarantees safety, rather than on the presence of danger cues. Thus, in the short term, Sam's active and passive avoidance strategies temporarily worked by reducing his uncertainty and associated distress. However, they also prevented Sam from disconfirming his obsessional fears. That is, when there were no injuries at work, and when no child died as a result of consuming Sam's medication, Sam erroneously interpreted this to mean that his avoidance and checking rituals were crucial (i.e., "Someone would have been hurt if I didn't check"). Because Sam believed that his ritualistic behavior was successful, it was reinforced and became habitual.

Foa and Kozak (1986) proposed that the reduction of pathological fear requires confrontation with the feared stimulus to activate the fear network, along with presentation of corrective information (i.e., that disastrous consequences are unlikely). Therefore, the formulation of Sam's case led to the use of exposure therapy as the principle treatment procedure. Repeated and prolonged exposure to obsessional fear cues and to the intrusive doubts themselves would help Sam discover that such stimuli do not portend disastrous consequences. Exposure is thought to weaken anxiety responses by changing the meaning of obsessional intrusions. At the same time, Sam was required to resist all avoidant and safety-seeking rituals so that the only explanation when disastrous consequences did not occur was that the fear was unfounded.

TREATMENT PROTOCOL

In our clinic, basic CBT strategies are applied in the case of doubting and checking concerns. Patients initially receive a 2- to 3-hour consultation during which the diagnosis of OCD is established and treatment recommendations are discussed. For patients who begin CBT, individual therapy sessions are typically scheduled on a twice-weekly basis, with about 3 or 4 days between sessions (e.g., therapy sessions on Tuesdays and Fridays). This frequency ensures a briefer period between sessions than weekly sessions, allowing the therapist to more rapidly correct any adherence problems that occur between sessions. Each session lasts approximately 90 minutes. The following subsections describe the treatment protocol in more detail and illustrate how the treatment procedures were implemented in Sam's case.

Psychoeducation and Information Gathering (Sessions 1 and 2)

Goals of the first two sessions include developing rapport, taking a general history, socializing the patient to the cognitive–behavioral model of OCD (e.g., Figure 7.1) and its treatment, and conducting a functional analysis of the patient's obsessional doubts and checking rituals. The functional analysis entails collecting detailed information about the patient's current fear cues, feared consequences, avoidance patterns, rituals, and other safety-seeking behaviors (Abramowitz, 2006).

Current fear cues. The therapist should elicit information about external sources of anxiety. Obsessional doubts are highly idiosyncratic and may be triggered by routine activities, as they were for Sam. The most straightforward way to identify situational triggers is to ask questions such as "What kinds of things do you check?" "What do you need to seek reassurance about?" and "What situations do you try to avoid because you are afraid of harming someone?" Common fear cues include leaving the home (fear of fires), driving (fear of hitting pedestrians), seeing sharp or "dangerous" objects (that could result in injury), and completing paperwork (errors could cause negative consequences). Words (e.g., *accident*) or numbers (e.g., 13) may also trigger obsessional fear. For Sam, handling his medication and walking through the bookstore (or other crowded public areas where children might be present) were significant fear cues.

Feared consequences. Next, the therapist assesses the feared consequences of exposure to the fear cues. Images and ideas of feared disasters are common among patients with checking symptoms, and these often take the form of doubts and rhetorical questions about mistakes, negligence, or mishaps such as "What if I accidentally killed someone?" "Did I give him sufficient warning that the stairs are slippery?" "I might have written 'fuck you' instead of 'thank you' in my letter to the boss!" Individuals with scrupulosity often have doubts pertaining to unanswerable issues concerning divine punishment. Sam reported intrusive obsessional thoughts about responsibility for innocent people being injured, such as by slipping on a fallen book or spilled water or ingesting medicines.

Avoidance patterns. The particular tactics used to avoid obsessional cues and feared consequences vary widely from patient to patient. Examples include refraining from actions associated with "high-risk" cues, such as driving on certain roads, using the stove, completing paperwork, reading articles about disasters, and being the last person to leave the house (or to go to sleep). Sometimes avoidance is subtle, such as not listening to music while driving for fear of being too distracted to recognize that one has hit a pedestrian. Sam avoided the children's section of his bookstore and other places (e.g., malls, playgrounds, his daughter's nursery school) where he thought children could pick up stray items off the floor and ingest them.

Rituals and other safety-seeking behaviors. The therapist must determine the specifics (frequency, intensity, duration, antecedents, and consequences) of checking, reassurance seeking, and other safety-seeking rituals and must determine the relationship between these responses and obsessional fear. For example, Sam engaged in persistent checks of the floors whenever he saw young children or had doubts that he might have dropped his pills. He also repeatedly counted his pills to ensure that none were missing. He kept his pill bottle wrapped in several bags to avoid dropping pills unknowingly. Sam believed that he had to perform these rituals and safety behaviors in order to prevent harm or injury for which he was ultimately responsible.

Treatment Planning

Exposure Hierarchy

Once the functional assessment is complete (usually by the end of the second session), the therapist and patient use this information to assemble the exposure hierarchy. Because in this presentation of OCD anxiety is evoked by both tangible environmental cues and by elusive thoughts or doubts about possible disasters, the treatment plan should involve situational exposures to external fear-evoking situations or stimuli, coordinated with imaginal exposures to thoughts (images, doubts, uncertainty) about the feared consequences of not performing checking or reassurance-seeking rituals (Abramowitz, 2006). The procedures for developing exposure hierarchies based on patients' Subjective Units of Discomfort Scale (SUDS) ratings are explained in chapter 4 of this volume. Exhibit 7.1 presents examples of hierarchies for two patients with doubting and checking concerns, and Exhibit 7.2 contains Sam's exposure hierarchy.

Response Prevention Plan

Once the exposure hierarchy is complete, therapist and patient establish a response prevention plan. Patients must refrain from all checking rituals, all reassurance-seeking efforts, and all other attempts to prevent feared disasters. They must avoid, for example, picking up objects off the ground, counting, reporting possible hazards to others, and list making. Family members must also refrain from performing these rituals by proxy. If checking involves simply looking (e.g., at the door lock), the object can be obscured from view (e.g., with a piece of paper). For patients afraid of making mistakes, important paperwork (e.g., financial documents) may be briefly reviewed once. Redoing mathematical calculations is not permitted (unless an egregious error has been made). Mental checking (e.g., reviewing behaviors) and seeking information or advice that has already been given (e.g., from authorities) are likewise not permitted. Patients who perform behavioral or

EXHIBIT 7.1
Sample Exposure Hierarchies for Two Patients With Doubting and Checking Concerns

Patient 1
Obsessional Doubts About Responsibility for House Fires

Situational exposure	Subjective Units of Distress Scale Rating	Imaginal exposure
Leave lights on while out of the house for the day.	45	Images of fires.
Leave computer turned on while in a different room.	50	Images of fires.
Leave computer on while out of the house for the day.	60	Images of house fires.
Leave iron and toaster plugged in while away from the house for the day.	75	Images of house fires.
Turn oven on and go outside for 15, 30, and then 45 minutes.	75–85	Images of house fires.

Patient 2
Obsessional Fears About Unknowingly Hitting Someone While Driving

Situational exposure	Subjective Units of Distress Scale Rating	Imaginal exposure
Back out of driveway (while only checking the mirror once).	40	Doubts about whether the neighbor's child was killed.
Drive around mall parking lot at off peak time.	45	Doubts about whether someone was injured.
Drive around mall parking lot on a weekend afternoon.	60	Doubts about whether someone was injured.
Drive at night on a street where there are joggers.	75	Doubts about whether someone was injured.
Drive past an elementary school at dismissal time.	75	Thoughts of injuring a child.
Drive through a neighborhood where children are playing.	75	Thoughts of injuring a child.
Drive with the car radio turned up loud.	85	Thoughts of hitting a pedestrian by mistake.
Drive while speaking on cell phone.	90	Thoughts of hitting a pedestrian by mistake.

mental rituals that are difficult to stop altogether can purposely perform them incorrectly or in a way that leaves them feeling uncertain about feared consequences. The following rules for response prevention were developed for Sam:

- no checking;
- no use of bags to contain pill bottles;
- no counting pills;
- no calling work to check on safety issues; and
- no calling doctors or poison control.

EXHIBIT 7.2
Sam's Exposure Hierarchy: Obsessional Fears About
Responsibility for Harm Befalling Innocent Children

Situational exposure	Subjective Units of Distress Scale Rating	Imaginal exposure
Put "hazards" on the floor of the bookstore (e.g., books, food).	55	Images of someone tripping and being injured.
Drop a banana peel in the middle of the mall food court.	65	Images of someone tripping and being injured.
Drop objects (e.g., scissors, pins) on the floor in the bookstore or the mall.	75	Doubts about causing injury; responsibility for injury.
Handle Celexa (citalopram hydrobromide) pills while in the mall.	80	Doubts about whether pills were dropped; responsibility for injury.
Handle Celexa pills while in a playground or park full of children.	82	Doubts about whether pills were dropped; responsibility for injury.
Handle Celexa pills while walking through an elementary school.	85	Doubts about whether pills were dropped; responsibility for injury.
Handle Celexa pills while walking through the children's section of the bookstore.	90	Doubts about whether pills were dropped; responsibility for injury.
Place "dangerous" objects where there are children.	Scissors = 85 Pills = 95	Responsibility for injury to a child.

Exposure Therapy and Response Prevention

Conducting Exposure Exercises

Once therapist and patient agree on the treatment plan, therapist-supervised exposure exercises are conducted during each session. Because many situations that evoke obsessional doubts for patients with checking rituals cannot be re-created in the therapist's office, flexibility with regard to implementing exposure exercises outside the office (i.e., on field trips) is necessary. Sam and his therapist, for example, met at Sam's bookstore, where he placed "dangerous" objects on the floor with the therapist's supervision. They subsequently went back to the office, where the therapist helped Sam conduct imaginal exposure until his anxiety associated with obsessional doubts subsided.

Exposures may be compromised if the patient remains in the situation for an extended period. For example, staying in the house after plugging in the television or turning on the stove is inherently reassuring; the patient can see that no fire has started. Therefore, when in vivo exposures evoke uncertainty about negative outcomes, precautions should be taken to ensure that no de facto reassurance seeking occurs. Instead, imaginal exposure to the feared outcomes should be commenced to prolong the exposure exercise. After Sam's exposure to walking through his son's elementary school, during which he had handled a few of his pills and then returned them to their container, Sam and the therapist returned to the therapist's office and conducted imaginal exposure to uncertainty and doubt about possible disasters, as reflected in the following script:

> I walked through the school holding my pill container open. There were young children everywhere; some were unsupervised. I might have dropped some pills, because I didn't count to make sure I still had all of them. I even took a few pills out. Some might have spilled to the floor without my realizing it. I feel like I was careless. I want to go back and check all of the floors for loose pills. I want to warn the principal that there might be dangerous drugs loose in the hallways. But I know that I'm not supposed to do this. I need to remain uncertain about the possible outcomes. It is possible that I dropped some of my medicine on the floor and that one of the young students picked it up and swallowed it. Who knows what could happen next? He or she might get very sick, or even die. It would be my fault. I can imagine the headlines: "Student Dies After Finding Loose Pills at School." How *awful* that would be. I might have to live with this for the rest of my life. Why was I so careless?

Sam devised this imaginal script by first writing a description of his feared consequences of exposure. After some collaborative editing, the therapist or Sam read the contents of the thought into a tape recorder with a loop tape that replayed after 2 minutes. Sam was instructed to listen to the loop tape for about 30 minutes (with instructions to engage in the doubt) or until his SUDS rating subsided by about 50%.

Using Cognitive Interventions During Exposure

Although research suggests that exposure therapy is just as formidable an agent of cognitive change as are cognitive therapy interventions (Whittal, Thordarson, & McLean, 2005), it is probably useful to embed the cognitive techniques described in chapter 5 (this volume) within exposure exercises to facilitate the modification of problematic beliefs about risk, uncertainty, and the importance of intrusive thoughts. Informal Socratic questioning and the use of the pie chart technique for allocating responsibility (Van Oppen & Arntz, 1994) are two of the more useful cognitive interventions in the context of exposure for obsessional doubts and checking rituals. Continued psychoeducation about the normalcy of intrusive doubts and the cognitive–behavioral model in Figure 7.1 also serve as useful cognitive techniques.

TROUBLESHOOTING

In this section, we address five obstacles often encountered in the treatment of doubting and checking symptoms: balking, fears of future consequences, transfer of responsibility, persistent requests for reassurance, and the use of cognitive techniques as reassurance-seeking rituals. Suggestions for troubleshooting these obstacles are also presented.

When Patients Balk at Exposure Exercises

Patients sometimes question the need to perform as exposure exercises activities that "people wouldn't normally do," such as purposely spilling water on the floor of a public place and not warning people about the potential danger. The therapist can explain that the aim of exposure is not simply to do what "most people do," but instead to demonstrate that feared consequences are highly unlikely. The therapist can also point out that the situations encountered during exposure can and do occasionally happen under normal circumstances (even if by accident) but do not necessarily lead to disastrous outcomes and that this type of exposure is meant to help the patient learn not to be fearful that these situations could occur.

Fears of Disastrous Consequences in the Distant Future

Obsessions about feared consequences that could occur in the distant future (e.g., going to hell when one dies) appear to present barriers to conducting exposure, because such outcomes cannot be disconfirmed within the session. However, the cognitive underpinnings of OCD (especially doubting symptoms) include the intolerance of uncertainty (Tolin, Abramowitz, Brigidi, & Foa, 2003). Therefore, exposure exercises for such fears can be designed to weaken associations between uncertainty and high levels of anxiety. In vivo exposures should incorporate situations that arouse feelings of uncertainty, and imaginal exposure should focus on not knowing for sure whether the feared consequence has happened or will happen (Abramowitz, 2001). From the behavioral perspective, such exercises encourage habituation to feelings of uncertainty. From the cognitive point of view, such exercises decatastrophize uncertainty and help patients better manage acceptable levels of doubt without resorting to compulsive rituals.

Transfer of Responsibility During Exposure

To be maximally effective, exposures for obsessional doubts and checking symptoms must be engineered to make the patient feel directly responsible for any feared consequences. Even the therapist's presence during exposure can invalidate the task if the patient can easily transfer responsibility for any harm to the therapist. For example, a patient with obsessional doubts about whether he or she has hit a pedestrian while driving might feel more comfortable if the therapist accompanies him or her on a driving exposure than when driving alone (e.g., "The therapist would never let anything terrible happen"). Thus, during each exposure it is important to routinely assess the degree to which the patient feels responsible for the feared outcome. In this instance, the therapist might accompany the patient on a driving exposure at first but then instruct the patient to conduct this exercise on his or her own.

Persistent Requests for Reassurance

The goal of exposure therapy is to reduce the patient's need for absolute certainty without resorting to checking and other forms of reassurance seeking. Some patients, however, persistently question the therapist to try to gain assurance of safety and have difficulty resisting this behavior even during exposure exercises. In such instances, the first inclination may be to ease the patient's anxiety by guaranteeing that he or she is not in any danger. However, this undermines the goal of teaching patients to live with acceptable levels of risk and uncertainty. The recommended response is to communicate compassion while focusing on how exposures are purposely designed to evoke uncertainty for the patient. It is often useful to explain to patients that although exposure exercises present low risk, there can never truly be an absolute guarantee of safety. For example, the therapist can say,

> It sounds like you're feeling uncomfortable and are searching for that guarantee right now, and that's your obsessional doubting. Because I already answered that question, it would not be helpful for you if I answered it again. The best way to stop the obsessional doubts is for you to work on tolerating your distress and uncertainty—how can I help you to do that?

We have worked with some individuals who were completely unable (or unwilling) to stop their persistent reassurance-seeking behavior in and between sessions. Because failing to refrain from seeking assurance interferes with exposure (it is equivalent to refusing to abstain from rituals) and inevitably compromises outcome, therapy had to be suspended in these cases. Suspension is the last resort when patients refuse to comply with treatment procedures. If this option is chosen, it is important that the therapist convey in the most sensitive way why he or she recommends discontinuation of treatment (i.e., because the patient is unable to carry out the treatment procedures in ways that would be beneficial) and what alternatives might be available.

Use of Cognitive Techniques as Reassurance-Seeking Rituals

On occasion, we have observed that patients use cognitive techniques (e.g., rational responses) as reassurance-seeking rituals to allay doubt about feared consequences. It is important that therapists avoid trying to convince the patient that feared consequences are "impossible" or that exposure situations are "not dangerous." This is for the patient to discover for himself or herself through experience. Risk levels are best described as "acceptably low" rather than "zero." Occasionally, patients will appear as if they are straining to obtain reassurance. This might take the form of subtle reassurance-seeking strategies (e.g., watching the therapist's facial expression closely). As a general rule, the therapist should answer questions about the risk of particular feared consequences only once.

Doubting obsessions and checking rituals occupy a significant quadrant within the diverse landscape of OCD symptoms. Yet, even within this symptom dimension, the topography is quite heterogenous; patients present with an endless variation of anxiety-evoking doubts and uncertainties that typically relate to a finite number of personally relevant themes (e.g., responsibility for harm befalling loved ones, religious salvation). Rituals that involve various forms of checking and reassurance seeking, although superficially diverse, all serve the same function: they are attempts to obtain an unobtainable, unqualified guarantee that feared outcomes will not occur. A thorough functional assessment of these symptoms (as described in this chapter and in earlier chapters of this volume) is the best means by which to gain an appreciation of the rich and internally consistent patterns of phenomenology present in this presentation of OCD. Using the cognitive–behavioral theoretical framework as a guide, effective treatment consists of helping patients confront the particular situations, stimuli, and thoughts that evoke anxiety and uncertainty (exposure), while simultaneously resisting urges to use maladaptive anxiety-reduction strategies such as checking, reassurance seeking, and transferring responsibility. Cognitive therapy techniques further reinforce the overall aims of treatment, which are to help patients reduce their exaggerated sense of responsibility and focus on what is probable as opposed to what possible.

REFERENCES

Abramowitz, J. S. (2001). Treatment of scrupulous obsessions and compulsions using exposure and response prevention: A case report. *Cognitive and Behavioral Practice, 8,* 79–85.

Abramowitz, J. S. (2006). *Understanding and treating obsessive–compulsive disorder: A cognitive–behavioral approach.* Mahwah, NJ: Erlbaum.

Abramowitz, J. S. & Braddock, A. E. (2006). Hypochondriasis: Conceptualization, treatment, and relationship to obsessive–compulsive disorder. *The Psychiatric Clinics of North America, 2,* 503-519.

Abramowitz, J. S., Franklin, M. E., Schwartz, S. A., & Furr, J. M. (2003). Symptom presentation and outcome of cognitive–behavioral therapy for obsessive–compulsive disorder. *Journal of Consulting and Clinical Psychology, 71,* 1049–1057.

Abramowitz, J. S., Schwartz, S. A., & Moore, K. M. (2003). Obsessional thoughts in postpartum females and their partners: Content, severity, and relationship with depression. *Journal of Clinical Psychology in Medical Settings, 10,* 157–164.

Abramowitz, J. S., Schwartz, S. A., & Whiteside, S. P. (2002). A contemporary conceptual model of hypochondriasis. *Mayo Clinic Proceedings, 77,* 1323–1330.

Antony, M. M., Downie, F., & Swinson, R. P. (1998). Diagnostic issues and epidemiology in obsessive–compulsive disorder. In R. P. Swinson, M. Antony, S. Rachman, & M. Richter (Eds.), *Obsessive–compulsive disorder: Theory, research, and treatment* (pp. 3–32). New York: Guilford Press.

Eisen, J. L., Phillips, K. A., Baer, L., Beer, D. A., Atala, K. D., & Rasmussen, S. A. (1998). The Brown Assessment of Beliefs Scale: Reliability and validity. *American Journal of Psychiatry, 155,* 102–108.

Foa, E. B., & Kozak, M. J. (1986). Emotional processing of fear: Exposure to corrective information. *Psychological Bulletin, 99,* 20–35.

Goodman, W. K., Price, L. H., Rasmussen, S. A., Mazure, C., Fleischmann, R. L., Hill, C. L., et al. (1989). The Yale–Brown Obsessive–Compulsive Scale: I. Development, use, and reliability. *Archives of General Psychiatry, 46,* 1006–1011.

Hamilton, M. (1960). A rating scale for depression. *Journal of Neurological and Neurosurgical Psychiatry, 18,* 315–319.

Obsessive–Compulsive Cognitions Working Group. (2003). Psychometric validation of the Obsessive Beliefs Questionnaire and the Interpretation of Intrusions Inventory: Part I. *Behaviour Research and Therapy, 41,* 863–878.

Rachman, S. (1976). Obsessional–compulsive checking. *Behaviour Research and Therapy, 14,* 269–277.

Rachman, S. (1997). A cognitive theory of obsessions. *Behaviour Research and Therapy, 35,* 793–802.

Rachman, S. (2002). A cognitive theory of compulsive checking. *Behaviour Research and Therapy, 40,* 625–639.

Rachman, S., & de Silva, P. (1978). Abnormal and normal obsessions. *Behaviour Research and Therapy, 16,* 233–248.

Rachman, S. J., & Hodgson, R. J. (1980). *Obsessions and compulsions.* Englewood Cliffs, NJ: Prentice Hall.

Tolin, D. F., Abramowitz, J. S., Brigidi, B. D., & Foa, E. B. (2003). Intolerance of uncertainty in obsessive–compulsive disorder. *Journal of Anxiety Disorders, 17,* 233–242.

van den Hout, M., & Kindt, M. (2003). Repeated checking causes memory distrust. *Behaviour Research and Therapy, 41,* 301–316.

van Oppen, P., & Arntz, A. (1994). Cognitive therapy for obsessive–compulsive disorder. *Behaviour Research and Therapy, 32,* 79–87.

Whittal, M., Thordarson, D., & McLean, P. (2005). Treatment of obsessive–compulsive disorder: Cognitive behavior therapy versus exposure and response prevention. *Behaviour Research and Therapy, 43,* 1559–1576.

8

TREATING INCOMPLETENESS, ORDERING, AND ARRANGING CONCERNS

LAURA J. SUMMERFELDT

The pairing of symmetry obsessions with ordering and arranging compulsions is one of the most reliable findings in the empirical literature on obsessive–compulsive disorder (OCD) symptom subtypes (see Mataix-Cols, do Rosario-Campos, & Leckman, 2005). However, symmetry and ordering, like other OCD symptoms, can be driven by different underlying motivations. On the one hand, ordering may serve to offset fears about potential harm. For example, an individual with obsessive thoughts about being responsible for bad things happening to others might feel compelled to arrange elements of the environment in order to prevent or undo this possibility. Functionally, this harm-avoidant symptom configuration does not differ from that of cases described in traditional accounts, and in other chapters in this volume, of OCD and its treatment. There is another common manifestation of this symptom profile, however, in which the individual feels driven to order and arrange to preserve the pristine state and sameness of his or her environment, with little sense of threat or anticipated harm. Instead of anxious apprehension, the individual describes being plagued by tormenting dissatisfaction, a feeling of things being "not just right." This form of ordering and arranging symptoms is the focus of this chapter.

This sense of things being not just right can manifest through any sensory modality, including the visual (e.g., appearance of belongings or documents), auditory (e.g., preference for sameness in ambient noise), tactile (e.g., checking textures by touching or tapping), and proprioceptive (e.g., having to "even up" actions). It may also apply to more complex experiences that do not easily fall under the sensory category, such as cognition (e.g., expressing one's thoughts unambiguously, in the best words). Such diversity of presentation means that ordering and arranging may be either literal or figurative. These are not uncommon experiences in OCD; in studies with clinical samples, Leckman et al. (1995) and Miguel et al. (2000) found that well over half of participants endorsed the need to perform compulsions to quell feelings of things being not just right.

In his writings on OCD a century ago, French physician, psychiatrist, and philosopher Pierre Janet described this experience as *les sentiments d'incomplétude*—literally, feelings of incompleteness—an inner sense of imperfection connected with the perception that actions or intentions have been incompletely achieved (see Pitman, 1987b, for a translated précis). This form of sensory-affective dysregulation is now well recognized and has been captured in different terms by different writers. Rasmussen and Eisen (1992) described it, following Janet, as *incompleteness*. The conceptualization of deficits in the *feeling of knowing* in OCD (Rapoport, 1991) also shows overlap. Other more recent examples include *not just right* experiences (Coles, Frost, Heimberg, & Rhéaume, 2003; Leckman, Walker, Goodman, Pauls, & Cohen, 1994), *sensory phenomena* (Miguel et al., 2000), *sensitivity of perception* (Veale et al., 1996), and *yedasentience* (Szechtman & Woody, 2004).

Our group has found the term *incompleteness* to be comfortingly familiar to patients (see Summerfeldt, Antony, & Swinson, 2002). Building on earlier work by Rasmussen and Eisen (1992), my colleagues and I have incorporated this concept into a dimensional model of OCD that posits the existence of two continuous orthogonal dimensions—*harm avoidance* and *incompleteness*—that cut across overt symptoms and may in combination underlie most manifestations of this disorder. We hypothesize that the two dimensions may be associated with quite different features, vulnerabilities, and causal factors.

ETIOLOGIC ISSUES

Existing research and clinical observations suggest that at the core of incompleteness OCD is a deficit in the ability to use emotional experience and sensory feedback to guide behavior (Summerfeldt, 1998). Phenomenologically, this deficit seems to reflect malfunction in some internal signal that terminates behaviors by producing what Rapoport (1991) termed a *feeling of knowing*—an emotional indicator that lets one know when a state has been satisfactorily achieved (see Szechtman & Woody, 2004, for a similar account applied to OCD in general). At the macro level, incompleteness OCD may exemplify the effects of lifelong deficits in this function. This formulation converges with a long-standing literature pointing to dysfunction in OCD in neural circuits involving the basal ganglia. Although models of the specific mechanism vary, there is some consensus that it manifests as impairments in the selection of behavioral responses, the production of coherent subsequences of goal-oriented actions, and the switching of task priorities in response to feedback. In other words, these connections may contain the self-quenching circuit that provides people with a subjective sense of completeness. Malfunctions in this circuit may manifest as persistent "error signals" (Pitman, 1987a; Schwartz, 1999), incorrectly prompting the individual to (futile) corrective action.

TREATMENT OUTCOMES

There has been no direct investigation of treatments for incompleteness OCD. However, existing empirical accounts provide some indirect evidence that the outcomes of conventional psychological interventions, such as cognitive–behavioral therapy (CBT) using exposure and response prevention (ERP; also called exposure and ritual prevention), may not be entirely generalizable to this manifestation of OCD.

In a review of rates of OCD symptom subtypes in behavioral treatment outcome studies, Ball, Baer, and Otto (1996) found that compulsions not related to cleaning (e.g., checking, hoarding, symmetry, and counting rituals—plausibly those most characterized by incompleteness) were significantly underrepresented. These figures may reflect a greater likelihood that patients with these symptom profiles refuse or drop out of treatment, as well as the difficulty of designing interventions in such cases and their consequent exclusion from treatment studies. In contrast, Mataix-Cols, Marks, Greist, Kobak, and Baer (2002) reported few differences among symptom factors, including the symmetry or ordering dimension, in predicting compliance with or response to behavior therapy. At the midpoint between these two reports, another study found that although hoarding symptoms alone were unique in predicting poorer response to CBT than other OCD symptom clusters, of the remaining symptom domains, the one most similar in response rates to hoarding was symmetry related (Abramowitz, Franklin, Schwartz, & Furr, 2003).

Other reports, relying less on symptom subtypes, also suggest that incompleteness may predict poor response to treatment. Tallis (1996) described four patients with cleaning rituals driven by a need to maintain belongings in "just so" condition. All showed negligible long-term therapeutic response to ERP, although their response was better than that achieved using cognitive therapy or medication. OCD patients unable to articulate feared consequences have been found to show a trend toward less posttreatment improvement (45% compared with 69%) than those with clear feared consequences (Foa, Abramowitz, Franklin, & Kozak, 1999). In short, the overt symptoms and underlying characteristics most associated with incompleteness are often those identified as being least responsive to ERP. Such accounts suggest that individuals with incompleteness OCD may show modest gains in response to treatment using standard CBT models and techniques.

APPLYING COGNITIVE–BEHAVIORAL PRINCIPLES

Faced with the theoretical and research literature, a therapist may be worried about the applicability of key principles of effective CBT to incompleteness OCD. Foa et al. (1999), for example, suggested that individuals who can identify specific feared consequences may best benefit from ERP because the content of their obsessions allows for disconfirmatory exposure exercises. Similar caveats may apply to treatment incorporating cognitive principles. Foa and Kozak (1986) proposed that reductions in OCD symptoms are mediated by reductions in estimates of the probability of feared consequences and resultant modifications of fear structures, achieved through the repeated disconfirmations of the expected outcome that occur during ERP. By these accounts, CBT not only may be difficult to apply for individuals with incompleteness OCD, but also, even if applied, may ultimately be less effective. However, my clinical experience, as well as the limited research evidence currently available, suggests that ERP is still indicated. The sections that follow outline ways of adapting key behavioral and cognitive principles to this form of OCD (see also Summerfeldt, 2004).

The Behavioral Component

Behavioral treatment of OCD derives from Mowrer's (1960) two-stage model of phobic behavior. This model proposes that obsessions, through conditioning, come to elicit distress that then fails to extinguish because of avoidance behavior or its functional equivalents, such as compulsive rituals. As these behaviors alleviate anxiety, they are negatively reinforced; thus, compulsions and avoidance are self-perpetuating. ERP is designed to address the second stage of this process. The basic premise behind the effectiveness of exposure is the principle of extinction, or the gradual loss of a learned involuntary response, such as anxiety, by repetition of an event in the absence of objective threat or reinforcement (see chap. 4, this volume).

Although this model is most commonly applied to anxiety, its basic principles should apply to other emotional experiences, such as incompleteness, despite the fact that it appears to be an internally generated, rather than acquired, emotional state. Indeed, the term *habituation* is usually used to describe this same process applied to unlearned or reflexive behaviors. When the therapist is familiarizing a patient with the treatment model, a useful parallel is the familiar experience of getting accustomed over time to a persistent situation, such as street noise or a spot on the windshield.

The Cognitive Component

Behavioral principles, which appear to be applicable to incompleteness OCD, constitute only a part of the full cognitive–behavioral account of OCD. Prevailing cognitive models of OCD derive from the premise that emotional responses are mediated through the problematic interpretations, or appraisals, that the person gives to otherwise innocuous experiences (i.e., intrusive thoughts). Such appraisals are thought to take place because of dysfunctional core beliefs, or schemata, acquired through experience (see chap. 5 in this volume).

This model has difficulty accommodating incompleteness experiences in OCD. In line with cognitive appraisal theory, cognitive contents are thought of as proposition-like beliefs that can be expressed and assessed as declarative phrases, such as "Thinking about a bad thing happening makes it more likely." More important, these appraisals are thought to lead to negative affect, such as anxious apprehension. The critical underlying premise is that emotions arise as the consequence of the operations of cognitive beliefs and appraisals. According to this perspective, although the behavioral component of the model is useful in explaining the perpetuation of the problem, the cognitive component is seen to be its source. There is little place in such models for inherent dysfunction or pathological process.

This perspective poses the greatest challenge for applying the model to incompleteness in OCD. According to the standard cognitive–behavioral model, the cognitive component is etiologic; affect is conceptualized as a reaction rather than a self-standing phenomenon. However, in cases of incompleteness OCD, intrinsic affective disturbance appears to be an essential feature, which itself serves as a trigger and motivation for problematic behaviors. This factor may account for why traditional cognitive restructuring techniques aimed at challenging irrational appraisals, and ultimately modifying causal core beliefs, may be minimally helpful for individuals with incompleteness OCD (see Tallis, 1996).

In my clinical experience with individuals high in incompleteness, two useful ways of adapting the conventional cognitive–behavioral perspective to their OCD treatment have presented themselves. The first involves the recognition that although the sensory-affective disturbance may be primary, the person's interpretation of that experience still has implications for his or her behavior and emotional responses. In other words, an important treatment focus is the individual's cognitions about his or her emotional experiences rather than about external stimuli. Conventional cognitive appraisal models suggest that in such cases, the usual appraisal is that discomfort will be uncontrollable or lead to sickness or "madness," with anxiety increasing as a result (see Rachman, 1997, 1998). However, it may not be necessary to adopt the causal model implicit in this account or to posit that appraisals must be catastrophic to be influential. In the case of incompleteness OCD, it may be most useful to help the person alter the basic subjective value he or she places on feelings of incompleteness. For such individuals, this affect feels real; they interpret it as a legitimate indicator of some change in the environment that requires an immediate response. Schwartz (1996, 1998, 1999), whose accounts of OCD emphasize its neurobiological bases, has written most about the therapeutic implications of this concept. He used the term *relabeling* to refer to the step of recognizing obsessions and behavioral urges as OCD and the term *reattributing* to refer to the subsequent recognition that the intensity of these experiences is caused by a malfunction in the brain sending invalid signals into consciousness.

Building on the concept of mindful awareness, Schwartz (1999) suggested that reframing these experiences as false messages from the brain allows the patient to acquire a distance between his or her sense of self and the experience of symptoms and to observe "one's own internal sensations with the calm clarity of an external witness" (p. 123). In the case of incompleteness OCD, such acceptance-based cognitive strategies can be included in the psychoeducation stage of a standard course of ERP.

The second way of adapting the conventional cognitive appraisal perspective for incompleteness OCD involves expanding it to allow for the causal role of sensory-affective dysregulation. As Teasdale (1997, p. 67) suggested, it may be necessary to go beyond the mainstream position that cognitions always precede emotional states and to acknowledge that cognitions may also arise as a consequence of these same states. In OCD high in incompleteness, sensory-affective disturbance may be the distal causal factor behind symptoms. It is entirely possible that core beliefs may be secondary to the individual's potentially lifelong experience of this disturbance and related symptoms, rather than being their antecedent, as proposed by the standard cognitive–behavioral model. For example, the lifelong experience of tormenting perceptions that things are not just right may bring about such beliefs as "There must, then, be a perfect solution." The result may be a pattern of interdependent affective, cognitive, and behavioral symptoms. In short, for incompleteness OCD, the full cognitive–behavioral model may be best applied by expanding it to include a revised causal sequence.

In summary, there is evidence that incompleteness OCD reflects intrinsic sensory-affective dysfunction, likely with a neurophysiological origin. Nonetheless, both behavioral and cognitive treatment methods can be applied to its understanding and treatment, with some adaptations. Although such primarily cognitive techniques as restructuring may be useful, they likely do not address the primary cause. Behavioral techniques such as ERP may be most essential.

CASE VIGNETTE

Client Description

Julie was a married 31-year-old mother of a small child who worked part-time as an administrative assistant after having resigned from a position which was a prestigious promotion. Julie presented at the anxiety disorders clinic where I work in response to a recruitment poster for a study of "compulsive perfectionism." Julie reported that although she had always been perfectionistic, she began to experience her perfectionism as irresistible and distressing soon after her marriage at age 18. She believed that it was at its worst during the previous year, when she had held the since-resigned position.

Julie reported experiencing hyperawareness about her environment and the adequacy of her actions in several everyday activities. This hyperawareness manifested in two obsessional themes: (a) the need for symmetry and sameness in the physical environment and (b) the need for exactness and precision, both of appearance and of expression, in written words. To quell feelings of discomfort associated with these preoccupations, Julie was engaging in several compulsive behaviors, including arranging and ordering of items in her home; cleaning, not to remove germs, but to render her home pristine and perfect; and rereading and rewriting documents.

Julie identified her primary difficulty as distress arising from extreme perfectionism regarding her home. She described a chronic preoccupation with the need for things to conform to a flawless appearance (e.g., surfaces, mirrors, alignment of wall trim and furniture cushions, items in cupboards, carpet texture). There were literally no elements in Julie's home that were not involved. In response to these thoughts, which were present almost chronically when she was at home, Julie was spending 3 to 4 hours daily (and up to 4 to 5 hours on days off) cleaning, "tidying," and ordering. She performed these activities ritualistically—"doing the circuit," in Julie's words—with much distress arising from circumstances that had to be prevented or delayed. Avoidance was particularly pervasive: Julie went to extreme lengths to preserve the pristine state of rooms, including edging around walls to avoid walking on carpets and keeping lights low so she could not see marks on walls. She recounted vacuuming each morning before work, then arranging her daughter's clothing on the stairs to prevent her from crossing the carpets and thus necessitating an additional vacuum.

Although she initially downplayed the presence of OCD symptoms in her professional life, assessment revealed difficulties related to the wording and appearance of written documents. Julie identified difficulty with chronic doubts about the adequacy of her choice of words, layout, content, and overinclusiveness (i.e., not knowing how much information was enough before terminating a writing task). Julie noted that her inability to cope with the promotion likely had much to do with the fact that that position had required her to write more documents and e-mail messages. She reported still taking much longer than necessary to complete routine writing-related tasks at work. As with her ordering compulsions, despite this effort, Julie still felt plagued by the sense that documents were not just right. Julie stated that in anticipation of this unshakeable dissatisfaction, she started to feel anxious even before initiating writing tasks. It became evident that these difficulties were present in most life domains involving writing (e.g., she needed to draft multiple versions of wordings for greeting cards and gift tags). She often managed this anxiety with avoidance or, for unavoidable writing tasks at work, procrastination.

Case Formulation

Julie was diagnosed with OCD. Her obsessions, although taking two discrete forms, both revolved around feelings of incompleteness. No specific triggers dominated, she could identify no feared consequences, and she described the primary affect as discomfort and tension. Anxious apprehension, when present, was a secondary reaction (i.e., in anticipation of feelings of dissatisfaction). Like most individuals with incompleteness OCD, her greatest difficulties were with open-ended activities, for which the criteria for adequate completion are governed by emotional impressions. These criteria, in Julie's case, seemed to be malfunctioning. In their place, rigid rules and considerable time were devoted to cleaning and writing in the hope of getting things just right. Despite her efforts, feelings of incompleteness persisted. As a consequence, rituals had become increasingly time consuming and avoidance more pervasive.

Treatment Plan

A standard time-limited course of ERP was planned aimed at desensitizing Julie to the negative affect associated with her incompleteness experiences and motivating her compulsions. The plan was to progress through a hierarchy of exposure tasks designed to provoke in Julie feelings of incompleteness coupled with prevention of the rituals and avoidance she used to alleviate the associated discomfort. In Julie's case, the pervasiveness of these feelings at home meant that single circumscribed exposure tasks, performed in isolation, might be less relevant than daylong exposures to perpetual states of change in her environment. Standard cognitive restructuring techniques (focusing on irrational beliefs) were not used.

Treatment consisted of 16 sessions of ERP modelled after the treatments described by Steketee (1999) and Kozak and Foa (1997). Twice-weekly 60- to 90-minute sessions were used for the first 5 weeks, followed by 4 weekly and then 2 biweekly sessions. This course of therapy included the following components:

- psychoeducation to familiarize Julie with the behavioral model of OCD, especially as it applies to incompleteness;
- information gathering and treatment planning to collect baseline data through self-monitoring of cues, avoidance, and rituals and to assign discomfort ratings to identified cues to design a hierarchy of exposure situations;
- graduated ERP involving in-session exposure tasks and daily homework tasks, with self-monitoring of discomfort levels during self-administered exposure; and
- home visits.

Treatment Phase 1: Psychoeducation, Monitoring, and Planning (Sessions 1–3)

The first three sessions were devoted to educating Julie about treatment; further evaluating the components of her OCD through monitoring of avoidance, triggers, and rituals; and designing an exposure hierarchy on the basis of this monitoring. During this phase, emphasis was placed on helping Julie to internalize the treatment model by applying each of its components to her own symptoms. The aim of ERP for the treatment of incompleteness OCD is to help the individual habituate to feelings of sensory-affective discomfort. The goal is to decrease the power of this experience to guide behavior or, in the words of one patient, "to build up an immunity to the feeling."

Initiating Treatment and Psychoeducation

Julie had grown used to most of her obsessive–compulsive tendencies and had engaged in little reflection on their uncontrollability or the problematic motivation behind them. Furthermore, in the case of her ordering symptoms, almost all areas of her life at home were affected. It was thus necessary that she reframe these difficulties as OCD in order to address them therapeutically. My colleagues and I have found that the assessment itself (including the extensive self-monitoring) can be useful to this end, because the individual acquires a language to apply to otherwise perplexing experiences. Julie was receptive to the treatment formulation summarized in the preceding section and stated that she could see the value of gradually building up her "immunity" so that she could have some normality in her daily life. A necessary part of the educational component entailed some cognitive reframing of her experiences as OCD; the strategies used for this were similar to those described by Schwartz (1996) as *relabeling* and *reattributing*.

Feelings of incompleteness are often longstanding and ego syntonic. Consequently, ambivalence about treatment and initially lower motivation for change can be expected at the outset of treatment. Julie, for example, expressed concern about becoming careless and messy: "That just isn't me." Ambivalence about treatment can be addressed by identifying these feelings as an understandable consequence of apprehension about change and about the duration and strength of OCD. We have found it helpful to correct the individual's perception that the goal of treatment is to bring to an end to all habitual ways of doing things by pointing out that there is a difference between having to do and choosing to do a behavior. Another valuable technique is to increase the patient's awareness of the cost of symptoms, such as their impact on relationships, mood, and plans for the future. This analysis can be done either as a separate recording task (see Antony & Swinson, 1998, for adaptable "perfectionism forms") or as part of a general discussion about the results of initial symptom assessment and self-monitoring. Julie reported that until her assessment, she had not reflected on how much of her day-to-day conduct was actually avoidance.

The emotional state seen in incompleteness OCD can also pose challenges to treatment. In discussing the treatment plan, Julie initially expressed doubt about relinquishing behaviors (e.g., cleaning and tidying) that were comforting and sometimes even gratifying. Compulsions are often distinguished from other driven behaviors, such as impulsions, by their association with an offset of negative affect (e.g., anxiety) rather than the onset of positive affect. This distinction may be difficult in incompleteness OCD, for which temporary partial relief from baseline discomfort can be subjectively positive and may lower the individual's motivation to refrain from rituals. This reluctance can be addressed by building the individual's ability and confidence in identifying his or her compulsions as such in early sessions and by promoting CBT as a way of gaining control over daily behaviors that are being driven by emotions rather than choice.

Self-Monitoring and Recording

In the early stages of treatment, self-monitoring of triggers for obsessions, avoidance behaviors, and rituals provides the patient and therapist with a detailed picture of the functional components of the patient's OCD. Given the pervasiveness of incompleteness experiences and compensatory ritualizing, self-monitoring for cues can become overwhelming. Furthermore, features of OCD can themselves interfere with necessary recording and self-report activities. Julie's obsessional doubts and need for exactness were both evident in her self-monitoring activities. Her 8-page, much-revised record of triggers for obsessions and rituals had to be substantially pruned to make a workable exposure hierarchy. Despite this level of detail, Julie reported that she still had had difficulty distinguishing obsessions and compulsions from other experiences. A useful strategy was to strengthen Julie's ability to label obsessions and compulsions as such by identifying key ways they differ from other experiences. For Julie, and for other clients with incompleteness OCD, such differences commonly revolve around the strength of the emotion felt if the behavior is resisted or modified in some way. In one patient's words, "The emotions are running the show."

An additional benefit of monitoring is that it enables the person to make a personal distinction between legitimate needs and actions versus obsessions and emotion-driven compulsions. Whereas for Julie a complete cataloguing of all environmental triggers might be impossible and minimally useful, a core group could be identified on the basis of the similarity of their subjective flavor. We have found it useful to encourage patients to recognize that "if it feels like OCD, it probably is." Practice in session using the subjective units of distress scale (SUDS) to rate discomfort levels from 0 to 100, a necessary tool for building the exposure hierarchy, further helped Julie select triggers to address.

The final goal was to compile a representative list of 15 to 20 exposure items for each obsessional theme, with items described in enough detail to distinguish them from similar items with different ratings. The exposure hierarchy must be based on the level of discomfort felt in the absence of the usual compulsive accompaniment (i.e., if the activities were deritualized). For example, Julie reported that bedtime for her daughter was minimally problematic. However, the same situation without ritualizing had a SUDS rating of 40 because of her attunement to the disarray of her daughter's toys, making that specific "subtrigger" a suitable low-level item on her hierarchy.

Involving Family Members

Julie declined the recommended opportunity for her husband to attend an early session. Family accommodation is known to reinforce and perpetuate compulsions (Calvocoressi et al., 1995). Certain familial variables, such as amount of critical interactions with the patient, may also predict poor response to therapy. We have found several potentially detrimental family responses to be anticipated for patients with incompleteness OCD:

- Because there is no objective threat to identify with and because the patient's preoccupations are often objectively trivial (i.e., the need for alignment of belongings), family members may show a lack of empathy.
- Because symptoms are often not circumscribed, the impact on the family may be great, provoking resentment and anger.
- Family members may consider many of the behaviors associated with incompleteness OCD (e.g., procrastination, slowness)

to be controllable and therefore the result of a "lack of effort" on the part of the client.

- Family members may become impatient with the speed of change once therapy has begun.

Therapists should be prepared to address these issues when discussing with the client variables likely to influence the practicability and outcome of treatment.

Treatment Phase 2: Exposure and Response Prevention (Sessions 4–16)

By Week 4, a satisfactory exposure hierarchy had been drawn up, and Julie was ready to engage in her first session of therapist-assisted exposure. The following are sample items from Julie's exposure hierarchy related to symmetry and order and cleanliness, together with their SUDS ratings:

- leaving footprints, residue, or lint on the carpet in the bedroom and living room (100);
- leaving hairs or lint on the floor in the upstairs bathroom (85);
- leaving and looking at residue or water marks on the coffee table (70);
- leaving knickknacks out of place on bedroom surfaces (50); and
- seeing disarray in the doll's hair, clothing, and position in the child's bedroom (40).

Symptom themes in incompleteness OCD, although similar in form, can have widely different content. To minimize confusion for the client, particularly in the early days of treatment when he or she is still becoming familiar with ERP principles, the therapist may find it useful to have parallel exposure hierarchies. Sample items appearing on the hierarchy used for treating Julie's need for exactness and precision related to written documents included the following:

- writing a professional report to be submitted at work (100),
- drafting a professional report in point form (80),
- drafting a point-form version of a cover letter for a promotion application (75),
- writing a letter to actually be sent to a family member (65), and
- writing a point-form summary of the last hour's activities (45).

Implementing Exposure and Response Prevention

In-session exposures are particularly valuable for the therapist to help the patient practice techniques for SUDS monitoring and to be on the lookout for rituals or other activities that might limit the effectiveness of exposure. In incompleteness OCD, creativity is required to identify valid yet portable cues for assisted exposure. For Julie, whose incompleteness was mostly expressed through symmetry and exactness obsessions, her therapist included such in-session tasks as "messing things up" (e.g., putting hand cream and mustard fingerprints on mirrors and picture glass, leaving lint on fabrics), writing (e.g., documents, greeting cards), recording (e.g., documenting activities), and sorting belongings (e.g., CDs, books). Some ideas for portable exposure stimuli suitable for incompleteness OCD, organized by symptom theme, are as follows.

- *Symmetry and exactness:* Belongings, clothing, books, documents, greeting cards, recipe cards, novel items provided by therapist.
- *Cleaning:* Household items, clothing.
- *Doubt:* Documents and bills, writing tasks, reading tasks, lists, timed leaving task.
- *Tactile and motor stimuli:* Posture, textiles, speeded leaving of room, spurned clothing to be worn.
- *Fear of not saying just the right thing:* Greeting cards, writing tasks, answering machine recording, pen pal "helper."

Julie and her therapist began with exposure to seeing residue on mirrors or the glass in picture frames (SUDS rating of 45). Julie recounted how she would avoid this scenario and described cleaning and rearrangement strategies she would feel driven to use. They then brainstormed discomfort-inducing alternatives focusing on randomness, disarray, and sensory change (i.e., touching the glass with greasy fingers, staring at the messy surfaces, changing the placement of pictures on the desk to maximize the visibility of the residue, putting mirrors and pictures on the floor to attract lint). The therapist modeled these activities, then Julie proceeded with exposure and monitored her SUDS level at 5-minute intervals. During this exercise, the therapist acted as coach, keeping Julie focused, taking discomfort ratings, and making encouraging statements while also prompting exploration, as Julie's SUDS level decreased, of how the task could be made most discomforting. The goal was to continue active and continuous exposure until her SUDS level returned to baseline or half of her maximum experienced level.

This objectively simple in-session task and its SUDS ratings provided valuable evidence for a discussion of parallels with other less mundane aversive experiences and the power of the feeling state to drive behavior. Julie was surprised to see that her SUDS level had declined, even when she tried to make the task the most discomfort provoking. Within half an hour, her SUDS level had returned to baseline. This finding provided an opportunity to discuss how giving in to the behavior had prevented her from seeing that this decline in distress would happen, and she quickly applied this insight to other, more difficult, situations. She left the session with the homework of continued self-administered exposure to messy pictures, to an item lower in the hierarchy (i.e., the doll in her daughter's room), and to a corresponding item in her writing hierarchy.

Implementing Exposure

Julie's exposures continued to progress, with evidence of habituation at each stage. For all hierarchy tasks, satisfactory reduction of SUDS level took place within 60 to 90 minutes. However, frequent readjustments to ERP strategies were required. At the center where I work, therapists encourage patients to move laterally within exposure stages (i.e., to do self-exposure to nonplanned situations of equivalent discomfort value) and to think of ERP as a lifestyle change, rather than a situation-specific strategy. Julie also knew that even the planned exposures were cumulative; each week, she would continue exposures to previous items and add new items as well.

After the first few sessions, it became clear that circumscribed exposure to specific items did not allow Julie and her therapist to monitor progress with the wide range of home situations in which Julie had been ordering and arranging and in which she was now instead cultivating disarray, change, and randomness. Exposure was becoming a daylong activity, and single-session plotting became impractical. Two useful adaptations for incompleteness OCD are "day plots," in which the patient monitors SUDS levels at hourly intervals while engaging in exposure as part of daily activities, and weekly hierarchy item reratings, in which the patient rates current SUDS for all exposure items at a set time, such as in session. Both of these were found to be effective for Julie.

However, by Session 8 the plotting itself presented a new obstacle. Julie reported that the rules and format for plotting and journaling of difficulties in home exposures had themselves become ritualized and similar to the problems she had had with other documentation tasks. This is a common challenge with this patient population and can often extend to the very work of exposure (e.g., the order, timing, and duration of exercises). Therapists can address this challenge by generating ways of introducing randomness and spontaneity into the treatment itself. For example, Julie was encouraged to randomly change recording methods, to do abbreviated (e.g., word-count-restricted or timed) notation, and to plot data on hand-drawn forms. Other tactics might include skipping the plotting on random days and tackling planned and nonplanned exposures in random order.

Implementing Response Prevention

During treatment planning, attention must be paid to what aspects of compulsions to prevent, particularly in the case of incompleteness OCD, in which many activities have a compulsive quality and rituals often mature into elaborate and subtle forms (e.g., Julie's tactics for getting out of the house each morning). Aspects of rituals can include time spent on specific behavior (e.g., in reading over a document, making a bed), context control (e.g., no interruptions or distractions), time spent on a sequence of behaviors, necessitating further analysis of the source of the slowness (e.g., checking, mental review, repeating, or meticulous performance of each component), and ritualization of single behaviors or ritualized sequencing of multiple behaviors.

For many individuals with incompleteness OCD, a primary feature is the ritualized and inflexible quality of nearly all daily activities—"It's not the time; it's the manner," one patient observed. Thus, in planning response prevention, therapists should generate methods for reducing not only the duration of behaviors, but also their inflexible configuration. For example, one client (see Summerfeldt, 2004) reported that he spent only about 30 minutes on his morning grooming routine. However, this activity had to follow an invariable sequence, with each subcomponent performed in precisely the same way and with perfect consistency in all aspects of his surroundings. In Julie's case, primary features were the excessive time she spent on behaviors because of her need to repeat and perform meticulously, as well as her well-elaborated avoidance strategies. Both creativity and a thorough grasp of symptoms were needed to attempt the treatment goal of completely deritualizing these activities. For example, for her problems with initiating and efficiently completing writing tasks, response prevention guidelines similar to the following were implemented:

> Draft one point-form letter to a friend. Take a maximum of 10 minutes to complete it, and use a maximum of 5 points, with a maximum of 4 to 5 words per point. In 10-minute sessions, flesh out the draft to qualify as a "good" letter. Combine this with other 10-minute writing tasks into a sitting of ½ hour, working on them sequentially and plotting SUDS throughout.

As treatment progressed and rituals were being deconstructed and avoidance undermined, Julie became aware of other discomfort-alleviating "quick-fix" strategies in her life. Rituals and obvious avoidance strategies may not be the only self-perpetuating characteristics of incompleteness OCD that clients need to refrain from. Other functionally equivalent features can include difficulty delegating, general inflexibility, reassurance seeking (to alleviate feelings of uncertainty about one's perceptions), primary obsessional slowness, and indecisiveness and procrastination. The breadth of such behaviors may complicate design of the response prevention component of treatment.

The form of response prevention—complete or partial—is an important consideration. Complete response prevention from the outset is often advised, but this may not always be practical. In the case of incompleteness OCD, in which most of the person's daily activities may be compulsive in form, several response prevention variants should be considered (see Steketee, 1999, for a discussion). Two types of partial response prevention—ritual restriction and ritual abbreviation—may be particularly useful. Prompting, shaping, and pacing, for example, have been reported to be effective methods for modifying perfectionism-related slowness (Rachman, 1974). For individuals with very high discomfort, a stepwise approach to response prevention using response delay may be another option (see Schwartz, 1996). In this approach, the waiting period can be gradually increased until the person is refraining altogether from ritualizing. Ritual interruption and interference may also be essential. Following a few initial exposures, Julie reported that simply refraining from compulsions was less distressing than engaging in the behaviors in a way deliberately contrary to the ritual, which prompted maximal levels of incompleteness feelings, obsessions, and general discomfort. At the outset of each hierarchy step, Julie and her therapist generated ideas for ritual interference strategies for each item. In her homework, Julie began with these guidelines and then modified them using her own judgment about how to maximize her SUDS level, with the ultimate goal of making spontaneity and choice, rather than discomfort reduction, the basis for behavioral choices. It is particularly important with this patient population to be attuned to the possibility of inadvertent rigidity and rule-driven ritualizing of the exposure itself.

By Session 7, Julie was applying ERP principles to most domains of her home life; she had adopted an "exposure philosophy." By Session 11, Julie had tackled the most difficult items in both hierarchies. Between these two points, she noted an interesting consequence of the ritual disruption technique: Her cognitions about the utility of her perfectionistic cleaning and writing rituals appeared to have been altered. She now regarded them as ultimately futile symptoms, rather than as logical and potentially improvable strategies. She reported that until this point she had not truly internalized the therapy, thinking that it would be possible to recoup her cleaning and ordering tactics if discomfort became unbearable in treatment. A noticeable improvement in her mood state accompanied this shift.

Treatment Phase 3: Relapse Prevention and End of Treatment (Sessions 15 and 16)

In the last two (biweekly) sessions, Julie's therapist turned to strategies for maintaining gains. For Julie, and commonly for others with incompleteness-related symptoms, two issues warrant particular attention: guidelines to be used for "normal" behavior (in the absence of rituals) and management of emergent symptoms. Both concerns were partly addressed in a review of key issues that had arisen throughout the course of treatment, including the ritualization of therapy strategies (e.g., plotting and monitoring) and Julie's experience and mastery of setbacks, as well as the skills she had built, which included her ability to recognize obsessions and compulsions using distress and preoccupation as signs and her use of ERP as a new response style that must be kept strong through regular practice. In the last two sessions, Julie did a trial run of how to conduct basic activities (e.g., sending a letter to an old friend) and reported, surprised, that her ERP skills had generalized to those activities. She noted that the self-determined lateral exposures had likely been crucial; she had been generating spontaneous guidelines since early in treatment. We ended with a plan for contact if needed and booked follow-ups.

Outcome

At the posttreatment session, Julie reported continued feelings of mastery over her symptoms. Although incompleteness experiences were still a part of her day-to-day life, their power to influence her behavior, including in the form of avoidance, seemed much reduced. This impression was supported by posttreatment assessment data. However, subsequent follow-ups using the interviewer-rated Yale–Brown Obsessive–Compulsive Scale (Y–BOCS) showed some regression. Pretreatment, posttreatment, and 3- and 6-month follow-up total scores showed a substantial early improvement of 68% in total symptom severity at posttreatment but some loss of gains subsequently. The greatest decline occurred in the 3-month interval posttreatment in compulsion severity, primarily because of less resistance to compulsions. Julie revealed that she had ceased practicing daily ERP for the physical ordering and arranging at home; that it was simply easier, given her busy life, to use her old strategies; and that because she knew she could control her symptoms "if I have to," using them helped her function.

At this point, the therapist reviewed the rationale for undertaking CBT and earlier treatment data and observations. Julie agreed that her symptoms would likely only worsen, and she decided to reimplement daily ERP on her own in response to any experience that she felt was primarily driven by incompleteness feelings. Support phone calls over the next month confirmed that she was doing this. At 6-month follow-up, at which Julie reported continued use of daily ERP, despite regular ritual violations, 3-month gains had been retained.

In short, although Julie retained an overall 35% improvement at 6 months following cessation of treatment, substantial loss of gains had taken place. At both follow-ups, her OCD was still clinically significant according to usual norms. Although symptom severity stabilized between the 3- and 6-month follow-ups, it had done so only with the help of continued daily ERP. The drive to ritualize, although controllable, still persisted. Although the power of her obsessions to drive Julie's behavior had lessened, the occurrence of incompleteness experiences seemed to be untouched.

Improving Long-Term Treatment Outcome

Difficulties maintaining gains in incompleteness OCD are likely the direct consequence of such clinical features as early onset and degree of ego syntonicity, which may interfere with the motivation for, and ease of, self-directed ERP after treatment ends. Efforts to improve long-term treatment outcomes can focus on two interrelated issues: (a) ability to recognize symptoms and (b) efforts spent in resistance.

An important task early in treatment is to help the individual label incompleteness OCD symptoms as such. In the absence of the therapist's coaching, following treatment patients' ability to identify their symptoms in this way may become less sharp. One individual noted at follow-up, "During treatment, I knew it was the OCD, but now it just feels like me." Several tactics may help to revitalize the person's ability to maintain perspective on his or her symptoms and the practical skills acquired in therapy. One tactic, if feasible, is to continue with treatment part-time, perhaps indefinitely; our center offers once-monthly CBT group booster sessions to this end. It may also be useful to join a local OCD support group, such as one affiliated with the Obsessive–Compulsive Foundation. In addition to the social support offered, the opportunity to hear about and discuss others' and one's own symptoms helps keep alive the ability to recognize OCD-driven emotional experiences and behaviors. Finally, educational materials are often valuable not only at the beginning of treatment (e.g., to help the patient become familiar with the premises of ERP), but also as reference tools after treatment has ended. I usually provide clients with a list of popular self-help books, but many people with incompleteness OCD have reported back that many of the "classic" OCD profiles described in them seemed irrelevant. Several patients like Julie have found it easiest to identify with the examples and formulations provided in *Brain Lock* (Schwartz, 1996). Although there are fundamental differences between the treatment protocol described in this chapter and that described in the book, it has been my experience that individuals high in incompleteness OCD find this book particularly helpful. Selected OCD-related readings from *When Perfect Isn't Good Enough* (Antony & Swinson, 1998) can also be useful.

Even if patients correctly identify compulsions as such, another juncture at which treatment gains can be lost is in the lessened effort spent on resisting them, a principal source of Julie's increased Y–BOCS score at 3-month follow-up. As discussed earlier in this chapter, a useful strategy for helping patients sustain levels of effort, and one that can be instituted while treatment is under way, is to instill ERP as a default and overlearned response, or lifestyle, rather than symptom-bound intervention. Motivation for treatment, always a consideration in OCD (see chap. 3 in this volume), may be particularly important for this group of patients. Making issues of motivation and ambivalence explicit at the outset of treatment, rather than addressing them after difficulties arise, is another proactive strategy.

CONCLUSION

OCD dominated by incompleteness feelings poses a challenge to therapists hoping to apply prevailing psychological treatments. Contrary to conventional cognitive appraisal models, which maintain that affect has its origins in core beliefs and appraisals, in incompleteness OCD cognitive contents appear to be secondary to a primary sensory-affective disturbance. The behavioral component of CBT, aimed at habituation to the disturbing sensory-affective experience, may be key to treatment success.

The case vignette presented in this chapter provides evidence for the partial effectiveness of carefully conducted ERP in a complex case of incompleteness OCD. However, the long-standing, ego-syntonic nature of Julie's compulsive rituals and their association with a baseline internal state rather than an acquired aversion to specific triggers resulted in substantial loss of gains once the therapist took a less active role. Thus, therapy appeared to contain, but not eliminate, her compulsions. Only with sustained self-administered ERP efforts was Julie able to stabilize her symptoms. In a less highly motivated individual, a much poorer outcome would have been likely. At this point, it is not known to what extent decreased adherence to rituals can be maintained once therapy sessions have ended, particularly in the face of symptom shift, life stress, or fluctuations in mood. Long-term support and supervision of ERP may be necessary.

REFERENCES

Abramowitz, J. S., Franklin, M. E., Schwartz, S. A., & Furr, J. M. (2003). Symptom presentation and outcome of cognitive–behavioral therapy for obsessive–compulsive disorder. *Journal of Clinical and Consulting Psychology, 72,* 1049–1057.

Antony, M. M., & Swinson, R. P. (1998). *When perfect isn't good enough: Strategies for coping with perfectionism.* Oakland, CA: New Harbinger.

Ball, S. G., Baer, L., & Otto, M. W. (1996). Symptom subtypes of obsessive–compulsive disorder in behavioral treatment studies: A quantitative review. *Behaviour Research and Therapy, 47,* 47–51.

Calvocoressi, L., Lewis, B., Harris, M., Trufan, S. J., Goodman, W. K., McDougle, C. J., & Price, L. H. (1995). Family accommodation in obsessive–compulsive disorder. *American Journal of Psychiatry, 152,* 441–443.

Coles, M. E., Frost, R. O., Heimberg, R. G., & Rhéaume, J. (2003). "Not just right experiences": Perfectionism, obsessive–compulsive features and general psychopathology. *Behaviour Research and Therapy, 41,* 681–700.

Foa, E. B., Abramowitz, J. S., Franklin, M. E., & Kozak, M. J. (1999). Feared consequences, fixity of belief, and treatment outcome in patients with obsessive–compulsive disorder. *Behavior Therapy, 30,* 717–724.

Foa, E. B., & Kozak, M. J. (1986). Emotional processing of fear: Exposure to corrective information. *Psychological Bulletin, 99,* 20–35.

Kozak, M. J., & Foa, E. B. (1997). *Mastery of obsessive–compulsive disorder: A cognitive–behavioral approach (therapist guide).* Toronto, Ontario, Canada: Psychological Corporation.

Leckman, J. F., Grice, D. E., Barr, L. C., de Vries, A. L. C., Martin, C., Cohen, D. J., et al. (1995). Tic-related vs. non-tic-related obsessive compulsive disorder. *Anxiety, 1*, 208–215.

Leckman, J. F., Walker, D. E., Goodman, W. K., Pauls, D. L., & Cohen, D. J. (1994). "Just right" perceptions associated with compulsive behavior in Tourette's syndrome. *American Journal of Psychiatry, 151*, 675–680.

Mataix-Cols, D., do Rosario-Campos, M. C., & Leckman, J. F. (2005). A multidimensional model of obsessive–compulsive disorder. *American Journal of Psychiatry, 162*, 228–238.

Mataix-Cols, D., Marks, I. M., Greist, J. H., Kobak, K. A., & Baer, L. (2002). Obsessive–compulsive symptom dimensions as predictors of compliance with and response to behaviour therapy: Results from a controlled trial. *Psychotherapy and Psychosomatics, 71*, 255–262.

Miguel, E. C., do Rosario-Campos, M. C., Prado, H. S., do Valle, R., Rauch, S. L., Coffey, B. J., et al. (2000). Sensory phenomena in obsessive–compulsive disorder and Tourette's disorder. *Journal of Clinical Psychiatry, 61*, 150–156.

Mowrer, O. H. (1960). *Learning theory and behavior*. New York: Wiley.

Pitman, R. K. (1987a). A cybernetic model of obsessive–compulsive psychopathology. *Comprehensive Psychiatry, 28*, 334–343.

Pitman, R. K. (1987b). Pierre Janet on obsessive–compulsive disorder (1903). *Archives of General Psychiatry, 44*, 226–232.

Rachman, S. (1974). Primary obsessional slowness. *Behaviour Research and Therapy, 12*, 9–18.

Rachman, S. (1997). A cognitive theory of obsessions. *Behaviour Research and Therapy, 35*, 793–802.

Rachman, S. (1998). A cognitive theory of obsessions: Elaborations. *Behaviour Research and Therapy, 36*, 385–401.

Rapoport, J. L. (1991). Basal ganglia dysfunction as a proposed cause of obsessive–compulsive disorder. In B. J. Carroll & J. E. Barrett (Eds.), *Psychopathology and the brain* (pp. 77–95). New York: Raven Press.

Rasmussen, S. A., & Eisen, J. L. (1992). The epidemiology and clinical features of obsessive compulsive disorder. *Psychiatric Clinics of North America, 15*, 743–758.

Schwartz, J. M. (1996). *Brain lock: Free yourself from obsessive–compulsive behavior*. New York: HarperCollins.

Schwartz, J. M. (1998). Neuroanatomical aspects of cognitive–behavioral therapy response in obsessive–compulsive disorder: An evolving perspective on brain and behavior. *British Journal of Psychiatry, 173*, 38–44.

Schwartz, J. M. (1999). A role for volition and attention in the generation of new brain circuitry: Toward a neurobiology of mental force. *Journal of Consciousness Studies, 6*, 115–142.

Steketee, G. (1999). *Overcoming obsessive–compulsive disorder: A behavioral and cognitive protocol for the treatment of OCD (therapist protocol)*. Oakland, CA: New Harbinger.

Summerfeldt, L. J. (1998). Cognitive processing in obsessive–compulsive disorder: Alternate models and the role of subtypes (Doctoral dissertation, York University, Toronto, Ontario, Canada, 1998). *Dissertation Abstracts International, 60,* 4288B.

Summerfeldt, L. J. (2004). Understanding and treating incompleteness in obsessive–compulsive disorder. *Journal of Clinical Psychology, 60,* 1155–1168.

Summerfeldt, L. J., Antony, M. M., & Swinson, R. P. (2002). Reply to Bilsbury and others: More on the phenomenology of perfectionism: "Incompleteness" [Letter to the editor]. *Canadian Journal of Psychiatry, 47,* 977–978.

Szechtman, H., & Woody, E. (2004). Obsessive–compulsive disorder as a disturbance of security motivation. *Psychological Review, 111,* 111–127.

Tallis, F. (1996). Compulsive washing in the absence of phobic and illness anxiety. *Behaviour Research and Therapy, 34,* 361–362.

Teasdale, J. D. (1997). The relationship between cognition and emotion: The mind-in-place in mood disorders. In D. M. Clark & C. G. Fairburn (Eds.), *Science and practice of cognitive behavior therapy* (pp. 67–93). New York: Oxford University Press.

Veale, D., Gournay, K., Dryden, W., Boocock, A., Shah, F., Willson, R., et al. (1996). Body dysmorphic disorder: A cognitive behavioural model and pilot randomised controlled trial. *Behaviour Research and Therapy, 34,* 717–729.

9

TREATING RELIGIOUS, SEXUAL, AND AGGRESSIVE OBSESSIONS

S. RACHMAN

The content of most repugnant obsessions falls into three categories: intrusive and unacceptable blasphemous thoughts, intrusive and unacceptable sexual thoughts, and intrusive and unacceptable thoughts of harming others. As a further twist, patients can fall into reverse reasoning—for example, "The fact that I am anxious in the presence of children proves that I am weird and untrustworthy." According to the cognitive model, the essential problem in these obsessions, as in other obsessions in obsessive–compulsive disorder (OCD), is that people interpret their thoughts as signifying that they are bad, crazy, or dangerous. Cognitive–behavioral treatment (CBT) relies on cognitive techniques to help people modify such misinterpretations, and the supplementary behavioral component is used to help patients reduce the behavioral consequences of their obsessions. Over the course of CBT, the personal meaning of the thoughts gradually changes from threatening to benign. After successful treatment, the obsessions have declined or disappeared, and the associated avoidance and compulsive behaviors have become insignificant.

EXAMPLES AND FEATURES OF REPUGNANT OBSESSIONS

Examples of religious obsessions include a fear of making sacrilegious gestures in a holy place (e.g., "I will shout foul, obscene language in church"), repeated sacrilegious images, the pollution of prayers or other rituals by impure or disgusting thoughts, and a fear of devilish temptations. Examples of sexual obsessions include a fear of committing inappropriate acts or gestures (e.g., "I will sexually molest a young child") and repeated images of sex with inappropriate partners (e.g., "I see myself having sex with the priest"). Examples of aggressive (or harm) obsessions include a recurrent fear of harming other people (e.g., "I will push an elderly man under the oncoming train"; "I will stab my mother") or of harm coming to relatives or friends (e.g., "My parents will be killed by an intruder"). Some obsessions combine the themes; for example, sacrilegious obsessions can involve images of having sexual relations with religious figures.

A unique quality of sexual obsessions is that they often are preceded or accompanied by bodily sensations that are interpreted as signs of sexual arousal or desire. When the person believes that these sensations indicate sexual arousal, such as when they occur in the wrong place or in an inappropriate context (e.g., near children), he or she can feel distressed, ashamed, and frightened. Many patients end up avoiding situations or people around whom the sensations are evoked.

THE COGNITIVE MODEL OF OBSESSIVE–COMPULSIVE DISORDER

Because of the intrusive, disrupting qualities of the obsessive thoughts and the unacceptability of their repugnant content, individuals with OCD resist their thoughts. They try to block the intrusive ideas, to oppose them, to debate with them, or to reject them altogether. The obsessions commonly produce feelings of shame, fear, self-doubt, and self-distrust. People tend to question their view of themselves and their morality, and they may begin to feel that they are unsafe, evil, weird, or on the verge of going crazy. The thoughts are so shameful or embarrassing that people prefer to conceal them and feel guilty for having such unacceptable and objectionable ideas.

People keep most of these obsessions secret—in one patient's words, "It is my dirty little secret." Another patient said, after successful treatment, "The number of my secrets was a measure of my illness." Before entering therapy, people with OCD tend to believe that their obsessional experiences are unique to them, and this belief is conserved by keeping the experiences secret. It follows that they feel they are freakish or weird. Given that most of the people who are seriously affected by obsessions have high moral or religious standards, these ideas are acutely unacceptable to them and give rise to corrosive self-doubting. They fear that they may have lurking inside their seemingly virtuous character secret thoughts and ideas that are dangerous, wicked, disturbing, sinful, and unsafe (e.g., "I must be a very bad person"). Many patients believe that they should control their thoughts as well as their behavior, and they come to fear that one day they will lose control and carry out the repugnant acts that invade their thoughts.

Overinterpretations of the significance of one's intrusions can become entangled with an exaggerated sense of responsibility (Purdon, 1999; Rachman, 1997; Salkovskis, 1985, 1999). For example, the belief "My immoral sexual thoughts reveal something important and unflattering about the kind of person that I really am" may be entangled with a thought such as "I am sinning because I am responsible for all of my thoughts." Another example of a belief representing exaggerated responsibility is the thought "I keep seeing horrible images of my parents involved in a serious vehicle accident, and I feel responsible for placing them in danger" (this not uncommon expression of the cognitive bias is called *thought–action fusion*). The majority of people dismiss or ignore their unwanted intrusive thoughts and regard them as nonsense. However, if a person attaches important meaning to these unwanted thoughts, the thoughts tend to become distressing and adhesive.

Cognitive–behavioral treatment is based on the cognitive explanation that obsessions are caused by catastrophic misinterpretations of the significance of one's unwanted intrusive thoughts, images, and impulses. The obsessions persist for as long as the misinterpretations continue, and they diminish or disappear as a function of the weakening or elimination of the misinterpretations. The aim of treatment is to assist patients in modifying their interpretations of the unwanted intrusions, normalizing them, and decatastrophizing them. When some progress has been made in the cognitive work, attention is turned toward dealing with the self-defeating safety behavior that helps to sustain the maladaptive cognitions.

The cognitive work involves an analysis of the thoughts and the corresponding meanings and interpretations patients ascribe to them, the therapeutic collection of evidence (especially using behavioral experiments), the generation of reasons for and against the interpretations, and the formulation of alternative interpretations. This work is supplemented by exposure exercises; behavioral experiments; and recommendations to cease avoidance, concealment, thought suppression, internal debates, and neutralization.

ASSESSMENT

Once OCD has been identified as the primary focus of treatment, the therapist formulates a specific treatment plan on the basis of a thorough understanding of the person's symptoms and the appraisals driving them. A semistructured interview examining the nature of the person's obsessions and compulsions can be useful in conjunction with administration of the Personal Significance Scale (PSS), which is designed to assess the personal significance the individual places on his or her obsessions (e.g., that the thought signifies the presence of a nasty and vicious hidden character flaw that puts the person in danger of losing control; see Rachman, 2003, for both of these tools). Other useful measures include the Thought Action Fusion Scale (Shafran, Thordarson, & Rachman, 1996) and the second edition of the Beck Depression Inventory (Beck, Steer, & Brown, 1996).

In cases in which avoidance behavior is a significant contributor to the problem, the use of behavioral avoidance tests is advisable. The therapist and patient compile a list of avoidances, and the most manipulable and relevant are selected for testing (e.g., knives, sharp objects, supermarkets). The tests are carried out in the conventional way; the patient is asked to approach the object or situation as closely as possible and to rate his or her anxiety using a simple measure of anxiety, such as a "fear thermometer," a scale of 0 (calm or no anxiety) to 100 (terrified or extremely anxious). The therapist observes the degree and extent of the person's avoidance of each specific object or situation. At the completion of treatment, little or no avoidance should remain. To track therapeutic changes, the PSS can be given at the start of every session. In addition, the person is asked at the beginning of each session about the nature, frequency, and distress of any obsessions experienced in the previous week. For this purpose, a simple report sheet can be used.

TREATMENT

The therapist begins treatment by providing information about obsessions and OCD, introducing the treatment rationale, and examining the nature and genesis of the individual's obsessions. Treatment then focuses on collecting evidence relevant to the person's interpretation of the meaning of the obsession via cognitive and behavioral strategies.

Didactic Phase

The therapist describes the nature of normal and abnormal obsessions, noting in particular that the content of normal and abnormal obsessions is indistinguishable and that almost everyone experiences such intrusions from time to time (Niler & Beck, 1989; Purdon & Clark, 1994; Rachman & de Silva, 1978; Salkovskis & Harrison, 1984). A list of normal and abnormal obsessions can be used as a focal point of this discussion (e.g., see Rachman, 2003). During the discussion, the therapist emphasizes the universality of the phenomenon and encourages the person to speak openly and freely about his or her experiences, in recognition of the fact that intrusive thoughts are a common experience and need not be kept secret. Not infrequently, patients receive this information and explanation with surprise, followed by relief ("I always thought that I was a complete freak and concealed my struggle with the thoughts from everyone, from the world"). Some anxiety evaporates.

The therapist then introduces the treatment model, emphasizing that unwanted intrusive thoughts become clinically significant when the person interprets them as being of great personal significance. The therapist can provide examples of unwanted intrusive thoughts that are regarded as being trivial and others that are regarded as being of great personal significance and can elicit examples from the person himself or herself. The therapist can provide patients with a written copy of the rationale for the treatment, plus references (see Rachman, 2003). The following is an example of an introduction to the treatment model:

> Most drivers get angry on occasion and even curse under their breath or openly (e.g., "I'll kill you!"). However, they seldom take seriously the aggressive feelings they experience while at the wheel. They soon calm down and dismiss their aggressive reactions as unimportant. They do not interpret the angry thought as personally significant or as a sign of lurking homicidal tendencies. Do you ever have silly thoughts while driving? Or at other times? Do you ever have unwanted thoughts about religion, or sex, or aggression? If so, which of these silly thoughts bother you, and which do not? Do you know why some thoughts bother you and others do not?

Following this introduction, a therapist may find it helpful to discuss the particular content of the person's main obsessions. After establishing the category into which the obsessions fall, the therapist should ask why other themes do not feature in their obsessions. Generally, this exploration leads people to recognize that the content of their obsessions is closely connected to their values. For example, people with strong religious beliefs and values may experience objectionable blasphemous thoughts, whereas those for whom religion is of little interest are not vulnerable to blasphemous thoughts. The therapist then explains that as the personal significance attached to the unwanted thoughts increases, the frequency of and distress caused by the thoughts also increase. Likewise, when the personal significance attached to an unwanted intrusive thought is lowered, the level of distress and frequency of the obsessions will decrease. The therapist then explains why unwanted intrusive thoughts arise in the first place and describes how stress or anxiety can significantly increase the frequency of such unwanted thoughts.

Next, the therapist explains the nature of both overt and covert neutralizing activities and how they can have an adverse effect on the obsessional experience. *Neutralizing* refers to any attempt made to "put right," correct, change, or cancel the obsession. In the short term, attempts at neutralization often are successful in reducing a certain amount of anxiety or discomfort, and these effects are typically achieved quite promptly. In the longer term, however, acts of neutralization serve to protect the idea that the thoughts are indeed of great personal significance and that the feared event might well have occurred if the patient had failed to carry out the neutralizing act. In fact, the distress that arises from an unwanted intrusive thought would diminish spontaneously, albeit a little more slowly than occurs after a deliberate act of neutralization (Rachman, Mitchell, Trant, & Teachman, 1996). When appropriate, the therapist can illustrate this point using a demonstration in which he or she asks the person to deliberately form one of his or her less disturbing obsessions and first to follow it with a deliberately neutralizing act and then to refrain from neutralizing. The therapist can observe the following about efforts to suppress such thoughts:

> Unwanted thoughts can cause distress, and it is quite natural for people to resist them or to fight them off. However, trying to suppress these intrusive thoughts can unfortunately cause them to increase. The harder you try, the worse they become.

Attention is then turned to the effects of persistent avoidance behavior (e.g., avoidance of sharp objects, school playgrounds, churches). The immediate effect of escape or avoidance behavior is to achieve a degree of relief from anxiety in the short term, but in the long term the troublesome beliefs are protected from extinction (e.g., "If I had not taken care to avoid the children's playground, I would certainly have experienced the aggressive thoughts and might have lost control and acted on them"). Individuals are encouraged to reduce their maladaptive avoidance behavior at an early stage, perhaps Session 4. They are also discouraged from concealing the obsession; concealment protects the person from shame and embarrassment but has the longer-term effect of passively confirming the exaggerated significance that he or she has attached to the obsession. Concealment also inadvertently protects the catastrophic misinterpretations, because the person is not exposed to the views of other people or to evidence that might disconfirm the interpretation. The person may be extremely reluctant to seek treatment, or even comfort, because it would involve disclosure of what they believe to be shameful, morally repugnant ideas.

Next, the therapist provides education about biases in information processing, in particular the thought–action fusion bias (Rachman, 1993; Shafran & Rachman, 2004). This bias involves the belief that having an intrusive thought of harm coming to someone increases the probability of the feared event actually occurring or the feeling that having the thought or image is morally equivalent to carrying out the repugnant action. The therapist explains that OCD involves feelings of inflated responsibility for the care and protection of others and the need to take steps to deflate any exaggerated tendencies the patient may experience.

The therapist then provides information pertaining to the relationship between depressive mood and obsessions. Often, the obsessions cause depressive mood, but in other instances, a depressive mood is followed by an increase in obsessional activity. Many patients are taking medication, and the therapist should elicit their medication-related experiences, including side effects and withdrawal effects, as well as their interpretations of their obsessions in light of their reactions to their medications.

To conclude the didactic stage of treatment, the therapist gives the patient a written account of the model of OCD to refer to as needed (see Rachman, 2003). The therapist draws attention to the important distinction between the patient's thoughts and his or her actions. Typically, patients have experienced the thoughts many thousands of times, and very rarely, if ever, has a thought been followed by an action. It is worth emphasizing that the clinical problem is one of thoughts, not actions. The therapist reviews the nature and genesis of the individual's obsessions, with most attention paid to the specific content of their obsessions. The examination then evolves into an analysis of the evidence for and against the person's interpretation of the personal significance of the intrusions.

Collection of Evidence For and Against the Interpretation of the Thought

The next stage of treatment consists of the collection of evidence that is relevant to the person's construal of the significance of intrusive thoughts and to his or her expectations of the awful consequences of changing obsession-generated behavior (e.g., "What exactly will happen if I cease avoiding children?" "What will happen if I cease trying to neutralize my blasphemous thoughts?"). This process can begin with identification of the different interpretations the person has of the obsession, followed by exploration of the reasons for believing the interpretation and identification of areas of doubt as to whether that interpretation is the most viable. An initial strategy is to ask the individual how he or she would view a friend if the friend reported having the same thought and how useful his or her concealment and avoidance strategies have been (see Rachman, 2003).

The therapist then asks the person to consider some alternative explanations. This inquiry is supplemented by specific questions, such as the following:

- "How many times have you had these thoughts?"
- "How many times have these thoughts been followed by acts of aggression (e.g., toward children, an older person), embarrassment (e.g., shouting obscenities), or other unacceptable acts (e.g., sexual or blasphemous)?"
- "How many times have you experienced these disturbing sexual or anxious sensations?"
- "How many times have these sensations been followed by unacceptable acts of aggression or sex?"

Inquiries about other mental experiences can be helpful—for example, "Have you ever had disturbing dreams about yourself behaving unacceptably or disturbingly badly? If so, were the dreams followed by the unacceptable acts you dreamed about?" Finally, the therapist can ask about the meaning others place on the thoughts, such as "Has any doctor said that you are in danger of ending up crazy?" or "When you disclosed to your family or friends that you experience unwanted, intrusive thoughts of harming people, did they avoid being alone with you?"

It is important to note that many patients, especially those who have recurrent impulses, fear that one day they will lose control and carry out a horrible act. As a result, they consistently impose on themselves iron self-control and self-discipline. They may reply to these questions with answers like the following:

- "I would have lost control if I hadn't been careful, vigilant, and self-disciplined."
- "I would have lost control if I hadn't locked away all the knives, but some day I might lose that control."
- "I might become so anxious that I lose control."
- "I might be so drugged by medication that I will become confused and lose control."
- "I might carry out the horrible action in my sleep."

Many of these reasons readily lend themselves to behavioral experiments (described later in this chapter). For example, the therapist may describe specific circumstances and ask, "Under these circumstances, if you refrain from using your usual self-discipline, what happens?"

Some people engage in excessive self-monitoring of thoughts and are endlessly vigilant in the attempt to block unacceptable thoughts. Such people report feeling on guard all the time, reflected in the following comments:

- "I have to be on guard all the time."
- "I am constantly examining my thoughts."
- "Bad things will happen if I don't control my thoughts."
- "I will feel responsible [or guilty, or to blame] if a bad thing happens because I failed to control my thoughts."
- "Failing to control my thoughts would mean that I am an inadequate or weak person."
- "I will be punished if I don't control my thoughts."
- "I am responsible for controlling all of my thoughts at all times."

The therapist can address this excessive vigilance by setting up a behavioral experiment in which the person predicts what would happen if he or she refrains from such monitoring and then actually refrains for an arranged period or in an arranged place. Some individuals find the idea of an "off-duty" period helpful—they can even make themselves a simple badge to wear during such periods to remind themselves that they are off-duty. The therapist can then draw their attention to the contrast when they remove the badge and resume duty. Did a disaster occur during the off-duty period? Are they truly safer, or do they even feel safer, when they go back on vigilance duty? Were their specific predictions confirmed or not? Did they lose control?

Some people find the analogy of radio noise useful in appraising their unwanted intrusive thoughts. These thoughts can be regarded as the noise and not the signal—they are not significant. The true signals—that is, the person's values and beliefs—are what count, and not the irrelevant noise.

Addressing Self-Defeating Safety Behaviors

When they feel upset and threatened, people with obsessional problems do what all people do—they seek safety. The main forms of safety behaviors are concealment, thought suppression, reassurance seeking, avoidance and escape behavior, and neutralization. Questions about the role and effects of safety behavior crop up at various points in treatment. The therapist can observe, "Your safety behavior has not worked for you. Despite using your thought suppression [or blocking, concealment, neutralizing, or reassurance seeking], you continue to be tormented by the obsessions. Let us consider some preferable alternatives." The notion that safety behavior can be harmful comes as a surprise to many, and therapists may often find it necessary to carry out some simple demonstrations that enable the patient to experience the effects of these types of safety behavior.

Concealment

Concealing the nature and, especially, the repugnant content of the obsessions from friends and relatives seemingly protects the patient from rejection or worse. However, the very act of concealment can sustain the obsession, because it ensures that the patient never hears the balanced, calm, and moderating views of trusted others. People tend to leak the details slowly, bit by bit, until they feel secure in therapy; some feel that disclosure of the obsession weakens or even invalidates their "magical" powers of control. Others resist disclosure because they feel responsible for protecting their relatives and friends, and they worry that by revealing the obsessions, they might jeopardize these other people. These obstacles can be overcome with patience, and the very process of disclosing the concealed material can reduce its inflated significance. Useful questions therapists can ask to encourage disclosure include the following:

- "Whom have you told, when, and with what reaction?"
- "Were they sympathetic or not?"
- "Did they interpret the thoughts in the same way that you do?"
- "Did they attach great significance to the meaning of the thoughts?"

- "When you told them about your obsessions, did they avoid you, shout at you, bug you, or have any other negative reaction?"
- "Did any of them change their attitude toward and behavior around you? If not, why not?"

Disclosure to a friend or relative should be planned with care, because an ill-conceived disclosure can backfire. The therapist should encourage the patient to select trusted people who are sympathetic and psychologically minded, and the patient may even need to practice with the therapist the type and amount of disclosure he or she contemplates. As a safeguard, the patient may want to plan and practice disclosures to more than a single person.

Thought Suppression

Many people are understandably confused and troubled by the fact that their obsessions are so frequent and keep coming back (e.g., "They must be important and revealing, because they are so frequent and so intrusive"). When the therapist provides the educational component and introduces the idea that obsessions may be insignificant, mere noise in the system, it is not uncommon for people to feel confused at first. The patient may ask, "If they are so insignificant, why do I keep having them?" The explanation contains two parts. As noted in the section on the initial phase of treatment, people pay more attention to significant matters than to insignificant matters, so if the intrusive thoughts are regarded as important, people pay more attention to them. Second, attempts to suppress unwanted thoughts often produce the opposite result: They become more frequent, not less frequent. The therapist can point out that the person's attempts to suppress the obsessions have not worked and that the obsessions keep coming back, no matter how hard the person tries to block them.

There are some simple, brief demonstrations that can be used to illustrate the effects of trying to block the thoughts. A popular method is to ask the person to "think about whatever you wish, anything at all. However, there is one exception—you are not to think about elephants! Whatever happens, block out and fight against any thoughts of elephants. You are forbidden to think of elephants." In most instances, people report some thoughts of elephants. The attempt at suppression can produce a paradoxical increase in the forbidden thought. In a second demonstration, the therapist can ask the person to select one of his or her common but not too distressing obsessions, and the therapist repeats the instructions substituting the obsessional thought for elephants. The results provide a basis for recommending that the patient desist from trying to fight off, block, or suppress the obsessions: "Let them simply float through your mind. Regard them as noise, just noise. Don't try to fight them off, or block them, or cancel them."

Some people feel that there is a moral need for them to fight off the thoughts; if they cease fighting them, they feel, it means that they accept the thoughts. Others believe that if they cease fighting off the thoughts, something bad will happen, and they will be responsible. They may even feel that a dreaded misfortune (often vague and diffuse) has been prevented precisely because of their efforts at suppression. In these instances, behavioral experiments are advisable. Depending on the patient's beliefs, the experiments are directed at the inflated sense of responsibility and the belief that thought suppression makes people safer. As with all behavioral experiments, a simple six-step plan is devised. The following is an example:

1. The purpose of the experiment is to test whether or not people are safer when I suppress the thought than when I refrain from suppression.
2. I predict that when I suppress the thought for an entire week, no misfortune will befall someone close to me.
3. I will implement the experiment and report back to the therapist in session.
4. The purpose of the opposite experiment is to test whether or not people are safe even when I totally refrain from thought suppression.
5. I predict that when I refrain from all suppression for one week, something bad will happen to a person close to me.
6. I will implement the experiment and report back to the therapist in session.

Reassurance Seeking

The repeated seeking of reassurance about one's own safety or the safety of others, like neutralizing and compulsions, provides short-term relief but sustains obsessions. Contrary to appearances, requests for reassurance are not requests for fresh information, but rather are attempts to reduce anxiety; typically, the person already knows what answer is going to be given. The therapist can advise the patient to ask friends and relations to withhold such reassurance and instead to state, "It will interfere with your progress in treatment if I give that reassurance."

Avoidance and Escape Behavior

When fear or anxiety occurs in objectively safe conditions or when it is excessive, escape or avoidance is unnecessary, and behaviors perceived as leading to a "successful" escape from a falsely perceived danger can help to preserve the false belief in the danger. The person who fears that he or she might molest a child ensures that he or she avoids children and never learns that the fear is a false one. The most effective way to reduce false or exaggerated fears is the well-established method of repeated, graded, planned exposures to the situation that is feared and avoided. In my experience, this exposure seldom fails. To maximize the effects of exposures, the therapist should initiate a full discussion of the reason for and the details of the repeated exposures. In some circumstances, a therapist may find it helpful to start with a modeling exercise in which the therapist models the desired behavior a few times before the patient copies it. The patient rates the amount of fear or anxiety he or she experiences during each exposure trial using the fear thermometer. The planned exercises are self-correcting: The fear and associated avoidance should decline progressively. If they do not, it indicates the presence of an error or omission; the plan or specific instructions may be confused or misleading or the planned exercises too challenging. The therapist should correct the plan as appropriate.

A careful and progressive series of exposure exercises should be planned in advance. The significance of any sensations the patient experiences needs to be clarified, with particular attention to the similarities and differences between sensations of anxiety and those of sexual arousal. Patients often fear that they will lose control, and such fears need to be addressed and disconfirmed in the course of the exposure exercises.

When questions of a religious character arise (e.g., "What is the exact nature and purpose of prayer?"), the therapist can encourage the patient to seek advice from a priest, minister, vicar, rabbi, or other spiritual guide. With the permission of the patient, the therapist also can discuss the patient's concerns with a religious authority, and, generally, it is easy for the therapist and religious authority to sort out the differences in a manner that directly benefits the patient. Are unwanted, intrusive obscenities truly blasphemous, or are they better regarded as an unsettling psychological phenomenon? The thoughts are by definition unwanted and, hence, resisted and rejected. They are ego dystonic. The patient or therapist can select specific blasphemous acts to explore, in keeping with the person's views and personality.

Harm obsessions tend to be the most complex, but they are not necessarily the most difficult to tackle. They can be complex because of the potential mixture of a cognitive bias in the form of thought–action fusion, inflated responsibility, and fear of losing control. The fear of losing control produces maladaptive avoidance behavior that needs to be reversed. The occurrence of thought–action fusion requires a full account of the role of cognitive biases and their insupportability, coupled with behavioral experiments that enable the patient to test the validity of the thought–action fusion. Inflated responsibility has pervasive effects and may underpin the patient's misinterpretations of these thoughts; progress can be facilitated when patients recognize the inflated sense of their perceived responsibility and redraw their "map" of responsibility to more realistic, acceptable levels.

Neutralization

Thought suppression refers to attempts to block the obsessions and *neutralization* to attempts to cancel out the effects of the obsessions. Neutralization may take the form of attempting to substitute an acceptable thought or trying to form a safely reassuring image to cancel out the unacceptable thought (e.g., reanimating a "victim") or somehow "put matters right." Neutralization can be internal, as in saying a corrective phrase or prayer, and it can be external, as in handwashing. Like handwashing or compulsive checking, neutralizing generally provides some relief, but this relief rarely lasts; and more neutralizing is needed. The trap for patients is to believe that the dreaded misfortune has been averted because they neutralized; this consolidates the fundamental misinterpretation of the significance of the intrusive thoughts. Attempts at neutralization may make it more difficult for the patient to overcome the problem, and the therapist should therefore discourage any attempts.

To demonstrate that the discomfort that is reduced by neutralization has a natural tendency to decline even if the neutralizing act is omitted, the following exercise can be used (if the patient feels morally compelled to cancel out the obsession to neutralize it, the demonstration should be complemented by an examination of the "moral" component of the neutralization):

1. Select a clear and reproducible act of neutralization that the patient engages in (e.g., blanketing the obsession with a counterthought or a counterimage, saying a neutralizing phrase such as "they are safe" or "peace").
2. Ask the person to form one of his or her obsessions, signal when he or she has it, hold it for 2 minutes or so, and then carry out the neutralizing action.
3. Did the formation of the obsession produce anxiety or discomfort? Have the patient rate his or her level of distress on a 0–100 scale.
4. Was the neutralization action performed correctly? What effect did it have on the anxiety? Again, have the patient rate his or her level of distress.

Generally, the obsession will cause some discomfort, in the region of 30 to 40 on the 100-point scale, but less than the discomfort produced by the patient's spontaneous obsessions. When the neutralizing act is completed, the anxiety usually declines promptly, to 10 or so. In the second part of the demonstration, the therapist again asks the patient to form the obsession, but this time to refrain from any neutralizing. If the obsessions provoked moderate anxiety (i.e., 30–40), this level of anxiety will remain for a few minutes. Then the therapist engages the person in a 10-minute discussion of some unrelated subject, after which time the patient again rates his or her level of anxiety. Usually, it will have declined to about 0.

A variant of this exercise is to have the person delay carrying out neutralizing for specified periods, such as 1, 5, or 10 hours. Typically, patients find that when the agreed time to neutralize finally arrives, they no longer feel the urge to do so. When encouraging people to delay neutralizing (or checking, or any other such activity), the therapist should also have them refrain from carrying out internal debates about the validity of their obsessions, which are seldom resolved.

Developing Alternative Views of the Thought's Significance

The removal of a mistaken interpretation is not sufficient; therapists should strive to help the person formulate an alternative, more accurate interpretation (Teasdale, 1999). The therapist and patient can list the alternative interpretations and reasons for and against each one. The following sections discuss various tactics that can be used in collecting new information that has a bearing on the patient's alternative interpretations.

Behavioral Experiments

In addition to helping the individual overcome avoidance and safety behaviors, behavioral experiments can be used to develop alternative interpretations of the obsession itself. The purpose of the experiments is to allow the patient to collect direct, personal information pertaining to important OCD beliefs and to do so in a thoughtful, planned manner, rather than merely hoping for random events to occur.

Behavioral experiments are particularly helpful when the person is hesitant or skeptical about considering fresh interpretations of the obsessions or when he or she endorses benign interpretations only in the clinic but not in external situations. These experiments are designed to collect information, and in this way they differ to some extent from exposure exercises. Exposures certainly can uncover fresh information, but this is incidental; in most instances, the primary aim is to reduce fear.

To be effective, a behavioral experiment should be planned with a specific stated purpose. For example, for people who overpredict the likelihood and unpleasantness of fear or other aversive events, a behavioral experiment can be designed to reduce unwanted overpredictions. In some circumstances, the patient may want to be accompanied by a therapist during the behavioral experiment—for example, to test doubts (e.g., "Am I safe with children?") In planning specific exercises, the patient may find it helps to prepare a simple written plan along the following lines:

1. The exact fear is that I may molest a child.
2. I predict that if I spend 10 minutes near children in the park, then my anxiety will reach a level of _____ (on a scale of 0–100).
3. The probability of my molesting a child is _____ (0%–100%).
4. In session, I will report the amount of time I spent on the exposure, the level of anxiety I experienced, and the probability of my taking the action.

5. Together with the therapist, I will review conclusions from the experiment.

Another type of behavioral experiment is the minisurvey. The reactions of friends and relatives are potentially important sources of alternative information and interpretations about the obsessions, and patients can conduct minisurveys to gather such information. The therapist can asks the patient,

> Have you told anyone about your thoughts? If yes, have people changed their behavior toward you since you told them? Do they show signs of fearing you? Do they avoid you? Do they avoid being seen in public with you? Do they exclude you? Do they call you sinful, immoral, or wicked? If their behavior has not changed in these ways, can you say what significance they attach to those thoughts of yours?

The aim of a minisurvey is to collect evidence about people's thoughts and attitudes from the people themselves, rather than relying on patients' inferences or guesses about what they think. The patient selects a few people whom he or she trusts and whose opinions he or she values and asks them, for example, "Do you ever have unwanted intrusive thoughts? Has your attitude toward me changed since I told you about my thoughts? What do you do about your thoughts?" These surveys should be carried out with more than one person.

Analyzing Past Obsessions and Past Treatments

The patient's experiences with past obsessions, what provoked them, and especially what led to their decline can be of considerable relevance and importance. The therapist can ask questions such as the following:

- "When you experienced your first obsessions, what did you think they meant? What did you conclude?"
- "What did you do about them, if anything?"
- "Did you tell anyone else about your obsessions? If not, why not? If yes, whom did you tell, and what was their reaction?"
- "Have any of your earlier or past obsessions decreased in frequency or intensity? Can you explain why they decreased? What do you conclude from the decline or disappearance of earlier obsessions?"
- "Were any of your past obsessions followed by unacceptable or catastrophic behavior? violent acts? unacceptable sexual acts? obscene acts? shouting in public? making a nasty scene in church? any other acts? What exactly prevented you from carrying out any of these acts?"

The patient's replies can identify incisive questions to be tackled in behavioral experiments.

Patients' reactions to previous treatments, psychological or pharmacological, can be revealing. Their explanations of the positive, negative, and neutral effects of the treatment can also reveal a good deal about the significance they attach to their thoughts and give clues as to what sort of information or experiences may have an impact on the obsessions.

Obsessions and Moods

The interpretation that patients place on their intrusive thoughts can be strongly influenced, in a positive or negative direction, by their mood states, and this recognition often helps patients loosen the rigidity of their beliefs about the nature of their obsessions. The information about mood–thought interactions can also make a useful contribution to patients' understanding of the mood-dependent nature of most obsessions and helps to account for the effects of mood-influencing medications. Patients can also learn that they are likely to be vulnerable to obsessions when depressed.

Responsibility

Many people with obsessional disorders struggle with an inflated sense of responsibility. They feel that they are pivotally responsible for caring for others and for preventing harm coming to them, and so they feel obliged to carry out protective, preventive actions such as compulsive checking to prevent harm coming to other people. Frequently a therapist may find it necessary to explore the range and depth of a person's sense of responsibility and to take steps to modify it if possible. Because the elevated sense of responsibility imposes an oppressive burden and drives compulsive urges to check and to avoid, the threat of additional or increased responsibility can promote intense anxiety. Therefore, it is common for affected people to go to great lengths to avoid any additions to their existing responsibilities (e.g., refusing promotion to a more responsible job, delaying or refusing marriage). This sense of responsibility plays into the obsessions and is a particular problem when thought–action fusion occurs. The therapist should describe the concept of inflated responsibility and, if it is present, discuss more realistic and acceptable limits on the patient's sense of personal responsibility. Patients should be encouraged to list their main responsibilities and examples of how they often overstep them.

Cognitive Biases

Many people who are troubled by obsessive–compulsive problems display particular biases in their thinking. The inflated sense of responsibility that is common in OCD is associated with these biases. One example is the biased belief that the probability of the feared event is greatly increased if the person feels responsible for preventing the event—for example, "If I feel responsible for ensuring that our house is safe from fire, then the probability of the house burning is increased; but if someone else is responsible for protecting the house from fire, then the probability of the house burning down is decreased." They feel that "when I am responsible, things are sure to go wrong."

The most researched cognitive bias in OCD is *thought–action fusion*, in which patients believe that their thoughts influence external events (Shafran & Rachman, 2004). The *probability bias* is the feeling that one's thoughts can influence external events by making them more probable. For example, if a patient has the thought that a relative will have a car accident, the patient perceives that the risk is increased because he or she had the thought. *Morality bias* is the belief that one's thoughts influence one's moral standing—for example, "Having an unwanted, unacceptable sexual image is as morally offensive as carrying out the unacceptable action."

The therapist begins by identifying the biases, explains how they work, draws attention to their self-defeating effects, and emphasizes the need to refrain from attempts to suppress the thoughts. The person is encouraged to identify the occurrence and effects of the cognitive biases and to take corrective steps, mainly by combating the false conclusions that emerge from thought–action fusion and other biases.

The Use of Pragmatic Tests

A. T. Beck (personal communication, July 15, 1995) recommended using pragmatic tests to assist people in overcoming their maladaptive beliefs and interpretations. Beck asked patients whether they would be better off or worse off if they shed the maladaptive cognitions (e.g., "Would your life be easier, or more fulfilling, if you set aside these cognitions?" "Would your life be easier, or more fulfilling, if you substituted more accepting, realistic cognitions?"). The therapist can put these questions to patients, asking them whether their specific interpretations of the significance of their unwanted, intrusive thoughts are a help or a hindrance in their lives (e.g., "Would your life be more peaceful if you could substitute an accepting, benign interpretation of these thoughts to replace your self-critical interpretations?").

The therapist can help the patient construct two contrasting interpretations: self-critical interpretations (e.g., "These thoughts mean that I am a bad person, hypocritical, and possibly dangerous") versus accepting, benign interpretations (e.g., "These thoughts are mere noise. They tell me nothing of importance about myself. My behavior and my principles are those I value and have chosen for myself. These thoughts are irrelevant"). The therapist again asks the person whether he or she would be better off or worse off if he or she engaged in the self-critical interpretation; the same question is then asked about the benign interpretation ("Pragmatically, which interpretation is best for you?").

The alternate interpretations are then used as the basis for a behavioral experiment: Patients adopt the self-critical interpretation for a full week, convince themselves of its validity, and record the effects of the interpretation on their feelings and behavior and on the frequency and intensity of their obsessions. In the second week, patients adopt and endorse, with conviction, the validity of the contrasting and benign interpretation. As before, patients record their feelings and behavior during the week, as well as the frequency and intensity of their obsessions. For greater and more enduring effects, patients may repeat the behavioral experiment or extend the test period from 1 week to 2 or 4 weeks.

Assessing Progress and Dealing With Problems

The primary aim of treatment is to achieve a decrease in the frequency of the obsessions and in the distress that they produce. If the person reinterprets the intrusive thoughts as benign events that are neither threatening nor personally damaging, the obsessions should diminish and then disappear. In practice, changes in interpretations of what had been a dominating feature of the person's daily life are seldom abrupt and complete. Rather, the patient's interpretations change in a gradual and erratic fashion; sometimes the person experiences changes in the degree of conviction or the believability of the interpretations, rather than a complete switch to a fresh interpretation.

How, then, is progress assessed? The weekly recordings made by the patient reveal the frequency and distress caused by the symptoms and are therefore of paramount importance. The recordings also provide a basis for the self-correcting aspect of the treatment. The person's recordings should be supplemented by those of the therapist. No treatment program is satisfactory until the frequency and distress scores come down to within tolerable, or even normal, levels. In the short term, significant reductions in frequency and distress are sufficient signs of improvement, but for the longer term, more effort is needed. Broader changes are necessary to consolidate the improvements.

Evidence of important changes in the interpretation of intrusive thoughts is needed to ensure that the causes of the obsessions have been dealt with. The scores the patient regularly reports on the Personal Significance Scale are essential evidence. At the conclusion of therapy, these scores should be supplemented by the patient's responses during the readministration of all of the pretreatment measures. Another very important index of change is the patient's behavior: Has the avoidance behavior ceased? Has the unnecessary concealment been abandoned? Has the patient abandoned neutralization? Has he or she resumed former social activities? Other measures that can be useful in assessing progress include the following:

- session-by-session changes, such as in the patient's weekly recordings of frequency, distress, and content and in the therapist's overall assessment at the conclusion of each session;
- qualitative reports of enhanced social behavior, improved mood and concentration, and reductions in avoidance; and

- posttreatment status as assessed by tracking all of the session-by-session changes and by administering a structured interview (preferably completed by someone other than the therapist), psychometric exams (e.g., PSS, Beck Depression Inventory, Thought–Action Fusion Scale, Yale–Brown Obsessive–Compulsive Scale [Goodman et al., 1989]), and behavior tests.

In some cases, the patient's misinterpretations prove to be inflexible and persist unchanged, despite the educational or other components of treatment. A related problem is encountered when the patient gradually endorses a more benign interpretation of the intrusive thoughts within the sessions, but in some outside situations remains as convinced as ever that the intrusive thoughts are dangerous, damaging, or uniquely revealing. This gulf can be difficult to overcome. In both of these problems—inflexible misinterpretations and nongeneralizing changes in interpretations—the use of behavioral experiments can be extremely helpful. They provide fresh, direct, personal information and carry far greater evidential weight for the patient than do reams of statistics and "cold" technical information about obsessions in general.

If any of the strongly endorsed interpretations fail to decline, a reconsideration of the problem and the cognitive tactics is called for. In numerous instances, the lack of change can be traced to the evidence that bolsters the patient's maladaptive interpretation and the weakness of the contrary evidence. A search for fresh, direct, personal evidence is then required. This evidence can be obtained by specifically designed behavioral experiments, minisurveys, and tests of the effects of the tactics developed specifically for dismantling obsessions.

Similarly, changes in behavior, especially reductions in avoidance, can have a big impact on beliefs and interpretations. Quite often it is the combination of these two tactics—implementing behavioral experiments and reducing avoidance behavior—that leads to changes in misinterpretations. Some common questions include "What will happen if I refrain from suppressing the thoughts?" "What will happen if I refrain from trying to put right or to correct the thoughts?" "What will happen if I resume attending church?" "What will happen if I tell my parents about my thoughts?" Some misinterpretations are slower to change than others. Beliefs such as "People will reject me if they learn about the obsessions" tend to shift more slowly, because the ideas and attitudes of other people are not directly accessible in the same way as one's self-appraisals. The cognition "I am a wicked, immoral person" is directly accessible, but "They will think badly of me, that I am wicked" is not so accessible, nor is the relevant information.

Obsessive–compulsive disorder and depression often are associated, and many patients with obsessions are or have been depressed. The recurrence or exacerbation of depression can certainly interfere with treatment but should not preclude it. Obviously, steps should be taken to reduce the depression. Practically speaking, many patients with accompanying depression are taking medications, and changes in drugs or dosage levels are not infrequently associated with emotional turbulence. At times, a therapist may find it necessary to slow therapy until the patient's emotional state or mood is stable. Typically, these episodes of emotional disturbance retard progress but do not have a lastingly adverse effect on improvements already made in overcoming the maladaptive misinterpretations of one's intrusive thoughts.

Follow-Up and Prevention

At the end of treatment, it is important for a therapist to remind people that unwanted intrusive thoughts are a universal experience and that such thoughts become obsessional only if they are misinterpreted as having catastrophic meanings. Hence, therapists should advise people to continue regarding the thoughts as benign and neither dangerous nor uniquely revealing. They can encourage patients to collect and evaluate the reasons for their interpretations of any newly troubling thoughts, to block the temptation to avoid, to forgo attempts at suppressing the unwanted thoughts, and to refrain from neutralizing and concealment. In general, if patients use the methods they have acquired during therapy, they should be well equipped to deal with any threatened recurrences. Follow-up evaluations can be scheduled for intervals of 1 month, 3 months, 6 months, and 1 year, with more frequent consultations if necessary.

REFERENCES

Beck, A. T., Steer, R. A., & Brown, G. (1996). *Beck Depression Inventory manual* (2nd ed.). San Antonio, TX: Psychological Corporation.

Goodman, W. K., Price, L. H., Rasmussen, S. A., Mazure, C., Fleischmann, R. L., Hill, C. L., et al. (1989). The Yale–Brown Obsessive–Compulsive Scale: I. Development, use, and reliability. *Archives of General Psychiatry, 46,* 1006–1011.

Niler, E. R., & Beck, S. J. (1989). The relationship among guilt, anxiety and obsessions in a normal population. *Behaviour Research and Therapy, 27,* 213–220.

Purdon, C. (1999). Thought suppression and psychopathology. *Behaviour Research and Therapy, 37,* 1029–1054.

Purdon, C., & Clark, D. A. (1994). Obsessive intrusive thoughts in non-clinical subjects: Part II. Cognitive appraisal, emotional response and thought control strategies. *Behaviour Research and Therapy, 32,* 403–410.

Rachman, S. (1993). Obsessions, responsibility and guilt. *Behaviour Research and Therapy, 31,* 149–153.

Rachman, S. (1997). A cognitive theory of obsessions. *Behaviour Research and Therapy, 35,* 793–802.

Rachman, S. (2003). *The treatment of obsessions*. Oxford, England: Oxford University Press.

Rachman, S., & de Silva, P. (1978). Abnormal and normal obsessions. *Behaviour Research and Therapy, 16,* 233–248.

Rachman, S., Mitchell, D., Trant, J., & Teachman, B. (1996). How to remain neutral: An experimental analysis of neutralization. *Behaviour Research and Therapy, 34,* 889–898.

Salkovskis, P. M. (1985). Obsessional–compulsive problems: A cognitive–behavioural analysis. *Behaviour Research and Therapy, 23,* 571–583.

Salkovskis, P. M. (1999). Understanding and treating obsessive–compulsive disorder. *Behaviour Research and Therapy, 37,* S29–S52.

Salkovskis, P. M., & Harrison, J. (1984). Abnormal and normal obsessions—A replication. *Behaviour Research and Therapy, 22,* 1–4.

Shafran, R., & Rachman, S. (2004). Thought–action fusion: A review. *Journal of Behavior Therapy and Experimental Psychiatry, 35,* 87–108.

Shafran, R., Thordarson, D. S., & Rachman, S. J. (1996). Thought–action fusion in obsessive–compulsive disorder. *Journal of Anxiety Disorders, 10,* 379–391.

Teasdale, J. (1999). Emotional processing, three modes of mind and the prevention of relapse in depression. *Behaviour Research and Therapy, 37,* 553–577.

10

TREATING COMPULSIVE HOARDING

ANCY E. CHERIAN AND RANDY O. FROST

Compulsive hoarding is a potentially disabling syndrome that includes three primary symptoms: (a) the acquisition of and failure to discard a large number of possessions that appear to be useless or of limited value, (b) living spaces sufficiently cluttered so as to preclude activities for which those spaces were designed, and (c) significant distress or impairment in functioning caused by hoarding (Frost & Hartl, 1996). Compulsive acquisition can include compulsive buying and the collecting of free things as well as discarded items (e.g., from trashcans or dumpsters). It is often associated with euphoria or positive mood states or can be used as a compensatory behavior to soothe negative moods (Kyrios, Frost, & Steketee, 2004). The failure to discard worthless or worn-out objects results from the view that possessions have value in excess of their true worth (Steketee & Frost, 2003). The final defining feature is extreme clutter in the home (or surrounding areas), office, or car. Clutter typically prevents the normal use of space and such daily activities as cooking, cleaning, and bathing. As a result, the home may pose risks for fire, falling (especially for elderly people), poor sanitation, and other health risks (Damecour & Charron, 1998).

This chapter reviews some of the recent diagnostic questions that have emerged regarding the classification of compulsive hoarding as a clinical syndrome. We also present a cognitive–behavioral model of compulsive hoarding that should assist with case formulation and treatment planning. We cover assessment and specific treatment components and present a case example to help illustrate the application of treatment techniques and ways to manage clinical challenges.

DIAGNOSIS, COMORBIDITY, COURSE, AND PREVALENCE

Compulsive hoarding is typically conceptualized as a symptom of obsessive–compulsive disorder (OCD). Studies of OCD populations report hoarding frequencies in adults of 18% to 33%, with moderate correlations among hoarding and OCD symptoms (Samuels et al., 2002). Saxena et al. (2002) found hoarding to be the primary symptom in 11% of their large sample of OCD clients. Research on symptom subtypes suggests that hoarding may be a distinct subtype of OCD (see Steketee & Frost, 2003, for a review). Hoarding has also been associated with a number of other disorders, including social phobia, depression, dementia, schizophrenia, eating disorders, and mental retardation (Samuels et al., 2002).

Compulsive hoarding is also comorbid with several personality disorders, including avoidant, dependent, compulsive, schizotypal, and paranoid personality disorders. Some findings suggest, however, that only dependent and schizotypal traits differentiate hoarding versus nonhoarding OCD, with both occurring more frequently among hoarders (see Steketee & Frost, 2003).

Several studies suggest that hoarding runs a chronic and unchanging course. A study using retrospective assessment of onset with a timeline to facilitate recall indicated that hoarding symptoms (acquisition, difficulty discarding, and clutter) had a mean age of onset of about 13, although extreme levels of hoarding did not develop until 1 to 2 decades later (Grisham, Frost, Steketee, Kim, & Hood, 2006).

MODEL OF COMPULSIVE HOARDING

We have proposed a cognitive–behavioral model of compulsive hoarding based on student, community, and clinical samples examined in studies of the psychopathology and treatment of hoarding (e.g., Frost & Hartl, 1996; Steketee & Frost, 2003). This model suggests that the manifestations of hoarding (acquisition, saving, clutter) result from basic deficits or problems in information processing, beliefs about and attachments to possessions, and emotional distress and avoidance behaviors that develop as a result.

Deficits in Information Processing

Information processing deficits associated with hoarding are reflected in attention, organization and categorization, memory, and the use of information to make decisions. Each is thought to be linked to the disorganization and clutter experienced by those who hoard. Hoarders often describe problems with attention and relate them to difficulties staying focused when dealing with their possessions. Hartl, Duffany, Allen, Steketee, and Frost (2005) found hoarding participants to have significantly higher scores on measures of adult attention-deficit/hyperactivity disorder (ADHD); childhood symptoms of ADHD; and current cognitive failures in perception, memory, and motor function. Whereas some people with hoarding problems can focus attention only for a short time, others report being distracted by the memories invoked by a possession. Both difficulties may result in the person attempting to sort and organize for hours, making little to no progress.

People with hoarding problems have trouble categorizing objects. A tendency to regard each possession as unique and special renders the grouping and organizing of possessions difficult (Steketee & Frost, 2003). Rather than organizing possessions into categories and storing them out of sight, people with hoarding problems attempt to remember the location of each item.

People who hoard frequently complain about memory problems. Specifically, they report less confidence in their memory, concern about the catastrophic consequences of forgetting, and a strong desire to keep possessions in sight so they will not forget them (Hartl et al., 2004). They often doubt their ability to remember where possessions are kept, what they have read, and life experiences generally. Hoarding behaviors may be an attempt to compensate for these deficits. For example, to remember a specific life event, such individuals may save memorabilia, or in an attempt to avoid forgetting what they read, they may keep a whole magazine or newspaper. Saving gives people who hoard the impression that they have access to potentially important information. Hartl et al. (2004) found evidence for actual memory deficits in severe hoarders compared with nonclinical control participants, which suggests that people with this problem may keep important items in sight to not forget them. Paradoxically, attempts to keep important items in plain sight—and many items are thought to be important—often result in items being lost among the many other items. As the clutter increases, this visual organizational system loses effectiveness.

Another common problem associated with hoarding is difficulty with decision making (Frost & Gross, 1993). As a consequence of problems with categorization and organization, people with hoarding problems require too much information to make decisions. This indecisiveness may be caused by difficulties in identifying what information is essential and what information is irrelevant.

Emotional Attachment and Beliefs

Findings from several studies indicate that attachments to possessions in hoarding are often highly emotional (Cermele, Melendez-Pallitto, &

Pandina, 2001). Research on how these attachments are formed suggests four basic qualities of these attachments: emotional attachment, memory-related concerns, responsibility for possessions, and control over possessions (Steketee & Frost, 2003). These are generally exaggerations of the types of attachments that most people form with personal objects.

For people with hoarding problems, objects that are reminders of relatively unimportant events take on sentimental or emotional significance. As a result, they save a large number of ordinary possessions. Objects become reminders of the past, and they seem to feel that the loss of the object would equal the loss of the life experience. Similarly, many people who hoard consider possessions to be a part of their identity. Clients report that throwing something away would be like losing a part of themselves.

Another form of emotional attachment involves the role possessions have in making people feel comfortable. People who hoard may overestimate the probability of bad things happening to them and look to their possessions as signals of safety. Clients often describe their houses as "cocoons" or "bunkers" and their possessions as things that protect them. Removing these possessions can violate feelings of safety.

When attempting to discard a possession or resist acquiring a new possession the most common feeling people who hoard report is a sense of loss. This feeling appears to be a grief-like reaction that is often accompanied by the belief that the feeling will last forever. The desire to avoid this grief often contributes to difficulty discarding. In addition to the emotional experience of loss, people with hoarding problems report concerns about the loss of information or opportunities. People who hoard believe that if they discard a newspaper, the information it contains will be lost forever, or if they resist acquiring a newspaper, they will miss an opportunity to gather potentially important information. This perception can lead to the accumulation of countless pieces of information that, ironically, are often impossible to find should the need arise.

Another reason people with hoarding problems save things is a sense of responsibility to ensure that possessions are not wasted. This sense of responsibility can lead people to "rescue" things from the trash or recycle items that can be used or repaired. For example, one client described how she "rescued" a plastic bag from the train station because "it is a perfectly good plastic bag." Preoccupations with saving, recycling, and not wasting are a time-consuming endeavor that leaves little time and energy to address the actual problem of clutter.

Most people who hoard develop a sense of control over their possessions and find it quite anxiety provoking to have anyone else touch or use their possessions (Steketee & Frost, 2003). This difficulty may be related to beliefs that the possession is an extension of the self; removal or touching of the item may be experienced as a violation.

Avoidance and Reinforcement

Behavioral avoidance is closely linked with, and used to compensate for, the deficits that accompany compulsive hoarding. For example, saving possessions allows people with hoarding problems to postpone or avoid making decisions about possessions, perhaps for fear of making a mistake (Frost & Hartl, 1996). Saving also allows individuals to avoid emotional upset associated with discarding a valued possession.

Assessment

A multimethod assessment should be done both in the clinic and in the client's home. Self-report measures of hoarding and of the interference it causes, as well as measures of hoarding-related beliefs, can be collected in the clinic (for reviews, see Frost, Steketee, & Grisham, 2004; Steketee & Frost, 2003). An initial home visit is essential in establishing a baseline and developing a case formulation. Observational and client measures of clutter are important to collect at the first home visit, as are photos that can be used to track progress. Therapists should expect clients to be worried and embarrassed about the first home appointment. To facilitate their comfort and cooperation, the therapist should provide information about what will occur during the visit and review treatment rules in advance (e.g., that the therapist will not touch client's possessions and will safeguard confidentiality).

CASE VIGNETTE AND FORMULATION

Betty was a 62-year-old married woman with three grown children. She lived in a two-family home with her husband. Although the second unit was once a source of income, at the time of treatment it was used for storage. Betty worked in an office while pursuing a career in art on the side. Although she did not acquire excessively in childhood, she recalled having significant difficulty parting with her possessions. For example, in junior high school, Betty saved all of her textbooks and class notes for future reference. These were stored in boxes in her parents' basement until she moved, at which point they went into her own basement. Although she had never used the notes, she planned to organize them so that in the event she needed the information, it would be easily accessible.

Her home was significantly cluttered. The clutter consisted mainly of paperwork, magazines, books, containers, travel information, gardening tools, clothing, and art supplies. The level of clutter significantly interfered in Betty's life in that she no longer had visitors to the home. She had difficulty finding important things that she needed, and she had to buy duplicates of things to compensate for the lack of organization.

In addition to problems discarding, Betty experienced problems with acquiring. On an average day she accumulated at least a shopping bag full of things from the objects she encountered during her day. Items typically included the paper coffee cup from her morning coffee, the daily paper (sometimes multiple copies), plastic utensils, plastic bags, napkins, and other objects she found interesting. She collected not only for herself but also for friends and family. For instance, if someone in her office was disposing of books, she would consider whether they might be of interest to one of her friends or children. She also had trouble declining free things and often accepted things she did not need or want. At the end of each day, she placed the bag of collected items in a corner, and she rarely sorted or organized the items later.

Organization was another area of difficulty for Betty. Although certain areas of the home were clutter free, others were in a state of chaos. Any attempted system of organization was overburdened by large quantities of things. Betty stated that many people perceived her to be quite organized; she was often the "go-to person" when others were in need of information. They were unaware of the incredible ordeal involved in finding these things in her cluttered home. She tried various methods to organize, including keeping things in plain sight and taping important papers to the wall. Unfortunately, these systems failed because "important things" were covered with "more important things," resulting in a pile of items of varying importance. Bills and checks got mixed in with magazines and newspaper clippings, causing both financial and emotional distress.

Betty was a difficult client to work with. She was very critical of the therapist and demanding about what should and should not be done in treatment. Despite this kind of interpersonal behavior, she admitted that she greatly feared criticism from others: "I live in a frame of mind that everyone will criticize me."

A major goal of treatment was to develop, with Betty, a working model or formulation for understanding her hoarding symptoms. Treatment formulation is an ongoing process that continues over the course of treatment as additional information is uncovered about the beliefs, behaviors, and emotions that contribute to the individual's hoarding. Creating a case formulation involves several techniques designed to clarify the variables contributing to saving, acquiring, and clutter. These techniques include assessment, which is a major component of the functional analysis and often includes a clinical interview designed to assess the extent of the clutter and the level of functional impairment. At this point, the therapist will begin to conceptualize the types of items that are typically acquired and saved and the thought and behavior patterns that maintain the problem. Visualization tasks in which the client is asked to imagine the home in its current state of clutter or to imagine the home completely clear of clutter can help both the therapist and the client understand emotional reactions to clutter and clutter-free space

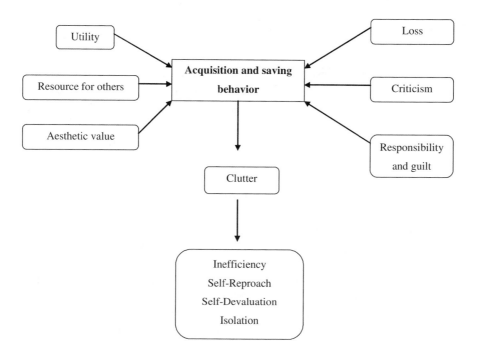

Figure 10.1. Factors influencing Betty's hoarding.

and subtle avoidance strategies. The information the therapist gathers is then integrated in a working model that depicts the contributing and maintaining factors of compulsive hoarding. Using these techniques, six major factors contributing to Betty's hoarding behavior were revealed. Three of these involved the positive qualities or outcomes associated with saving things, and three involved fears about the negative consequences of discarding. Figure 10.1 is a schematic representation of her case formulation.

The attractions of saving included the belief that the objects might be useful some day. For example, she saved information related to art galleries, because it would be useful once she was ready to show her work. Similarly, she saved newspaper articles, magazines, and other paper goods for the information they contained. In addition, she thought of herself as a resource for others. She believed that people came to her when they needed something, and she collected not just for herself, but for others as well. Third, she found an intrinsic or aesthetic value in objects. Objects made her feel good, and she could re-create this experience by saving them.

The fear engendered by the thought of discarding things involved a fear of losing a part of her life. For example, she saved most of her children's toys and clothing because they reminded her of the time when both she and they were young. She also saved old photographs, memorabilia, and all personal mail to help her gain access to her past. She believed that if she were to discard these items, she would have no trigger for these memories, and they would be lost forever. Losing these memories would be like losing a piece of her history and ultimately herself. Another fear was that if she discarded something, she might be subject to criticism from others, especially her husband. Finally, Betty saved things because she felt responsible for not wasting resources. She expressed guilt to the point of tears during one behavioral experiment in which she was discarding a sock with a hole in it. She felt that this meant that she was a wasteful, and therefore bad, person.

TREATMENT

Treatments of compulsive hoarding have developed and changed over time. The first attempts involved labor- and time-intensive treatment (Hartl & Frost, 1999), as well as group approaches (Steketee, Frost, Wincze, Greene, & Douglass, 2000). These experiences have led us away from using a strict session-by-session protocol; the variability within this population and the amount of time needed for this treatment do not lend themselves to such structure. For most hoarding clients, 6 months to 1 year of treatment is necessary. The focus on treatment is on three deficits: disorganization, difficulty discarding, and compulsive acquisition. Before focusing on these deficits, motivation for change must be addressed.

Problems with motivation and compliance are legendary in clients with hoarding problems (Christensen & Greist, 2001). In our experience, even clients who report being highly motivated at the beginning of treatment have difficulty sustaining that motivation. We now begin treatment by carefully emphasizing the nature and extent of the work clients will have to do. Furthermore, we incorporate motivational interviewing techniques during the early case conceptualization phase and throughout treatment when needed. We discuss motivation issues in more detail in the next section.

Session location is an important issue in the treatment of hoarding. Although holding sessions in the clinic may be more convenient for the therapist, sessions should be conducted, as much as possible, in the client's home or at locations where acquisition is a problem. Holding sessions in the client's home accomplishes four things. First, hoarding clients are often socially isolated; most have not had anyone in their home in years. Visits by a therapist habituate them to having other people in their home. Getting people to visit clients' homes is crucial to preventing relapse once the home is clear. Second, we have observed that many hoarding clients can work effectively when the therapist is with them at home, but not by themselves. Having the therapist present interrupts their pattern of avoiding the sorting and discarding that are necessary components of therapy. Furthermore, people with hoarding problems show the same tendency as most people to tidy up their home when a visitor is expected. Anticipating a visit from the therapist increases homework compliance. Third, visits to the home allow the therapist and client to establish realistic homework plans that can be the start of fading procedures to teach clients to work on their own. Fourth, during the home visit the therapist can help the client select items to bring to the clinic for sorting and discarding exercises. When this task is left to clients, subtle forms of avoidance emerge, such as bringing in items that are easily discarded or items about which the client has already made a decision.

When working in the home is problematic, therapists can use photos of specific areas of the client's home in treatment. Therapist and client can plan behavioral experiments for items in the pictures. The client's homework assignment would then be to carry out the decision or experiment.

Because of their excessive concern with maintaining control over possessions and the shame they experience at the thought of other people seeing their home, many hoarding clients are terrified of the therapist's visit. It is crucial that the therapist and client establish ground rules for home visits. The most important rule is that the therapist not touch or move anything without the client's permission. The client must make all decisions about possessions. Most people with hoarding problems have faced relatives, friends, or authorities who argued with them and pressured them into getting rid of cherished possessions. Loss of possessions in this way results not in habituation, but rather in sensitization to any form of loss. This sensitivity can be difficult to deal with for the therapist, who may have found subtle forms of pressure successful with other OCD patients. For habituation to occur in the treatment of hoarding, the client must make the decision without attributing it to the therapist.

We include five components in treatment for compulsive hoarding:

1. motivation for treatment,
2. skills training,
3. imaginal and in vivo exposure,
4. cognitive strategies, and
5. relapse prevention.

Motivation for Treatment

Many clients with obsessive hoarding enter treatment because they are pressured by friends and family to do so (Christensen & Greist, 2001; Steketee et al., 2000). This pressure not only drives a wedge between the client and family members, but also leaves the client suspicious about the intentions of those identified as "helpers." Clients are unlikely to change their behavior substantially unless they first decide that they would be better off if they did so. Many clients recognize the problems hoarding creates for them and express a desire to change, but when faced with the task of actually discarding a cherished possession, their motivation evaporates. Encouraging clients to discuss their ambivalence about change sets the stage for later therapy, when they are asked to challenge their beliefs about losing possessions. This discussion also clarifies the specific beliefs that are interfering with recovery. The therapist must fully explore these issues using motivational interviewing techniques before commencing with the active treatment. It is best for the therapist to address these problems as early as possible rather than waste effort on a treatment that will be inadequate because ambivalence on the part of the client will prevent them from engaging in the necessary work. Ambivalence about change must be identified and discussed. If it is not identified, subtle forms of noncompliance and a lack of common goals will undermine the activities, exercises, and discussions that make up this treatment.

Therapists treating compulsive hoarding are strongly urged to read Miller and Rollnick's (2002) book *Motivational Interviewing* to become familiar with its concepts and principals. In our experience, motivational interviewing techniques have been essential tools for addressing the constant struggle with ambivalence found in this client population. The motivational interviewing approach, originally developed for substance abuse problems, is "a directive, client-centered counseling style for eliciting behavior change by helping clients explore and resolve ambivalence" (Rollnick & Miller, 1995, p. 325). Motivational interviewing involves the collaboration or formation of "a partnership that honors the client's experience and perspectives" (Miller & Rollnick, p. 35), evocation of motivation within the client, and the assumption that the client is autonomous and has the right and capacity to exercise self-direction and informed choices.

Direct attempts at persuasion should be avoided. Most clients have faced family, friends, and authorities who have been very direct in telling them what to do, but to no avail. Similar attempts by the therapist are not likely to succeed. As with all forms of cognitive therapy, changes in attitudes are elicited by Socratic techniques and various methods described in the next section. Therapists can become familiar with Socratic methods by reading examples of therapeutic dialogue in Beck (1995).

Skills Training

We believe that there are three major skills necessary in successfully managing one's possessions: (a) learning how to solve problems, (b) learning how to make decisions and tolerate mistakes, and (c) learning how to categorize and put objects out of sight. Many people with hoarding problems spend considerable amounts of time trying, but failing, to get organized. Therapists should begin by discussing if and how these skills deficits contribute to the hoarding problem. The goal of this part of treatment is to help clients learn to efficiently solve problems, make decisions, and organize possessions so they do not have to rely on memory to find items when they need them.

Problem Solving

People with hoarding problems frequently have difficulty identifying the important features of a problem and generating solutions other than avoidance. We follow six simple steps in working with clients to solve problems:

1. identify and define the problem;
2. generate as many solutions as possible (be creative and silly to help keep thinking flexible);
3. evaluate possible solutions and select the one or two that seem most feasible;
4. implement the solution;
5. evaluate the outcome; and
6. if necessary, repeat the process until a good solution is found.

The most common problem we have observed in this treatment involves clients' inability to do homework between sessions. When this occurs, we use problem-solving steps to generate solutions. All solutions, however impractical from the client's point of view, are carefully evaluated.

Decision Making

With regard to decision making, it is first necessary for the client to understand the decision-making problem. Hoarding clients tend to be perfectionistic and fear making mistakes (Frost & Gross, 1993) which frequently results in avoidance of making decisions. Cognitive (e.g., downward arrow, described later in this chapter) and behavioral strategies (e.g., behavioral experiments) can be used to evaluate the consequences of making a mistake and to challenge catastrophic thinking.

Additionally, difficulties with attention can interfere with the process of decision making. Clients can get distracted and move on to something else without ever making a choice. Friends and family can be enlisted to help the client maintain his or her attention on the task at hand. Setting a timer to remind clients to work on a particular task at that time or working for shorter periods at a time can be helpful.

Finally, decisions about possessions are emotionally charged and thus aversive for people who hoard. Not making a decision allows them to avoid this negative experience. It may be helpful for the therapist to simplify the task by asking clients to focus on one small decision at a time so that they may experience some success; positive emotions can then be associated with the decision-making process. Another problem that contributes to indecisiveness is an overly complex thought process. Clients consider too many variables when trying to make a decision and have difficulty evaluating the relative importance of each piece of information. One strategy involves having clients consider only the three most important pieces of information in making the decision.

Organization

People who hoard have problems categorizing possessions. Clients often identify each possession as special or unique and deserving of its own category. The result is extreme disorganization, and clients must remember the location of each possession. To assist clients in organizing, we work with them to define a relatively small number of categories for each type of possession, simplifying the decisions about where items go. We create an organizing plan, which includes a list of categories of saved items (e.g., mail, photos, clothing, newspapers) and a list of locations these may be placed in a typical home. Next, we develop a plan for sorting, categorizing, and moving saved items. These activities include obtaining storage containers and labels to hold possessions once they have been sorted. For clients whose homes are fully cluttered, it may be necessary for the therapist to have them create a working space where possessions can be sorted into categories. Additional things to consider include scheduling times to work on sorting, specifying a length of time to work on sorting, and establishing a time frame for discarding items or putting items away.

A basic sorting system might include the following basic steps: The client must decide whether to keep or discard the item. The number of undecided items should be kept to a minimum and a plan made for when and how to determine their ultimate destination. If the decision is to remove the item, the client must determine where it should go and how to get it there. If the decision is to keep the item, the client must determine what category it belongs to and where it should be placed.

Imaginal and In Vivo Exposure

The therapist must fully understand the nature of the client's avoidance before implementing exposure. Avoidance behaviors in hoarding can be subtle. For instance, when the hoarding behavior has been going on for a long time, clients sometimes avoid noticing or recognizing the clutter. This perceptual avoidance may improve mood and make them feel less overwhelmed, but it interferes with their ability to resolve the clutter problem. For one of our clients, part of her exposure homework was to take a full minute every time she came home and look around her apartment to notice the clutter. Another form of exposure might involve having clients review and describe pictures of their home. In our experience, this strategy often produces more recognition of clutter than either simply describing it or even being there.

Yet another kind of avoidance seen in hoarding is the tendency to put everything in sight. We have shown elsewhere that this is related to a fear of losing or forgetting (Frost & Gross, 1993). For Betty, one exposure exercise involved putting things out of sight and asking at various intervals whether she remembered where the item was located. One good strategy for doing this is creating a filing system, because one bonus outcome will be improvement in client's ability to find important papers.

The inability to make decisions is a classic feature of compulsive hoarding, and much of the problem with saving possessions arises from this difficulty. In addition to the skills training described earlier in this section, decision making can be made part of the exposure. The work of sorting possessions and excavating portions of the home involves a protocol that requires decision making. During these sequences it is important for the therapist to limit the number of outcomes for each decision. The first decision involves one of two choices—save or get rid of the item. The second decision involves where the item goes. The locations should be worked out ahead of time in a planful way so that clients will have cleared spaces ready for the saved possessions. It is essential that sorted material be placed in the appropriate location so that clients can be reinforced for decisions made with organized belongings. Sorting possessions exposes clients to evaluating and making decisions about their possessions. It is critical that clients begin this right away and get used to doing it regularly and often. Betty used a similar system, tailored to her own needs, to manage her incoming mail, something she generally avoided because she found the task overwhelming and anxiety provoking. She began by deciding which pieces of mail were important to keep and which were not. Bills were placed in a priority pile, unwanted papers were immediately discarded, and catalogues were placed in a separate pile. Catalogues were separated because Betty made a decision during treatment to limit the amount of clutter coming into the home by calling companies and asking them to take her off their mailing lists.

Typical exposure scenarios are difficult to implement in compulsive hoarding. Although the client may find it possible to create exposure hierarchies, unless the exposure is set up as an experiment to test a hoarding-related belief, it is not clear that the exposure will result in habituation. If the client is discarding just to go along with the therapist's agenda or the therapy protocol, the exposure will have little effect on the hoarding behavior. The client may find it is more productive to set up the exposure as a way of testing out the beliefs that form the attachment to the possession. Much of the exposure work in treating hoarding is done in the context of cognitive restructuring of beliefs. In Betty's case, discontinuing receipt of catalogues tested the belief that she would not be able to make purchases without the appropriate catalogues. Over time, she learned that she could access the information in other ways (e.g., using the computer) if she needed to make a purchase.

Exposures for compulsive acquisition are far easier to implement than those for saving behavior. More is involved, however, than with typical exposures for other OCD symptoms. In addition to distress from not acquiring, people with compulsive acquisition problems have high levels of positive affect and attraction to the desired object. In creating an exposure hierarchy, both the attractive qualities and the level of distress at not acquiring must be considered. Habituation involves both the development of the ability to tolerate attraction to an object without acquiring it and tolerance of the subsequent discomfort from not acquiring.

Understanding the avoidance pattern with compulsive acquisition is crucial as well. Many people with acquisition problems have gained some degree of control over them by avoiding the places where they have trouble controlling their acquisition. To gain complete control over their acquisition problem, they must identify these places and incorporate them into the exposure hierarchy. The hierarchy typically begins with situations that can be resisted, like driving by a favorite thrift store, and end with having the client walk away from an item they have handled and talked about acquiring.

Imagined exposure can be used to structure the feared outcome and sometimes works better than in vivo exposure. For example, at the core of much saving behavior is the fear of losing information. An exposure that involves the client imagining the loss of information in a specific newspaper not only provides useful information about the nature of the attachment to objects but also facilitates the decision to get rid of the newspaper. The structure of imagined loss may vary, depending on the needs of the client. Rather than a hierarchy, the exposure can focus on just one object and allow for cognitive elaboration to help in the decision-making process regarding discarding.

Typical exposure sequences focus on the distress and negative experiences of the exposure. With hoarding, the situation is more complicated. For exposure to be effective, the client must make the decision to discard. For most clients, the distress occurs mostly during the decision-making process and is often minimal after the decision has been made. Clients frequently need help in the decision-making process to work through the pros and cons of discarding. Thus, the focus is more on the reasons for the decision and less on the distress.

Cognitive Strategies

As discussed earlier in this chapter, several characteristic beliefs contribute to hoarding problems, including beliefs about the value of objects, responsibility to avoid waste, importance of maintaining control over possessions, and memory concerns. Furthermore, a frequent style of thinking associated with compulsive hoarding is a perfectionistic fear of making mistakes. In contrast to other forms of OCD, these beliefs are often ego syntonic and may not be viewed by clients as erroneous or maladaptive. Correcting these beliefs requires a skillful application of Socratic questioning and motivational interviewing techniques to get clients to consider the validity and adaptiveness of beliefs. Before applying cognitive techniques, the therapist should be familiar with the general use of cognitive therapy procedures and the style of collaborative work between the therapist and client. In general, these strategies are designed to help clients step back from their thoughts and consider alternative perspectives on their hoarding problems. A more complete description of these techniques can be found in Steketee and Frost (in press). Three are described in the sections that follow: making predictions, the downward arrow method, and listing advantages and disadvantages.

Making Predictions

Early in the sorting process, the therapist asks the client to make predictions about what would happen if specific items were discarded—in particular, the probability of bad outcomes, the consequences of these bad outcomes, and how well the client could cope with such an outcome. Similar questions should be asked about how upset clients would feel about getting rid of the item, how long that distress would last, and how well they think they could cope with that feeling. The answers to these questions frequently frame the hoarding problem and provide opportunities for behavioral experiments to test the predictions. Examining these predictions frequently allows the therapist to suggest which items might be good to use for a discarding experiment. The experiment might involve testing the prediction regarding bad outcomes and distress.

Downward Arrow Method

The downward arrow method involves a series of questions designed to identify catastrophic fears and beliefs associated with hoarding (see chap. 5, this volume, for a general description). In the case of Betty, when discussing whether or not to discard a travel brochure for Hawaii, the therapist asked, "What would happen if you let this item go?" Betty responded, "I may want to visit Hawaii someday. It would be helpful to keep this, just in case." The therapist followed this with questions designed to uncover the meaning this information had for the client (e.g., "What would happen if you did want to visit Hawaii and you did not have the brochure? What would be the worst part about that? How else can you find the information? Would anything else happen? And then what?"). By following this line of questioning, clients invariably provide information about core beliefs that drive their hoarding (e.g., "I need to be prepared" or "I need to be perfect"). Once such core beliefs are elicited, they can be carefully examined and challenged.

Listing Advantages and Disadvantages

Having clients list the advantages and disadvantages of hoarding versus not hoarding can be a good starting point for treatment. People who hoard tend to focus on the immediate costs associated with discarding or not acquiring something and ignore the costs of acquiring, not organizing, and saving and the benefits of getting rid of them. Listing and examining the costs and benefits of hoarding behaviors can be a useful strategy to help clients consider less obvious alternatives. Clients may need assistance in identifying the costs of their hoarding behavior, because they usually rarely consider or actively avoid making such an analysis. Once the lists are completed, the therapist can highlight discrepancies using a motivational interviewing approach to facilitate change-oriented talk in the client.

RELAPSE PREVENTION

Relapse prevention begins with a review of the compulsive hoarding models developed during the early phases of treatment to determine whether they are still accurate. The therapist reviews the general principles of treatment in a way that emphasizes the skills the client developed during the therapy, with particular attention to those found to be most successful. The therapist then provides clients with information about the likely course of symptoms after treatment, noting that it is unlikely that they will be completely free of their hoarding problem. The therapist helps clients identify stressors that may trigger hoarding and ways to handle them, and discuss strategies for managing setbacks; planning will help clients not to overreact in response to minor setbacks.

TROUBLESHOOTING

A number of treatment-interfering behaviors can surface in the treatment of compulsive hoarding. Many of these behaviors are part of the syndrome. For example, subtle yet powerful forms of avoidance keep clients from doing the work necessary for change. Three of the most common problems are (a) not working between treatment sessions, (b) diverting attention to other topics during the session, and (c) hypersensitivity to mistakes and criticism.

In our experience, homework problems seem to occur more frequently in hoarding than other forms of OCD. The reasons clients give for not doing homework are varied. Many focus on the themes of being too busy, tired, or stressed. Therapists who treat hoarding should anticipate hearing these things frequently. We have adopted the strategy of treating these as avoidance behaviors that are part of the syndrome of hoarding. With people who are too tired or stressed to do homework, we use the analogy of physical fitness: When they begin treatment, their stamina for sorting possessions is low, but by regularly working for longer and longer periods of time, they will experience less fatigue and stress when faced with sorting their possessions, just as their physical fitness would improve with regular physical exercise. Other strategies are helpful as well, including finding friends or relatives who can sit with them while they sort.

Many hoarding clients can and do talk extensively about hoarding, as well as other problems. If the therapist is not careful, these topics will dominate sessions, and little time will be left to work on organizing possessions. We also view this as a subtle form of avoidance; it is more palatable for clients to talk than to work on sorting and discarding. If sorting is made a standard part of sessions from the outset, this problem should be minimized.

A third frequently observed problem is a high level of perfectionism and sensitivity to perceived mistakes and criticism. Changing their current pattern of behavior (i.e., discarding) leads clients to feel that they are making serious mistakes or violating some sort of moral code (i.e., they have become a wasteful and thus bad person). The therapist can deal with these issues directly using the cognitive therapy techniques described in this chapter and elsewhere (Steketee & Frost, in press).

The study of compulsive hoarding is relatively recent and, therefore, limited information is available regarding the treatment of this challenging condition. Although most researchers consider hoarding to be a symptom or subtype of OCD (Christensen & Greist, 2001; Samuels et al., 2002), hoarding appears to differ from OCD in several significant ways including treatment response. Poor treatment outcomes indicate a need for further research on the etiology and maintaining factors associated with hoarding.

The treatment described in this chapter is based on a cognitive–behavioral model of compulsive hoarding (Frost & Hartl, 1996; Frost & Steketee, 1998) which presumes that problems with acquiring, saving, and clutter result from personal vulnerabilities, information processing deficits, beliefs about and attachments to possessions, and emotional distress and avoidance behaviors. The intervention relies on collaboration between the therapist and the client to develop a shared understanding of the client's hoarding problem and to apply the treatment techniques that are designed to address the specific facets of compulsive hoarding. Preliminary studies based on the model presented here show encouraging evidence for the efficacy of cognitive–behavioral treatments specifically designed to treat hoarding (Cermele et al., 2001; Hartl & Frost, 1999; Saxena et al., 2002; Steketee et al., 2001). While complete remission of hoarding symptoms is infrequent, most experience a significant reduction in clutter, difficulty discarding, and excessive acquiring and have gained skills to continue their work long after treatment ends.

REFERENCES

Beck, J. S. (1995). *Cognitive therapy: Basics and beyond.* New York: Guilford Press.

Cermele, J. A., Melendez-Pallitto, L., & Pandina, G. J. (2001). Intervention in compulsive hoarding: A case study. *Behavior Modification, 25,* 214–232.

Christensen, D. D., & Greist, J. H. (2001). The challenge of obsessive–compulsive disorder hoarding. *Primary Psychiatry, 8*, 79–86.

Damecour, C. L., & Charron, M. (1998). Hoarding: A symptom, not a syndrome. *Journal of Clinical Psychiatry, 59*, 267–272.

Frost, R. O., & Gross, R. C. (1993). The hoarding of possessions. *Behaviour Research and Therapy, 31*, 367–381.

Frost, R. O., & Hartl, T. L. (1996). A cognitive–behavioral model of compulsive hoarding. *Behaviour Research and Therapy, 34*, 341–350.

Frost, R. O., & Steketee, G. (1998). Hoarding: Clinical aspects and treatment strategies. In M. A. Jenike, L. Baer, & W. E. Minichiello (Eds.), *Obsessive–compulsive disorder: Practical management* (3rd ed., pp. 533–554). St. Louis, MO: Mosby Yearbook Medical.

Frost, R. O., Steketee, G., & Grisham, J. R. (2004). Measurement of compulsive hoarding: Saving Inventory—Revised. *Behaviour Research and Therapy, 42*, 1163–1182.

Grisham, J., Frost, R. O., Steketee, G., Kim, H.-J., & Hood, S. (2005). Age of onset in compulsive hoarding. *Journal of Anxiety Disorders, 20*, 675–686.

Hartl, T. L., Duffany, S. R., Allen, G. J., Steketee, G., & Frost, R. O. (2005). Relationships among compulsive hoarding, trauma, and attention-deficit/hyperactivity disorder. *Behaviour Research and Therapy, 43*, 269–276.

Hartl, T. L., & Frost, R. O. (1999). Cognitive–behavioral treatment of compulsive hoarding: A multiple baseline experimental case study. *Behaviour Research and Therapy, 37*, 451–461.

Hartl, T. L., Frost, R. O., Allen, G. J., Deckersbach, T., Steketee, G., Duffany, S. R., & Savage, C. R. (2004). Actual and perceived memory deficits in individuals with compulsive hoarding. *Depression and Anxiety, 20*, 59–69.

Kyrios, M., Frost, R. O., & Steketee, G. (2004). Cognitions in compulsive buying and acquisition. *Cognitive Therapy and Research, 28*, 241–258.

Miller, W. R., & Rollnick, S. (2002). *Motivational interviewing: Preparing people for change* (2nd ed.). New York: Guilford Press.

Rollnick, S., & Miller, W. R. (1995). What is motivational interviewing? *Behavioural and Cognitive Psychotherapy, 23*, 325–334.

Samuels, J., Bienvenu, O. J., III, Riddle, M. A., Cullen, B. A. M., Grados, M. A., Liang, K. Y., et al. (2002). Hoarding in obsessive–compulsive disorder: Results from a case-control study. *Behaviour Research and Therapy, 40*, 517–528.

Saxena, S., Maidment, K. M., Vapnik, T., Golden, G., Rishwain, T., Rosen, R., et al. (2002). Obsessive–compulsive hoarding: Symptom severity and response to multimodal treatment. *Journal of Clinical Psychiatry, 63*, 21–27.

Steketee, G., Chambless, D. L., & Tran, G. Q. (2001). Effects of axis I and axis II comorbidity on behavior therapy outcome for obsessive–compulsive disorder and agoraphobia. *Comprehensive Psychiatry, 42*, 76–86.

Steketee, G., & Frost, R. (2003). Compulsive hoarding: Current status of the research. *Clinical Psychology Review, 23*, 905–927.

Steketee, G., & Frost, R. (in press). *Treatment manual for compulsive hoarding.* New York: Oxford University Press.

Steketee, G., Frost, R. O., Wincze, J., Greene, K., & Douglass, H. (2000). Group and individual treatment of compulsive hoarding: A pilot study. *Behavioural and Cognitive Psychotherapy, 28,* 259–268.

III

STRATEGIES FOR SPECIFIC POPULATIONS

11

TREATING OBSESSIVE–COMPULSIVE DISORDER IN CHILDREN AND ADOLESCENTS

MARTIN E. FRANKLIN, JOHN S. MARCH, AND ABBE GARCIA

Epidemiological data suggest that at least 1% of children and adolescents experience clinically significant obsessive–compulsive disorder (OCD; Flament et al., 1988) and that among adults with OCD, one third to one half developed the disorder during childhood or adolescence (Rasmussen & Eisen, 1990). The disorder often disrupts academic, social, and vocational functioning; is associated with significant psychiatric comorbidity; and can lead to derailment from achieving important developmental milestones that have major implications for successful functioning as an adult. Thus, in addition to reducing OCD and related symptoms, early identification and successful treatment may reduce adult morbidity and comorbidity as well (March, 1995).

Cognitive–behavioral therapy (CBT) involving exposure and response prevention (ERP; also known as exposure and ritual prevention) has emerged as experts' preferred initial treatment option for OCD across the developmental spectrum (March, Frances, Kahn, & Carpenter, 1997), and within the past 2 years, two randomized controlled trials have provided further empirical support for the efficacy of CBT in children and adolescents (Barrett, Healy-Farrell, & March, 2004; Pediatric OCD Treatment Study Team, 2004).

However, the paucity of CBT expertise for pediatric OCD in most communities limits the accessibility of this form of treatment, leaving many families searching for other mental health services for their children. Pharmacotherapy with selective serotonin reuptake inhibitors (SSRIs) has also been established as efficacious for pediatric OCD (e.g., sertraline; March et al., 1998) and is widely available. However, partial response to SSRIs appears to be the norm, and safety concerns have been raised about their use with younger patients. Furthermore, the largest randomized controlled trial in pediatric OCD conducted thus far supported the superiority of combined treatment over SSRI monotherapy (Pediatric OCD Treatment Study Team, 2004). It is clear that training mental health professionals to implement CBT for children and adolescents with OCD is now a major priority among clinical researchers, and such dissemination is likely to be of substantial public health value.

Toward that end, this chapter focuses on some of the clinical subtleties of treating children and adolescents with OCD. Many excellent texts have already been devoted to the conduct of psychotherapy with children and adolescents more broadly speaking, and because of space considerations, we focus in this chapter on the nuts and bolts of conducting OCD treatment specifically. Given the apparent formal similarity between adult and pediatric OCD, the other chapters in this volume are also informative for those interested in treating younger patients. Nevertheless, we emphasize that children and adolescents with OCD should not be viewed as little adults with OCD, and thus it is of paramount importance for the therapist to attend to the developmental stage and needs of the child, as well as to the family and school contexts in which the child lives, when implementing ERP in a clinically sensitive manner. March and Mulle (1998) published the manual for the protocol that was empirically evaluated in the "Pediatric OCD Treatment Study."

ASSESSMENT: WITH WHOM, AND WITH WHAT?

An adequate assessment of pediatric OCD should include a comprehensive evaluation of current and past OCD symptoms, current OCD symptom severity, and associated functional impairment and a survey of comorbid psychopathology. In addition, the strengths of the child and family should be evaluated, as well as their knowledge of OCD and its treatment. There are many self-report and therapist-administered instruments that can be used to guide this type of assessment. We typically mail several relevant self-report questionnaires (e.g., Children's Depression Inventory, Kovacs, 1996; Multidimensional Anxiety Scale for Children, March, 1998; Children and Parents' OCD Impairment Scales, Piacentini, Bergman, Keller, & McCracken,

2003) to the family for completion before intake and then review these materials before meeting with the child. If it is apparent from these materials that comorbid depression or anxiety problems other than OCD are prominent, we focus on these symptoms as well in the intake. For surveying the history of OCD symptoms and current symptom severity, we use the interviewer-rated checklist and severity scale of the Children's Yale–Brown Obsessive–Compulsive Scale (CY–BOCS; Scahill et al., 1997) and recommend its use even in the clinical context, because it provides a wealth of information about the topography and severity of the child's OCD and can be used to guide treatment.

Before conducting the clinical interview, it is particularly important for the therapist to determine whether the child should be seen with or without the parents present. We typically recommend a conjoint interview, directing questions to the child but soliciting parental feedback as well; clinically, we feel this establishes the expectation that the child will be the primary player in treatment, with parents in a secondary and primarily supportive role depending in part on the age and social maturity level of the child. The decision to interview the child alone or with a parent present is made on the basis of developmental factors, discussion with the parent in advance, observations of the child's and family's behavior in the waiting area, and even discussion during the interview if necessary. Our mantra is "get the data," meaning that if parental presence increases the validity of the assessment, we include them; if not, then we interview the child alone. With older children and adolescents in particular, when there are discrepancies in the reporting of the patient and the parents, we tend to weigh the patient's report of obsessions more heavily, while recognizing that parents may be more attuned to the amount of time the child spends engaged in overt behavioral rituals. We also emphasize to the family that these discrepancies are quite common and that as treatment progresses, everyone will become more attuned to how OCD is affecting the child and the family. We state this specifically to minimize the possibility of family bickering about whether the child was being "truthful" in reporting the symptoms.

Occasionally, we deviate from the strategy of interviewing the child in the presence of the parents when we are asking about potentially sensitive content areas, such as sexual or violent obsessions. Sometimes the referral source has already specified that these obsessions are present, in which case we recommend the interview be set up to include some time with the child alone; occasionally, the child has already discussed the details of these obsessions with his or her parents, and thus the therapist may find it unnecessary to treat this part of the interview differently. With adolescents in particular, or when the therapist doesn't know whether the patient has these kinds of intrusions, he or she can make a general statement, such as "Some kinds of obsessions might be really uncomfortable to talk about in front of other people, especially family members—does your OCD give you any of those that we should discuss with Mom and Dad out of the room?"

If the patient confirms that he or she would like to have some time alone to discuss certain obsessions, it is imperative for the therapist to lead into this discussion with some basic psychoeducation about the nature of thoughts in general, the reportedly frequent occurrence of sexual and violent obsessions in OCD across the developmental spectrum, the concept of thought–action fusion (i.e., failure to differentiate thoughts from actual behavior), and a careful definition of sexual and violent obsessions that clearly differentiates them from pleasurable sexual thoughts and from angry ruminations or violent fantasies. These points covered, the therapist should again convey a knowledgeable and accepting tone when asking about specific sexual and violent obsessions. To facilitate this inquiry, we use "hip-pocket patient" examples (e.g., "Some kids with sexual obsessions involving younger children have images of losing control and acting on them, whereas others think much more about the consequences of doing so") and place these thoughts, regardless of their content, in a neurobehavioral framework (e.g., "They're just brain hiccups and don't have any real meaning or importance"). This framework is a useful heuristic that can help patients and families avoid the pattern of recrimination and blame that so often accompanies pediatric disorders (empirical support for all aspects of the model has yet to be garnered).

As part of a comprehensive intake process, we suggest that pediatric OCD patients' medical histories be surveyed, with particular attention to the presence of recurrent streptococcal infection. Current research diagnostic criteria for pediatric autoimmune neuropsychiatric disorders associated with streptococcal infections (PANDAS) require at least two documented episodes of exacerbations in OCD and tic symptoms associated with streptococcal infection (Swedo et al., 1998). Unfortunately, an unambiguous retrospective diagnosis of PANDAS is next to impossible in a clinically referred population of youths with OCD (Giulino et al., 2002). Clinically, children who have unambiguous evidence of PANDAS should be referred for appropriate treatment of their group A β-hemolytic streptococcal infection. Once treated for the infection, the therapist should then consider CBT and/or SSRI pharmacotherapy strategies. Increasingly, we have found that families come to the clinic already knowledgeable about PANDAS, so when surveying this area the therapist is likely to be received favorably. Even in cases in which PANDAS is improbable (e.g., gradual onset, no reported strep infection or illness before onset), this discussion provides an opportunity to emphasize that OCD is a neurobehavioral disorder likely to have various biological precipitants and underpinnings and is certainly not the result of bad parenting, stubborn children, or other such inaccurate and unhelpful causes.

More generally, we place OCD firmly within the medical context, akin to diabetes, supporting later discussions that externalize OCD as a separate entity causing the child and family distress and discomfort; this approach makes it easier to conceptualize the struggle to tame OCD as one in which the child, therapist, and family are aligned to fight against the OCD, rather than against each other. The therapist should make this point throughout the initial interview process and can further underscore it by phrasing questions about OCD symptoms and related dysfunction along the following lines: "What kind of trouble has the OCD been giving you this week?" "How has OCD gotten the family all knotted up in its web?" "Does your OCD tell you that something bad will happen if you don't wash, or does it just say that you'll be uncomfortable until you do?" The therapist should refer to OCD as an entity that is separate from the child from the beginning; this serves as a model of how to speak and think about OCD so as to clearly establish this critically important stance for treatment.

PSYCHOEDUCATION

Session 1 of our center's treatment manual is devoted specifically to psychoeducation and the presentation of a neurobehavioral model of OCD and to a discussion of the theory behind how ERP works to reduce fear and correct mistaken beliefs (Foa & Kozak, 1985, 1986). We consider the entire evaluation and treatment context an ongoing opportunity for teaching children and their families about OCD. For example, early in the initial interview and before administering the CY–BOCS, the therapist should explain the concepts of obsessions and compulsions, using specific examples if the child or parent has difficulty grasping the concepts. We also take this opportunity to tell children and their parents about the prevalence, nature, and treatment of OCD, which may increase their willingness to disclose specific symptoms. Children may be particularly vulnerable to feeling as if they are the only ones on earth with obsessive fears, so therapists may find it useful to preface the examples with "I once met a kid who . . ." to dispel this myth and minimize the accompanying sense of isolation. During the interview, it is also important for therapists to observe the child's behavior and inquire whether certain behaviors (e.g., unusual movements, vocalizations) are compulsions designed to neutralize obsessions or to reduce distress. This information is critically important for the therapist, and the opportunity to identify obsessions and compulsions as they occur can be very helpful for families and for children as well. For example, in the midst of an initial evaluation, one child asked the evaluator if a certain carving in his office was made of wood. When the answer—"Yes, it's made of wood"—did not help the now increasingly anxious child, the therapist asked "whether OCD is telling you that you have to hear a one-word answer." The child confirmed the therapist's suspicion, and the therapist then was able to ask several other questions about "what OCD tells you" in these situations, thus demonstrating knowledge of OCD generally that the family had found reassuring while simultaneously learning more about the child's particular flavor of OCD.

Another common opportunity for psychoeducation during the early interviews involves identification of feared consequences. For example, some children who are aware of their obsessional content may be fearful of saying the fears aloud. The therapist surveying common obsessions with the CY–BOCS checklist instead of asking the child to disclose the fears helps with this problem, as does encouragement by the therapist (e.g., "Lots of the kids I see have a hard time talking about these kinds of fears"). We have found that flexibility in the manner of disclosing the obsession is warranted. Thus, we would encourage the child to write down the fears or to nod his or her head as the therapist describes examples of similar fears in order to help the child share his or her OCD problems. In this way, the therapist conveys to the child and family that he or she recognizes the difficulty associated with disclosure. The therapist can also use examples from children he or she has evaluated in the past (e.g., "I remember a few months ago when a kid about your age told me she would be scared to pet her hamster because when she's holding him, OCD might tell her that she is going to lose control and hurt him"), although it is important for the therapist to let the children and families know that he or she is careful not to violate confidentiality when citing such examples.

Among the most critical points the therapist should convey during psychoeducation for OCD is that treatment will focus on changing the child's response to the obsession, rather than trying to make obsessions go away directly. This may strike the child and family initially as counterintuitive, because it is evident to many that obsessional distress is causing the urge to ritualize. We make ample use of Mowrer's two-factor theory (Mowrer, 1939, 1960) when explaining that obsessions are involuntary thoughts that give rise to anxiety, whereas compulsions are intentional behaviors or mental acts that reduce obsessional distress but unfortunately in the process "feed the OCD" through the process of negative reinforcement. Given that people cannot exercise much control over their thinking anyway and that OCD is analogous to a "brain hiccup" that is especially impervious to voluntary control, therapists should instead focus on helping patients learn to control what they can actually control, namely compulsions and avoidance behaviors; put another way, the task is to try to weaken OCD by not doing what it asks one to do. We emphasize that if the child learns how to "say no" to OCD, the frequent and scary obsessions will decrease, the demands that OCD places on the child will become less onerous, and the job of saying no will get easier and easier. With younger children in particular, the image of a favorite dog begging at the dinner table is a useful and nonthreatening way for therapists to convey the effects of withdrawing reinforcement (especially if the child has a dog at home who engages in such behavior):

As long as you slip the dog some scraps at the table, she will continue to sit next to you and beg. When you stop doing so, she might beg a bit louder at first, but if not reinforced, she will stop begging and move on.

The therapist should get to know his or her patient sufficiently well so that he or she can judge which analogies will work best and tailor the discussion of these core concepts to the interests and developmental level of the child.

EXPOSURE HIERARCHY DEVELOPMENT

Working with information the therapist gathered at intake about the topography of the patient's OCD, the next stage of treatment is the development of an exposure hierarchy. The therapist must convey to the child that the treatment will proceed at the child's chosen pace: Situations and thoughts that trigger obsessional distress are first ranked on a fear thermometer (March & Mulle, 1998) from 0 (*easiest*) to 10 (*hardest*) to guide selection of treatment targets. Once the targets are selected, the collaborative task of resisting OCDs demands (response prevention) and intentionally finding opportunities to "give OCD a hard time" (exposure) begins in earnest. The therapist may encounter several clinical challenges at this stage. Some children have a difficult time distinguishing among the levels of distress, conveying to the therapist that "everything is a 10," and some focus during the hierarchy development task on what they cannot do, rather than what they can do.

The therapist can help the child make better distinctions by clearly defining the anchor points with salient stimuli. For example, if a child with contamination fears says that drinking out of an unopened bottle of soda that was just dispensed from a vending machine is a 10, the therapist might counter by saying, "Well, it sounds like your OCD would give you a really hard time on that one. What about if the soda bottle was just opened and you saw somebody drink out of it—what number would that be?" The child might respond by saying, "That would be a 20." The therapist could then ask the child, "Now, let's say we went to the bottling factory, and you took the first bottle right out of the first box, before it even got to the stores—what would that be on the thermometer?" The therapist could use these clear distinctions to recalibrate the fear thermometer ratings and to convey to the patient that distinctions can indeed be made on the contamination hierarchy.

With contamination, it is also important for the therapist to know whether an item that has touched a highly contaminated item, such as a paper towel that has been brushed against a public toilet seat, is equally contaminated. Such questions also convey a way that the therapy can proceed from lower to more difficult items.

The therapist must be familiar with key dimensions associated with the difficulty level of particular symptom clusters. For example, for contamination symptoms, level of contact with the contaminating source (e.g., brushing past it vs. prolonged, complete contact with it) and location of the contamination (e.g., on the body, such as head or face, vs. in the world, such as a highly public place) are two dimensions along which a therapist can ask pointed questions to elicit variations in anticipated fear ratings from the client. Another way to break out of a rating conundrum is for the therapist to examine the effects of context: For example, a child might say that refraining from his touching ritual is invariably a 10 on the fear thermometer, but the therapist can counter with questions about whether the rating would be different if the child was running late for a play date or on his or her way to see a movie that he or she had looked forward to all year. Examining home versus school, Mom's house versus Dad's house, and other such contextual shifts can also facilitate hierarchy development. When a therapist encounters a child who says "I couldn't possibly do that," we recommend a first response during this stage such as, "OK, it sounds as if OCD would give you a terrible time resisting that exposure, but can you think of something that you might be able to do instead?"

EARLY TREATMENT SESSIONS

The early stages of ERP can be very fulfilling for patients, parents, and therapists alike: Children and adolescents begin to take on OCD in a way that seemed impossible just weeks before, and early successes breed confidence in the conceptual model and allow the child to take bolder and seemingly riskier steps up the hierarchy. The therapist may occasionally encounter difficulties with parental eagerness to change the original agreement and race to more difficult terrain: "I see that he's already able to touch the floor in his room, so we want him now to go back to collecting the trash in the house and taking the cans to the road on garbage night." The therapist should reiterate the principle of hierarchy-driven treatment, especially if direct contact with trash is rated a 9 and the floor of the child's room a 2. The therapist might respond,

> I think we all have the same goal in mind, which is that your child functions as if OCD isn't giving him a hard time, but we don't want to lose sight of the fact that there's a lot of OCD territory to take back between the 2s and the 9s. I'd be concerned that if we move up quickly now, without finding out if the 3s, 4s, and 5s respond as nicely as the lower items have already, we could take on too much and actually wind up losing ground to OCD.

Such a response communicates empathy with the parents about their desire to get OCD out of the picture as soon as possible but does not deviate from the previously agreed on game plan to move systematically through the hierarchy at a pace that the child sets. Although tempting in the face of significant progress on the lower end, the therapist skipping rungs on the ladder without explicit agreement from the child that he or she is ready to do so is a potentially risky strategy that may threaten both the alliance and outcomes, especially if the adjustment is made in response to parental pressure rather than to clinical considerations.

Another clinical challenge that tends to arise early on in ERP is how the therapist should best use praise and external reinforcers. Young children especially may not be attuned to the long-term implications of leaving OCD untreated, and thus the fear and discomfort associated with confronting OCD may be much more salient than the risks of strengthening it by giving in to its demands. Social reinforcement from the therapist and parents may help motivate a child who is not inherently motivated to do the work; we often refer to "throwing a ticker tape parade" when a child successfully completes an exposure, fills out monitoring sheets, and participates actively in conceptualizing and implementing treatment. We ask the child and the parents about their responses when the child successfully completes treatment tasks to gauge whether more praise for efforts would be helpful.

When social reinforcement alone is insufficient to motivate a child to actively engage in the battle against OCD, external reinforcers can be used. With explicit agreement with the parents about the frequency and value of the rewards, the therapist can establish a schedule to track homework compliance, successful monitoring of rituals, and so forth that includes points the child can redeem when he or she meets the target behavior. The therapist can remind families that these reinforcers should be set not very far in the future (e.g., a trip to the zoo during the upcoming weekend), once earned should not be rescinded, and should generally focus on the use of treatment techniques rather than on levels of symptom reduction. Older children and adolescents may also profit from the use of reinforcer systems and should be encouraged to reward themselves for efforts using tangible reinforcers readily available to them (e.g., 1 hour of listening to favorite music after completing assigned treatment tasks).

MOVING UP THE EXPOSURE HIERARCHY

The goal of treatment is to teach the child to go about his or her business without getting tangled up in OCD's demands. As the child moves up the hierarchy and encounters more intense affect associated with the obsessions, it is especially important for therapists to emphasize this goal. The therapist should make clear throughout ERP that the goal of treatment is to teach the child to recognize OCD's demands for what they are, which is benign electrical noise from a brain hiccup, and then to go about the day's business without getting entangled in OCD's demands. When the child does so, his or her obsessional distress will decrease in the short run, and the frequency and intensity of these obsessions will weaken in the long run because he or she has successfully refrained from engaging with OCD. We tell our patients that obsessions are simply not worth the expenditure of energy they crave, and declining OCD's invitations to engage is the best way to weaken the OCD. Given that obsessions are likely to be more prominent as the patient moves into more difficult terrain during treatment, this message is worth reiterating before, during, and after exposure exercises.

For example, we once treated a patient who would have intrusive images of a grizzly bear's face growling at him and, on occasion, telling him to ritualize. Assessment during intake indicated that this phenomenon was obsessional rather than psychotic, and the patient cited these particular images as among the most difficult to confront without engaging in neutralizing behaviors (e.g., repeating actions until the image went away). We decided to conduct exposures that would specifically assist the patient in moving up the hierarchy to confront the bear images directly. We asked the patient to manipulate the bear image by conjuring it up intentionally and then having it engage in a variety of silly acts (e.g., reciting the Gettysburg Address, singing insipid pop songs); this raised the patient a temporary rung on the ladder to be able to allow the image to remain without engaging in behavioral rituals designed to make it go away immediately. Once the patient became more adept at holding the image rather than neutralizing, we asked him to let the image remain regardless of whether it was growling, singing, or helping him with history homework and to treat it like background noise. The patient's affect evoked by the presence of the image reduced with these exposures; he began to experience more and more success in refraining from neutralizing the image when it occurred spontaneously, the affect associated with the spontaneous image decreased, and eventually the frequency and intensity of these obsessions diminished. We emphasized throughout this several-week-long process that the presence or absence of the image was not a useful yardstick by which to evaluate how well he was doing in treatment and that, rather, he should pay careful attention to whether he was sufficiently detached from the image to avoid paying it much attention, should stop trying desperately to make it go away, and should go about the business of living his life and pursuing his interests.

Although there is some confusion in the field on this point, the goal of ERP is not to make obsessions go away directly, but rather to change the person's reaction to these thoughts so that he or she refrains from ritualizing and avoiding and instead moves forward with daily activities. The frequency and intensity of obsessional distress can be expected to decrease, because this more detached stance and successful response prevention expose the patient to corrective information. Trying to make obsessions go away directly is likely a futile endeavor that can lead only to frustration and further engagement with the OCD, which then strengthen the illness.

MAINTENANCE AND RELAPSE PREVENTION

Children and adolescents who have worked hard in CBT and have reaped its benefits, such as decreased OCD symptoms and improved functioning, can sometimes become increasingly fearful as treatment winds down, as might their families. Therapists can allay their concerns up front by emphasizing that ERP is really a teaching model in which the therapist imparts knowledge to the patient about how to fight back against OCD and teaches the patient the necessary skills to move forward long after the therapy has been completed. Nevertheless, trepidation at this stage is common for patients and their families, especially if the acute treatment phase is much shorter than the period of OCD dysfunction that preceded it. We use teaching and coaching metaphors liberally to make this process seem comparable to experiences the family has had before (e.g., "After your first season of soccer, did you suddenly forget that you're not supposed to touch the ball with your hands unless you're the goalie, or did you remember that?"), and social reinforcement of the patient's creativity in combating OCD can also assist with the transition (e.g., "It seems like last week you really outsmarted your OCD by recontaminating your hands and your body with that used towel right after you showered so that OCD wouldn't be so happy that you were super clean").

We also try to reinforce the learning of core concepts at the end of each exposure session by having patients summarize the session's exposure for their parents and explain the theoretical rationale for the week's homework assignment, rather than doing this ourselves. In this way, the therapist can check the patient's grasp of core concepts and reinforce the child's newfound knowledge about OCD and its treatment. We supplement learning reinforcement with another technique that is familiar to students: the pop quiz. Toward the end of treatment, we prepare several questions about hypothetical children with OCD symptoms other than the patient's, to see if patients can successfully recognize obsessions and compulsions and generate treatment exercises for the other children. The familiarity with the format helps children understand the point of the exercises and allows the therapist an opportunity to check on their understanding of core concepts and to provide more "ticker tape parades" for correct responses. We often structure these questions to match those used on a psychology licensing exam or in a residency training program, and when patients ace the quizzes, we remind them that their knowledge of how to use CBT to treat OCD is on par with that of mental health professionals. Most patients respond very favorably to this comparison, and many have reported that their improved confidence in their own ability to recognize and combat OCD plays a key role in their ongoing success in keeping the illness at bay.

CONCLUSION

We believe that the following are important priorities in pediatric OCD treatment research:

- more studies comparing medications, CBT, and combination treatment to control conditions to determine whether medications and CBT are synergistic or additive in their effects on symptom reduction;
- follow-up studies to evaluate relapse rates, including the utility of booster CBT for reducing risk for relapse;
- component analyses, such as a comparison of ERP, cognitive therapy, and their combination, to evaluate the relative contributions of specific treatment components to symptom reduction and treatment acceptability;
- comparisons of individual- and family-based treatments to determine the optimal degree of family involvement in the treatment of younger children;
- development of innovative treatments for OCD in children ages 4 to 8 years;
- treatment innovations targeted to factors, such as family dysfunction, that may constrain the application of CBT to patients with OCD;
- export of research treatments to divergent clinical settings and patient populations to judge the acceptability and effectiveness of CBT as a treatment for child and adolescent OCD in real-world settings; and
- once past initial treatment, the management of partial response, treatment resistance, and treatment maintenance and discontinuation.

REFERENCES

Barrett, P., Healy-Farrell, L., & March, J. S. (2004). Cognitive–behavioral family treatment of childhood obsessive–compulsive disorder: A controlled trial. *Journal of the American Academy of Child and Adolescent Psychiatry, 43*, 46–62.

Flament, M. F., Whitaker, A., Rapoport, J. L., Davies, M., Berg, C. Z., Kalikow, K., et al. (1988). Obsessive compulsive disorder in adolescence: An epidemiological study. *Journal of the American Academy of Child and Adolescent Psychiatry, 27,* 764–771.

Foa, E. B., & Kozak, M. J. (1985). Treatment of anxiety disorders: Implications for psychopathology. In A. H. Tuma & J. D. Maser (Eds.), *Anxiety and the anxiety disorders* (pp. 421–452). Hillsdale, NY: Erlbaum.

Foa, E. B., & Kozak, M. J. (1986). Emotional processing of fear: Exposure to corrective information. *Psychological Bulletin, 99,* 20–35.

Giulino, L., Gammon, P., Sullivan, K., Franklin, M., Foa, E., Maid, R., & March, J. S. (2002). Is parental report of upper respiratory infection at the onset of obsessive–compulsive disorder suggestive of pediatric autoimmune neuropsychiatric disorder associated with streptococcal infection? *Journal of Child and Adolescent Psychopharmacology, 12,* 157–164.

Kovacs, M. (1996). *The Children's Depression Inventory.* Toronto, Ontario, Canada: MultiHealth Systems.

March, J. S. (1995). Cognitive–behavioral psychotherapy for children and adolescents with OCD: A review and recommendations for treatment. *Journal of the American Academy of Child and Adolescent Psychiatry, 34,* 7–18.

March, J. S. (1998). *Manual for the Multidimensional Anxiety Scale for Children (MASC).* Toronto, Ontario, Canada: MultiHealth Systems.

March, J. S., Biederman, J., Wolkow, R., Safferman, A., Mardekian, J., Cook, E. H., et al. (1998). Sertraline in children and adolescents with obsessive–compulsive disorder: A multicenter randomized controlled trial [Comments]. *Journal of the American Medical Association, 280,* 1752–1756.

March, J., Frances, A., Kahn, D., & Carpenter, D. (1997). Expert Consensus Guidelines: Treatment of obsessive–compulsive disorder. *Journal of Clinical Psychiatry, 58*(Suppl. 4), 1–72.

March, J., & Mulle, K. (1998). *OCD in children and adolescents: A cognitive–behavioral treatment manual.* New York: Guilford Press.

Mowrer, O. H. (1939). A stimulus–response analysis of anxiety and its role as a reinforcing agent. *Psychological Review, 46,* 553–565.

Mowrer, O. H. (1960). *Learning theory and behavior.* New York: Wiley.

Pediatric OCD Treatment Study Team. (2004). Cognitive–behavioral therapy, sertraline, and their combination for children and adolescents with obsessive–compulsive disorder: The Pediatric OCD Treatment Study (POTS) randomized controlled trial. *Journal of the American Medical Association, 292,* 1969–1976.

Piacentini, J., Bergman, R. L., Keller, M., & McCracken, J. (2003). Functional impairment in children and adolescents with obsessive compulsive disorder. *Journal of Child and Adolescent Psychopharmacology, 13*(Suppl. 1), S61–S69.

Rasmussen, S. A., & Eisen, J. L. (1990). Epidemiology of obsessive compulsive disorder. *Journal of Clinical Psychiatry, 53*(Suppl.), 10–13, discussion 14.

Scahill, L., Riddle, M. A., McSwiggin-Hardin, M., Ort, S. I., King, R. A., Goodman, W. K., et al. (1997). Children's Yale–Brown Obsessive–Compulsive Scale: Reliability and validity. *Journal of the American Academy of Child and Adolescent Psychiatry*, *36*, 844–852.

Swedo, S. E., Leonard, H. L., Garvey, M., Mittleman, B., Allen, A. J., Perlmutter, S., et al. (1998). Pediatric autoimmune neuropsychiatric disorders associated with streptococcal infections: Clinical description of the first 50 cases. *American Journal of Psychiatry*, *155*, 264–271.

12

TREATING OBSESSIVE–COMPULSIVE DISORDER IN PEOPLE WITH POOR INSIGHT AND OVERVALUED IDEATION

DAVID VEALE

In this chapter, I discuss a model for understanding overvalued ideas (OVIs) and poor insight in obsessive–compulsive disorder (OCD) and the clinical implications of such a model. This chapter is the probably the least evidence based in this book, and much research is needed to develop and evaluate novel interventions for OVIs and poor insight. The presence of an OVI in a client often requires the therapist to sail in uncharted water and may be a frustrating or challenging experience. For an individual with an OVI, the intervention of a therapist or relatives may be an unwanted intrusion.

The first problem that bedevils this practice area is that authors do not agree on what an OVI or poor insight is and how it is best measured. The fourth edition of the *Diagnostic and Statistical Manual of Mental Disorders* (DSM–IV; American Psychiatric Association, 1994) defined an OVI as

> an unreasonable and sustained belief that is maintained with less than delusional intensity (that is, the person is able is to acknowledge the

possibility that the belief may or may not be true). The belief is not one that is ordinarily accepted by other members of the person's culture or subculture. (p. 769)

This definition has been echoed by a number of U.S. authors (Hollander, 1993; Kozak & Foa, 1994; Neziroglu, McKay, Yaryura-Tobias, & Stevens, 1999; Phillips & McElroy, 1993), who have emphasized the strength of a belief as one of the key criteria for an overvalued idea. Thus, individuals with OVIs are extremely certain that the feared consequences of their obsessions are generally reasonable but also acknowledge that they may possibly be mistaken. The term *overvalued idea* has thus become, for U.S. authors, shorthand for poor insight. On a continuum from obsessional doubts to delusional certainty, individuals with obsessional doubts at one end are regarded as having good insight and those at the other end with delusions as having no insight. Patients with no insight believe that the feared consequences are entirely reasonable and do not alter this belief when presented with evidence to the contrary. This notion, however, is becoming outdated with the development of cognitive therapy for delusions and schizophrenia. The term *insight* has also been used to describe a continuum of awareness of having a mental disorder (Amador & Seckinger, 1997), which is not usually an issue in individuals with OCD, who rarely disagree with their diagnosis.

The older European concept of an OVI is broader and emphasizes a number of dimensions other than the strength of the belief and abnormality (Hamilton, 1974; Jaspers, 1963; McKenna, 1984, Wernicke, 1900). Such authors have conceptualized an OVI as an isolated sustained belief that meets the following criteria:

- is held strongly, but with less than delusional intensity;
- usually preoccupies the individual's mental life, more than many delusions;
- is ego syntonic, unlike most obsessions;
- often develops in an abnormal personality;
- is usually comprehensible with knowledge of the individual's past experience and personality;
- has content usually regarded as abnormal compared with the general population (but is not as bizarre as some delusions);
- causes disturbed functioning or distress to the individual or others;
- is associated with a high degree of affect (e.g., anxiety or anger at a threat of loss of the goal or object of the belief);
- compared with many delusions, is more likely to lead to repeated action that is considered justified;
- could progress to a delusion;
- may not prompt the individual to seek help from mental health services but may be brought to the attention of the services by a concerned relative or another agency; and

- has some similarities to passionate religious or political convictions in which the individual remains functional.

Obsessive–compulsive disorder may be classified as with or without poor insight in the *DSM–IV*, which further suggests that when an obsession reaches "delusional proportions," an additional diagnosis of delusional disorder or psychotic disorder not otherwise specified may be made. OVIs and strength of conviction were found to be a poor prognostic indicator in four case series treated with exposure and response prevention or cognitive–behavioral therapy (CBT; Foa, 1979; Foa, Abramowitz, Franklin, & Kozak, 1999; Neziroglu, Stevens, Yaryura-Tobias, & McKay, 2000; Salkovskis & Warwick, 1985) although Lelliott, Noshirvani, Başoğlu, Marks, and Monteiro (1988) found the opposite results. O'Dwyer and Marks (2000) discussed the role of delusions in OCD, although it is not clear whether some of their cases should be classified as involving OVIs. A major problem is that studies have used different measures or conceptualizations of OVIs; the first step in improving this literature is for authors to use standardized measures and concepts. There are also individuals with OCD who find it difficult to articulate any feared consequences other than feeling uncomfortable or "not right," and it is difficult to measure the awfulness of experiencing emotion on scales that measure conviction of belief.

BELIEFS, VALUES, AND EVALUATIONS

To develop a better understanding of overvalued ideas and delusions in OCD, it is important for therapists to first consider the differences between beliefs and values. Philosophers have long distinguished between the two and debated their relationship (Hudson, 1970).

Normal Beliefs and Values

A *belief* (or an *inference*) is something thought to be true because of observation or evidence. It can usually be subjected to empirical testing or logic to derive facts, which tend to be objective and universally agreed on. In contrast, a *value* is something thought to be good or important to an individual. Hence, strongly held values are principles that one will not yield on and cannot be subject to empirical testing. Normal values may be divided between those that are terminal (e.g., the importance of happiness) and those that are instrumental (e.g., the importance of being honest). Values (like beliefs) are on a continuum in terms of the degree of importance attached. Some values might be viewed as extreme (e.g., those held by a racist organization or an orthodox religious group), but they are not classified as mental disorders.

Values are more abstract and global than concrete goals but may make sets of goals more coherent. Values are not the same as *evaluations* (or judgments), which are ratings of an event or person on a scale of good to bad. They do, however, have some similarities with evaluations: Unlike beliefs, neither values nor evaluations are subject to empirical testing. Values are more difficult to measure or challenge because they are subjective and personal. The division between beliefs and values is often confused and has had relatively little impact on psychology or psychotherapies other than acceptance and commitment therapy (see Hayes, Strosahl, & Wilson, 1999). Beliefs and values are a neglected distinction in descriptive psychopathology and may be important in the development of a better understanding of individuals with treatment-resistant OCD.

Abnormal Beliefs

In abnormal mental states, the inference goes beyond the data available in the development of negative thoughts or delusions. Delusions may arise out of the blue but are more usually a misinterpretation of an abnormal perception and are regarded as absolutely true by the individual. They are conceptualized as being on a continuum with normal beliefs and are considered to be multidimensional (Peters, Joseph, & Garety, 1999).

Most negative or catastrophic thoughts in OCD are beliefs. The feared consequences in OCD are derived from such beliefs. For example, a person who has an obsession about contamination may overestimate the likelihood of harm resulting from touching a toilet seat. The strength of such beliefs tends to be state dependent (e.g., the person may be 100% convinced about harm when highly anxious but 90% when not anxious). A related concept in OCD that is also a belief is an overinflated sense of responsibility for preventing harm (Salkovskis, 1999). Beliefs are thus conceptualized as having a spectrum of conviction from obsessional doubt to delusional conviction, with overvalued ideas being held with less than delusional certainty (Phillips, Kim, & Hudson, 1995). The definition of an overvalued idea as a belief held with less conviction than a delusion, although at first attractive, ignores the multidimensional aspects of overvalued ideas described by the European psychopathologists. It also ignores the only empirical data on OVIs, in anorexia nervosa, that highlight the role of imagination and introspection over time, the association with affect, and the likelihood of repeated action (Jones & Watson, 1997).

Abnormal Evaluations

In abnormal mental states, evaluations are more extreme than normal ratings on a continuum of good to bad (or some variant such as *awfulness* or *evilness*). Fulford (1991) described evaluative delusions, which are usually associated with depressive psychosis. Beliefs and evaluations are like two sides of a coin, although more attention or importance is often paid to one than to the other. For example, a person with OCD might believe that thinking about having sex with his daughter may make him a pedophile and evaluate himself as a "wicked sinner" for having such thoughts. This is *thought–action fusion*, which has both a belief and an evaluative (or moral) component. Therapy for beliefs in OCD focuses on normalizing the intrusive thought and helping the individual to test out or strengthen an alternative belief repeatedly in a series of behavioral experiments. The approach for abnormal evaluations is based on a functional analysis, which is described later in this chapter.

Abnormal Values

The values that exist in an abnormal mental state are not usually described in psychopathology or cognitive theories. Cognitive theories usually incorporate values in the form of rules or demands (e.g., "I must have order and symmetry in my possessions") or according to how important a value is (e.g., "My health and preventing harm to myself are paramount in my life"). One way of conceptualizing OVIs is that they are beliefs that are associated with specific values, which have become dominant, idealized, and excessively identified with the self (Veale, 2002). To differentiate a value from a belief, I continue with the common usage of the term *overvalued idea* to refer to a belief that is held with less than delusional conviction and that preoccupies an individual's mental life (e.g., an obsession that an item is contaminated). I use the term *idealized value* for the other side of the coin, which is the value that has become dominant and excessively identified with the self (e.g., the importance of preventing anxiety or harm in someone who has difficulty expressing any feared consequences of his or her obsession of order).

Idealized Values

Identification of the Value With the Self

The first characteristic of an idealized value is its excessive identification with the self or the personal domain. Beck (1976) first used the term *personal domain* to describe the way a person attaches meaning to events or objects around him or her. At the center of a personal domain are a person's characteristics—his or her physical attributes, goals, and values. Clustered around the center are the animate and inanimate objects in which he or she has an investment, such as family, friends, and possessions. An idealized value occurs when a value develops such overriding importance that it defines the self or identity of the individual or becomes the center of his or her personal domain. The thinking error is similar to that described for *personalization*, in which the value has overgeneralized from one aspect to (almost) the whole of the self. Normal cognitive processing involves complexity and flexibility in implicit views of the self. For example, I might view myself as a psychiatrist or teacher when I go to work, as a father when I return home, as a biological object when I consult my doctor about a serious illness, and so on. There is complexity and flexibility in the views of my self, and these views are not associated with any particular value.

Idealized values, in contrast, are associated with a view of the self that is identified with specific values. For example, the possessions of an individual with compulsive hoarding have become of paramount value and importance to the self. An individual might view his- or herself as a custodian or caretaker. He or she thus experiences his or her possessions as being like a shell on his or her back and, not surprisingly, has great difficulty throwing away part of his- or herself. In obsessional jealousy, the person might define a large part of his or her identity using his or her partner. He or she views his or her self as small and inadequate, and his or her partner is therefore the most important part of his or her life and regarded as part of his or her self, hence the enormous investment in avoiding the threat of losing the partner.

Rigidity of an Idealized Value

A second characteristic of idealized values is the rigidity with which they are held. Rigidity is different from the poor insight and the conviction of an overvalued idea (or belief), which is best described as being held extremely strongly. In the case of an idealized value, the essential feature is its inflexibility: Individuals are unable to adapt to different circumstances and ignore the consequences of acting on their value. For example, a man with OCD restricted his eating because of his belief that his bowels were excessively sensitive and might be damaged by eating the wrong type of food, and he subsequently died from malnutrition. This person rigidly ignored the consequences of his actions. Idealized values may take different forms in different types of OCD. Individuals with OCD characterized by order, symmetry, and precision believe that they have to have things "just so" or "complete" or that they must never make a mistake. These symptoms are sometimes associated with obsessional slowness (Rachman & Hodgson, 1980; Veale, 1993). Order and symmetry (like hoarding) have been identified as a subtype of OCD and are associated with obsessive–compulsive personality disorder and tics (Baer, 1994). Such symptoms are often associated with discontent or irritation rather than excessive anxiety. Affected individuals usually do not articulate any feared consequences or beliefs (e.g., about causing harm). They may, however, place great importance on preventing feelings of being uncomfortable or not right. Their values about the importance of order and precision then become a dominant aspect of their identity and provide valued direction in their lives.

MEASUREMENT OF OVERVALUED IDEAS
AND IDEALIZED VALUES

Three scales have been developed for the measurement of overvalued ideas. Eisen et al. (1998) developed the Brown Assessment of Beliefs Scale (BABS), which includes such dimensions as degree of conviction, perception of others' views of beliefs, explanation of differing views, fixity of the belief, attempts to disprove the belief, and insight concerning the belief. The scale was designed not to be content specific and to cover a range of disorders. This scale is based on a conceptualization of beliefs as occupying a continuum of insight including good insight, poor insight (overvalued ideas), and no insight (delusional thinking). Overvalued ideas occur when the patient acknowledges the possibility that the belief may or may not be true. Factual accuracy or truthfulness is not an issue for values, however, which involve emotional and subjective judgment. Neziroglu et al. (1999) developed an Overvalued Ideas Scale, which is more specific to beliefs in OCD. There is some overlap between this scale and the BABS, as both measure similar dimensions. Lastly, Foa et al. (1995) described a Fixity of Beliefs questionnaire that assesses the degree to which individuals with OCD recognize their obsessions and compulsions as being unreasonable.

None of these scales have face validity for measuring values, which require a different approach. Instruments for the measurement of normal values exist (Hayes et al., 1999; Rokeach, 1973) in which respondents are asked to rate the importance of a list of values such as family relations or health. But most values in OCD, such as the importance of possessions or order, are not included in such questionnaires because they are regarded as abnormal. There are at least three dimensions in the measurement of idealized values: (a) the degree of importance attached to the value, (b) the rigidity with which the value is held, and (c) the strength of identification of the value with the self. An underlying assumption in the use of *degree of importance attached* to operationally idealized values is that values are finite, and if enormous importance and mental energy are attached to one value, less importance is attached to other normal values, such as happiness or family security. Thus, if 90% of a hoarder's values are attached to his or her possessions, only 10% is left for remaining values such as friendships, health, achievement, and so on. A person's strength of identification of the values with the self may be closely correlated with degree of importance, and this concept remains to be tested empirically.

The rigidity of a value can be measured by the degree to which it causes functional disability. We normally conceptualize the functional disability caused by a disorder as the degree to which it interferes with occupational, social, or other important areas of functioning. In measuring idealized values, one can measure the degree to which a patient is prepared to risk or sacrifice certain domains in life, such as occupation, savings, health, or relationships, in pursuit of the value. When functional disability is severe, a patient is prepared to end his or her life or commit murder if he or she cannot obtain the goal. For example, the female patient with obsessive–compulsive hoarding was virtually housebound, because she had to guard her possessions. She would not allow anyone into her apartment and spent the day checking her memory to ascertain whether anything was lost. She had completely cut herself off from relationships and friends. The apartment was a fire hazard, but she felt that if her home were to catch fire, she would stay with her possessions rather than escape and be left with nothing of her self. If a person with morbid jealousy believed that he or she would lose his or her partner, he or she might murder the partner.

STRATEGIES FOR OVERCOMING OVERVALUED IDEAS AND IDEALIZED VALUES

Individuals with OVIs or idealized values do not always seek help from mental health services. They may pursue inappropriate help from other agencies (e.g., the police or courts) or be brought to the attention of the mental health services by concerned relatives or another agency. Such individuals may be highly avoidant and may not see themselves as having a mental disorder. When they do seek help to accommodate their obsessions, they may become angry and frustrated with therapists who do not help them pursue their goals. In my experience, the most difficult patients to treat are those who are highly avoidant of experiencing any anxiety and who express little or no feared consequences. The importance of not experiencing distress at all costs appears to have become the idealized value, and they may desire only medication. Several strategies may be useful for engaging individuals with idealized values in a program of exposure or behavioral experiments, including engaging in competing hypotheses and behavioral experiments, using creative hopelessness, identifying healthy values, disentangling the self from the value, and examining values in context.

Engaging in Competing Hypotheses and Behavioral Experiments

The competing hypotheses approach was described by Salkovskis, Forrester, Richards, and Morrison (1998), who argued that there is no difference in approach to helping individuals with OVIs in OCD compared with those with other obsessions. The therapist works collaboratively with a patient to ascertain the evidential or historical basis for the beliefs and then evaluates the evidence for these beliefs against more realistic alternatives. However, evaluating beliefs is not always possible (e.g., when feared consequences may occur many years in the future or cannot be tested). Salkovskis et al. therefore advocated setting up two alternative hypotheses to test during therapy. For example, a woman with OCD had intrusive thoughts about being in a parallel world and feared that her family and friends around her could be "false." The therapist regarded these beliefs as OVIs. The patient was extremely functionally disabled because of elaborate and complex rituals and avoidance behaviors to prevent her remaining in a parallel world. Her quality of life was appalling and objectively far worse an experience than if her obsession ever came true.

The model suggests that the therapist present two competing theories to the patient to test out. According to Theory A (which the patient had been following), her problem was that she was stuck in a parallel world. Logically, she had to do everything she could to get herself back to the real world before any harm could occur. In Theory B, her problem was that she worried excessively about being stuck in a parallel world. Thus, her problem was caused by her solution of trying too hard to prevent herself from not being in parallel world, because it increased her worries. A behavioral experiment involves testing out which theory best explains the phenomenon. This patient might deliberately try to jump into a parallel world and to stay there without any safety-seeking behaviors or rituals to determine if her worries decreased. If she refused to test her obsession or expose herself to the risk of being in a parallel world, the therapist could change tack by identifying her valued directions in life and conducting a functional analysis of the consequences (or costs) of her current solutions. This patient valued the importance of being a good mother and having a good relationship with her family. The therapist then helped her realize that by following her current solutions, she was driving her family away and ending up alone (i.e., as if she were in the parallel world). Hence, the strategy was to use pragmatism to determine if the patient's feared consequences might metaphorically or literally be happening as a result of pursuing her solutions.

Using Creative Hopelessness

A second approach is the use of metaphors for instilling "creative hopelessness," as described in acceptance and commitment therapy (Hayes et al., 1999). This approach is usually more helpful than the use of logic or evidence. If the patients' identified goals and values are abnormal, the therapist might ask them questions about whether they would teach their children or loved ones this value or solution or whether their children or loved ones would be grateful that they pursued this value or solution on their behalf. If not, the therapist expresses surprise and tries to draw from the patients the reasons why their family would not want them to use the value or solution. If so, the therapist accepts the consistency of their position and reverts to the functional consequences of pursuing their idealized values.

Idealized values may also be overcompensations for past failures (e.g., perfectionism) or traumas (e.g., avoidance and compulsive washing after rape;

de Silva & Marks, 1999). Again, the patient is trying too hard to prevent harm from recurring, and the ghosts of the past have not been updated with current experiences. It may be possible for the patient to focus on the functional consequences of persisting with a solution that is understandable or functional in the short term but has many consequences in the long term or now causes a conflict with a patient's valued directions in life. The emphasis is on the consequences of the current solution. Reverse role-playing or two-chair techniques (Greenberg, 1979) can be used to strengthen an alternative value; the patient can practice arguing the case for an alternative value while the therapist or patient sitting in another chair argues the case for the idealized value.

Identifying Healthy Values

Some individuals struggle to identify healthy valued directions. Treatment may need to focus on values and goals that they have forgotten or that were important before the idealized values and OCD took hold. The therapist should encourage any flicker of enthusiasm from past positive experiences that helps patients define their healthy values. One approach advocated by Hayes et al. (1999) is to ask patients to imagine being a spirit at their own funeral and to identify what they would like friends and relatives to remember them by or what epitaph they would want written on their tombstone to reflect their real valued directions. Therapy is then focused on actions or concrete steps that individuals can take to achieve their valued directions. This approach provides a different experience in therapy from defining a problem in increasing detail and trying to solve problems that do not exist or that cannot be solved.

Disentangling the Self From the Value

The strategy in disentangling the self from the value is to challenge the logic of identifying one's value so closely with one's self. For example, individuals with obsessional hoarding have difficulties letting go of things, which they perceive as the loss of a major part of their "self," and holding on to things becomes their dominant value. The fundamental thinking error in an idealized value is overgeneralization, in which a patient identifies his or her self with the value, and all other aspects of his or her identity are diminished. The therapist may help a patient by questioning the logic of this position. The concept of Big *I* and Little *i* can be useful: The self, or Big *I*, is defined by thousands of Little *i*'s in the form of other identities, values, likes and dislikes, and characteristics accumulated since the person was born (Dryden, 1998; Lazarus, 1977). The patient is encouraged to focus on his or her many other functional values and identities to develop a more flexible and complex view of the self. In cases of obsessional hoarding or morbid jealousy, one of the Little *i*'s (one's possessions or partner) may need to become less close to the center of the personal domain so that healthy boundaries can be formed with one's possessions or partner.

Examining Values in Context

Idealized values usually are reduced only by small degrees over time and crucially depend on performing actions that are opposed to the old values. Helping the patient develop a contextual functional analysis of the problem and consider the long-term consequences of pursuing his or her current solutions and values is the single most important strategy. Paradoxically, individuals who seek help because they want to keep their partner, family, or occupation may have a better prognosis. Disorders in which success is more dependent on the individual being ready or wanting to change rather than being pressured by others are less likely to have positive outcomes. Thus, individuals with idealized values who have no spouse or family or who are financially comfortable are more likely to drop out of treatment because they are less ready to change. They have adapted their lives to suit their overvalued ideas and can continue to live in this way as long as their disorder does not interfere with society.

The best known example of the interaction between life circumstances and amenability to treatment is Howard Hughes, who could pay aides to accommodate his OCD and avoided contact with any contaminants by extensively controlling his single-room environment, sealed with masking tape to prevent the ingress of germs. His aides were instructed to follow numerous detailed rituals that could take hours to perform. Tissues were spread everywhere on the bed, chair, and bathroom floor to prevent contact with contaminants. Later in his life, he discarded his clothes and went about naked in his "germ-free zone" and paid no attention to his personal hygiene. He would urinate on the floor or against the bathroom door (presumably because it was too anxiety provoking to open the door or go into the bathroom) and refused to allow anyone to clean it up, preferring instead that paper towels be spread around. He neglected his self-care, and the consequences of his OVIs were a very poor quality of life and premature death. He continued to promote his values even after death; the Howard Hughes Medical Institute was set up to prevent disease caused by bacteria, malignant growth, or otherwise and has a current endowment of $11 billion (Brown & Broeske, 1996). If Howard Hughes had been born slightly later, or had his OCD been diagnosed and treated, perhaps his inheritance and values would have been devoted to research into OCD.

PHARMACOTHERAPY FOR OVERVALUED IDEAS

No randomized controlled trials in pharmacotherapy have examined the effect of serotonin reuptake inhibitors (SSRIs) on the strength of a belief in OCD. There is some evidence for the benefit of antipsychotic drugs in low doses augmenting an SSRI in resistant OCD, but these studies do not identify whether the subjects had OVIs (National Collaborating Centre for Mental Health, 2006). Research is very difficult in this area; individuals with OVIs are unlikely to be recruited into trials because they are usually far too occupied with the pursuit of their symptom-related goals. The best advice in pharmacotherapy, after trying at least two SSRIs and clomipramine, is to follow clinical guidelines with augmenting agents or a combination of an SSRI and clomipramine (National Collaborating Centre for Mental Health, 2006) and to encourage psychopharmacologists to use measures of OVIs and idealized values in their research.

Cognitive–behavioral therapists have a good evidence base for altering negative automatic thoughts, metacognitions, and even delusions. One of the last frontiers in psychological therapies is the development of effective interventions for OVIs. Pharmacotherapy is unlikely to develop a solution for OVIs—for example antipsychotic drugs are more effective in psychosis than treating hallucinations than delusions. I have proposed a model for understanding OVIs in OCD (and other disorders) which will now need evaluation and refinement.

REFERENCES

Amador, X. F., & Seckinger, R. A. (1997). The assessment of insight: A methodological review. *Psychiatric Annals, 27,* 798–805.

American Psychiatric Association. (1994). *Diagnostic and statistical manual of mental disorders* (4th ed.). Washington, DC: Author.

Baer, L. (1994). Factor analysis of symptom subtypes of obsessive–compulsive disorder and their relation to personality and tic disorders. *Journal of Clinical Psychiatry, 55,* 18–23.

Beck, A. T. (1976). Meaning and emotions. In A. T. Beck (Ed.), *Cognitive therapy and the emotional disorders* (pp. 47–75). London: Penguin.

Brown, P. H., & Broeske, P. H. (1996). *Howard Hughes: The untold story.* London: Little, Brown.

de Silva, P., & Marks, M. (1999). The role of traumatic experiences in the genesis of obsessive–compulsive disorder. *Behaviour Research and Therapy, 37,* 941–951.

Dryden, W. (1998). *Developing self-acceptance.* Chichester, England: Wiley.

Eisen, J. L., Phillips, K. A., Baer, L., Beer, D. A., Atala, K. D., & Rasmussen, S. A. (1998). The Brown Assessment of Beliefs Scale: Reliability and validity. *American Journal of Psychiatry, 155,* 102–108.

Foa, E. B. (1979). Failures in treating obsessive–compulsives. *Behaviour Research and Therapy, 17,* 169–176.

Foa, E. B., Abramowitz, J. S., Franklin, M. E., & Kozak, M. J. (1999). Feared consequences, fixity of belief, and treatment outcome in individuals with obsessive–compulsive disorder. *Behavior Therapy, 30,* 717–724.

Foa, E. B., Kozak, M. J., Goodman, W. K., Hollander, E., Jenike, M. A., & Rasmussen, S. A. (1995). *DSM–IV* field trial: Obsessive–compulsive disorder. *American Journal of Psychiatry, 152,* 990–996.

Fulford, K. W. M. (1991). Evaluative delusions. *British Journal of Psychiatry, 159*(Suppl. 14), 108–112.

Greenberg, L. S. (1979). Resolving splits. *Psychotherapy Theory, Research and Practice, 16,* 316–324.

Hamilton, M. (1974). *Fish's clinical psychopathology.* Bristol, England: John Wright.

Hayes, S. C., Strosahl, K. D., & Wilson, K. G. (1999). *Acceptance and commitment therapy.* New York: Guilford Press.

Hollander, E. (1993). Introduction. In E. Hollander (Ed.), *Obsessive–compulsive related disorders* (pp. 1–16). Washington, DC: American Psychiatric Press.

Hudson, W. D. (1970). *Modern moral philosophy.* London: Macmillan.

Jaspers, K. (1963). *General psychopathology* (J. Koenig & M. W. Hamilton, Trans.). Manchester, England: Manchester University Press. (Original work published 1959)

Jones, E., & Watson, J. P. (1997). Delusion, the overvalued idea and religious beliefs: A comparative analysis of their characteristics. *British Journal of Psychiatry, 170,* 381–386.

Kozak, M. J., & Foa, E. B. (1994). Obsessions, overvalued ideas and delusions in obsessive–compulsive disorder. *Behaviour Research and Therapy, 32,* 343–353.

Lazarus, A. (1977). Towards an egoless state of being. In A. Ellis & R. Grieger (Eds.), *Handbook of rational emotive therapy* (Vol. 1, pp. 113–118). New York: Springer Publishing Company.

Lelliott, P. T., Noshirvani, H. F., Başoğlu, M., Marks, I. M., & Monteiro, W. O. (1988). Obsessive–compulsive beliefs and treatment outcome. *Psychological Medicine, 18,* 697–702.

McKenna, P. J. (1984). Disorders with overvalued ideas. *British Journal of Psychiatry, 145,* 579–585.

National Collaborating Centre for Mental Health, et al. (2006). *Obsessive–compulsive disorder: Core interventions in the treatment of obsessive–compulsive disorder and body dysmorphic disorder.* London: Gaskell and British Psychological Society.

Neziroglu, F., McKay, D., Yaryura-Tobias, J. A., & Stevens, K. P. (1999). The Overvalued Ideas Scale: Development, reliability, and validity in obsessive–compulsive disorder. *Behaviour Research and Therapy, 37,* 881–902.

Neziroglu, F., Stevens, K. P., Yaryura-Tobias, J. A., & McKay, D. (2000). Predictive validity of the Overvalued Ideas Scale: Outcome in obsessive–compulsive and body dysmorphic disorder. *Behaviour Research and Therapy, 39,* 745–756.

O'Dwyer, A.-M., & Marks, I. M. (2000). Obsessive–compulsive disorder and delusions revisited. *British Journal of Psychiatry, 176*, 281–284.

Peters, E. R., Joseph, S. A., & Garety, P. (1999). Measurement of delusional ideation in the normal population: Introducing the PDI (Peters et al. Delusions Inventory). *Schizophrenia Bulletin, 25*, 553–576.

Phillips, K. A., Kim, J. M., & Hudson, J. I. (1995). Body image disturbance in body dysmorphic disorder and eating disorders: Obsessions or delusions? *Psychiatric Clinics of North America, 18*, 317–334.

Phillips, K. A., & McElroy, S. L. (1993). Insight, overvalued ideation, and delusional thinking in body dysmorphic disorder: Theoretical and treatment implications. *Journal of Nervous and Mental Disease, 181*, 699–702.

Rachman, S. J., & Hodgson, R. (1980). *Obsessions and compulsions*. Englewood Cliffs, NJ: Prentice Hall.

Rokeach, M. (1973). *The nature of human values*. New York: Free Press.

Salkovskis, P. M. (1999). Understanding and treating obsessive–compulsive disorder. *Behaviour Research and Therapy, 37*(Suppl. 1), S29–S52.

Salkovskis, P. M., Forrester, E., Richards, C., & Morrison, N. (1998). The Devil is in the detail: Conceptualising and treating obsessional problems. In N. Tarrier, A. Wells, & G. Haddock (Eds.), *Treating complex cases—The cognitive behavioural therapy approach* (pp. 47–80). Chichester, England: Wiley.

Salkovskis, P. M., & Warwick, H. M. C. (1985). Cognitive therapy of obsessive–compulsive disorder: Treating treatment failures. *Behavioural Psychotherapy, 13*, 243–255.

Veale, D. (1993). Obsessional slowness revisited. *British Journal of Psychiatry, 19*, 6–19.

Veale, D. (2002). Over-valued ideas: A conceptual analysis. *Behaviour Research and Therapy, 40*, 383–400.

Wernicke, C. (1900). *Grundriss der Psychiatrie* [Foundations of psychiatry.]. Leipzig, Germany: Verlag von Georg Thieme.

13

TREATING COMORBID PRESENTATIONS: OBSESSIVE–COMPULSIVE DISORDER, ANXIETY DISORDERS, AND DEPRESSION

DEBORAH ROTH LEDLEY, ANUSHKA PAI, AND MARTIN E. FRANKLIN

Obsessive–compulsive disorder (OCD) rarely occurs in isolation. Rather, most individuals with OCD experience one or more additional psychological disorders, including other anxiety disorders and depression. In this chapter, we review comorbidity rates and provide guidelines for differentiating OCD from other anxiety disorders and depression. The impact of comorbid disorders on treatment outcome is also reviewed. Finally, we suggest ways to modify OCD treatment when other conditions are present.

Comorbidity rates between OCD and other disorders differ across studies because of differences in population selection and methodology, but comorbidity is generally high. Weissman et al. (1994) conducted an epidemiological study of individuals with OCD in seven countries and found that 49% of people with OCD experienced a comorbid anxiety disorder and 27% experienced comorbid major depressive disorder. Among studies conducted in anxiety clinics, there is great variability (see Table 13.1), but in general, comorbid conditions are common. It is interesting that when OCD co-

TABLE 13.1
Prevalence Rates of Comorbid Anxiety Disorders and Depression
Among Obsessive–Compulsive Disorder Patients in Anxiety
Disorder Clinic Samples

Disorder	Prevalence in obsessive–compulsive disorder
Specific phobia	0.95%–17%
Generalized anxiety disorder	0.95%–12%
Posttraumatic stress disorder	2%–7%
Social phobia	4%–35%
Panic disorder	4%–29%
All anxiety disorders	13%–76%
Major depression	14%–40%

Note. Prevalence rates were taken from Brown, Campbell, Lehman, Grisham, and Mancill (2001); Denys et al. (2004); Perugi et al. (1997); Sanderson, Dinardo, Rapee, and Barlow (1990); Steketee et al. (1999, 2001); and Tukel et al. (2002).

occurs with other anxiety disorders, OCD is typically the principal diagnosis (i.e., the diagnosis of greatest severity; see Antony, Downie, & Swinson, 1998).

A consistent picture has not emerged of the chronology of symptom presentation when OCD occurs with other disorders. Antony et al. (1998) reported that social phobia predated OCD in an anxiety disorder clinic sample, whereas specific phobias and agoraphobia onset after OCD. This finding could be explained by the differential ages of onset of the anxiety disorders (e.g., OCD typically has a later age of onset than social phobia). Major depression tends to begin after OCD, suggesting that depression might be a response to OCD symptoms (e.g., Diniz et al., 2004).

Many disorders besides OCD are also characterized by intrusive thoughts, compulsive behaviors, and avoidance. Similarly, some symptoms seen in OCD, such as panic attacks, occur in other disorders. Clinicians thus must carefully assess each patient and make decisions about the best diagnostic match for a patient's unique concerns. Sometimes symptoms that overlap with other disorders are best accounted for by OCD. At other times, symptoms may in fact be signs of another disorder, and an additional diagnosis with OCD is warranted. The next section offers guidelines for arriving at these diagnostic decisions (see also Table 13.2).

COMMON COMORBID CONDITIONS

Panic Disorder

Many patients with OCD experience panic-like symptoms or panic attacks in response to OCD triggers. This calls to question whether an additional diagnosis of panic disorder is warranted. It is essential for clinicians to

TABLE 13.2
Clues for Establishing a Sole Diagnosis of Obsessive–Compulsive Disorder Versus Diagnoses of Obsessive–Compulsive Disorder and a Co-occurring Anxiety Disorder

Other disorder	Clues for a sole diagnosis of obsessive–compulsive disorder	Clues for assignment of an additional diagnosis
Panic disorder	Panic occurs only in response to OCD triggers. The patient fears consequences of the OCD trigger, not the panic symptoms. If the patient fears consequences of panic symptoms, it is often because he or she fears losing control and acting on intrusive thoughts.	The patient has unexpected panic attacks. The patient fears the consequences of panic symptoms (e.g., having a heart attack). The patient avoids situations because of the feared consequences of panic symptoms.
Social phobia	The patient primarily fears having others notice his or her OCD symptoms (e.g., washing, checking).	The patient fears being judged for his or her everyday actions (e.g., stating a dissenting opinion or asking someone to change his or her behavior). The patient also has other social concerns, such as performing in front of others or initiating and maintaining conversations.
Posttraumatic stress disorder (PTSD)	Despite having experienced a trauma, the patient does not meet criteria for PTSD. Intrusive thoughts and compulsive behaviors extend beyond those that could be seen as reasonably connected to the trauma the patient experienced.	The patient meets the full criteria for PTSD. Some intrusive thoughts and compulsive behaviors are tied to the trauma that the patient experienced, and others extend beyond those that could be seen as reasonably connected to the trauma.
Generalized anxiety disorder (GAD)	The patient worries about things that would not be considered everyday concerns. The patient engages in compulsions, which often have to be done in a strictly defined or repetitive way, to ward off feared outcomes.	The patient worries about everyday concerns such as finances and the health and safety of loved ones. The patient engages in behaviors to try to distract himself or herself from worries or to provide reassurance (e.g., calling a loved one who is late coming home from work).
Specific phobias	The patient's concerns about specific objects or situations are not everyday concerns, but rather are more unusual or magical (e.g., getting AIDS from a bee sting).	The patient is concerned about specific objects or situations that are more reality based (e.g., fearing that a bee sting will be terribly painful).

ask patients what provokes the panic and what they fear will occur as a result of it. For patients with OCD, panic attacks are typically brought on by exposure to OCD triggers. Patients with OCD typically do not worry about the consequences of the panic itself (e.g., having a heart attack), but focus instead on consequences tied to their OCD, such as getting sick from others' germs.

Some patients, however, do worry that the panic symptoms will lead them to lose control or go crazy. Even for these patients, though, the feared outcome is often tied to OCD concerns. For example, many patients with OCD fear harming others. They worry that if they panic in response to an OCD trigger (e.g., chopping up vegetables for dinner with the baby playing close by), they might lose control and inflict harm. In these scenarios, panic symptoms are best accounted for by OCD.

An additional diagnosis of panic disorder is warranted, however, if patients experience panic attacks out of the blue, if they fear the consequences of the attack itself (e.g., having a heart attack), and if they change their behavior because of these fears (e.g., discontinuing all exercise, not riding the subway because help might not be available in the event of a panic attack).

Social Phobia

OCD and social phobia can share overlapping features, presenting the question of whether these features are best accounted for by OCD or whether an additional diagnosis of social phobia is warranted. For example, some patients with OCD worry a great deal about offending others. When patients with OCD worry about offending others, their concerns are often more unusual than those seen in social phobia, and they typically seek a great deal of reassurance regarding their behavior. For example, a young patient we treated constantly asked her friends if she had offended them by the way that she dressed, walked, or held her body. An additional diagnosis of social phobia would be warranted if the patient feared offending others during more everyday social situations such as expressing dissenting opinions or asking others to change their behavior. Similarly, other fears such as concern about being judged negatively when speaking up at meetings, initiating conversations, or going on dates might point toward an additional diagnosis of social phobia.

Posttraumatic Stress Disorder

Intrusive thoughts and compulsive behaviors are often seen in posttraumatic stress disorder (PTSD), making it difficult to decide whether a patient has a sole diagnosis of PTSD or whether an additional diagnosis of OCD is warranted. When intrusive thoughts and compulsions appear to be directly related to the traumatic event the patient experienced, these symptoms are best accounted for by PTSD. For example, a patient may frequently check locks and windows after being robbed. These symptoms would be considered part of PTSD, and an additional diagnosis of OCD would not be warranted.

However, some patients go on to develop OCD symptoms that seem unrelated to the trauma. For example, a patient began experiencing classic trauma symptoms after a car accident. While driving, she also started to fear that she had hit a pedestrian, causing her to drive around block to check that this had not occurred. Soon after this symptom appeared, the patient became concerned with harming her patients in her work as a nurse. She began checking medications over and over again before administering them, checking on patients many times before leaving in the evenings after already completing her rounds, and mentally reviewing all of her activities once she got home in the evening. These symptoms seemed unrelated to her trauma, even though the trauma seemed to be the triggering incident for them. In this case, an additional diagnosis of OCD was warranted.

Generalized Anxiety Disorder

Obsessive–compulsive disorder and generalized anxiety disorder (GAD) are both characterized by ruminative thoughts (obsessions in the case of OCD and worries in the case of GAD) and by attempts to reduce anxiety brought on by these thoughts. In OCD, obsessions (and their accompanying compulsions) are typically superstitious or unrealistic. For example, an OCD patient worried that she would be responsible for her daughter developing autism by coming in contact with contaminants like household cleaners and plastics used in toys, baby bottles, and other common products. She made every effort to prevent her daughter from coming in contact with these objects, and when such contact occurred, the patient would wash her child excessively and pray that she would not get autism. It is clear that these worries and compulsions were unrealistic.

An additional diagnosis of GAD might be warranted in patients with OCD when they also experience everyday or real-life worries about such things as finances, performance at work or school, or the health and safety of loved ones. For example, a patient might fear that his wife will be involved in a car crash when driving home from work (highly unlikely, but still more likely than one's child developing autism from plastic or chemicals). Furthermore, in response to such worries, patients with GAD often try to distract themselves or engage in behaviors that are logically connected to their worries, such as calling a loved one who is late coming home.

Specific Phobias

Patients with OCD exhibit fear of specific objects or situations, some of which overlap with cues for specific phobias. Patients with OCD typically have unusual or unrealistic fears of these triggers and engage in compulsive behaviors to prevent feared outcomes. For example, patients with OCD who fear blood often fear getting HIV or some other illness from blood and might engage in elaborate washing rituals when they believe they have come in contact with blood. An additional diagnosis of specific phobia might be warranted when patients have more realistic concerns about a particular trigger. For example, a patient might fear being bitten by a dog simply because the dog bite would hurt and be frightening, but not because an obscure disease could be contracted from the dog. In specific phobias, avoidance of feared stimuli is more common than elaborate rituals to ward off the feared consequences of such stimuli.

Depression

From time to time, patients with OCD present with symptoms that mirror some of those seen in depression. For example, one teenage patient presented for treatment reporting that she had a very hard time having fun. She had stopped doing virtually all of the activities that she enjoyed and was spending a lot of time watching TV and aimlessly wandering around the house. On first glance, this teenager looked depressed. However, with further questioning, it became clear that her symptoms were better explained as OCD. She reported having intrusive thoughts that she should not have fun and worried that if she did have fun, she would lose her ability to detect suffering in the world and she would go to hell. In response to these thoughts, the patient avoided having fun and prayed a great deal that she would have a place in heaven. These experiences sounded very much like OCD, and the patient denied any other symptoms of depression. Certainly, if she also reported loss of appetite, suicidal thoughts, and other classic symptoms of depression, an additional mood disorder diagnosis would be warranted.

COMORBIDITY AND OBSESSIVE–COMPULSIVE DISORDER PRESENTATION AND TREATMENT

With comorbidity being so common in OCD, it is clear that many patients experience not only the impairment caused by OCD but also experience the impairment caused by co-occurring mood and anxiety disorders. This raises the question of how comorbidity affects the presentation of OCD and its treatment. Anecdotally, clinicians point to comorbidity as complicating the nature of OCD and its treatment. However, many research studies do not address the effect of comorbid depression or anxiety disorders on OCD presentation, because concurrent diagnoses are often exclusionary criteria.

The research that has been conducted is inconsistent. One study (Denys, Tenney, van Megan, de Geus, & Westenberf, 2004) found that having comorbid disorders did not affect the severity of OCD symptoms, whereas others (Angst, 1993; Tukel, Polat, Ozdemir, Aksut, & Turksov, 2002) found a relationship between comorbidity and OCD symptom severity. A more consistent finding is that comorbidity is associated with poorer quality of life, particularly in the case of comorbid depression (Lochner et al., 2003; Masellis, Rector, & Richter, 2003). A few studies have examined whether anxiety disorder comorbidity affects treatment outcome. Generally, the presence of additional anxiety disorders has not been found to influence treatment outcome of OCD. However, one study reported that OCD patients with GAD terminated treatment at higher rates than other patients (Steketee, Chambless, & Tran, 2001), and another found that the presence of PTSD in patients with OCD hindered response to exposure and response prevention (ERP; Gershuny, Baer, Jenike, Minichiello, & Wilhelm, 2002). Unfortunately, few studies have looked specifically at how anxiety disorder comorbidity affects OCD treatment outcome.

More research attention has been paid to the impact of depression on OCD treatment outcome. Some studies have found that higher levels of depression at pretreatment were related to poorer outcome (Foa et al., 1983; Keijsers, Hoogduin, & Schaap, 1994; Steketee et al., 2001), whereas others have found little or no effect (Mataix-Cols, Marks, Greist, Kobak, & Baer, 2002; O'Sullivan, Noshirvani, Marks, Monteiro, & Lelliott, 1991; Steketee, Eisen, Dyck, Warshaw, & Rasmussen, 1999). Abramowitz, Franklin, Street, Kozak, and Foa (2000) found that only patients who were severely depressed were less likely to respond to ERP therapy for OCD. Similarly, highly depressed OCD patients seem to be at greater risk for relapse following treatment discontinuation (Abramowitz & Foa, 2000; Başoğlu, Lax, Kasvikis, & Marks, 1988).

MODIFYING TREATMENT FOR COMORBID OBSESSIVE–COMPULSIVE DISORDER AND OTHER ANXIETY DISORDERS

As we discussed in the preceding section, many patients with OCD also have other anxiety disorders, and for most, these additional diagnoses do not interfere a great deal with treatment for OCD. There are times, however, when additional diagnoses can impede treatment. Because there is little research on how to manage such situations, this section draws on our clinical experience to address this issue. As a caveat, we believe that OCD treatment is best carried out with an exclusive focus on OCD. Exposure and response prevention therapy for OCD (Kozak & Foa, 1997) is a time-limited treatment, and in the 17 sessions we slate for it, we consider it best for clinician and patient to stay focused on resolving the OCD. With this in mind, this section does not focus a great deal on combined treatments that tackle two or more disorders concurrently. Rather, we discuss the ways in which comorbid diagnoses can interfere with ERP, as well as the sequence that might be used for tackling co-occurring problems (e.g., when to treat panic disorder before treating OCD).

Treating Patients With Comorbid Panic Disorder or Panic Attacks

Even though patients who experience panic-like symptoms or panic attacks only in response to OCD triggers do not meet criteria for panic disorder, clinicians may find it likely that the panic symptoms will be a focus of attention during ERP. The clinician must learn what the patient fears will happen because of the panic attacks. Learning about these idiosyncratic fears allows the clinician to tailor psychoeducation to the patient (e.g., teaching the patient that even severe anxiety does not lead to psychotic breaks) and to ensure that exposures are set up in such a way that patients can test out their beliefs.

For example, if a patient fears that he or she will remain anxious forever in response to anxiety from touching doorknobs and then not washing his or her hands, the exposure can be set up to test this belief out (e.g., "How likely do you think it is that you will stay anxious forever after this exposure?"). The experience of the exposure then teaches the patient that the anxiety actually decreases over the course of the exposure. Of course, the patient also learns that other feared consequences of touching doorknobs and not washing hands (e.g., getting sick) also do not occur. Some patients may also benefit from interoceptive exposure in which panic symptoms are brought on in isolation of OCD-related concerns to help patients to learn that such symptoms are not dangerous.

When patients have both panic disorder and OCD, pursuing treatment can sometimes be difficult, particularly if patients have a hard time leaving the house or using available modes of transportation to get to sessions. In these cases, the panic disorder should be attended to first to facilitate attendance at treatment.

Treating Patients With Comorbid Social Phobia

In individual therapy, treatment for OCD is rarely complicated by comorbid social phobia. Although patients might be nervous interacting with the clinician in the first few sessions of treatment, most acclimate to the situation and can complete treatment with little problem. It is occasionally necessary, however, for clinicians to address social concerns concurrently with OCD concerns, particularly when exposures involve other people. This was the case with the patient who feared that her daughter would develop autism. For one exposure, the patient was asked to go into a hardware store, touch the containers of different products, and then feed her daughter a snack. Because she also had social phobia, she was very anxious about going into the hardware store to just touch things without buying anything. Indeed, she was so anxious initially that she refused to do the exposure. Her clinician asked her what she thought would happen if she did not buy anything, and she predicted that the store owner would say something nasty to her as she left. The clinician simply considered this another prediction to be tested during the exposure. In fact, when the patient, her baby, and the clinician left the store, the store owner wished them a great day and asked them to come back soon. The patient was very surprised by the owner's response. In the process of this one exposure, she confronted both her social beliefs ("I will be judged negatively if I go into a store and don't buy something") and her OCD beliefs ("If I touch things in the store and then feed my baby, she will develop autism"). In other words, although treatment was focused on OCD, the same principles of exposure were used to help the patient confront some of her beliefs related to social anxiety.

There are times when co-occurring social phobia must be treated before initiating treatment for OCD, such as when group treatment for OCD is the only available option. If social anxiety is so severe that it precludes participation in group treatment, such patients will need to seek treatment for social phobia first. We treated a patient with severe social phobia who worried that people were looking at him and judging him negatively on the train as he rode to treatment sessions. His social anxiety was so severe that he dropped out of OCD treatment; we recommended that he seek treatment for social phobia closer to his home and then resume ERP when social anxiety was less interfering.

Treating Patients With Comorbid Posttraumatic Stress Disorder

Because many patients with PTSD experience intrusive thoughts and exhibit compulsive behaviors that have some functional relationship to the trauma they experienced, it is appropriate for clinicians to proceed with PTSD treatment to deal with both of these difficulties. For other patients with PTSD, behaviors aimed at alleviating anxiety related to the trauma can grow into a full-blown case of OCD. Often, the best way to decide which disorder to treat first is to ask the patient which is causing the most significant distress and impairment. In the case of the nurse who developed both PTSD and OCD after a car accident, her PTSD symptoms lessened with the passage of time, but her OCD symptoms worsened, extending far beyond intrusive thoughts and compulsive behaviors related to the car crash. The clinician asked the patient which problem she wanted to work on first, and she quickly answered that the OCD was causing the most significant distress and impairment. During OCD treatment, she worked on her obsessive thoughts and compulsive behaviors related to driving, as well as on her difficulties with her nursing work. At the end of treatment, both her OCD and her PTSD symptoms had resolved, despite the fact that she received no specific treatment for the PTSD. The clinician was empathic when the patient raised trauma-related symptoms in session and encouraged her to continue to seek support from family and friends about what she had been through, but direct exposure to traumatic memories was not incorporated into the ERP regimen.

Treating Patients With Comorbid Generalized Anxiety Disorder

GAD rarely interferes to such a degree that OCD treatment is not feasible. Rather, patients may have a hard time focusing on OCD treatment; they may want to discuss both obsessions and worries because they do not distinguish between these states in the same ways that clinicians do. This confusion can be particularly difficult to resolve when treatment is carried out according to a strict protocol and there is not much flexibility for deviation. In such situations (e.g., in research studies), patients can be educated about the difference between OCD and GAD and can be encouraged to try to focus on OCD for the allotted time and then re-evaluate their GAD at the end of treatment.

In more flexible clinical environments, clinicians may find it is acceptable to allow time during OCD treatment to discuss patients' worries and strategies for dealing with them. This dual focus works particularly well when clinicians' methods for treating GAD are similar to their methods for treating OCD.

MODIFYING TREATMENT FOR PATIENTS WITH COMORBID OBSESSIVE–COMPULSIVE DISORDER AND DEPRESSION

As noted earlier in this chapter, many patients with OCD also have a depression diagnosis. In our experience, only when depression is very severe does it seem to interfere in treatment for OCD. In the case of severe depression, or when patients are having prominent suicidal thoughts, it is always advisable for patients to seek treatment for their depression first. With improved mood and energy and less risk of self-harm, patients will be much more ready to focus on the hard work of OCD treatment.

Clinicians should not overlook even more minimal depression because it can affect a patient's motivation for treatment and hopefulness about treatment outcome. Patients who are depressed may come to sessions late, miss sessions regularly, or not be able to carry through with homework. When the clinician queries them, often they reveal that they are also having difficulties with other activities, like doing household chores and accomplishing tasks at work. These patients can benefit a great deal from the behavioral activation techniques used in the treatment of depression. Activity monitoring can be assigned for homework, and one session can be dedicated to examining the patient's activities. Plans can be made for incorporating more pleasurable and mastery-related activities. Most importantly, the clinician can help patients see how OCD treatment sessions and homework can provide a great source of mastery and, by extension, can lead to improvements in mood. Activity monitoring can continue throughout OCD treatment, with 10 minutes spent at the beginning of each session reviewing the week. During this review, it is essential for the clinician to confirm that the patient has committed time to OCD homework and is deriving a sense of accomplishment from such activities. This method of integrating behavioral activation with a structured anxiety disorder treatment has yielded promising results for patients with both social phobia and depression (see Huppert, Roth, & Foa, 2003).

CONCLUSION

Comorbidity is very common in OCD. For the most part, comorbid anxiety and mood disorders do not interfere greatly in OCD treatment. When very severe depression or anxiety disorders interfere with clients' engagement in OCD treatment, these conditions must be treated first. However, because OCD is often the most severe of co-occurring disorders, proceeding first with OCD treatment may make the most sense. With slight modifications to treatment for co-occurring problems, clinicians can often minimize their interference. By the end of treatment, it is not unusual for problems besides OCD to be significantly improved despite the lack of direct focus on them.

REFERENCES

Abramowitz, J. S., & Foa, E. B. (2000). Does major depressive disorder influence outcome of exposure and response prevention for OCD? *Behavior Therapy, 31*, 795–800.

Abramowitz, J. S., Franklin, M. E., Street, G. P., Kozak, M. J., & Foa, E. B. (2000). Effects of comorbid depression on response to treatment for obsessive–compulsive disorder. *Behavior Therapy, 31*, 517–528.

Angst, J. (1993). Comorbidity of anxiety, phobia, compulsion and depression. *International Clinical Psychopharmacology, 8*(Suppl. 1), 21–25.

Antony, M. M., Downie, F., & Swinson, R. P. (1998). Diagnostic issues and epidemiology in obsessive–compulsive disorder. In R. P. Swinson, M. M. Antony, S. Rachman, & M. A. Richter (Eds.), *Obsessive–compulsive disorder: Theory, research and treatment* (pp. 3–32). New York: Guilford Press.

Başoğlu, M., Lax, T., Kasvikis, Y., & Marks, I. M. (1988). Predictors of improvement in obsessive–compulsive disorder. *Journal of Anxiety Disorders, 2*, 299–317.

Brown, T. A., Campbell, L. A., Lehman, C. L., Grisham, J. R., & Mancill, R. B. (2001). Current and lifetime comorbidity of the *DSM–IV* anxiety and mood disorders in a large clinical sample. *Journal of Abnormal Psychology, 110,* 585–599.

Denys, D., Tenney, N., van Megan, J. G., de Geus, F., & Westenberf, H. G. (2004). Axis I and II comorbidity in a large sample of patients with obsessive–compulsive disorder. *Journal of Affective Disorders, 80,* 155–162.

Diniz, J. B., Rosario-Campos, M. C., Shavitt, R. G., Curi, M., Hounie, A. G., Brotto, S. A., & Miguel, E. C. (2004). Impact of age at onset and duration of illness on the expression of comorbidities in obsessive–compulsive disorder. *Journal of Clinical Psychiatry, 65,* 22–27.

Foa, E. B., Grayson, J. B., Steketee, G. S., Doppelt, H. G., Turner, R. M., & Latimer, P. R. (1983). Success and failure in the behavioral treatment of obsessive–compulsives. *Journal of Consulting and Clinical Psychology, 51,* 287–297.

Gershuny, B. S., Baer, L., Jenike, M. A., Minichiello, W. E., & Wilhelm, S. (2002). Comorbid posttraumatic stress disorder: Impact on treatment outcome for obsessive–compulsive disorder. *American Journal of Psychiatry, 159,* 852–854.

Huppert, J. D., Roth, D. A., & Foa, E. B. (2003). Cognitive behavioral treatment of social phobia: New advances. *Current Psychiatry Reports, 5,* 289–296.

Keijsers, G. P. J., Hoogduin, C. A. L., & Schaap, C. P. D. R. (1994). Predictors of treatment outcome in the behavioural treatment of obsessive–compulsive disorder. *British Journal of Psychiatry, 165,* 781–786.

Kozak, M. J., & Foa, E. B. (1997). *Mastery of obsessive–compulsive disorder: A cognitive–behavioral approach (Therapist guide).* New York: Oxford University Press.

Lochner, C., Mogotsi, M., du Toit, P. L., Kaminer, D., Niehaus, D. J., & Stein, D. J. (2003). Quality of life in anxiety disorders: A comparison of obsessive–compulsive disorder, social anxiety disorder, and panic disorder. *Psychopathology, 36,* 255–262.

Masellis, M., Rector, N. A., & Richter, M. A. (2003). Quality of life in OCD: Differential impact of obsessions, compulsions, and depression comorbidity. *Canadian Journal of Psychiatry, 48,* 72–77.

Mataix-Cols, D., Marks, I. M., Greist, J. H., Kobak, K. A., & Baer, L. (2002). Obsessive–compulsive symptom dimensions as predictors of compliance with and response to behaviour therapy: Results from a controlled trial. *Psychotherapy and Psychosomatics, 71,* 255–262.

O'Sullivan, G., Noshirvani, H., Marks, I., Monteiro, W., & Lelliott, P. (1991). Six-year follow-up after exposure and clomipramine therapy for obsessive compulsive disorder. *Journal of Clinical Psychiatry, 52,* 150–155.

Perugi, G., Akiskal, H. S., Pfanner, C., Presta, S., Gemignani, A., Milanfranchi, A., et al. (1997). The clinical impact of bipolar and unipolar affective comorbidity on obsessive–compulsive disorder. *Journal of Affective Disorders, 46,* 15–23.

Sanderson, W. C., Dinardo, P. A., Rapee, R. M., & Barlow, D. H. (1990). Syndrome comorbidity in patients diagnosed with a *DSM–III–R* anxiety disorder. *Journal of Abnormal Psychiatry, 99,* 308–312.

Steketee, G., Chambless, D. L., & Tran, G. Q. (2001). Effects of axis I and II comorbidity on behavior therapy outcome for obsessive–compulsive disorder and agoraphobia. *Comprehensive Psychiatry, 42,* 76–86.

Steketee, G., Eisen, J., Dyck, I., Warshaw, M., & Rasmussen, S. (1999). Predictors of course in obsessive–compulsive disorder. *Psychiatry Research, 89,* 229–238.

Tukel, R., Polat, A., Ozdemir, O., Aksut, D., & Turksov, N. (2002). Comorbid conditions in obsessive–compulsive disorder. *Comprehensive Psychiatry, 43,* 204–209.

Weissman, M. M., Bland, R. C., Canino, G. J., Greenwald, S., Hwu, H.-G., Lee, C. K., et al. (1994). The cross national epidemiology of obsessive compulsive disorder: The Cross National Collaborative Group. *Journal of Clinical Psychiatry, 55*(Suppl.), 5–10.

14

TREATING COMORBID PRESENTATIONS: OBSESSIVE–COMPULSIVE DISORDER AND DISORDERS OF IMPULSE CONTROL

ADAM S. RADOMSKY, ANTJE BOHNE, AND KIERON P. O'CONNOR

Impulse control disorders (ICDs) are problems that involve repeated behavior that causes distress, harm, or interference. ICDs include problems such as intermittent explosive disorder (pathological and unreasonable or unprovoked outbursts of rage), kleptomania, pyromania, pathological gambling, and trichotillomania (TTM, or pathological hair pulling; American Psychiatric Association, 2000). Although not strictly an ICD, many have argued that Tourette's disorder (TD) also belongs in this list. Some researchers have even proposed that repeated nose picking, or rhinotillexomania, should be included (Jefferson & Thompson, 1995). Unlike obsessive–compulsive disorder (OCD), in which compulsions are usually designed to reduce anxiety or prevent unwanted or catastrophic events from occurring, the repeated behavior in ICDs is commonly carried out to reduce feelings of tension or to generate certain soothing or pleasurable sensations.

Although some researchers have argued that just about all problems that share repeated behavior as a feature or symptom must somehow be related, it is clear that ICDs are not only different from OCD, but also different from each other. One other way of describing the differences between compulsions in OCD—which reduce fear, anxiety, or the perceived likelihood that something awful will happen—and the kind of repeated behavior seen in ICDs—which reduce tension or discomfort and can lead to pleasurable sensations—is to call the ritualistic behavior in OCD *compulsions* and the repeated behavior in ICDs *impulsions*. Impulsive behavior is generally considered to be more habitual or automatic than compulsive behavior. Clients who engage in compulsive behavior can often describe a host of reasons why their compulsions are necessary. These reasons may seem somewhat irrational (e.g., "I must wash my hands exactly eight times if I want to avoid spreading cancer germs to my family"), but they do provide a cognitive or belief-driven explanation for the ritualistic behavior. Impulsive behavior, in contrast, is often described as something habitual or automatic that is done without much thought, for no particular reason, or sometimes to alleviate or bring on particular sensations.

Even though there are fundamental differences between impulsive and compulsive behaviors, it is important for us to include ICDs in this book for a variety of reasons. As we discuss in a later section, some authors have argued that almost all disorders in which there is repetitive behavior should be thought of as being within the construct of an "obsessive–compulsive spectrum" of disorders. This controversial concept has recently become prevalent in the thinking in this field. As such, we thought it important to describe how treatment for ICDs is quite different from treatment for OCD. Furthermore, because it has been proposed that impulsions and compulsions are similar, it is possible or even probable that diagnostic errors can lead clinicians to apply treatment techniques commonly used for OCD to ICDs. When the two co-occur, it is extremely important for clinicians to carefully assess the repeated behavior to determine the best treatment approach or approaches.

In this chapter, we do not describe treatment issues associated with comorbid OCD and each ICD, partly because of limited space and partly because some ICDs have virtually no controlled treatment research to speak of. We have decided instead to focus on the treatment of OCD when it is comorbid with tics, pathological hair pulling, and pathological skin picking. We chose these problems because viewed together, they can provide an understanding of how to treat the co-occurrence of OCD and ICDs.

CO-OCCURRENCE OF OBSESSIVE–COMPULSIVE DISORDER WITH IMPULSE CONTROL DISORDERS

Studies show that between 28% and 63% of adults with Tourette's disorder also show comorbid OCD, whereas 17% of those with OCD show comorbid tics (Comings, 1990; Kurlan et al., 2002). In children, the comordidity may be even higher (Budman & Feirman, 2001). The wide range in estimates likely results from problems in applying the diagnostic criteria. Shapiro and Shapiro (1992) have been strong advocates of the position that many of the apparent compulsions in TD are in fact tic-like, and they called them "impulsion compulsions." This idea was supported by George, Trimble, Ring, Sallee, and Robertson (1993), who developed a scale to distinguish tics from rituals on the basis that tics are ego-syntonic, sensory, self-directed actions, whereas rituals are more elaborate, ego-dystonic, other-directed actions.

Cath, Spinhoven, Landman, and van Kempen (2001) noted that the same repetitive behavior could be defined as either impulsive or compulsive. They suggested that impulsion can be distinguished from compulsion on the basis of emotion and goal directedness. As noted earlier in this chapter, impulsions are associated not with anxiety, but with stimulation. It is interesting that TD has a higher overlap with habit disorders (e.g., skin picking, hair pulling, nail biting) than would normally be expected (Woods, Miltenberger, & Flach, 1996). Habits may serve the same function (emotional or sensory regulation) as tics and hence may be a variant of the same problem (Christenson, Ristvedt, & Mackenzie, 1993; O'Connor, 2005). There is little evidence, however, of high rates of comorbidity between tic disorders and other impulse disorders such as gambling, kleptomania, and pyromania. Furthermore, several studies have shown that individuals with TD and tic disorders do not score highly on measures of impulsivity (Summerfeldt, Hood, Antony, Richter, & Swinson, 2004) or impulsive personality (Cath et al., 2001; O'Connor, 2001). In sum, the relationship between tics and rituals needs to be clarified before comorbidity can be reliably estimated (Comings, 1990). Probably of more use to clinicians than statistics about comorbidity would be some description of the functional and other relationships between OCD and disorders of impulse control.

RELATIONSHIPS BETWEEN IMPULSE CONTROL DISORDERS AND OBSESSIVE–COMPULSIVE DISORDER

Hollander and Benzaquen (1997) have been the principal advocates of the notion of the obsessive–compulsive spectrum, which they have proposed within a framework of "hyperfrontality" versus "hypofrontality" and increased versus decreased serotonin activity. According to their model, OCD and TD appear on opposite ends of the spectrum. However, there is little evidence that TD and OCD represent opposing ends of any biological dimension. Both OCD and TD have brain serotonin activation, but in distinct ways. OCD may have higher attentional arousal and TD higher motor arousal, but this is not a continuum of arousal. Likewise, there is no evidence of a relationship between serotonin measures and impulsivity or compulsivity (Cath et al.,

2001), nor has serotonin receptor hyposensitivity been reported in OCD (Khanna, John, & Lakshmi Reddy, 2001). The serotonin hypothesis of OCD relies almost exclusively on the positive treatment response of OCD to selective serotonin reuptake inhibitor (SSRI) medication, but not all people with these problems respond to SSRIs, and these medications have been shown to affect other systems as well (Lavoie, 2002).

In practically every cognitive or behavioral aspect, tics and rituals appear to be distinct. People with TD do score high on perfectionism, but only on two aspects: personal standards and personal organization (O'Connor et al., 2001), thought to be the least related to the core concept of perfectionism (Frost, Marten, Lahart, & Rosenblate, 1990). In contrast, people with OCD score highly on perfectionism dimensions of doubts about actions and concern over mistakes, but not on personal standards or personal organization (Frost, Rhéaume, & Novara, 2002; Rhéaume, Freeston, Dugas, Letarte, & Ladouceur, 1995).

The same behavioral parameters do not characterize TD and OCD (Petter, Richter, & Sandor, 1998), and people diagnosed with OCD do not show any more overactivity or motor arousal than normal. If people with TD score high on measures of obsessionality, it is on instruments such as the Leyton Inventory (Cooper, 1970), which assesses routine and ordering (Robertson, 1989). Tics and obsessions occur in distinct contexts. O'Connor, Brisebois, Brault, Robillard, and Loiselle (2003) showed that tic onset is situation specific and may be more linked to activity than to objective stimulus parameters. For example, socializing activities are associated with face tics, manual work with shoulder tics, and hair pulling with intellectual work (O'Connor et al., 2003). In OCD, it is usually the interaction between intrusive thoughts (and/or beliefs) and the surrounding context that provokes compulsions, not simply activity level or type.

"Just right" experiences seem to sit on the border between obsessions (and compulsions) and tics. The person arranges objects or performs symmetrical movements until he or she feels right, apparently with no other visible consequences. However, the absence of visible external consequences does not mean that there are no internal consequences about how the person judges himself or herself. As Coles, Frost, Heimberg, and Rhéaume (2003) and Radomsky and Rachman (2004) pointed out, some symmetry compulsions relate to superstitious fears, or the belief that bad placement may lead to bad consequences. A functional analysis of the emotions and goal directedness behind similar actions can help to distinguish tics from compulsive rituals.

A particularly thorny problem is distinguishing mental tics from obsessions. Mental tics are basically mental repetitions, such as repeating a song or phrase just for the feel of it or to release tension. These should not be confused with obsessions, in which there is a clearly catastrophic interpretation of the thought or fear of a specific problem, situation, or event and possible associated mental neutralizations (Rachman, 1997, 1998).

EFFECTS OF COMORBIDITY ON OBSESSIVE–COMPULSIVE DISORDER PRESENTATION AND TREATMENT

There is scant research on how the co-occurrence of other disorders, specifically ICDs, might affect the presentation of OCD and treatment outcome. The consensus among clinicians is that the presence of both TD and OCD leads to greater treatment difficulty. Such conclusions are largely drawn from medication studies, particularly from cases of child comorbidity, in which the presence of TD, OCD, and ADHD can imply serious behavioral problems (Budman & Feirman, 2001). Frequently, these other behaviors are more problematic than tics, obsessions, or compulsions.

Lochner et al. (2005) did a cluster analysis of data from OCD patients with comorbid obsessive–compulsive spectrum disorders. They identified three spectrum clusters, with OCD + TTM falling in Cluster 1 ("reward deficiency"), which was associated with early OCD onset, the presence of tics, and harm-related, sexual, or religious obsessions and compulsions, but not with treatment response.

du Toit, van Kradenburg, Niehaus, and Stein (2001) compared OCD patients with and without comorbid obsessive–compulsive spectrum disorders, including ICDs such as TTM and pathological skin picking. They found that the comorbid group included a larger proportion of female patients and had significantly more, but not more severe, obsessions and compulsions. Individuals in this group also spent more time on, and reported greater resistance against, their OCD symptoms than those without comorbid spectrum disorders, but they did not differ in any other associated psychopathology.

In a study by Matsunaga et al. (2005), OCD patients with a current or past comorbid impulse disorder showed a younger age at onset, lower levels of functioning, and more severe psychopathological features (i.e., OCD, anxiety, and depressive symptoms) and were more likely to show poor treatment response, as assessed by scores on the Yale–Brown Obsessive Compulsive Scale (Y–BOCS; Goodman et al., 1989), than OCD patients without any history of impulse disorder. With respect to treatment outcome, Neudecker (2005) reported the similar finding that TTM patients with obsessive–compulsive traits were significantly more likely to be treatment nonresponders than those without OCD traits.

TREATMENT APPLICATIONS: OBSESSIVE–COMPULSIVE DISORDER AND TICS

If tics and symptoms of OCD coexist in adults, they can usually be treated independently and sequentially in either order, often depending on the priority of the client. The bigger problem comes when the two interact with each other, especially if it is not clear to the clinician at what point the tics end and the obsessions and compulsions begin. As Summerfeldt et al. (2004) and others have noted, when tics and OCD become intertwined, it is usually in the context of beliefs about superstition or bad luck. For example, a person may view his or her tics as a superstitious sign and integrate the feel of completing the tic into a general good luck prediction for the day or the future.

Alternatively, what begins as an incidental tic can be elaborated into or followed up with compulsive behavior. For example, a ticlike head turn may become followed up by a full stare to check that the initial look was not missing anything. Conversely, the opposite can apply, and sometimes in the course of treating OCD, the compulsive ritual (e.g., checking) becomes reduced to a token look that serves a sensory rather than a cognitive purpose. For example, a woman with tics and a "hit and run" obsession who repeatedly resisted going back to check whether she had hit a person while driving a car eventually was able just to turn her head toward the rear view mirror without even looking into it and to feel relief.

CASE DESCRIPTION OF A CLIENT WITH TICS

L was a single 39-year-old man with OCD and TD whose tics and rituals were intertwined. L worked in a management position in an international firm that required much travel. His primary complaint was superstitious rituals, which had invaded his life over the past 10 years. If he thought badly of someone or inadvertently forgot to think of someone in the right way, he would neutralize the thought or omission by repeating an action. He would also constantly replay conversations to see if he had said or thought anything of bad consequence during the day. He also had a series of improvised rules about daily activities. He worked a lot on the computer and had recently changed, for example, the word *start* to *begin* on the initial icon because he had made the association between "starting" and things "starting to go badly wrong." He erased software programs with superstitious names like "Demon."

L also had mild eye-blink tics, as well as a head tic; several times an hour, he turned his head to the left and sniffed. The tic was more prevalent when he was unoccupied or in a social situation. L also had cognitive tics. He said that his head was constantly full of ideas, and the need to perform a superstitious ritual could come spontaneously out of nowhere, inspired by a cognitive tic. He might be walking along and suddenly get the idea that he had to go back and retrace his steps, or something bad would happen. When asked about this, he stated that he had never worried about anything specific happening, but he would get a mild feeling of discomfort that he would often later interpret as signifying some sort of nonspecific impending doom.

L's mental tics included repeating phrases or songs, and often he would have metacognitive thoughts about his mental tics (e.g., "Why am I thinking this?"), which would spiral off into a number of repetitive behaviors to superstitiously neutralize his fear of "wrong thinking." It is interesting that the thought about causing harm or bad luck could be triggered by a mental tic, but the resolution was that he "felt right" sensorially after the repetition.

Treatment Strategy

The clinician began therapy by providing psychoeducation on how the strategies L was using, such as trying to ignore, distract, and suppress the thoughts, were counterproductive. The clinician pointed out another tactic of his: to question himself to see if he could work out why he was thinking as he was, which became compulsive questioning. The reasons for his magical thinking and superstitious behavior, the clinician observed, were linked to an insecure coping strategy. To address these symptoms, the clinician implemented reality tests of L's "thought power" to demonstrate his lack of magical ability.

The clinician first addressed the cognitive tics by identifying them as tics, and not obsessions or compulsions. Hence, like other tics, they were more likely to arise in only some situations, and their content could vary. The clinician encouraged the client to "catch the thought" as soon as it came and "not go any further," tolerating the discomfort while carrying on with his next activity. L discovered that the discomfort was short lived, and he soon forgot about the thought. The head tic was more likely to occur in social situations, and the clinician taught L relaxation techniques to use as an incompatible response (relaxation training is part of habit reversal training [HRT], discussed later in this chapter). Treatments ran in parallel, and after 10 weeks, both tics and OCD symptoms were markedly reduced, at which point L was transferred to work in another city.

TREATMENT APPLICATIONS: OBSESSIVE–COMPULSIVE DISORDER, HAIR PULLING, AND SKIN PICKING

As with tics, it is important for clinicians to clarify whether pathological hair pulling and skin picking each constitute a disorder or whether such grooming behaviors are OCD symptoms. In general, TTM and pathological skin picking might independently co-occur with, have caused, or have resulted from OCD. Pathological grooming behaviors can serve a similar function to compulsions (e.g., anxiety reduction, satisfaction of perfectionist needs) or might be differentially motivated (e.g., stimulation and pleasure seeking), or sometimes even both, varying intraindividually over time. Careful case conceptualization is needed to ascertain the functional connections, if any, between impulsive and compulsive symptoms.

Case Description of a Client With Skin Picking

P, a 32-year-old woman, lost her job because of compulsive checking and ordering. Since her early teens, she felt compelled to have everything "perfect, neat, and in order." She spent hours a day checking work documents for mistakes and rearranging her desk and files, which kept her from finishing her work. In addition, she picked daily and extensively at her skin (face and feet) to "clean up and smooth" her skin of perceived irregularities (slight acne, dry skin), having the opposite effect (skin lesions, scabs, scars) and leading to significant pain while walking. She mainly picked at her skin in front of a mirror (satisfying perfectionistic needs), but also while engaged in sedentary activities like watching TV (habitually), when feeling bored (stimulation seeking), or after having arguments (emotion regulation). Because the compulsions and skin picking were determined to be fairly independent of each other, treatment began with exposure and response prevention for her checking and habit reversal training for her pathological skin picking.

Treatment Strategy: Habit Reversal Training

Habit reversal training (Azrin & Nunn, 1973) is considered the nonpharmacological treatment of choice for tics and nervous habits. It is a multicomponent intervention including awareness training, competing response training, relaxation training, and contingency management. The rationale behind HRT is that people with nervous habits and tics can be taught to recognize early signs of their pathological behavior and to perform incompatible responses that prevent or interrupt the unwanted behavior. In the long term, the patient aims to adopt the competing response and, thus, replace the unwanted (and often harmful) behavior with more functional (and less harmful) behavior.

Awareness Training

In the first step, the clinician conducts an interview to identify the problematic behavior and the functions it serves (i.e., positive and negative reinforcing consequences such as bodily sensations, emotions, or social interaction) and provide the basis for a functional analysis of the problem. In addition, the client is trained to self-monitor his or her problematic behavior and to identify and record its antecedents, or warning signs, such as particular sensations, rising urges, or the presence or absence of identifiable triggers. The purpose of awareness training is to train the client to notice the unwanted behavior or a rising urge as early as possible. This step is particularly important if the behavior shows any automatism or tends to occur out of conscious awareness (e.g., while engaged in sedentary activities). This step frequently results in a significant, albeit only temporary, positive effect by itself, by reducing the frequency of the unwanted behavior. Awareness training can serve as an important initial motivator for the client to agree to engage in the long-term and challenging process of overcoming a habit that is often self-reinforcing because of the pleasurable or relaxing sensations it provides.

Competing Response Training

In the second step, an appropriate competing response that physically interferes with the tic or pathologic grooming behavior is chosen and established. It is called a *competing response* because the muscles involved in the preventive behavior compete with the muscles involved in the to-be-eliminated behavior. For TTM clients, for example, the competing response might be to make a fist with the thumb against the palm until a slight tension is felt and to maintain this pressure for several minutes. Whenever the client senses one of the identified warning signs or as soon as he or she realizes that the problematic behavior has already been initiated, the client engages in the competing activity. Thus, his or her muscles are trained to execute a different movement in response to the urge, preventing the performance of the pathological behavior. It is extremely important that the client practice the competing response daily and persistently so that it becomes as automatic as the to-be-eliminated behavior.

Relaxation Training

In the relaxation training component of HRT, the clinician instructs patients to use breathing, postural adjustment, or other relaxation techniques (e.g., progressive muscle relaxation) to reduce the urge that triggers the tic or pathological grooming behavior. In contrast to OCD urges, which subside if rituals are consistently resisted, urges in TTM or tic disorders usually do not subside without the application of relaxation. Once the client is familiar with and competent in the use of a relaxation technique, this component is incorporated into HRT. Clients learn to apply relaxation during the full period they are performing the competing response until they feel a significant reduction in the urge to perform the problematic behavior.

Contingency Management

To establish durable change in behavior, new behavior should be reinforced, which can be done by clients themselves or by a support person. Each time clients are successful in resisting an urge to engage in the problematic behavior (or in using the competing response), they should be rewarded or reinforced. Suitable rewards are specified for each individual and can include material incentives; positive, commending self-talk; and encouragement by friends and family. The implementation of token economies (earning points and exchanging them for pleasurable activities of choice) can be helpful for children and adolescents. In the long term, reinforcement might become more and more intrinsic, resulting from decreasing negative long-term consequences such as the diminishment of bald spots in TTM or, more generally, the lessening of embarrassment, suffering, and functional impairment.

Although not an integral component of HRT, attention to social support is important (Keuthen, Bohne, Himle, & Woods, 2005) not only for social reinforcement, but also for treatment compliance. Clients may identify a person to help them remember to use the competing response. The support person should receive some brief training, including an explanation of the HRT rationale and the role of a support person. Moreover, the support person needs to be informed about the individually identified warning signs of the problematic behavior and the correct use of the competing response. The training also includes the practice of properly praising the client for the correct use of the competing response and prompting when he or she is seen performing the to-be-eliminated behavior but not using the competing response.

Habit reversal training is the most empirically researched behavioral approach for tics and pathological grooming behaviors, and it has been shown to be an effective treatment for these disorders (for a review, see Keuthen et al., 2005; for HRT with tics, see Wilhelm et al., 2003). However, not all clients with pathological habits and tics respond to HRT equally well, and partial remission of symptoms and relapse are not uncommon. Among other things, treatment response might depend on the specific functions the problematic behaviors serve. If irrational or dysfunctional thoughts are related to the pathological grooming behavior (e.g., perfectionistic beliefs), an integration of cognitive techniques (e.g., cognitive restructuring) seems to be indicated.

ISSUES IN THE BEHAVIORAL COMPONENTS OF THERAPY

One important decision with impulse control disorders is when to limit exposure to trigger stimuli versus when to facilitate exposure to threatening stimuli. Treatment strategies for tics and rituals are often independent, although techniques may overlap. As stated earlier in this chapter, the treatment of choice for tics is HRT (Azrin & Peterson, 1988). There are no reported clinical trials applying competing response training to OCD, but it is recognized by researchers that other components of HRT, such as awareness training and relaxation, are ineffective by themselves as interventions for OCD (Greist et al., 2002).

The distinct functions of rituals (aversion reduction) and tics (tension reduction) indicate different targets for treatment. There is some overlap, however, in applying the same treatment principles in distinct ways. In both tics and rituals, exposure may be a useful technique. In the case of OCD, exposure is to the anxiogenic thought or stimulus, paired with response prevention, and this technique is recognized as a treatment of choice. There is growing evidence in severe cases of tics and self-mutilation that exposure to the urge to tic coupled with resistance to the tic can be effective (Hoogduin, Verdellen, & Cath, 1997; Verdellen, Keijsers, Cath, & Hoogduin, 2004).

ISSUES IN THE COGNITIVE COMPONENTS OF THERAPY

In cognitive therapy, similar techniques may be applied in distinct ways. For example, use of the thought suppression analogue in OCD encourages the person to let intrusive thoughts pass by rather than react to them and attempt to suppress them, because such suppression may lead to rebound. In the case of OCD, the thought is that something bad will happen. In the case of impulse control disorders, it may be the concern about doing something that attains importance. The person may become preoccupied with not making a noise or not inappropriately touching, which may be ideas they attempt to suppress but may finally lead them to give in to the urge and perform the action. Equally, spontaneous thoughts may be accorded importance in disorders of impulse control as guides or imperatives to action rather than viewed as just thoughts. In both types of disorder, metacognitive beliefs and appraisals about the problem can be distressing and counterproductive and are amenable to cognitive therapy.

CONCLUSION

Although the extent of the relationship is still under debate, it is clear that clients are not infrequently referred for help with comorbid OCD and ICDs. One of the most important things for a clinician to do during an assessment of these problems is to try to distinguish compulsive behavior from impulsive behavior. This is not an easy endeavor, but it is a critical one, because applying many of the techniques discussed in this book to ICDs is likely to be far less effective than using HRT. Similarly, using HRT to treat some of the core symptoms of OCD, such as compulsive washing or checking, is also unlikely to produce strong and durable treatment gains.

Once the clinician has obtained an understanding of the client's impulsive and compulsive behaviors, it is generally acceptable to treat these problems separately and preferably serially, unless compulsive and impulsive symptoms are intertwined. In these cases, a careful case conceptualization can help the clinician combine HRT with other CBT techniques. This is our clinical impression, and there is very little research in this area; our ability to make these claims would be better supported by additional empirical evidence.

Although there are many effective ways to obtain such evidence, one of them is accessible to all clinicians: We recommend ongoing assessment of both compulsive and impulsive symptomatology during treatment (and even during each session). The collection of empirical information about the status of specific, targeted symptoms not only can be a great help to clinicians faced with these comorbidities, but also can aid in the generation of single-case design investigations. Even these would be valuable to the field in understanding how to address the co-occurrence of OCD and ICDs. An excellent source of information on how to gather empirical evidence during treatment can be found in Woody, Detweiler-Bedell, Teachman, and O'Hearn (2002).

Although valuable, single-case design research will not answer all of the questions that remain about the comorbidity of OCD and ICDs and its treatment. In addition to larger outcome trials assessing the impact of HRT on impulsions and compulsions, research on the impact of CBT on impulsions and compulsions and, more interesting, on the degree to which gains in one domain transfer to the other would be of merit. However, before any of these trials can be conducted, more research into the connections—or lack thereof—between impulsive and compulsive behavior is warranted. Much debate remains about the connections between OCD and ICDs, and although available treatments for both can be effective, there is still a great deal of room for improvement.

REFERENCES

American Psychiatric Association. (2000). *Diagnostic and statistical manual of mental disorders* (4th ed., text rev.). Washington, DC: Author.

Azrin, N. H., & Nunn, R. G. (1973). Habit reversal: A method of eliminating nervous habits and tics. *Behaviour Research and Therapy, 11*, 619–628.

Azrin, N. H., & Peterson, A. L. (1988). Habit reversal for the treatment of Tourette's syndrome. *Behaviour Research and Therapy, 26*, 347–351.

Budman, C. L., & Feirman, L. (2001). The relationship of Tourette's syndrome with its psychiatric comorbidities: Is there an overlap? *Psychiatric Annals, 31*, 541–548.

Cath, D. C., Spinhoven, P., Landman, A. D., & van Kempen, G. M. J. (2001). Psychopathology and personality characteristics in relation to blood serotonin in Tourette's syndrome and obsessive–compulsive disorder. *Journal of Psychopharmacology, 15*, 111–119.

Christenson, G. A., Ristvedt, S. L., & Mackenzie, T. B. (1993). Identification of trichotillomania cue profiles. *Behaviour Research and Therapy, 31*, 315–320.

Coles, M. E., Frost, R. O., Heimberg, R. G., & Rhéaume, J. (2003). "Not just right experiences": Perfectionism, obsessive–compulsive features and general psychopathology. *Behaviour Research and Therapy, 41*, 681–700.

Comings, D. E. (1990). *Tourette syndrome and human behavior*. Duarte, CA: Hope Press.

Cooper, J. (1970). The Leyton Obsessional Inventory. *Psychological Medicine, 1*, 48–64.

Du Toit, P. L., van Kradenburg, J., Niehaus, D., & Stein, D. J. (2001). Comparisons of obsessive–compulsive disorder patients with and without comorbid putative obsessive–compulsive spectrum disorders using a structured clinical interview. *Comprehensive Psychiatry, 42*, 291–300.

Frost, R. O., Marten, P., Lahart, C., & Rosenblate, R. (1990). The dimensions of perfectionism. *Cognitive Therapy and Research, 14*, 449–468.

Frost, R. O., Rhéaume, J., & Novara, C. (2002). Perfectionism in obsessive compulsive disorder. In R. O. Frost & G. Steketee (Eds.), *Cognitive approaches to obsessions and compulsions: Theory, assessment and treatment* (pp. 91–106). Oxford, England: Elsevier.

George, M. S., Trimble, M. R., Ring, H. A., Sallee, F. R., & Robertson, M. M. (1993). Obsessions in obsessive–compulsive disorder with and without Gilles de la Tourette's syndrome. *American Journal of Psychiatry, 150*, 93–97.

Goodman, W. K., Price, L. H., Rasmussen, S. A., Mazure, C., Fleischmann, R. L., Hill, C. L., et al. (1989). The Yale–Brown Obsessive–Compulsive Scale: I. Development, use, and reliability. *Archives of General Psychiatry, 46*, 1006–1011.

Greist, J. H., Marks, I. M., Baer, L., Kobak, K. A., Wenzel, K. W., Hirsch, M. J., et al. (2002). Behavior therapy for obsessive compulsive disorder guided by a computer or by clinician compared with relaxation as a control. *Journal of Clinical Psychiatry, 63*, 138–145.

Hollander, E., & Benzaquen, S. D. (1997). The obsessive–compulsive spectrum disorders. *International Review of Psychiatry, 9*, 99–109.

Hoogduin, K., Verdellen, C., & Cath, D. (1997). Exposure and response prevention in the treatment of Gilles de la Tourette's syndrome: Four case studies. *Clinical Psychology and Psychotherapy, 4*, 125–135.

Jefferson, J. W., & Thompson, T. D. (1995). Rhinotillexomania: Psychiatric disorder or habit? *Journal of Clinical Psychiatry, 56*, 56–59.

Keuthen, N. J., Bohne, A., Himle, M., & Woods, D. W. (2005). Advances in the conceptualization and treatment of body-focused repetitive behaviors. In B. E. Ling (Ed.), *Obsessive–compulsive disorder research* (pp. 1–29). Hauppauge, NY: Nova Biomedical Books.

Khanna, S., John, J. P., & Lakshmi Reddy, P. (2001). Neuroendocrine and behavioral responses to mCPP in obsessive–compulsive disorder. *Psychoneuroendocrinology, 26*, 209–223.

Kurlan, R., Como, P. G., Miller, B., Palumbo, D., Deeley, C., Andersen, E. M., et al. (2002). The behavioral spectrum of tic disorders: A community-based study. *Neurology, 59*, 414–420.

Lavoie, M. E. (2002). Le traitement du trouble obsessionnel compulsif [The treatment of obsessive–compulsive disorder]. *Les Pages Bleues, Québec Pharmacie, 49*, 209–215.

Lochner, C., Hemmings, S. M. J., Kinnear, C. K., Niehaus, D. J. H., Nel, D. G., Corfield, V. A., et al. (2005). Cluster analysis of obsessive–compulsive spectrum disorders in patients with obsessive–compulsive disorder: Clinical and genetic correlates. *Comprehensive Psychiatry, 46,* 14–19.

Matsunaga, H., Kiriike, N., Matsui, T., Oya, K., Okino, K., & Stein, D. (2005). Impulsive disorders in Japanese adult patients with obsessive–compulsive disorder. *Comprehensive Psychiatry, 46,* 43–49.

Neudecker, A. (2005). *Multimodale Verhaltenstherapie versus Paroxetin-Behandlung bei Trichotillomanie* [Multimodal behavior therapy versus treatment with paroxetine in trichotillomania]. Unpublished doctoral dissertation, University of Hamburg, Germany.

O'Connor, K. P. (2001). Clinical and psychological features distinguishing obsessive–compulsive and chronic tic disorders. *Clinical Psychology Review, 21,* 631–660.

O'Connor, K. P. (2005). *Cognitive–behavioral management of tic disorders.* Etobicoke, Ontario, Canada: Wiley.

O'Connor, K. P., Brault, M., Robillard, S., Loiselle, J., Borgeat, F., & Stip, E. (2001). Evaluation of a cognitive–behavioural program for the management of tic and habit disorders. *Behaviour Research and Therapy, 39,* 667–681.

O'Connor, K. P., Brisebois, H., Brault, M., Robillard, S., & Loiselle, J. (2003). Behavioral activity associated with onset in chronic tic and habit disorder. *Behaviour Research and Therapy, 41,* 241–249.

Petter, T., Richter, M. A., & Sandor, P. (1998). Clinical features distinguishing patients with Tourette's syndrome and obsessive–compulsive disorder from patients with obsessive–compulsive disorder without tics. *Journal of Clinical Psychiatry, 59,* 456–459.

Rachman, S. (1997). A cognitive theory of obsessions. *Behaviour Research and Therapy, 35,* 793–802.

Rachman, S. (1998). A cognitive theory of obsessions: Elaborations. *Behaviour Research and Therapy, 36,* 385–402.

Radomsky, A. S., & Rachman, S. (2004). Symmetry, ordering and arranging compulsive behaviour. *Behaviour Research and Therapy, 42,* 893–913.

Rhéaume, J., Freeston, M. H., Dugas, M. J., Letarte, H., & Ladouceur, R. (1995). Perfectionism, responsibility and obsessive compulsive symptoms. *Behaviour Research and Therapy, 33,* 785–794.

Robertson, M. M. (1989). The Giles de la Tourette syndrome: The current status. *British Journal of Psychiatry, 154,* 147–169.

Shapiro, A. K., & Shapiro, E. (1992). Evaluation of the reported association of obsessive–compulsive symptoms or disorder with Tourette's disorder. *Comprehensive Psychiatry, 33,* 152–165.

Summerfeldt, L. J., Hood, K., Antony, M. M., Richter, M. A., & Swinson, R. P. (2004). Impulsivity in obsessive–compulsive disorder: Comparisons with other anxiety disorders and within tic-related subgroups. *Personality and Individual Differences, 36,* 539–553.

Verdellen, C. W. J., Keijsers, G. P. J., Cath, D. C., & Hoogduin, C. A. L. (2004). Exposure with response prevention versus habit reversal in Tourette's syndrome: A controlled study. *Behaviour Research and Therapy, 42,* 501–511.

Wilhelm, S., Deckersbach, T., Coffey, B. J., Bohne, A., Peterson, A., & Baer, L. (2003). Habit reversal versus supportive psychotherapy for Tourette's disorder: A randomized controlled trial. *American Journal of Psychiatry, 160,* 1175–1177.

Woods, D. W., Miltenberger, R. G., & Flach, A. D. (1996). Habits, tics, and stuttering: Prevalence and relation to anxiety and somatic awareness. *Behavior Modification, 20,* 216–225.

Woody, S., Detweiler-Bedell, J., Teachman, B., & O'Hearn, T. (2002). *Treatment planning in psychotherapy: Taking the guesswork out of clinical care.* New York: Guilford Press.

AUTHOR INDEX

Numbers in italics refer to listings in the reference sections.

Brisebois, H., 298, *308*
Broatch, J., 47, *55*
Broeske, P. H., *277, 278*
Brotto, S. A., *292*
Brown, G., 212, 228
Brown, J. M., 38, *58*
Brown, P. H., *277, 278*
Brown, T. A., 282n, *292*
Budman, C. L., 297, 299, *306*
Bujold, A., *142*
Burrows, G., *108*

Cahill, S. P., 67, *74*, 91, *105*
Calamari, J. E., 24, 26, *29*
Calvocoressi, L., 46, 47, *52*, 197, *205*
Campbell, L. A., 282n, *292*
Campeas, R., *53, 106, 141, 167*
Canino, G. J., *293*
Cardoner, N., *27*
Carmin, C., 21, *25*
Carpenter, D., 32, *56*, 152, 168, 253, 265
Carpenter, L. L., 12, *26*
Carroll, K. M., 33, 49, *52*
Carter, C., *105*
Carter, S. R., 44, *59*
Carter-Sand, S. A., 67, *74*
Cashman, L. A., 44, *51*
Cath, D. C., 297, *297–298*, 305, *306, 307, 309*
Caudwell, J., *108*
Cermele, J. A., *233–234, 247, 247*
Chambless, D. L., 13, 29, 33, 47, *52, 57*, 248, 287, *293*
Charney, D. S., *106, 142*, 228, *307*
Charron, M., 231, *248*
Cherones, T., 44, *52*
Christenson, G. A., 297, *306*
Christensen, D. D., 238, 239, *247, 248*
Clancy, G., *51*
Claridge, G. S., 14, *26*
Clark, D. A., 9, 13, 18, 20, 23, *25*, 67, *74*, 118, 124, 126, 127n, 130, 131, 134, 135, 136, 137, 139, 140, *141, 143*, 212, 228
Clark, D. M., 14, *25*, 207
Clary, C. M., *307*
Cobb, J., 48, *56*
Coffey, B. J., *206, 309*
Cohen, D. J., 188, *206*
Cohen, I., 115, *144*
Coles, M. E., 188, *205*, 298, *306*
Collins, K. A., 96, *106*

Comings, D. E., 297, *307*
Como, P. G., *307*
Cook, E. H., *265*
Cooper, J., 298, *306*
Cooper, M., 48, *52*
Corfield, V. A., *308*
Cottraux, J., 32, 33, 34, 36, 37, *52*, 81, *105*
Cowan, A., 44, *52*
Coyne, J., 36, *57*
Craske, M. G., 49, *57*, 90, *105, 109*
Cregger, B., 39, *57*
Crino, R., 32, *55*, 81, *107*
Crits-Christoph, P., 79, *105*
Cullen, B. A. M., *248*
Cuneo, P., *54, 106*
Curi, M., *292*

Damecour, C. L., 231, *248*
Dansky, B. S., 33, *52*
David, L., 44, *52*
Davidson, G. C., 71, *74*
Davidson, J., *105*
Davies, M., *264*
Davies, S., *53, 106, 141, 167*
Deacon, B. J., 21, *25*, 66, *74*
Deale, A., 82, *105*, 153, *167*
de Araujo, L. A., 34, *52*, 62, 65, *74*, 82, *105, 107*, 153, *167*
Deckersbach, T., *248, 309*
Deeley, C., *307*
de Geus, F., 286, *292*
de Haan, E., 33, 34, 46, *52, 53*, 58, 59, 65, *74, 75, 109, 144*
Dekker, J., 86, *105*
de Lange, I., 46, *53*
Delgado, P., 87, *106*
Den Boer, J. A., 14, *27*
den Hengst, S., 86, *105*
Denys, D., 282n, 286, *292*
DeRubeis, R. J., 79, *105*
de Silva, P., 11, 21, *25, 27, 107*, 124, 136, *143, 173, 186*, 212, 229, *275–276, 278*
Detweiler-Bedell, J., *306, 309*
Deus, J., *27*
Deuser, W., *105*
De Vries, A. L. C., *206*
DiClemente, C., 62, 66, *75, 76*, 97
DiClemente, C. C., 97, *108*
Diefenbach, G. J., 32, 39, 48, *58*
Dinardo, P. A., 282n, *292*
Diniz, J. B., 282, *292*

O'Dwyer, A.-M., 269, *280*
O'Hearn, T., 306, *309*
Okino, K., *308*
Oliver, N. S., 90, *108*
O'Neill, M. L., 36, *59*
Orsillo, S. M., *54*
Ort, S. I., *265*
O'Sullivan, G., 34, 56, 62, 65, 76, 81, *108,*
    287, *292*
Otto, M. W., 38, *57*, 189, *205*
Oya, K., *308*
Ozdemir, O., 287, *293*

Padesky, C., 121, 126, 128, 130, 140, *142*
Page, A. C., 90, *107, 108*
Palumbo, D., *307*
Pandina, G. J., 233–234, *247*
Park, J. M., *51*
Parkin, J. R., *54*
Parks, G. A., 49, *57*
Paterson, R., *142*
Pato, M. T., 39, 46, *59, 77*, 92, 94, *109*
Pauls, D. L., *57*, 188, *206*
Payne, L. L., 91, *106*
Pediatric OCD Treatment Study Team, 253,
    254, *265*
Pedrick, C., 69, *75*, 95, *107*
Pelissier, M.-C., 13, *27*
Penzel, F., 69, *76*
Perlmutter, S., *266*
Perugi, G., 282n, *292*
Peters, E. R., 270, *280*
Peterson, A. L., 304, *306, 309*
Petter, T., 298, *308*
Pfanner, C., *292*
Phelps, M. E., 43, *57*
Phillips, K. A., *186*, 268, 270, *278, 280*
Phoenix, E., 97, *109*
Piacentini, J., 254–255, *265*
Pinard, G., 70, 73, *77*, 115, *144*
Pitman, R. A., 14, *27*
Pitman, R. K., 188, 189, *206*
Polat, A., 287, *293*
Pollack, M. H., 38, *57*
Pollard, C. A., 47, *54*, 62, 63, 71, 72, 73, 76,
    77
Port, J. D., 23, *29*
Powers, M. B., 91, *108*
Prado, H. S., *206*
Presta, S., *292*
Price, L. H., *52, 54*, 87, *106, 142, 186, 205,*
    228, *307*

Prien, R. F., *106, 141*
Prochaska, J., 62, 66, *75, 76, 97, 108*
Przeworski, A., 20, 26, 44, *58*
Pujol, J., 23, *27*
Purdon, C., 21, 22, 25, *27*, 66, *76*, 82, 90,
    96, *108, 109*, 115, 118, 124, 126,
    127n, 129, 130, 134, 136, 137, 138,
    139, *143*, 211, 212, *228*

Rachman, S. J., 11, 12, 16, 17, 18, 21, 26,
    27, 28, 67, *76*, 80, 83, 84, *107, 108,*
    111, 114, 115, 117, 118, 124, 131,
    135, 136, *141, 142, 143, 144*, 153,
    168, 171, 172, 173, *186*, 192, 201,
    206, 211, 212, 213, 214, 215, 225,
    228, 229, 272, *280, 291, 298, 308*
Radomsky, A. S., 298, *308*
Rangé, B., *106*
Rapee, R. M., 28, *142, 144*, 282n, *292*
Rapoport, J. L., *55*, 188, 189, *206, 264*
Rasche-Ruchle, H., *55*
Rasmussen, S. A., 39, *53, 54, 59*, 63, *76*, 87,
    92, *106, 109, 142, 186*, 188, *206,*
    228, 253, *265, 278, 279, 287, 293,*
    307
Rassi, S., *55, 107*
Rauch, S. L., *206*
Rector, N. A., 287, *292*
Reed, G. F., 14, *27*
Resick, P., 71, *76*
Rettew, D. C., *55*
Rhéaume, J., 16, 21, 25, 26, 100, *109*, 114,
    121, *142, 143*, 188, *205, 298, 306,*
    307, 308
Richards, C., 28, 73, *76*, 274, *280*
Richards, H. C., 116, *144*
Richter, M. A., *141, 144, 186*, 287, *291, 292,*
    297, 298, *308, 308*
Richwain, T., *57*
Riddle, M. A., 248, *265*
Ring, H. A., 297, *307*
Rishwain, T., *248*
Ristvedt, S. L., 297, *306*
Robertson, M. M., 297, *307, 308*
Robillard, S., 113, *142, 298, 308*
Robinson, D., *28*
Rodriquez, B. L., 90, *109*
Roemer, L., *54*
Rogers, M. P., *54, 106*
Rokeach, M., *280*
Rollnick, S., 45, 56, 58, 62, 70, 71, *76*, 240,
    248

SUBJECT INDEX

Avoidance behavior, 190, 214, 219–220, 227
    in hoarding, 246
Avoidance patterns, 178–179
Avoidance strategies, 177
Awareness training, 302–303
    and OCD, 304

"Bad luck" events, 100
Balking at exposure exercises, 183
Beck, A. T., 225
Beck Depression Inventory, 212, 227
Behavioral avoidance tests, 212
Behavioral experiments, 222–223, 225–226,
    227, 241, 274–275
    for predictions in hoarding-compulsion
        treatment, 245
Behavioral interventions, 23
        and cognitive intervention, 36, 38
        See also Exposure and response preven-
            tion
Belief(s), 191, 269, 270
        abnormal, 270
        dysfunctional, 14, 173–174
        erroneous, 43
        and hoarding, 234
        normal, 269–270
        in overvalued idea, 268–269, 270
        protection of from extinction, 214
Belief and appraisal models, 14–15, 16–18,
    24
        empirical tests of, 18–23
        and needed research, 23–24
        of Salkovskis, 15–16
Betty (case vignette on hoarding), 235–238
Between-session work, 127–130. See also
        Homework
Biases, cognitive, 220, 224–225
Biology
        patients see as cause, 68
        See also Genetic factors
Brain, 23
        and OCD patients vs. others, 43
"Brain hiccups," 256, 258, 261
Brain Lock (Schwartz), 204
Brown Assessment of Beliefs Scale (BABS),
    176, 273
BT–STEPS program, 38–39

Carol (case composite), 150–151
        ERP for, 154
        homework, 166
        imaginal exposure, 153, 163

information gathering, 156, 157, 158
initial meetings, 154, 156
in vivo exposure, 161, 162
response prevention, 164, 165, 166
treatment plan, 159, 160
Case formulation, in hoarding vignette
        (Betty), 236–237
"Catastrophic misinterpretation," 16, 114
CBT. See Cognitive–behavioral therapy
Celexa, 175
CGI (Clinical Global Impression Scale),
        35
Challenger disaster, appraisal of responsibil-
        ity for, 118, 134
Checking compulsions or rituals, 11, 111,
        171–173, 185
        and behavioral treatment outcome stud-
            ies, 189
        in case study (Sam), 177
        and change in appraisals, 114
        cognitive–behavioral model of, 173–
            174, 175–176
        cognitive–behavioral therapy for, 174–
            178
            exposure therapy and response pre-
                vention,181–182
            obstacles in, 182–185
            psychoeducation and information
                gathering, 178–179
            treatment planning, 179–181
        covert (mental), 172
        as neutralization, 221
        overt, 171–172
        and perfectionism, 119
        and responsibility, 21
Childbirth, and personal responsibility, 21
Children and adolescents with OCD, 253
        assessment of, 254–257
        and grizzly-bear image, 262
        cognitive–behavioral therapy for, 253–
            254, 263
            as research priority, 264
        externalizing OCD as separate entity
            with, 256–257
        maintenance and relapse prevention for,
            263–264
        psychoeducation for, 256, 257–259
        treatment of
            early sessions in, 260–261
            exposure hierarchy in, 259–260,
                261–263
            as research priority, 264

and specific disorders
  anxiety disorders, 282, 287
  depression, 286, 287, 290–291
  generalized anxiety disorder (GAD),
    285, 287, 290
  of hoarding compulsion, 232
  impulse control disorders, 296–302,
    305–306
  panic disorder, 282–284, 288
  posttraumatic stress disorder, 284–
    285, 287, 289–290
  social phobia, 284, 288–289
  specific phobias, 285–286
and treatment
  modification of, 287–291
  timetable for, 40
Competing hypotheses, 274–275
Competing response training, 303
Compulsions, 11, 155, 258
  in client education template, 123
  vs. impulsions, 296
  loose use of term, 40
  mental, 98–99
    in case vignette (Rebecca), 103
  multiple types of, 119
  and negative affect, 196
  normal and clinical, 11
  overt and covert, 11
  in Salkovskis's approach, 15–16
  in two-process theory, 112
Compulsive checking. See Checking compulsions or rituals
Compulsive hoarding,. See Hoarding compulsion
Concealment, 217–218
  need to refrain from, 228
Conditioning model of OCD, 12–13
Consequences, 41
Consequences, feared. See Feared consequences
Contamination compulsions or fears, 11, 44
  case study on (Jim), 10–11
  in children, 259–260
  over depleted uranium (vignette), 132–
    133
  of Howard Hughes, 277
  uncertainty in (case example), 116
  See also Washing compulsion
"Contamination rag," 167
Contingency management, 303–304
Control
  in exposure practices, 89–90

and hoarding, 234
mental, 118–119, 138–139
"Costanza therapy," 44–45
Cost–benefit analysis
  of compulsions, 138
  in hoarding-compulsion treatment, 246
  of seeking certainty, 133
  of striving for perfection, 140
  of thought control, 139
  See also Functional analysis of behavior
Counting rituals, and behavioral treatment
  outcome studies, 189
Creative hopelessness, 275–276

Day plots, 200
Decision making, and hoarding, 233
  in treatment, 241–242, 243
Delusions
  evaluative, 270
  and overvalued ideas, 268, 269
Demographic characteristics, and behavioral
  treatment, 48
Depression
  and beliefs, 14
  comorbidity with, 286, 287, 290–291
  early acceptance of rationale in cogni-
    tive–behavioral therapy for, 83
  and ERP interventions, 31, 33
  and OCD, 227–228
Depressive mood, and obsessions, 214–215
Diagnostic and Statistical Manual of Mental
  Disorders, Fourth Edition (DSM–IV),
  149, 267–268
Diary records, 122
Didactic phase of treatment, 212–215. See
  also Psychoeducation
Diets, as analogy, 50
Disclosure, 218
Distraction
  in client education template, 123
  during exposure, 90–91, 99
    in case vignette (Rebecca), 104
  from intrusions, 15–16
  thought suppression as, 90
Doctors, reassurance seeking directed to, 172
Doubt, as stimulus for incompleteness OCD,
  199
Doubting, obsessional, 169–171, 185
  case study on (Sam), 175–177, 178,
    180–182
  cognitive–behavioral model of, 173–
    174, 175–176

cognitive–behavioral therapy for, 174–178
    exposure therapy and response prevention, 181–182
    obstacles in, 182–185
    psychoeducation and information gathering, 178–179
    treatment planning, 179–181
Downward arrow technique, 126, 241, 245
Dropout from treatment, 65, 277

Emotion, expressed, 47
Emotional attachment, in hoarding, 233–234
End-of-treatment issues, 49–50
    in case vignette on incompleteness OCD (Julie), 202–203
    decision about ending, 99
ERP. *See* Exposure and response prevention
Erroneous beliefs, 43
Escape behavior, 219–220
Etiology of OCD, questions about, 23
Evaluations, 270
    abnormal, 270–271
Evidence for and against hot thought, 140
Evidence for and against patient's interpretation, 215–217
Exactness concerns, 120
    as stimulus for incompleteness OCD, 199
    See also Symmetry compulsions or obsessions
Experiential avoidance, 44
Exposure hierarchy, 86–89, 153, 158–159
    in case composite (Carol), 160
    in case vignette on incompleteness OCD (Julie), 194, 197, 198
    in case vignette (Rebecca), 102
    for children and adolescents, 259–260, 261–263
    for doubting and checking concerns, 179, 180
Exposure and response prevention (exposure and ritual prevention) (ERP), 12–13, 31, 79–80, 111, 152–153, 154, 167, 219–220
    application and practice of
        conducting exposure practices, 89–92
        developing exposure hierarchy, 86–89
        manualized, 155
        presenting of treatment rationale, 83–86

and response prevention, 92–94
appropriate conditions for, 32–34
    and contraindications, 32
from belief and appraisal model, 18
in case composite on washing compulsion (Carol), 154 (*see also* Carol)
in case study on doubting and checking (Sam), 177, 181–182
in case vignette on incompleteness OCD (Julie), 194–203, 205
for children and adolescents, 253, 254, 257, 261–263
in cognitive–behavioral therapy, 22–23, 32, 36, 113
cognitive processes in, 84
and cognitive therapy
    combined with cognitive therapy, 36–37, 111–112, 140, 141
    compared with cognitive therapy, 81, 83, 113
in comparative meta-analysis, 114
cost of, 38
decision to stop, 99
detrimental results during, 100
as direct targeting, 19
empirical status of, 80–83
and extinction principle, 190
and fear structures, 112
as followed by "in recovery" period, 50
and general deficit models, 14
group, 39–40, 82
homework in, 164, 166–167 (*see also* Homework)
imaginal exercises in, 80, 82, 94–95, 152, 153, 163–164, 183
    for hoarding compulsion, 242–244
inclusion of family members in, 46
and incompleteness OCD, 189–190, 193
information gathering in, 156–158
initial meetings in, 154–156
inpatient vs. outpatient, 82
in vivo exercises in, 80, 82, 152, 153, 161–163, 183
    and feelings of uncertainty, 183
    for hoarding compulsion, 242–244
    and reassurance seeking, 298
lateral exposure changes in, 200, 202–203
as lifestyle change, 200
optimal formats for, 37–40
patients presenting obstacles to, 183–185

pharmacological augmentation of, 34–36, 46

premature termination of, 112, 114 (see also Dropout from treatment)

and pretreatment intervention, 70

problems arising in course of, 96–100

and quality of life, 48

and question of alternative treatment, 161

refusal rate for, 45, 96, 112

and relapse prevention, 49

response prevention, 152, 156, 164–166 (see also Response prevention)

self- vs. therapist-directed, 82, 83

and social phobia, 288–289

success (response) rate for, 62

and tic disorders, 304–305

treatment planning for, 158–161

and treatment readiness, 62

in two-process theory, 112

and unwanted thoughts, 44

for washing compulsion, 152

Expressed emotion, 47

Extinction, principle of, 190

and protection of beliefs, 214

Family intervention, 46–47

in case vignette on OCD (Julie), 197–198

in exposure, 93–94

and hoarding-compulsion clients, 239

Family stresses, in ERP, 48

Fear

as irrational but real, 167

two-factor theory of, 120

Fear cues, current, 178

Feared consequences, 178

and absence of insight, 268

and beliefs, 270

of children or adolescents, 258

and cognitive element of ERP, 36

and compulsive behavior, 171

in distant future, 183

and imaginal exposure, 94

and reassurance-seeking rituals, 184

Fear of losing control, 220

Fear of not saying the right thing, as stimulus for incompleteness OCD, 199

Fear reduction, 112

Fear structures, 112

Fear thermometer, 259, 260. See also Subjective Units of Distress Scale

Feeling of knowing, 189

deficits in, 188

Fixity of Beliefs questionnaire, 273

Flooding, 86

Fluvoxamine, plus ERP, 34

Follow-up, 228

Friends

of hoarding-compulsion clients, 239

involvement of in exposure, 94

Functional analysis of behavior, 41, 42, 178

in context, 277

in hoarding case (Betty), 236

in parallel-world example, 275

in preparing patient, 43

and tics vs. compulsive rituals, 298

See also Cost–benefit analysis

Functional disability, 273–274

General deficit models, 13–14

Generalized anxiety disorder

comorbidity with, 282, 285, 287, 290

and diagnosis, 283

vs. OCD, 40

and patient's readiness for change, 96

Genetic factors, 23–24, 24

Goals

in CBT, 129

difficulty in articulating, 67

in readiness treatment, 72

Grizzly bear, as example of intrusion, 262

Grooming behaviors, 301. See also Impulse control disorders

Group therapy

ERP in, 39–40, 82

vs. individual, 114

Guilt, and ERP interventions, 31

Habit disorders, 297

Habit reversal training (HBT), 302–304, 305, 306

Habituation, 191, 205

in case vignette of incompleteness OCD (Julie), 200

in hoarding treatment, 239, 243, 244

Hair pulling, 295, 298, 301

Hamilton Rating Scale for Depression, 176

Handwashing, as neutralization, 221. See also Contamination compulsions or fears; Washing compulsion

Harm avoidance, 188

Harm-avoidant symptom configurations, 187. See also Incompleteness OCD

Harm obsessions, 210, 220
  and appraisals, 126
  and treatment seeking, 65
Health, doubts about, 170–171
Healthy values, identifying of, 276
Hierarchies of exposure. *See* Exposure hierarchy
"Hip-pocket patient" examples, 256
Hit-and-run obsessions, 170, 300
Hoarding, obsessive–compulsive, 274
Hoarding compulsion, 231–232
  and behavioral treatment outcome studies, 189
  case vignette on, 235–238
  and CBT response, 189
  cognitive–behavioral model of, 232–235, 247
  comorbidity with, 232
  course of, 232
  and ERP, 33, 34
  frequency of, 232
  mini-model of, 18, 23
  and OCD, 232, 247
  and possessions as part of self, 272, 276
  relapse prevention in, 246
  research needed on, 247
  treatment of, 238–39, 247
    cognitive strategies in, 244–246
    exposure in (imaginal and in vivo), 242–244
    motivation for, 238, 239–240
    and motivational interviewing, 70
    skills training in, 240–242
    troubleshooting for, 246–247
  and withdrawal from treatment, 65
Hoarding obsession, 11
Home of client, as location of therapy session (hoarding compulsion), 238–239
Homework, 128, 164, 166–167
  with comorbid depression, 290–291
  for hoarding compulsion, 239, 241, 246
  in late treatment, 49
  and patient preparation, 69
  patient's summarizing of (children and adolescents), 263
Howard Hughes Medical Institute, 277
Hughes, Howard, 277

Idealized values, 271–272
  disentangling self from, 276–277
  and dropping out of treatment, 277

measurement of, 273–274
  strategies for overcoming, 274–277
Identity, doubts about, 170–171
Imaginal exposure, 80, 82, 94–95, 152, 153, 163–164, 183
  for hoarding compulsion, 242–244
Impact analysis, 69–70. *See also* Cost-benefit analysis
Impulse control disorders, 295–296, 305
  OCD comorbid with, 296–297, 299, 305–306
    case description of, 300–301
    and relationships between OCD and ICD, 297–298, 300
    and treatment applications, 299–300, 301–302
  OCD's relationships with, 297–298, 300
  treatment of, 301
    case description on, 302
    habit reversal training (HBT), 302–304, 305, 306
    and limiting vs. facilitating exposure, 304
    for tics, 299–301, 304
"Impulsion compulsions," 297
Impulsions, 296
Incompleteness, 188
Incompleteness OCD, 188, 204–205
  case vignette (Julie), 193–203, 204, 205
  and cognitive–behavioral principles, 190–193
  symptom labeling in, 204
  symptom themes in, 198, 199
  treatment outcomes for, 189–190
Inference, 269
Information, in explaining CBT to patients, 68
Information gathering (ERP), 156–159
  for checking and doubting, 178–179
Information-processing deficits
  and hoarding, 232–233
  and OCD, 14
Initial meetings (ERP), 154–156. *See also* Clinical interview
Insight, 268
  of OCD patients, 268
    and conditioning model, 13
    and ERP, 34
    with sexual or religious concerns, 33
    vs. superstitious thinking, 138
    therapist's facilitatilng of, 130
Integrative cognitive therapy, 70

Internet, preparatory information on, 69
Interpretation of Intrusions Inventory (III),
    19–20, 21, 122, 176
Interpretation of thought
    and "catastrophic misinterpretation,"
        16, 114
    change in, 226
    evaluating reasons for, 228
    evidence for and against collected, 215–
        217
    in OCD, 124–125
    self-critical vs. benign, 225
    See also Appraisals
Intolerance, of uncertainty, 115–116, 133,
    183
Intrusive thoughts (intrusions), 15, 191, 212–
    213
    changes in interpretation of, 226
    and comorbid disorders, 282
    and compulsions, 15–16
    in conflict with personal values, 171
    decatastrophizing of, 211
    and explaining CBT to patients, 68
    grizzly bear example of, 262
    and mental control, 118–119
    and mood states, 224
    normalizing of, 136, 271
    obsessional doubts from, 173
        in case study (Sam), 176
    in OCD vs. ICD, 305
    overemphasis on, 118
    pragmatic tests of, 225
    radio analogy for, 217
    suppression of, 218 (see also Thought
        suppression)
In vivo exposure, 80, 82, 152, 153, 161–163,
    183
    and feelings of uncertainty, 183
    and hoarding compulsion, 242–244
    and reassurance seeking, 181

Janet, Pierre, 188
Jealousy, obsessional, 272
Jim (case study, contamination problems),
    10–11
Jim (case study, successful treatment), 61
Julie (case vignette), 193–203, 204, 205
"Just right" experiences, 298
    and "not just right" experiences, 188

Knowing, feeling of, 189
    deficits in, 188

Kyle (case study), 10, 11

Lapse, vs. relapse, 50
Late-treatment components, 49
Learning histories, 21–22
Levels of Attribution and Change Scale, 66
Lifestyle changes, for long-term recovery from
    OCD, 50
Likelihood fusion, 137
Location of therapy sessions, for hoarding
    compulsion, 238–239
Long-term treatment outcome, 203–204
Loss, sense of, in hoarding, 234
Lynda (case study), 10, 11

Magical thinking, 138
Maintenance, for children and adolescents,
    263–264
Mal-learning, 21, 23
Manualized treatments, 155
McLean Hospital, Belmont, MA, 38
Memory problems, and hoarding, 233
Menninger Clinic, Houston, 38
Mental compulsions, 98–99
    in case vignette (Rebecca), 103
Mental control, 118–119, 138–139
Mental tics, 298, 300
Metaphors, in explaining CBT to patients,
    68
MFBT (multifamily behavioral treatment),
    46
Mini-models, 18, 23
Minisurvey, 223
Minority groups, and treatment, 64
Modeling of exposures by therapist, 39, 81–
    82, 92, 220
    in case composite Carol), 162
Models of OCD
    belief and appraisal, 14–15, 16–18, 24
        and needed research, 23–24
    empirical tests of, 18–23
    of Salkovskis, 15–16
    cognitive, 119–120, 210–211
        and incompleteness OCD, 191–192,
            204–205
        and reverse reasoning, 209
    cognitive–behavioral, 114–115
        of compulsive hoarding, 232–235,
            247
        of doubting and checking, 173–174,
            175–176
    conditioning, 12–13

contemporary, 16–18
criteria for, 12
general deficit, 13–14
patient's understanding of, 68
and subtype differences, 24
Monitoring forms, 87
in ERP case vignette, 101, 103
Moods, 224
"Moral fusion," 136
Morality bias, 225
Motivation
enhancing of, 68
by parents, 261
for treatment of hoarding compulsion, 238, 239–240
as treatment-readiness problem, 65
Motivational interviewing, 62, 69, 70, 240
for hoarding compulsion, 65, 240, 246
Motivational issues, in ERP, 96–97
Multidimensional Anxiety Scale for Children, 254
Multifamily behavioral treatment (MFBT), 46

National Anxiety Disorders Screening Day, 64
Neurobiological factors, 23, 24
Neuropsychological deficits, 14, 23
Neutralization (neutralizing), 213–214, 220–222
need to refrain from, 228
Nonadherence, 62, 65
Noncompliance, 128–129
and ambivalence, 130
with homework, 166
suspension as result of, 184
Normal beliefs and values, 269–270
Normalizing experience, 158
Normal obsessions, 11
Not just right experiences, 188
and "just right" experiences, 298

Objectives, in readiness treatment, 72
Obsessions, 11, 155, 258
from catastrophic misinterpretations, 16
in client education template, 123
in cognitive–behavioral model of OCD, 114
and depressive mood, 214–215
hit-and-run, 170
and intrusions, 16
loose use of term, 40

vs. mental compulsions, 98–99
vs. mental tics, 298
mood-dependent nature of, 224
normal and clinical, 11
pretreatment fear of reduced, 112
scrupulosity, 171
in two-process theory, 112
Obsessive Beliefs Questionnaire (OBQ), 19, 20, 21, 122, 176
Obsessive Compulsive Cognitions Working Group (OCCWG), 17–18
Obsessive–compulsive disorder (OCD)
behavioral explanation of, 83
classification schemes for, 149
comorbidity with, 281–282, 291
of anxiety disorders, 282, 287–290
of depression, 227–228, 286, 287
of generalized anxiety disorder (GAD), 282, 285, 287, 290
of impulse control disorders, 296–302, 305–306
of panic disorder, 282, 282–284, 288
of posttraumatic stress disorder, 282, 284–285, 287, 289–290
presentation of, 286–287
of social phobia, 282, 284, 288–289
of specific phobias, 282, 283, 285–286
treatment for, 287–291
cycle of, 83, 103, 124
exposure and response prevention for, 12–13, 31, 79–80, 111, 152–153, 154, 219–220 (see also Exposure and response prevention)
and feared consequences, 171 (see also Feared consequences)
vs. impulse control disorders, 295, 296
models of
belief and appraisal, 14–24
cognitive, 119–120, 191–192, 204–205, 209, 210–211
cognitive–behavioral, 114–115, 173–174, 175–176, 232–235, 247
conditioning, 12–13
criteria for, 12
general deficit, 13–14
patient's understanding of, 68
and subtype differences, 24
social costs of, 47–48
subtypes of
research needed on, 24

and treatment seeking, 64–65
symptoms of
  and comorbidity, 282, 283
  compulsive hoarding as, 232
  and grooming behaviors, 301
  heterogeneity of, 12, 14, 18
  major dimensions of, 11
  need to assess, 185
  need for complete description of, 157
  as senseless to patient, 120
  suppression of, 22
  as target of treatment, 122
  thought control in, 44
theories of, 9
  two-factor, 258
and therapeutic alliance, 121
treatability of, 3–4
treatment centers for, 38
See also Treatment, OCD
Obsessive–compulsive disorder in children
  and adolescents. See Children and
  adolescents with OCD
Obsessive–Compulsive Foundation, 47, 61,
  204
  Web site of, 69
Obsessive Compulsive Information Center,
  Web site of, 69
"Obsessive–compulsive spectrum," 296, 297
Obsessive hoarding. See Hoarding obsession
"Off-duty" period, 216–217
Ordering and arranging compulsions, 187–
  188, 272
Organization, and hoarding compulsion, 236,
  242
Overcompensations, idealized values as, 275–276
Overcorrection, 159–160
Overestimation of threat, 115, 130–133
Overgeneralization, 276
Overvalued ideas (OVIs), 267–269, 270
  of the financially secure and indepen-
   dent, 277
  measurement of, 273–274
  pharmacotherapy for, 277–278
  strategies for, 274–277
Overvalued Ideas Scale, 273

PANDAS (pediatric autoimmune neuropsychiatric disorders associated with
  streptococcal infections), 256
Panic disorder
  and beliefs, 14
  comorbidity of, 282, 282–284, 288

and patient's readiness for change, 96
Parallel world, patient's belief in, 275
Parents
  in interview with children or adolescents, 255
  social reinforcement from, 261
Patient liaison program, 69
Patient preference, and treatment outcome,
  36
Pediatric autoimmune neuropsychiatric disorders associated with streptococcal
  infections (PANDAS), 256
Pediatric OCD. See Children and adolescents
  with OCD
Perceptual avoidance, in hoarding compulsion, 242
"Perfection forms," 196
Perfectionism, 17, 20–21, 119, 139–140
  in case vignette (Julie), 193
  in hoarding-compulsion clients, 241,
   244, 247
  and OCD, 298
  slowness related to, 201
Personal domain, 271, 276–277
Personalization, 271–272
Personal Significance Scale (PSS), 212, 226,
  227
Pharmacotherapy
  in case composite (Carol), 151
  for children and adolescents with OCD,
   254
  in combination with psychotherapy, 81
  and ERP, 34–36, 46
  for overvalued ideas, 277–278
  and patient's readiness for change, 96
  See also Clomipramine; Selective serotonin reuptake inhibitors
Phobias, and obsessional fears, 120
Phobias, specific. See Specific phobias
Phobic disorders
  and spacing of exposure, 91
  two-stage model of, 190
Pie chart technique, 133–134, 182
Poor insight, 267
  overvalued ideas as, 268
Pop quiz, for children and adolescents, 263–
  264
Posttraumatic stress disorder (PTSD)
  comorbidity with, 282, 284–285, 287,
   289–290
  and diagnosis, 283
  and exposure therapy, 32, 33

Posttreatment status, assessment of, 227
Pragmatic tests, 225–226
    for parallel-world case, 275
Predictability, in exposure practices, 89–90
Predictions, in hoarding-compulsion treatment, 245
Pregnancy, washing compulsion increased in (case composite), 150
Probability bias, 225
Probability estimation, as technique for addressing threat, 131
Problem solving, for hoarding compulsion, 241
Processes of Change Questionnaire, 66
Protection of others, and appraisals, 126
Psychoeducation
    in case vignette on incompleteness OCD (Julie), 195–196
    for checking and doubting, 178–179, 182
    for children and adolescents, 256, 257–259
    in ERP case vignette, 101
    by ERP therapist, 39
    in preparation for CBT, 69
    about relapse, 49
    as therapeutic, 125
Psychological treatment for OCD. See Treatment, OCD
Psychometric exams, 227
Psychotherapy
    in comparative meta-analysis, 114
    pharmacotherapy in combination with, 81
Psychotherapy Decisional Balance Scale, 66

Quality-of-life issues, in treatment of OCD, 47–48
Questioning
    compulsive, 301
    for information gathering (ERP), 157
Questions about etiology of OCD, 23
Quiz, for children and adolescents, 263–264

Radio noise, and intrusive thoughts, 217
Rational–emotive therapy (RET), 36–37
    ERP combined with, 112–113
Readiness treatment, 71–73
    effectiveness of, 73
Readiness for treatment. See Treatment readiness
Reasoning abnormalities, 14, 23

reverse reasoning, 209
Reassurance
    as client goal, 129
    during ERP, 91–92
        in case vignette (Rebecca), 102–103
    self-reassurance, 164
Reassurance seeking, 97–98, 172–173, 219
    cognitive techniques as, 184–185
    persistent, 184
Reattributing, 192, 196
Rebecca's contamination fears (case vignette), 101–104
Recording, in case vignette on incompleteness OCD (Julie), 196–197
Reexposure, 93
Reinforcement and reinforcers
    in contingency management, 303–304
    external, 261
    and hoarding, 235
    immediate aftereffects as, 41
    withdrawing of (children), 258–259
Relabeling, 192, 196
Relapse
    from failure to take exposure far enough, 99
    vs. lapse, 50
Relapse prevention, 49–50, 228
    in case vignette on incompleteness OCD (Julie), 202–203
    for children and adolescents, 263–264
    for hoarding compulsion, 238, 246
Relaxation training, 303
    and OCD, 304
        vs. exposure, 80–81
Religious concerns and obsessions, 210
    and ERP, 33
Religious questions, 220
Repugnant obsessions, 210
Research
    on comorbidity of OCD and ICDs, 299, 305–306
    and Howard Hughes Medical Institute, 277
    neglected realms of, 23–24
    on OVIs and poor insight, 267
    on pediatric OCD treatment, 264
Resistance, 62–63
    to psychological models of OCD, 68
Response prevention, 152, 156, 164–166
    in case vignette on incompleteness OCD (Julie), 200–202
    complete vs. gradual, 92–93

Social reinforcement, for children or adolescents with OCD, 261
Socioeconomic stresses, in ERP, 48
Socratic dialogue, 36–37, 48, 130, 182, 240, 244–245
Sorting, in treatment of hoarding compulsion, 243
Specific phobias, comorbidity with, 282, 285–286
    and diagnosis, 283
Spiritual leaders, reassurance seeking directed to, 172
Spoiling, of mental compulsions, 99
SSRIs or SRIs (selective serotonin reuptake inhibitors), 34, 81, 113, 151, 254, 277–278, 298
Stages of Change Scale, 66, 67
Streptococcal infection, 23, 24, 256
Subjective units of distress scale (SUDS), 45, 159, 161, 165, 179, 182, 197, 199, 202. See also Fear thermometer
Substitute rituals, 162–163
Superstitious thinking, 138
    and symmetry compulsions, 298
    and tics plus OCD, 300
Supportive others, involvement of in exposure, 93–94
Suspension, for noncompliance, 184
Symmetry, as stimulus for incompleteness OCD, 199
Symmetry compulsions or obsessions, 11, 120, 187, 272
    and behavioral treatment outcome studies, 189
    exposure hierarchy for, 87
    and superstitious fears, 298

Tactile and motor stimuli, and incompleteness OCD, 199
Target behavior, 41
TD (Tourette's disorder), 295, 296, 297, 298
Therapeutic relationship or alliance
    clarifying to patient, 68–69
    in cognitive therapy for OCD, 121–122, 130
    and didactic interventions, 125
    in ERP, 153, 154, 155–156, 167
        as nonpunitive, 165
    for hoarding compulsion, 247
        in case vignette (Betty), 236
    and noncompliance, 129
    and traumatic outcome of exposure, 100

Therapist modeling, 39, 81–82, 92, 220
Thought–action fusion, 117, 138, 211, 214, 220, 225, 256, 271
Thought Action Fusion Scale, 212, 227
Thought–action relation, 136–137, 138
Thought control, 139
Thought records, 126–127, 130, 140
Thought recurrences, 137
Thoughts
    automatic (negative), 114
    interpretation of, 124–125, 215–217, 225 (see also Interpretation of thought)
    normalizing of, 136
    overimportance of, 117–118, 136–138
    significance of (alternative views), 222–226
    unwanted, 44
    See also Intrusive thoughts
Thought suppression, 90–91, 218–219, 220, 305
    and explaining CBT to patients, 68
Threat
    and obsession, 120
    overestimation of, 115, 130
TIB. See Treatment-interfering behavior
Tic disorders, 272, 298, 299–300
    case description on, 300–301
    cognitive, 300, 301
    as comorbid, 296–297
    habit reversal training for, 302
    mental, 298, 300
    treatment strategies for, 304
Tourette's disorder (TD), 295, 296, 297, 298
Training, for treatment of children and adolescents, 254
Traumas, idealized values as overcompensation for, 275–276
Treatment Ambivalence Questionnaire, 66
Treatment, for impulse control disorders, 299–305
    case description on, 302
    habit reversal training (HBT), 302–304
Treatment, OCD, 212
    addressing self-defeating safety behaviors, 217–222
    aims of, 185
    analyzing of past obsessions and past treatments, 223–224
    assessing progress and dealing with problems, 226–228
    and belief and appraisal model, 19, 22

ABOUT THE EDITORS

Martin M. Antony, PhD, ABPP, is a professor in the Department of Psychology at Ryerson University in Toronto, Ontario, Canada. He is also director of research in the Anxiety Treatment and Research Centre at St. Joseph's Healthcare in Hamilton, Ontario, Canada. He received his doctorate in clinical psychology from the University at Albany, State University of New York, and completed his predoctoral internship training at the University of Mississippi Medical Center in Jackson. Dr. Antony has published 20 books and more than 100 articles and book chapters in the areas of cognitive–behavioral therapy, obsessive–compulsive disorder, panic disorder, social phobia, and specific phobia. Dr. Antony has received career awards from the Society of Clinical Psychology (Division 12; American Psychological Association), the Canadian Psychological Association, and the Anxiety Disorders Association of America, and he is a fellow of the American and Canadian Psychological Associations. He has also served on the board of directors for the Society of Clinical Psychology and the Association for Behavioral and Cognitive Therapies and as program chair for past conventions of the Association for Behavioral and Cognitive Therapies and the Anxiety Disorders Association of America. Dr. Antony is actively involved in clinical research in the area of anxiety disorders, teaching, and education, and he maintains a clinical practice.

Christine Purdon, PhD, is an associate professor in the Department of Psychology at the University of Waterloo, Waterloo, Ontario, Canada, and is a consulting psychologist for the Anxiety Treatment and Research Centre at St. Joseph's Healthcare in Hamilton, Ontario, Canada. She received her doctorate in clinical psychology from the University of New Brunswick, Fredericton, Canada, and completed her internship at the Anxiety Disorders Clinic of the Centre for Addiction and Mental Health, Toronto, Ontario,

Canada. Dr. Purdon has published more than 30 journal articles and book chapters in the areas of obsessional thoughts, obsessive–compulsive disorder, and cognitive–behavioral approaches to anxiety disorders, and she has received several awards for her research. In addition, Dr. Purdon has coauthored a self-help book on the treatment of repugnant obsessions and has given numerous workshops and talks on the phenomenology and treatment of obsessive–compulsive disorder. She is chair elect of the clinical division of the Canadian Psychological Association and sits on the grants committee of a major mental health funding body. Dr. Purdon is actively involved in teaching and education and maintains a clinical practice.

Laura J. Summerfeldt, PhD, is an associate professor in the Department of Psychology at Trent University in Peterborough, Ontario, Canada. She is also on the adjunct faculty in the Department of Psychiatry and Behavioural Neurosciences at McMaster University in Hamilton, Ontario, Canada, and is a consulting psychologist at the Anxiety Treatment and Research Centre and the Psychology Residency Program at St. Joseph's Healthcare in Hamilton, Ontario, Canada. She received her doctorate from York University in Toronto, Ontario, Canada, and completed her postdoctoral training in the Department of Psychiatry and Behavioural Neurosciences at McMaster University. Dr. Summerfeldt has published numerous book chapters and scholarly articles in such areas as personality and psychopathology, obsessive–compulsive disorder, and social phobia. Her principal area of research interest is the phenomenology and taxonomy of obsessive–compulsive disorder and its links to personality and to clinical features such as comorbidity and age of onset. In addition to her clinical research, Dr. Summerfeldt is actively involved in teaching and education.